CHINESE CALLIGRAPHERS
AND THEIR ART

'Wang Hsi-chih Inscribing Fan,' a painting by Liang K'ai (*circa* 1140-1210)

CHINESE CALLIGRAPHERS
AND THEIR ART

CH'EN CHIH-MAI

MELBOURNE UNIVERSITY PRESS
LONDON AND NEW YORK : CAMBRIDGE UNIVERSITY PRESS

First published 1966

Printed and bound in Australia
at The Griffin Press, Adelaide, S.A.
for Melbourne University Press, Carlton N.3, Victoria

Registered in Australia for transmission
by post as a book

Dewey Decimal Classification Number 652·1
Library of Congress Catalog Card Number 65-22861

Text set in 12 point Garamond type

In Memory of My Father
CH'EN CH'ING-HO
1868-1959

Calligrapher, Collector,
Connoisseur and Critic

Preface

In his book *A Concise History of Modern Painting,* Sir Herbert Read, the distinguished English art critic and historian, says that Abstract Expressionism, the exciting movement in Modern Art, is but an extension and elaboration of Calligraphic Expressionism which has a close relationship with 'the Oriental *art* of calligraphy'. He goes on to say that some artists of the West—Henri Michaux, Mark Tobey, Morris Graves, among others—had travelled to China and Japan to study calligraphy and that as a result of their study their painting styles have come under its direct influence. What Sir Herbert says leads us to speculate that, as the art of Chinese calligraphy comes to be better known to the West, it may have as much to offer as Japanese prints to Post-Impressionism in Western art.

This is by way of introducing this book on Chinese calligraphy which, if I am not mistaken, is the first book in English on the subject since the publication of Chiang Yee's *Chinese Calligraphy*: *An Introduction to Its Aesthetic and Technique* (Methuen, London) a quarter of a century ago. Assuming that many of my readers have read Chiang Yee's book (if they have not, they are highly recommended to do so), I have chosen to approach the subject from a somewhat different angle and have refrained from making any further reference to and quoting from it.

The first portion of this book is a historical sketch of the evolution of the Chinese written language from its primitive beginnings down to the present day. In each historical period, I have chosen a few artists who in my opinion embody in their work the dominant trends of their time. There are literally thousands of calligraphers who deserve mention even in a general survey of this nature. I have elected to spare my readers the bewilderment of going over a plethora of unfamiliar names although many of them are household words in China. The choices I make, in the nature of things, are unavoidably arbitrary and subjective. The process of elimination is most difficult and often painful. Fortunately, there is surprisingly little disagreement among Chinese critics and art historians as to who are the giants. In this introductory discourse, I propose to confine myself to only the tablelands from which yet higher peaks may be scaled. The minor hills and mounds which dot the landscape in such profusion will have to be ignored.

'The style is the man himself' is an aphorism as applicable to Chinese calligraphy as to other forms of art. It is wise for us to know something of the man before we try to assess the merits of his artistic achievements. I have chosen as the title of this book *Chinese Calligraphers and Their Art* precisely for this reason. In introducing the calligraphers, I have therefore offered a reasonable amount of biographical data but only those aspects of their lives which I think are pertinent to our appreciation of their art. Chinese biographies are notorious for their undue emphasis on official posts. They generally include long lists of governmental positions the exact functions of which are ill-defined and often totally irrelevant, sometimes obscured by the mist of history. While we are naturally interested in knowing something of the artist's station in life, and in traditional China this is often best conveyed by the public honours bestowed upon him by his sovereign, there is after all a limit to this sort of thing. I often wonder whether Mi Fu, the protean genius of the Sung Dynasty, would resent being reminded a thousand years later that he was once, of all things, the military magistrate of Huaiyang!

A Chinese, especially a Chinese artist, is scandalous for the large number of ways by which he is identified: his surname (*hsing*), his personal name (*ming*), his courtesy name (*tzǔ*), his sobriquet (*hao*), and various other titles by which he has chosen to call himself from time to time. His friends and admirers are prone to add to the over-burdened list by identifying him by the governmental positions he held, the place in which he was born, the posthumous title bestowed upon him, and even the locality to which he was exiled. To cite a well-known example, Su Shih, the Sung Dynasty savant, besides being identified by his personal name Shih, had the courtesy name Tzǔ Chan. Because of his political quarrel with Wang An-shih, he was exiled to Huangchou where he lived for a time at a place called Tung-po. So he was known as Su Tung-po. After he was restored to favour, he occupied an official position called Yü-chü-kuan T'i-chü. He has therefore also become known as Su Yü-chü. Upon his death, he was honoured by the posthumous title Wên-chung. Hence the appellation Su Wên-chung. All these are exasperatingly confusing, but the Chinese art historians and critics are in the habit of using the different names indiscriminately, even in elementary textbooks, sometimes to show respect or affection for the artist, more often for pedantic or rhyming purposes. In a book intended for the non-Chinese reader such as this one, I propose to do away with this bad habit and identify one artist by only one name, that made up of his surname and personal name. I have stubbornly refused to call Su Shih by the name Su Tung-po, or the great Tsin Dynasty calligrapher Wang Hsi-chih by the name of his official title Wang Yu-chün. I have also dropped the Chinese practice of calling a man by only his personal name (*ming*) and eliminating the surname (*hsing*). Except for commonly accepted place names, all the proper names in this book are anglicised in accordance with Matthew's *Chinese-English Dictionary,* if only as a tribute to an Australian who has done so much to build a bridge between the Chinese and the English languages. I have not included an English-Chinese glossary of names and terms on the assumption that most of my readers do not read Chinese.

The second part of the book is devoted to the discussion of calligraphy as an art. This is a most difficult task because most of the terms and concepts of Chinese criticisms are untranslatable. An easy way out is to transliterate them, but then I shall have lost all justification for writing this book in English. It is not always possible or desirable to use terms and concepts of Western art in discussing a subject which is so uniquely Chinese. I enlist the help of Western art only when I find it appropriate. It is amazing how many avenues are open to me in this line of approach.

The eighty illustrations of this book are drawn from a variety of sources. The choice of illustrative materials, so basic to a book of this nature, is a most vexing problem indeed. It is manifestly impossible to exhibit the entire gamut of Chinese calligraphy between the covers of this book. Care must also be taken to focus our attention on the representative works of the artists. It is not always easy to lay our hand on the most authentic rubbings of the tablets (*pei*). Except for the works of the modern calligraphers, in which case the reproductions are made mostly from the originals, the bulk of the illustrations in this book are taken from the vast collection of the Chinese National Palace Museum in Taiwan and the *San Hsi T'ang Fa T'ieh,* compiled by order of the Ch'ing Emperor Ch'ien-lung in 1747, recently reissued in thirty-two volumes.

All my sources are Chinese. They number in the hundreds. One of the major references is the *P'ei Wên Tsai Shu Hua P'u,* the monumental encyclopaedia on calligraphy and painting compiled by order of the Ch'ing Emperor K'ang-hsi between 1705 and 1708. A most useful compilation is the *I Shu Ts'ung K'an* published by the *Shih Chieh Shu Chü* in Taiwan in 1963, being an expansion of the earlier *Mei Shu Ts'ung Shu* compiled by Huang Pin-hung and Têng Shih. I have given up the idea of a bibliography partly because it would be much too long (*P'ei Wên Tsai Shu Hua P'u* has a bibliography of 1,844 titles), and partly because most Chinese titles are untranslatable. A long list of book titles in transliteration would be too horrible to contemplate. For the same reasons I have abstained from indicating my authorities in footnotes.

Over the past years, I have been asked to give lectures on Chinese calligraphy and painting by a number of educational and art institutions in the United States, the Philippines, India, Australia and New Zealand. I have also contributed articles on the subject to Chinese and Australian magazines. Limited by time and space, the lectures and articles are highly condensed. This book is a separate and independent effort to explore the subject in greater depth.

I have been encouraged to write this book by Professor Harry Simon of the University of Melbourne, to whom I am also indebted for reading and correcting my manuscript. I wish also to thank the National Library of Australia and the Library of the Australian National University for allowing me to use their large collections, especially back numbers of Chinese art magazines. Last but not least, I wish to thank my wife Lilyan without whose understanding, constructive criticism and editorial assistance this book could never have been written.

Chronology

—2205 B.C.	Legendary Period	Huang Ti Ts'ang Chieh Shih Huang
2205-1766 B.C.	Hsia Dynasty (traditional)	
1766-1122 B.C.	Shang (Yin) Dynasty	Bronze inscriptions Oracle bones
1122-770 B.C.	Western Chou Dynasty	*San Shih P'an* *Chung Chou Chung* *Mao Kung Ting* Shih Chou (*Chou wên*) *Shih Ku* (stone drums)
770-222 B.C.	Eastern Chou Dynasty	
221-206 B.C.	Ch'in Dynasty	Li Ssŭ (d. 208 B.C.) Mêng T'ien (d. 209 B.C.)
207 B.C.-25 A.D.	Western Han Dynasty	*Han chien* (94 B.C.—) Shih Yu (middle of first century B.C.)

25-219	Eastern Han Dynasty	Hsü Shên
		Ts'ai Lun
		Chang Chih (d. 190)
		Ts'ai Yung (132-192)
		Chung Yu (151-230)
		I Ying Pei (153)
		Shih Ch'ên Pei (169)
		Ts'ao Ch'üan Pei (185)
219-265	Three Kingdoms	So Ching (239-303)
		T'ien Fa Shên Ch'ên Pei (276)
265-419	Tsin Dynasty	Lu Chi (261-303)
		Wei Shuo (272-349)
		Wang I (274-322)
		Huang Hsiang (304-361)
		Wang Hsi-chih (307-365)
		Wang Hsien-chih (344-388)
		Ku K'ai-chih (c. 344-406)
		Wang Hsün (349-400)
420-588	South and North Dynasties	*Ch'üan Lung Yen Pei* (458)
		I Ho Ming (514)
		Chih-yung (active latter half of sixth century)
589-617	Sui Dynasty	Ou-yang Hsün (557-645)
		Yü Shih-nan (558-638)
618-906	T'ang Dynasty	Ch'u Shui-liang (596-658)
		Emperor T'ai-tsung (reign 627-649)
		Chung Shao-ching
		Sun Ch'ien-li
		Li Yung (678-747)
		Hsü Hao (703-782)
		Chang Hsü
		Yen Chên-ch'ing (709-785)
		Emperor Hsüan-tsung (reign 712-756)
		Huai-su (725-789)
		Chang Huai-kuan
		Li Yang-ping

		Liu Kung-ch'üan (773-860)
		Chang Yen-yüan
906-960	Five Dynasties	Li Yü (937-978)
		Yang Ning-shih (863-955)
960-1276	Sung Dynasty	Ou-yang Siu (1007-1072)
		Ts'ai Hsiang (1011-1066)
		Wên T'ung (1019-1079)
		Su Shih (1036-1101)
		Li Kung-lin (1040-1106)
		Huang T'ing-chien (1050-1110)
		Mi Fu (1051-1107)
		Emperor Hui-tsung (1082-1135)
		Mi Yu-jên (1086-1165)
1277-1367	Yüan Dynasty	Chao Mêng-fu (1254-1322)
		Kuan Tao-shêng (1262-1319)
		Hsien-yü Shu (1256-1301)
		Ni Tsan (1301-1374)
1368-1643	Ming Dynasty	Shen Chou (1427-1509)
		Chu Yün-ming (1460-1526)
		Wên Chêng-ming (1470-1559)
		Tung Ch'i-ch'ang (1555-1636)
1644-1911	Ch'ing Dynasty	Fu Shan (1606-1685)
		Chin Nung (1687-1763)
		Chêng Hsieh (1693-1765)
		Liu Yung (1719-1804)
		Têng Shih-ju (1743-1805)
		Pao Shih-ch'ên (1775-1855)
		Ho Shao-chi (1799-1873)
		Chao Chih-ch'ien (1829-1884)
1912—	Republic	Wu Chün-ch'ing (1844-1927)
		K'ang Yu-wei (1858-1927)
		T'an Yen-k'ai (1876-1930)
		Tung Tso-pin (1895-1963)
		Yü Yu-jên (1878-1964)

Contents

Illustrations

Chapter One

Legendary Beginnings

Calligraphy, which the Chinese call *shu fa*, is the art of writing the characters, the semantic units, of the Chinese written language. The Chinese, it appears, are not content with writing the characters correctly and legibly and letting it go at that. Their love of beauty, their creative impulse, impels them to make each character into an artistic unit, and by putting many such units together, they strive to make the whole piece into an artistic composition. The Chinese, according to Sir Herbert Read, is 'the oldest surviving, the most persistent and aesthetically the most perfect civilisation known to the world'. He adds that 'at the base of all this plastic civilisation, this endless epoch of prevailing good taste, is the manual craft of calligraphy, or brush-writing'. Over many, many centuries of sustained and uninterrupted growth, calligraphy has indeed become the main stem of Chinese art, occupying a position which is equal to, if not on a higher plane than painting, and most certainly surpasses sculpture and architecture, not to mention porcelain-making and wood- and ivory-carving, in the hierarchy of the arts.

The origin of a language is understandably shrouded in myth, mystery and magic. We do not now have any material evidence as to how and when the Chinese language, spoken and written, came into being. What is lacking in material evidence, however, has been more than compensated for by the profusion of legends transmitted to us through the ancient classics. Foremost among the legends is that relating to the Three Emperors—Fu Hsi, Shên Nung and Huang Ti—the three pioneers of Chinese culture and civilization, all of whom appeared to us as extra-human if not supernatural creatures

[1]

with extraordinary capabilities. According to the legend, all the Three Emperors had some part to play in the creation and development of the fountainhead of Chinese culture and civilization: the written language.

Fu Hsi, 'the ox-tamer', who supposedly lived much more than an ordinary span of life in prehistoric times, was traditionally credited with devising the *pa kua* (sometimes translated as 'the eight trigrams'), consisting of a series of eight symbols formed by broken and unbroken straight lines arranged on three levels (Fig. 1). All sorts of mythical meanings have been read into the eight symbols until each has come to stand for a number of things through an amazingly liberal association of ideas. Thus *ch'ien,* the symbol of heaven, consisting of three unbroken straight lines parallel to each other, is also the symbol of *yang,* the male, while *k'un,* the symbol of earth, consisting of three broken straight lines parallel to each other, is also the symbol of *yin,* the female. All students of Chinese philosophy are, of course, familiar with the theory explaining how through the interaction of *yang* and *yin* the entire universe with its multitude of phenomena came into being. One Chinese scholar calculates that the eight trigrams may be taken to signify no less than 1,471 different things or concepts. Combinations of the symbols and their derivatives have formed the basis of a type of fortune-telling.

What is pertinent to our consideration is that some old Chinese etymologists held the view that the eight trigrams were the embryo of the Chinese written language. They advanced the proposition that the eight trigrams were the rudiments of a primitive language on the ground of their simplicity—parallel straight lines without curves or crosses. Modern students of the Chinese language are inclined to doubt the veracity of the long-established theory. Lü Fu-t'ing, a modern art historian, said:

Few people have questioned the validity of the theory held for several thousand years that the Chinese written language grew out of the *pa kua.* I think the theory is open to serious doubt. I venture this opinion on two grounds. First, the *pa kua* consists of only straight lines, while the earliest known characters of the Chinese written language are composed of curved lines. I fail to see how one could have been derived from the other. Secondly, the *pa kua* is a system by which things and phenomena are represented by simple, abstract symbols. The earliest known characters represent concrete things and abstract concepts by complicated pictures and designs. According to our general knowledge of the evolution of human wisdom, it is easier to create complicated pictures and designs than abstract symbols such as the *pa kua,* because images can be made by observation while symbols require a higher degree of mental effort. What is easier usually comes first; what is more difficult is likely to come later. The first point I make leads me to believe that there is probably no connection at all between the *pa kua* and the pictographs. The second point I make suggests that, if there were any relation between the *pa kua* and the pictographs, it is quite likely that the pictographs came before and not after the *pa kua.*

[2]

Fig. 1   *Pa Kua, 'The Eight Trigrams'*

Lü Fu-t'ing's deduction, logically speaking, seems to be unassailable. The only trouble with it is that it is nothing more than a deduction, with no material evidence to support it. The question of the *pa kua* and its relation to the Chinese written language must therefore remain in the realm of legend, and there is where it should belong. The chances of finding material evidence to answer it one way or another are remote indeed.

The second legendary pioneer of Chinese culture and civilization, Shên Nung, 'the god of agriculture', has been given credit for fashioning farm implements, 'bending wood for ploughs and hewing wood for ploughshares'; for the tasting and testing of a hundred varieties of herbs to find cures for the sick; for the custom of holding midday fairs for the exchange of goods. Like the *quipus* of the Incas, Shên Nung was said to have taught the people to tie knots with strings to record events and sanctify agreements or contracts. We are not at all sure how the string-knots later evolved into characters, as the authors of the ancient classics alleged. One theory is that the knots were originally used as a method of counting, such as the number of animals killed in a hunting expedition, and the shape of the knots inspired the characters for numerals. Another theory is that the shape of some of the knots inspired the characters denoting some concepts, such as the lobe of the string representing the concept of 'return'. While these theories may sound plausible, they must remain pure conjectures. However, classical etymologists, including Hsü Shên of the Han Dynasty, author of the earliest Chinese dictionary, *Shuo Wên Chieh Tzŭ* published in 100 A.D., were positive that there was a stage in the evolution of the Chinese written language when 'string-knots were used to record events and regulate affairs', and that such a stage occurred after the fashioning of the *pa kua* and before the formal making of characters. In the absence of any evidence to the contrary, we just have to take their word for it.

Down to the present day, the Chinese claim to be the direct descendants of the third pioneer of Chinese culture and civilization, Huang Ti, 'the Yellow Emperor'. Fu Hsi and Shên Nung, as we have seen, were legendary figures whose existence was based entirely on the accounts in classical literature. Huang Ti, on the other hand, was very probably a real figure, although many stories connected with his reign are hard to believe. He was supposed to have reigned for exactly one hundred years (the dates usually assigned to Huang Ti's reign are 2697-2597 B.C.) during which many important advances were said to have been made. His Queen, Lo Tsu (Hsi-ling Nü, 'the girl from Hsi-ling'), was given credit for the important invention with which China and the Chinese have since become indelibly identified—the rearing of silk-worms and the reeling of silk threads from their cocoons. Equally importantly, Huang Ti himself was said to have devised the 'south-pointing chariot', i.e. the compass. A warrior and an empire-builder, he pushed his frontiers forward in all directions by defeating in battle many other clans and set up a court in which hierarchical relationships were clearly designated. Inspired by the

[4]

rich colours and fancy patterns of natural objects, Huang Ti had one of his ministers, Shih Huang by name or title, copy the colours and patterns as decorations for his garments and pennants, not so much to appeal to the senses, but to denote and differentiate the ranks of officialdom and the levels of society—the beginnings of bureaucracy and aristocracy.

According to classical literature, it was during Huang Ti's reign that the formal making of written characters was inaugurated. The credit for this momentous invention is traditionally given to one of Huang Ti's ministers, Ts'ang Chieh. To the ancient Chinese, a man responsible for such a gigantic step forward in the evolution of culture and civilization must be endowed with unusual physical attributes. Thus the Han Dynasty writer Wang Ch'ung (*ca.* 27-100 A.D.), a man who fought valiantly against popular superstitions and well-schooled in astronomical knowledge, nevertheless maintained in his book *Lun Hêng* that Ts'ang Chieh was endowed with an extra pair of eyes, which was just another way of saying, according to the modern historian Chang Ch'i-yün, that Ts'ang Chieh was extraordinarily perceptive. Otherwise, how could he have invented so divine a thing as the Chinese written language?

How did he do it? According to the Han Dynasty etymologist Hsü Shên, Ts'ang Chieh, after studying the celestial bodies and their formations and the natural objects surrounding him, particularly the footprints of birds and animals, came to realize that things could be told apart by devising different signs to represent them, thereby making the first signs of the Chinese language. It is reasonable to assume that the Chinese people in Ts'ang Chieh's time must have uttered sounds to denote the objects with which they were in contact in their daily life. In other words, there must have been some sort of a spoken language among the people. According to one classical authority, some of the sounds must have corresponded somewhat with the sounds made by the objects denoted, presumably such sounds as those simulating the neigh of the horse and the moo of the cow. This is an intriguing theory, although the examples he adduced to support it are not entirely convincing. Theoretically, a character has three aspects: the sound used in the spoken language to denote a particular object, the image used in the written language to denote the same object, and the meaning attached to the sound and the image. The identification of the three aspects—sound, image and meaning—completes the process of character-making. Ts'ang Chieh, it appears, was the man who brought about the identification and is therefore accorded the honour of being the father of the Chinese written language, like Thoth and Isis of Ancient Egypt, Nebo of Babylon, Moses of the Jews and Hermes of the Ancient Greeks. Since the written language is the means by which the teachings of the sages are handed down from generation to generation, the written language has always been surrounded by an aura of sacredness by the Chinese, literate and illiterate alike, and Ts'ang Chieh, the man who fathered it, has come down in history as a man of extraordinary

Fig. 2   *Mo So* Characters. Reading from top to bottom, the characters signify Dog, Horse, Ox, Goat, Elephant, Pig, Mouse, Fish, Worm, Snake and Axe

accomplishments, one who succeeded in stealing the most jealously guarded secret of the gods. We have it on the authority of the classics that at the moment Ts'ang Chieh made the great invention, the gods wept unashamedly at night, so remorseful were they that man had found the key and broken the monopoly of the mysteries of the universe.

We would have liked nothing better than to subscribe wholeheartedly to this neat theory. Unfortunately there are many dissenting voices. The ancient philosopher Hsün-tzǔ, for instance, told us that Ts'ang Chieh really did not invent the written language all by himself. What he did, Hsün-tzǔ said, was merely to bring under some sort of system the signs and symbols which had become current in his day. Another ancient writer was even more sacrilegious. He believed that there was another man, Tsu Sung by name, who was engaged in the same task. All these are legends and speculations which the Chinese have been taught for a couple of thousand years. Modern scholars tend to support the proposition that, since the language situation in Huang Ti's time must have been utterly chaotic, its codification and systematization could not have been the handiwork of one or two individuals, however gifted they might be. The fact of the matter is that, Ts'ang Chieh notwithstanding, the Chinese language long after his time was far from being standardized. It still had a long way to go.

Chang Yen-yüan, the celebrated art historian and critic of the T'ang Dynasty, told us that in Ts'ang Chieh's time writing and picturing were one and the same thing. Although we have never seen a character of that remote period, it is quite possible, even probable, that it was a pictograph, a realistic and naturalistic representation of the object denoted. Hsü Shên was the man who classified the characters of the written language of his time into six categories (*lu shu*) of which *hsiang hsing,* 'simulation of form', was one of them. For instance, the character for 'sun' was a circle with a dot or a horizontal line in the middle; the character for 'moon' was in the form of a crescent; the character for 'turtle' was an outline of the turtle. Indeed it would be difficult to tell whether such an image is a character or a picture.

That this was probably the situation in remote antiquity is supported by the recent discovery by a group of scientifically-trained palaeographers of the primitive language of a small tribe known as *Na Hsi,* still living in the Linchiang District of Yunnan Province in South-western China. The tribe now consists of approximately 160,000 people, and is known as the *Mo So.* The most remarkable thing about this tribe is that it has a written language all its own. The *Mo So* people have been using their language to compose quite a number of religious books which have been collected and studied. The modern scholar, Li Lin-ts'an, has compiled a dictionary of the *Mo So* language. The entire vocabulary consists of 2,120 words, only two of which have yet to be defined. It is a beautiful language because all the words are in fact pictures. The words for animals, in particular, are sensitively drawn

outline pictures in profile done in considerable detail and vividness (Fig. 2).
It is a true delight to see the word for 'dog' which shows the pet in a
running posture complete with the hair of the tail. Similarly, the word for
'horse' shows the animal cantering with its beautifully described head turned
three-quarters sidewise. According to Li Lin-ts'an, an authority on the subject,
the *Mo So* language was formulated sometime in the T'ang Dynasty. It has
therefore lasted for about a thousand years. Amazingly, in all this time, the
Na Hsi people managed to keep their language and to keep it in the original
state. Imagine the palaeographers' astonishment when they first came upon
the *Mo So* language! It would have been no less had a live dinosaur been
seen roaming some untracked swamp in the twentieth century.

The Chinese written language, unlike the *Mo So,* has gone through a long
and involved process of development until it has shed practically all its
pictorial features and has become one of the most sophisticated and beautiful
languages of the human race. K'ang Yu-wei, the Ch'ing Dynasty calligrapher
and critic, who knew quite a bit about European languages, said: 'From the
very beginning, the Chinese have laid emphasis upon the form of the written
characters while the Europeans have laid emphasis upon the sound of the
words. The Chinese use their eyes; the Europeans use their ears.' What the
Chinese see with their eyes has become completely standardized long ago.
It is possible for a literate Chinese today to read and understand the works
of Confucius and Mencius without too much difficulty, less than that of
the Englishman reading Chaucer. The task of standardization allegedly started
by Ts'ang Chieh did not take long to fulfil. Perhaps the major landmark in
the evolutionary process was the publication of Hsü Shên's dictionary *Shuo
Wên Chieh Tzŭ* in 100 A.D.

However, what the Chinese hear with their ears is still divided into many
dialects. The Europeans, concerned as they are with pronunciations, are inclined
to exaggerate the diversities of the Chinese dialects. A European diplomat
visiting my house once asked me whether the calligraphic scroll on my wall
was in Mandarin or Cantonese. The professional philologists are of course
preoccupied with problems concerning the pronunciation of characters in
different periods and localities. Meanwhile, nationwide efforts have been made
in Republican China to make *kuo yü,* known to the west as Mandarin, the
uniform spoken language throughout the land. *Kuo yü* is now the medium
of instruction in all schools. As popular education spreads, the day is drawing
near when all Chinese will not only be able to read the same newspaper but
also listen in to the same radio broadcast. While the English-speaking peoples
are proud of their accents, the Chinese are ashamed of their dialects.

The emphasis on form instead of sound pointed out by K'ang Yu-wei is the
key to the art of calligraphy. William Willetts, the English student of Chinese
art, has explained the difference between Chinese calligraphy and English
handwriting in these words:

The basic units out of which Western writing is composed, the letters of the alphabet, are phonetic symbols and as such are simple in form, strictly limited in number, and relatively unchanging in appearance. Words are no more than linear combinations of these continually recurring basic elements; it follows that words cannot hold any inherent visual interest, since their forms are determined not by principles of structural design, but by the amount and nature of the phonetic material they have to carry. Each Chinese character, on the other hand, is organized within the boundaries of a square, and is conceived of and executed as an organic whole. Notwithstanding, therefore, that the elements out of which it is composed—the brush-strokes—must make an intellectually intelligible pattern, and notwithstanding that certain combinations of brush-strokes do recur from one character to another, each separate character in the amazingly rich Chinese vocabulary in fact constitutes a fresh problem in structural dynamics, an 'adventure of movement' whose successful resolution is a triumph of artistic management. And this, I maintain, is not a difference in degree, but an absolute difference in kind.

Although the origin of the Chinese language is still shrouded in mystery, the characters of which it is composed have long since inspired the visually sensitive to turn them into works of art. Ts'ang Chieh, in fathering the Chinese language, fathered also a special form of art which was destined to exert a tremendous influence on the art of the countries of East Asia and which, five thousand years later, is beginning to make its impact on Modern Art in Europe and America.

Chapter Two

The Oracle Bone Inscriptions

Long before the advent of modern archaeology the Chinese scholars have been collecting and studying the exquisite bronze utensils of antiquity. As far back as 1092, Lü Ta-lin of the Northern Sung Dynasty published his monumental work *K'ao Ku T'u* (Archaeological Diagrams), the first comprehensive treatise on the ancient bronzes. In his study the author undertook to describe each article by diagram accompanied by extensive explanatory notes, detailing the exact dimensions—height, width, depth, weight and capacity. He made extensive research into the various types and designs of the ancient bronzes, analysing and explaining the decorative patterns and deciphering the inscriptions. His purpose, as he stated it, was 'to probe into the articles' origins, to supplement the accounts in the classics, and to correct the errors of other scholars'. Thirty years later, the Sung Emperor Hui-tsung, the great collector and connoisseur of art, ordered the compilation of the *Hsüan-ho Po Ku T'u*, in which some fifty ancient bronzes in the royal collection were catalogued and described. Throughout the Sung Dynasty, many other scholars joined in the study, some with outstanding achievements, most notably the renowned scholar Ou-yang Siu and the famous painter Li Kung-lin.

Every lover of Chinese art is familiar with the bronzes of the Shang Dynasty, specimens of which are now found in almost every major museum in the world. They come in an amazing variety of shapes, types and ornamental motifs. Even the names by which they are called are delightfully musical to Chinese ears. The multifarious forms they assume show that the Shang people were gifted with the most fecund imagination, displaying great ingenuity in

Fig. 3   Bronze Wine Container and Inscription, Shang Dynasty

the broad range of the bronzes' graceful lines and elegant contours. The articles appear to possess an innate vitality and robust strength all their own. They seem to be quivering with life, ready at any moment, as someone said of the Parthenon, to soar into open space. The stylized creatures in the designs and ornaments, some mythical and some true to life, seem to dance in frenzied movement in a spirit of freedom and fancifulness.

It is not hard for us to fall in love instantly with these beautiful objects and to go on talking about them. But the study of Shang bronzes, however rewarding and satisfying, is not within the purview of this book. What interests us is that many of the ancient bronzes bear inscriptions composed of Chinese characters which are the oldest that we have seen. In some cases, the inscriptions consist of only a few characters indicating the name of the clan for which the bronzes were cast. After all, the the bronzes were extremely valuable objects reserved for the royal household and the aristocracy as some sort of a status symbol, and it was only fit and proper that they should be clearly identified. In some other cases, the inscriptions are longer and deal with a variety of subjects. Chinese scholars such as Ou-yang Siu and Li Kung-lin have been trying to decipher the characters with a remarkable measure of success. They call the script used on the ancient metal articles *chin wên,* characters on metal. Because of the great antiquity of the script, it has also been called simply *ku wên,* ancient characters.

The characters found on the most ancient metal articles may generally be classified as *hsiang hsing,* 'simulation of form', in other words, pictographs. This phenomenon has led the modern scholar Tung Tso-pin to advance the theory that the origin of *chin wên* may be traced back to the Neolithic Age in the period following the introduction of agriculture. It is Tung Tso-pin's contention that *chin wên* was in use as far back as 4,800 years ago, which is two hundred years before the date traditionally assigned to Huang Ti, a theory which tends to deny Ts'ang Chieh's claim as the father of the Chinese language. Whether we accept Tung Tso-pin's theory or not, there seems to be no question that the characters we find on the Shang bronzes must have evolved from something much more primitive, something that is comparable to the characters of the *Mo So* language. This is shown by the inscription on a Shang wine container in the shape of a rhinoceros (Fig. 3) where the characters, though still retaining some pictographic features, are really stylized abstractions, indicating unmistakably that in the mind of the Shang scribe a character should be a symbol of identification rather than merely a pictorial representation of the object denoted. This mental concept on the part of the Shang scribe constituted a major advance in the evolution of the Chinese written language, an advance which the *Na Hsi* people never made for their *Mo So* language for a period of almost a thousand years.

Our knowledge of the Shang script took a momentous step forward towards the end of the nineteenth century when a large quantity of tortoise shells

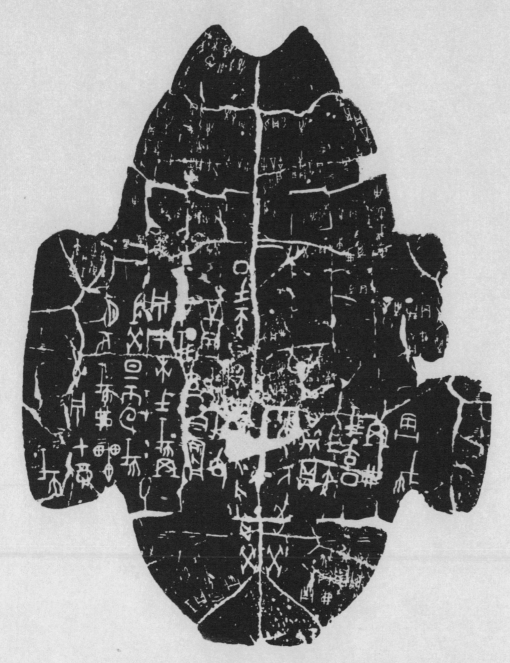

Fig. 4a   Oracle Bone, Inscription on Plastron

Fig. 4b Oracle Bone, Inscription on Bones

and animal bones bearing incised inscriptions were discovered at Anyang, one of the sites of the capital of the Shang Dynasty. We shall not relate the often repeated story of how the shells and bones were at first regarded as 'dragon bones' by the local inhabitants, how they were ground into powder to be sold as medicinal stimulants, and how the scholar Wang I-yung first doubted their authenticity and later congratulated himself in ecstasy for having stumbled upon one of the greatest discoveries of Chinese archaeology. Since then the study of Shang oracle bones, as they have come to be known in the West, has become a science in its own right. The oracle bones offer material evidence of a literate Bronze Age in China.

The oracle bones, which the Chinese call *chia ku,* were mostly made from plastron or from the scapulae of cattle. Sometimes they were made from the bones of other animals, such as deer-skull. On the face of the shells and bones the Shang priests inscribed questions and offered prayers to the gods. Heat was applied to the back of the shells and bones, and divine messages were read from the T-shaped cracks that resulted from the firing. The shells and bones were also used to record events and were carefully filed in the royal archives (Fig. 4).

Roughly 100,000 genuine oracle bones have been excavated and analyzed. The most exacting task is to decipher the inscriptions. Eliminating the many duplicates, more than two thousand characters have been found, of which the meaning of some 1,300 characters can be definitely ascertained. After more than half a century of intensive study, we are in a position to say that the oracle bones deal with such diverse subjects as ancestor worship, religious offerings, military campaigns, hunting expeditions, trips, inspection tours, eclipses, pregnancies, births, illnesses, deaths, prayers for rain, and other allied subjects. By far the bulk of the oracle bones deal with ancestor worship, thus underlining the Chinese saying: 'To serve the dead as the living, to honour the departed as the present—such is the basis of filial piety.' Some of the Shang rulers, it appears, believed in the oracles deeply. For instance, Emperor Wu-ting was in the habit of addressing all sorts of questions to his gods and asking for divine guidance—whether his queen was going to give birth to a boy or a girl, whether his beloved son was going to recover from his serious illness, what were the crops that would yield a bounty harvest in a particular year, whether there would be more rain to relieve the drought, which one of his ancestors was punishing him by giving him such a terrible toothache. In one oracle bone, reconstructed by Tung Tso-pin, the inscription tells of an incident during Emperor Wu-ting's reign some 3,240 years ago (Fig. 5a). The Shang Emperor addressed the gods: 'We are going to hunt at Kuei. Can we make captures?' The prediction was in the affirmative and the balance of the inscription gratefully records the catch: 1 tiger, 40 deer, 164 foxes, 159 fawns, a brace of pheasants, and 18 'double-red' birds. On the other hand, Emperor Tzu-chia, Emperor Wu-ting's son, apparently did not

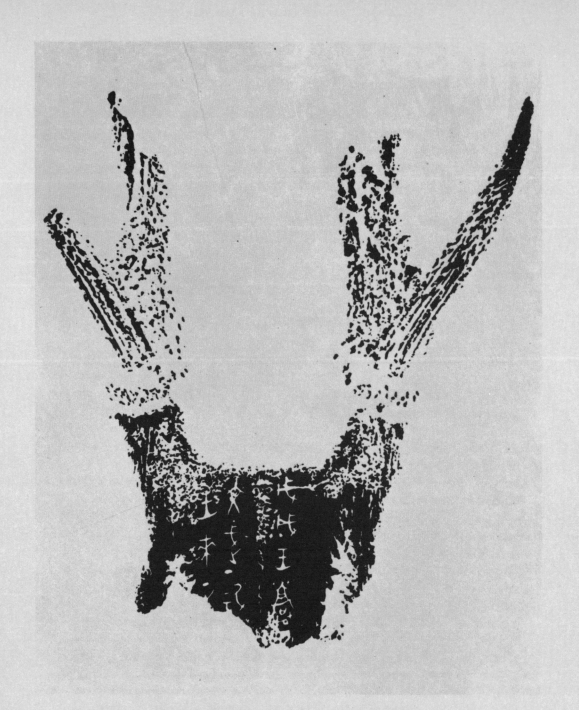

Fig. 4c Oracle Bone, Inscription on Deer-skull

think much of the oracles, and chose to confine himself to making routine questions relating to basic subjects such as ancestor worship, hunting expeditions, trips and tours.

The characters of the oracle bone inscriptions were engraved in vertical columns from top to bottom. The lines were arranged either from left to right or from right to left, a practice which made deciphering doubly difficult. Some characters were engraved upright, others were engraved sidewise. Because of the irregular shapes and surfaces of the shells and bones, the characters were uneven in size and the lines uneven in length. The same character might be written in a number of ways. For instance, the character *yang* (sheep) assumed no less than forty-five different forms on the oracle bones.

From the viewpoint of the art historian, the most intriguing aspect of the oracle bone script (the characters of the oracle bones have come to be regarded as a separate and distinct script, known to the Chinese as *chia ku wên*) is the deliberate effort on the part of the Shang scribes consciously to remove the pictorial image from the characters. Champions of Modern Art tell us that a recognizable image, an image that is the representation of something in the outside world, is not the necessary part of a picture. They go on to say that, if a picture's composition is to have its proper emphasis, references to the visual world should be eliminated. It would be going too far for us to argue that the theories of Modern Art were known to the Shang people. But it is nevertheless pertinent to observe that precisely the same tendency was manifested in the early development of the Chinese characters. For we can clearly see from the oracle bone inscriptions and those on the Shang bronzes that certain characters, in fact the majority of them, which started their career as pictorial representations of worldly objects (*hsiang hsing*), were wilfully transformed step by step into symbols and abstractions, thus becoming children of the imagination instead of pictures of familiar things. The primitive *Na Hsi* people make practically no distinction between the act of writing and the act of picturing. They write as they draw and they draw as they write. Judging by the large number of *hsiang hsing* characters in the Chinese written language, we may reasonably assume that substantially the same situation obtained with the Chinese people at the dawn of history. It was the later separation of the act of writing from the act of picturing which made it possible for the development of calligraphy as an art with a status as elevated as that of painting.

The oracle bone characters were incised with a sharp pointed instrument on the hard surface of the shells and bones. Writing in those days, therefore, was in fact an aspect of carving. Although here and there we come across traces of the brush (part of a character written with the brush is among the Shang relics at Anyang), the brush was then definitely not the common writing instrument. If calligraphy is understood to be the art of brush-writing, then we must conclude that in the Shang Dynasty the art of calligraphy was

[17]

yet unborn. However, modern calligraphers, impressed by the archaism of the oracle bone characters, have adopted the *chia ku wên* as a script and are using the brush to do the oracle bone characters. The reconstruction of oracle bone inscriptions was done by Tung Tso-pin with a brush on paper and not with a sharp-pointed instrument on hard surfaces (Fig. 5b). Tung Tso-pin was also fond of doing scrolls with oracle bone characters. Thus the *chia ku wên* has become an independent script in its own right and some calligraphers are specialized in it.

When the oracle bones were first discovered, there was great excitement among archaeologists and palaeographers somewhat comparable to that following the recent discovery of the Dead Sea Scrolls. The subsequent excavations carried out at Anyang and elswhere have been compared with that of Heinrich Schliemann at the site of Troy. For with these excavations the Shang Dynasty, which had existed for so long as something we only read about in the ancient classics, suddenly passed into the status of documented history, just as the age of Agamemnon, Menelaus, Helen and Hector came to be recognized as fact rather than fiction as a result of Schliemann's work. However, the high hopes entertained at first of reconstructing the entire history of the Shang Dynasty by the study of the oracle bones have not been fulfilled. Be that as it may, the art historian, on his part, is delighted by the large number of ancient artifacts excavated, all of which are of enchanting beauty and exquisite taste. He is particularly delighted, if he is interested in calligraphy, by the fact that in the oracle bones he is able to see the original writing of the Shang people, and thereby to acquire an intimate understanding of the evolution of the art of calligraphy before it was born. If the oracle bones do not tell us very much about the political, economic and social conditions of Shang China, they are certainly invaluable to the art historian, as invaluable as the cave paintings of Altamira.

Fig. 5a Reconstruction of Oracle Bone Characters by Tung Tso-pin

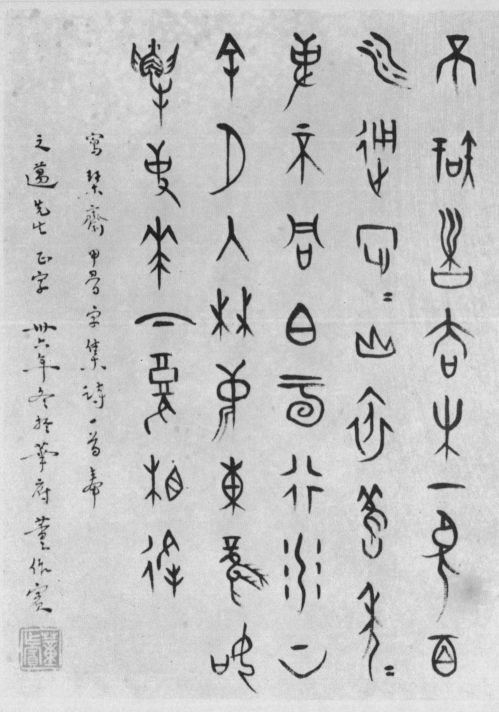

Fig. 5b Poem transcribed in Oracle Bone Characters by Tung Tso-pin inscribed to the author dated 'Winter, 1947, in Washington, D.C.'

Chapter Three

The Ancient Scripts

At the dawn of history, when the Chinese people were engaged in the important task of devising a writing system for themselves, and doing it in widely separated parts of the country, the overall situation must have been most chaotic and confusing. The drive for inventiveness, however, was truly breath-taking. We read in the ancient chronicles of all sorts of writing systems cropping up, as the Chinese say, like bamboo shoots after a spring shower, and the scripts were given descriptive names—the dragon script, the grain-ear script, the cloud script, the bird script, the worm script, the turtle script, the seashell script, the tadpole script, the tiger-claw script, the mosquito-foot script, and quite a number of others. Going over this list, we cannot help noticing that all of them bear some relation to natural objects. This is for a variety of reasons. The dragon script, we have been told, was supposed to have been devised by Fu Hsi, the first of the Three Emperors, after a dragon appeared auspiciously before him. The grain-ear script, on the other hand, was of course attributed to Shên Nung, the legendary ruler who taught the people to grow cereals. Ts'ang Chieh, we recall, was supposed to be the father of the Chinese written language. But his sovereign, Huang Ti, thought nothing of crossing him up by devising the cloud script and the turtle script independently when good omens, in this case a multi-coloured cloud and a turtle-spirit, visited the realm, and there was apparently nothing that Ts'ang Chieh could do about it. Being pioneers of Chinese culture and civilisation, the Three Emperors, and the Five Kings following them, it appears, were all most eager to get in the act of language-making. It is possible that the legend-makers of old, in order to underline the greatness of the figures they were dealing with, were compelled to make the figures into actors in the drama on a theme as sacred as the creation and formation of the writing system.

But there are other reasons for some of the scripts. The tadpole script (*k'o tou wên*) has been considered the grandfather of the Chinese written language. The invention of this script was credited to the second of the Five Kings, Chüan Hsü, who supposedly reigned in the third millennium B.C. It may be conjectured that it was called after the tadpole because the strokes forming the characters were suggestive of the tadpole. This may be due to the fact that in ancient times writing was done by dipping a needle into a thick liquid such as lacquer and dragging it across a hard surface such as a slab of wood or bamboo. Since the needle was hard and the liquid thick, the line drawn was heavy at the first point of contact and became thinner in the later stage, thus giving the impression of a tadpole with a large head and a slender tail. At least one writer has attributed the tadpole script to none other than Ts'ang Chieh himself.

The origin of the bird script (*niao shu*) is interesting from a different viewpoint. It was at first credited to Emperor Wên of the Chou Dynasty to whom various birds brought good tidings. He was also said to have devised the tiger script (*hu shu*) because a white tiger in his royal menagerie was particularly well behaved, 'refusing to step on the growing grass'. Emperor Wên of the Chou Dynasty was a towering figure in Chinese history, and of course he must have some part to play in the formation of the written language. Tung Tso-pin, however, has offered a new theory on the bird script. He maintains that the character for 'bird', usually a rather complicated representation of the feathered vertebrate (one version of the character for 'bird' may be seen as the first character of the third vertical line from the right in Fig. 3), might have been used not as a character but as a decoration to be attached to other characters. For instance, the character for 'spear', which even as a pictorial representation must have been rather simple, might have been considered too austere to satisfy the aesthetic sense. To liven up the character for 'spear', the ancient Chinese might think it proper arbitrarily to attach the character for 'bird' to it, perhaps showing the bird's beak holding the character for 'spear' in suspension. According to Tung Tso-pin, the addition of the character for 'bird' to the character for 'spear' did not mean that the bird had picked up the spear, or someone had used the spear to stab at the bird. The whole idea was a matter of decoration with no meaning attached. And since the character for 'bird' was a complicated design pleasing to the eye, it was attached to all sorts of characters more or less indiscriminately. Hence the bird script. Tung Tso-pin's theory, if true, naturally reminds us of the illuminated manuscripts of Medieval Europe in which the initial letters were richly adorned with flowers and vines, angels and animals, and of course birds.

Fig. 6   *San Shih P'an*

The many writing systems allegedly devised by the Three Emperors and Five Kings are known to us by name only. The most ancient forms of writing we have actually seen are the characters on the ancient bronzes and the two thousand odd characters on the oracle bones. Since these forms of writing are already reasonably stylized, it seems quite likely that they were preceded by more primitive and more pictographic forms. Perhaps the many scripts we have named belonged to this category.

The Chou Dynasty, which succeeded the Shang Dynasty in 1122 B.C., was a sprawling, feudalistic empire composed of many kingdoms and principalities. We are not at all sure what the language situation was at the time. In the later period, especially after the Chou capital was moved to the east in 771 B.C., the realm was in the process of fragmentation. Two separate cultures seemed to have existed side by side, one in the west and one in the east. The culture of the east was centred at the Kingdom of Lu, in which Confucius was born in 551 B.C. The written language, like the political situation, must have been extremely diversified.

The etymologist Hsü Shen tells us that a court chronicler named Shih Chou, who lived during the reign of Emperor Hsüan (827-788 B.C.) of the Chou Dynasty, made a valiant attempt to codify the then-existing writing systems into a standard vocabulary of some 9,000 characters. He arranged the characters into a text divided into fifteen chapters. This vocabulary was then officially adopted by the court for pedagogical purpose. The writing system he fashioned later came to be known as *Chou wên,* the character *Chou* being part of Shih Chou's name. Unfortunately, Hsü Shên did not tell us more about the man Shih Chou. We do not even know whether Shih Chou is the name of a man or a term used to designate 'the process of learning undertaken by the prince', as the modern scholar Wang Kuo-wei has asserted. The fifteen chapters of text Shih Chou was supposed to have compiled has also been irreparably lost. What we now have is only a term, *Chou wên,* which has come to mean the type of the script *chuan shu* used in the Chou Dynasty. In any case, whatever Shih Chou was supposed to have done could not have been very effective because we know as a fact that the Chinese written language long after his time was still far from uniform.

After a long period of disunion and internecine warfare, China finally came under the unified rule of the Ch'in Dynasty in 221 B.C. Dominated by the Legalist School of Philosophy, uniformity became the order of the day. Upon the order of the First Emperor, Shih Huang Ti, the Prime Minister Li Ssǔ was charged with the responsibility of reforming the written language and to devise a writing system which was to be generally used throughout the empire. The script submitted to his sovereign was a modification and improvement of all the scripts up to his time. It was a revolutionary step forward, the first uniform script for all China. Scholars of a later day have chosen to group all the different scripts before Li Ssǔ's time as the *ta chuan,*

Fig. 7   *Chung Chou Chung*

including *chin wên, chia ku wên* and *Chou wên,* to be distinguished from Li Ssŭ's script, which is known as the *hsiao chuan.**

With the coming into general use of Li Ssŭ's *hsiao chuan,* we have arrived at a major turning point in the evolution of the Chinese script, and we might well pause for a moment to take stock of the situation.

1. Before Li Ssŭ, a character might be written in any number of ways more or less at the whim of the writer. We have noted that the character *yang* (sheep) was written in no less than forty-five ways on the oracle bones. Some scholars have counted seventy-six ways by which the character *jên* (man) was written in the ancient relics. Li Ssŭ's great contribution was to standardize the way each character was to be written. His contribution to education and learning is wellnigh incalculable.

2. The ancient scribes used to do their characters in varying size and shape, some large and some small, some squat and some elongated, some upright and some sidewise. Li Ssŭ prescribed that all characters, irrespective of the number of strokes and elements they contained, must be written in uniform size and in upright position. With the *hsiao chuan,* therefore, it is possible to allocate equal space to each character and each line will contain an equal number of characters. Characters in *hsiao chuan* are generally slightly elongated, so that the spaces allocated to the characters are upright rectangles.

3. Characters in the ancient scripts, *ta chuan,* were often crude and unfinished, sometimes even childlike, which must have offended Li Ssŭ's methodical mind. In devising the *hsiao chuan,* Li Ssŭ made it a point to adhere strictly to geometric forms: the strokes were all of even width with no modulation, the lines perfectly straight, the curves fully rounded, the crosses at right angles. Artistry in doing *hsiao chuan* characters consisted in gaining complete mastery of the pliable tip of the brush, executing each stroke with even strength, making straight and circular lines without the aid of geometric instruments, and maintaining perfect symmetry on all sides. The lines in *hsiao chuan* were thin and strong, so the script has also come to be called *yü chin,* 'jade muscles', or *t'ieh hsien,* 'iron wires'.

The importance of the *hsiao chuan* in the evolution of the Chinese script cannot be over-estimated. When Hsü Shên compiled his dictionary *Shuo Wên Chieh Tzŭ* in 100 A.D., he used the *hsiao chuan* as the point of departure. When the Ch'ing Emperor K'ang-hsi ordered the compilation of the dictionary *K'ang-hsi Tzŭ Tien,* in the year 1716, characters in *hsiao chuan* were displayed on the margins for reference purposes.

The ancient scribes who experimented so boldly with the script have left us with a number of samples of their writing. We have already seen some of the characters on the Shang bronzes and oracle bones. They seem

---

* Up to this point, I have tried, however unsuccessfully, to supply a translation or explanation of the Chinese terms introduced into the text. I am compelled to depart from this practice in relation to the names of the several scripts partly because the terms are simply untranslatable and partly because they are technical terms which a student of Chinese calligraphy ought to know.

Fig. 8   *Mao Kung Ting*

to speak to us across the millenniums, telling us of the exploits of the ancient kings, the joy of marriages and births, the sorrow of deaths, the celebration attending a bounty harvest, the relief at the first drop of rain after a long drought, the glory of subduing the mighty tiger, the fear that was evoked by the appearance of bad omens, the solemnity at the ceremonies of ancestor worship. For the epigrapher, his reward is in deciphering the characters and in piecing together the stories they tell. The biographical sketch of the Sung painter Li Kung-lin contains the following entry: 'He knows many old characters.'

The most important documents left us by the Chou people are three bronze utensils bearing long inscriptions. The earliest one, *San Shih P'an,* is a ceremonial basin dating back to the reign of the Chou Emperor Li (reign 861-827 B.C.), a large shallow vessel supported on a broad circular foot flaring outward at the base, with two plain handles attached to the sides (Fig. 6). The basin is unusually large, being approximately twenty-five inches in diameter. While it is remarkably well cast and preserved, the feature that attracts our special attention is the inscription inside the basin consisting of 357 characters distributed in nineteen lines. Epigraphers have studied the inscription carefully and have found it to be a formal document settling a territorial dispute between two kingdoms, Ts'ê and San. It appears that the King of Ts'ê, for unexplained reasons, had launched an invasion upon some areas belonging to the King of San. Equally mysteriously, the King of Ts'ê was compelled to cede to the King of San some farmland as reparations. Officials of the two disputants were despatched to arrange for the transfer of the farmland, a transaction which was supervised by a representative of the Chou Emperor. The Ts'ê delegate took an oath pledging that his King would not make more trouble for the King of San. The Emperor's representative thereupon turned over the map of the farmland to the Ts'ê delegate while keeping a copy of the map himself. The San delegate, to solemnize the occasion, had the long statement made by the Emperor's representative engraved on the bronze basin as a documentary proof of the incident. After the exchange the basin was buried in the ground presumably for safe-keeping. It was a minor incident and was soon forgotten. The basin remained buried for twenty-five centuries until it was unearthed by accident in 1770 A.D. Immediately recognized as a priceless treasure, it passed through the hands of one collector after another. In 1809, it found its way into the Ch'ing imperial collection and was taken over by the National Palace Museum after the Republic.

A second Chou bronze is a large bell, known as *Chung Chou Chung,* which is 27½ inches in height. It is a hollow elliptical article surrounded by a vertical shank at the lower end of which is a flange with a ring for suspension. On the upper part of each face of the bell are two rectangular areas each framing nine 'nipples'. On the front of the bell in the centre panel are 32

Fig. 9 Inscription on *San Shih P'an* (detail)

characters in four lines; below, on the left side, are 57 characters in eight lines; and on the back at the lower right are 33 characters in five lines. Taken together, these three groups add up to a single inscription of 122 characters. Made during the reign of the Chou Emperor Li, the inscription is an account of some of the happenings of the time, mostly inconsequential (Fig. 7).

The third and perhaps the most important Chou bronze with inscriptions is a huge vessel with three legs, a type of utensil called *ting*, sometimes arbitrarily translated as 'tripod', which the legendary Emperor Yü of the Hsia Dynasty chose as a symbol of State authority. Generally placed as the product of the reign of the Chou Emperor Hsüan (reign 827-781 B.C.), the enormous vessel bears an inscription consisting of no less than 497 characters arranged in two groups totalling thirty-two lines. It records the gratitude of a certain Yin, Duke of Mao, for favours bestowed upon him by the Chou Emperor. The vessel, therefore, has come to be identified as *Mao Kung Ting*. The long inscription quotes the Emperor as saying to the Duke of Mao how the great founders of the Chou Dynasty were granted the Mandate of Heaven to rule the Empire, and how their successors must always be on the alert to the sacred duties of governance, how every care must be taken to be just and kind to the people, how the administrative edicts should be drafted and implemented, how the ruler must lead an upright and moral life as a model and lesson to the subordinates and the people. The inscription ends with a list of valuables bestowed upon the Duke of Mao—horses and carriages, bows and arrows, symbols of authority made of jade, wine and other things for sacrificial use. The Duke of Mao, having received such benevolence from the Emperor, undertook to cast the large *ting* in order to perpetuate the Emperor's admonitions 'to be handed down to descendants to treasure for ever and ever'. The *Mao Kung Ting*, like the *San Shih P'an*, was buried for twenty-five centuries. It was unearthed in the middle of the nineteenth century, and after passing through the hands of many collectors, was finally acquired by the Chinese Government in 1928, and is now in the collection of the National Palace Museum (Fig. 8).

The script used in the inscriptions on all three of the Chou bronzes belongs to the category of *ta chuan*, which ostensibly is the same as what is known as *Chou wên*. From the rubbing of the inscription of the *San Shih P'an* (Fig. 9), we can readily see that the characters, while still rather irregular, are considerably more stylized and more uniform than those on the Shang bronzes and oracle bones. The characters are also more 'modern', that is, nearer to the scripts used in a later age, so that deciphering them is no longer an insurmountable problem.

Some time in the seventh century, a series of ten 'stone drums' (*shih ku*) were discovered, all with inscriptions telling the story of a hunting expedition made by the Chou Emperor Hsüan. Due to their long exposure to the elements

Fig. 10　Inscription on Stone Drums (detail)

and their extremely eventful career, quite a number of the inscribed characters have become illegible. At present, only 321 out of a possible 500 characters may still be seen. One of the stone drums is undoubtedly a later replacement.

Considerable controversies have attended the question of the authenticity of the stone drums. That they are relics of antiquity is beyond dispute. The argument centres on the exact date of their origin. The T'ang essayist, the illustrious Han Yü, believed their authenticity as Chou relics enough to compose a long poem about them, pleading eloquently with the authorities to take good care of them and to instal them in the Temple of Confucius. Han Yü, and later the Sung savant Su Shih, attributed them to the reign of the Chou Emperor Hsüan, which made them contemporaries of the *Mao Kung Ting,* an attribution which was shared by many T'ang scholars, including the T'ang critic of calligraphy, Chang Huai-kuan. The scholar Su Hsü and the poet Wei Ying-wu, both of the T'ang Dynasty, even believed that the stone drum inscriptions were actually based on characters written by no less than Shih Chou himself. On the other hand, in the Sung Dynasty, the great student of antiquity, Ou-yang Siu, raised many doubts on the attribution, although he himself was unable to come up with a theory of his own. Ou-yang Siu, besides being a literary man of high stature, was a professional archaeologist, and his views, all carefully reasoned, are entitled to the utmost respect. In our time, with the aid of modern science, a scholar named T'ang Kuo-hsiang has offered seemingly incontrovertible evidence to support his theory that the stone drums were fabricated in the third year of the reign of King Ling of the Kingdom of Ch'in, namely, 422 B.C. Irrespective of whether or not the stone drums are genuine Chou products, they are beyond any doubt the oldest Chinese stone engraving extant.

The script of the inscriptions of the stone drums has become a script in its own right, known to the Chinese as *shih ku wên* (Fig. 10). It is quite obvious that the script belongs to the same family as the inscriptions on the Chou bronzes—*San Shih P'an, Chung Chou Chung* and *Mao Kung Ting.* In other words, it is a form of *ta chuan,* or *Chou wên.* However, it has been pointed out that the calligraphic style of the stone drum script seems to bear some resemblance to the *hsiao chuan* devised by Li Ssŭ. Calligraphically speaking, therefore, the stone drums should be somewhat later than the Chou bronzes, and the script of the inscriptions may be regarded as a transitory step between *ta chuan* and *hsiao chuan.*

The oracle bone characters were carved on plastron and animal bones; those on the Chou bronzes were cast on metal; and the stone drum characters were engraved on stone. The latter inaugurated the practice of engraving characters on stone, a practice which has been perpetuated down to the present day.

In the year 219 B.C., the First Emperor of the Ch'in Dynasty, Shih Huang Ti, made a grand tour of his far-flung Empire. At six different points of his

Fig. 11   *I Shan Pei* (detail)

journey, stone slabs were erected to commemorate his great deeds. Instead of just setting up stone markers, he was prevailed upon by his courtiers to record his glories in words which were to be engraved on the stone slabs. The characters were done by Li Ssǔ and the script, of course, was *hsiao chuan.*

All the stone slabs belonging to the Ch'in period have been either destroyed by fire or disintegrated beyond recognition. In the tenth century, a man by the name of Hsü Hsüan devoted fifty years of his life to the study of the Ch'in tablets. One of the tablets done by Li Ssǔ was erected at the mountain I Shan. Hsü Hsüan made a replica of it, carving the characters on hard date-wood instead of stone. From the Hsü Hsüan replica of the *I Shan Pei* (Fig. 11), we are privileged to get a glimpse of Li Ssǔ's *hsiao chuan.* But even from such an imperfect model, we can see the balance, the symmetry, the austerity of the characters, so dignified and formal that we cannot help being reminded of the totalitarian policies the Ch'in statesman pursued, policies which made China's first unification one of the most short-lived in her history.

Chapter Four

Han Innovations

Even as Li Ssǔ was mobilizing the highly centralized bureaucratic apparatus of the Ch'in government to make the *hsiao chuan* the standard script of all China, experiments were being made to devise something which was less formal and easier to execute. With the establishment of a central government wielding real and nationwide power for the first time in history, and with the extension of the Empire's frontiers to the far corners of the Asian continent, the *hsiao chuan,* with all its balance and symmetry and geometric forms, was demonstrably too cumbersome a script for the transcription of the torrents of edicts and proclamations flowing out of the capital city. A script with more easily and quickly executed characters was urgently called for.

According to classical art history, the answer to the call, oddly enough, came from a man named Ch'êng Miao who certainly had plenty of time on his hands, for he was an inmate of Li Ssǔ's crowded prisons. For ten years he experimented with a new script in his lonely cell. At last he produced something, a vocabulary of three thousand characters written in a way totally different from the *hsiao chuan*. The First Emperor, Shih Huang Ti, was pleased with what Ch'êng Miao showed him, and Ch'êng Miao was released from gaol and given, of all things, the office of a censor. The new script was called *li shu,* the character *li* being a general term for lowly persons. It was soon adopted as the script to be used by clerks and assistants for the drafting of documents while the *hsiao chuan* remained as the script for formal and official occasions.

[35]

Chinese art historians of old, especially Chang Huai-kuan, were fond of crediting a specific individual for the invention of each one of the scripts. Thus, Ch'êng Miao was given credit for fathering the script *li shu.* Modern archaeological research, however, has discovered many articles, such as coins and measuring instruments, made before the Ch'in Dynasty with characters executed more or less in the manner of *li shu,* suggesting therefore that Ch'êng Miao really did not invent the script all by himself. It was quite probable that a rudimentary form of *li shu* was in existence in the Ch'un Ch'iu Period and the Period of the Warring States, and that Ch'êng Miao was the man who turned it into a well-ordered script. His place in the history of Chinese calligraphy is, therefore, not entirely undeserved.

The introduction of *li shu* into general use, despite its humble origins, was a major breakthrough in the evolution of the Chinese script. It perhaps represented the most complete change from the past, opening entirely new vistas for the future. We may say that the *hsiao chuan,* however refreshingly novel, was in the nature of the summing up of the past. The *li shu,* on the other hand, was a revolution, the beginning of a brave new era. We are justified in saying this because *li shu* was the script which for the first time brought out the full capabilities of the brush.

Chinese calligraphy is the way of the brush, a most sensitive and versatile instrument, 'one of the most ingenious devices of man', with an almost limitless range of stylistic expressiveness. It used to be believed that the brush was the invention of the great Ch'in warrior Mêng T'ien, a contemporary of Li Ssǔ. Modern archaeology has exploded this long-held theory. Excavations carried out at Anyang have unearthed among the oracle bones a white pottery shard on which fragments of a character undoubtedly written with a brush can clearly be seen. In 1954, a brush was found in a grave in modern Changsha belonging to the Period of the Warring States. The brush has a round slender stem measuring about five inches in length, with a tuft of about an inch. These two archaeological finds have pushed back the date of the first use of the brush for writing way beyond Mêng T'ien's time. The prevailing opinion now is that, while the Chinese had been writing and picturing with the brush as far back as the Shang and Chou period, Chinese historians, in their habit of attributing an invention to a particular individual, gave the credit to Mêng T'ien because, while leading Ch'in troops to subdue the barbarians and supervising the building of parts of the Great Wall, he found time to fashion a brush of rabbit-hair with which he wrote his reports to his sovereign about his extraordinary exploits. In 1931, archaeologists found in North-western China (Chü-yen, Edsin Gol) a brush which dated back to the first century A.D. It is probably something very similar to what Mêng T'ien fabricated.

The Chinese brush is made of hairs or feathers or a combination of their varieties attached to a stem usually made of bamboo or wood. Because of the different qualities of the hairs and feathers used, there is a general distinction between what is known as a 'soft' and a 'stiff' brush. Whatever the material used, the tuft always comes to a sharp point, never spread out as the brush used by the Western painters. The Ch'ing scholar, Liang T'ung-shu, in a delightful little book on the brush, lists no less than thirty-six varieties of the brush, classified according to the materials with which they are made. Among the materials used animal hairs predominate: sheep, goat, rabbit, deer, wolf, musk-deer, tiger, fox, pig, horse, mouse, otter, gorilla, mongoose-tail, and others. Feathers used include those of goose, chicken and pheasant. One of the rare qualities favoured by some of the greatest calligraphers is the brush made of mouse-whiskers. Experiments have been made with materials of the vegetable kingdom: thorns, reeds, wood fibres, bamboo threads, though without appreciable success. The story is told that when a minor official in Canton lost the rabbit-hair brush belonging to his boss, and since the proper kind of rabbit-hair was unobtainable in his part of the country, he was driven to make a brush with his own whiskers and got away with it. Another man was reported to have made a brush with the tender hair of his infant child.

Brush-making is an exacting craft, and good brush-makers are highly honoured. Liang T'ung-shu, in his book, gives the names of ninety-two brush-makers over the centuries distinguished for the extraordinary qualities of their products. In the Chinese mind things associated with art and letters are surrounded by an aura of sacredness. Thus, the brush-makers, and even the brushes themselves, if they are of the finest quality, are endowed with super-natural attributes. We have been told that some particularly noted brush-makers, upon concluding their exalted profession on this earth, departed into the great beyond riding on a piece of rainbow-coloured cloud in a blaze of dazzling light, while others turned themselves into exotic birds eternally soaring in the heavens. Being responsible for so much beauty in our world, worn-out brushes have been buried by their owners like old heroes in solemn ceremonies.

The best brushes are, of course, made of the best hairs. In the old days, the most valued rabbit-hairs were those from the plains of North China because, according to Wang Hsi-chih, the Sage of Calligraphy, there were no weeds on the North China plains and the grass was long and fine, thus making the rabbits well-nourished and fat and their hairs firm and resilient. In the T'ang Dynasty, rabbit-hairs found in the deep mountains of Central China, especially in the Hsüan-ch'êng district, were considered the best. In the later centuries, Hu-chou in the Eastern Province of Chekiang became the centre of brush-making. Hence the term *Hu pi*, 'brushes from Hu-chou'.

Rabbit-hairs are at their best in mid-autumn when they are neither too soft nor too thick, especially those on the middle part of the animal's back and its flanks. When plucked, the hairs are first soaked in lime water to remove the oil and then tied together into tufts. We have been told that 'sheep-wool

[37]

is best in Chia-hsing, second best in Hsiu-shui, while that from Chia-shan and Hai-yen is inferior', with no further explanation. This typical Chinese statement is puzzling because all the four districts mentioned are in one of China's smallest provinces. Similarly, we are puzzled by the statement that brushes made of otter-hairs can be used to do eighty scrolls while those made of musk-deer hairs can do only forty scrolls.

The tuft of the brush is attached to a stem usually made of bamboo, which has the advantage of being inexpensive, light and durable. The rich and the ostentatious sometimes use more valuable materials for the stem—gold, silver, ivory, jade, crystal, tortoise-shell, rhinoceros-horn, porcelain, sandal-wood, and a special kind of speckled bamboo known as *Hsiang-fei chu* found in Hunan and Kwangsi. The valuable stems are often protected by brocade jackets, and the tufts may be replaced. Brush-stems almost always bear incised inscriptions indicating the variety and the maker. Occasionally they are decorated with pictures of human figures and landscape scenes. An ordinary brush comes with a bamboo container which is discarded in favour of a brass cap. A row of brass caps lined up on a stand, a normal equipment in a study, is called *han lin*, 'brush forest', a term which is also used to designate a scholar who has passed the advanced examination for public service. Worms may feast on the glue used to fasten the tuft on to the stem. One way to discourage the worms is to soak the brush in lime water. Immersing the brush in a sulphur-alcohol solution has the effect of prolonging its useful life.

The brush is an instrument to be handled with care and respect. The stiff tuft of a new brush should first be softened gently with clear water until about two-thirds of its length has become pliable. After use, the brush should be thoroughly rinsed to remove all remnants of ink. A brush is permanently ruined when the hairs are deranged. Liu Kung-ch'üan, the T'ang calligrapher, said that one misplaced hair would make a brush unserviceable. Some people, therefore, hang their brushes up to dry, and some brushes come with a string lobe on the stem for that purpose. A common way of arranging the hairs, to make them come to a sharp point, is to lick the tuft gently with the tongue and shape it with the lips. A well-ordered tuft should be in the shape of a tender bamboo shoot after a downpour in early spring. Liu Kung-ch'üan, in a letter thanking his friend who presented him with some brushes, defines a good brush in terms of long tuft, fine hairs, slender stem and even cut. Other calligraphers, however, may have other preferences. The fastidious calligraphers have brushes made to their personal specifications.

We have gone into a discussion of the brush at this point because when the *li shu* was being introduced for general use, the brush was becoming the prevailing instrument of writing. Without the brush, execution of characters in *li shu* would have been impossible. Thus, with the introduction of *li shu,* the art of calligraphy (brush-writing) was born.

[38]

Fig. 12 Han Inscription of Classics on Stone

The autocratic First Emperor, Shih Huang Ti, of the Ch'in Dynasty ordered the burning of the classics in 213 B.C. The Han Emperors, in a conscientious effort to repair the damage, were determined to encourage and intensify the study of the classics. Because the texts were salvaged from the Ch'in fire, a great deal of textual collation had to be done. In 175 A.D., when the collation task was completed, Ts'ai Yung, an outstanding scholar and calligrapher of the time, obtained the permission of the Han Emperor Ling-ti to have the entire body of the Five Classics engraved on stone. To train the scribes to perform this gigantic task, the Emperor set up the *Hung T'u Kuan,* the Academy of Calligraphy, in which the most accomplished scribes of the realm were assembled. Children over seventeen years of age were tested for their calligraphic capabilities by writing nine thousand characters in the major scripts. Those who showed talent were assigned to the Academy and in due course became court calligraphers. The promotion of calligraphy thus became a national policy and the standards were understandably high.

The text of the Five Classics was transcribed by Ts'ai Yung and the members of the Academy of Calligraphy. It was engraved on stone tablets. The process of transcription and engraving was completed in 183 A.D. The tablets stood like a forest in front of the National University outside K'ai-yang Gate of the City of Loyang. The tablets were sheltered by tiled roofs and protected by balustrades. They attracted nation-wide attention and, according to the chroniclers, thousands of carriages brought people from all over the country to admire them, while police squads were stationed on the spot to direct traffic and maintain order.

The tablets, unfortunately, soon ran into trouble. Fighting attendant to the Tung Cho Rebellion in 190 A.D. destroyed half of them, and subsequent disturbances destroyed more. In the past seventeen centuries, fragments of the tablets were unearthed from time to time. One of the largest and best preserved fragments was not unearthed until 1934. It is now in the collection of the Chinese National Historical Museum in Taiwan (Fig. 12).

The tablet transcriptions were done in *li shu,* the most commonly used script of the time. We cannot be sure whether or not the sample we have was done by Ts'ai Yung himself, but we should have no doubt that it was done by one of the best calligraphers available at the time. We can see readily that the Han scribe had taken full advantage of the pliability of the brush to achieve artistic effects radically different from those of the *hsiao chuan.* The strokes of the characters in *li shu* are purposely uneven and wavy, with terminations ending with a decided flick, giving the impression of a tail, with the obvious idea of producing a modulating and graceful effect. In the structure of the *li shu* characters, little if any effort is directed towards balance and symmetry, while distortions and exaggerations are deliberately introduced to enhance the formal appeal of the characters. *Li shu* is indeed an exhilarating liberation from the shackles of *hsiao chuan's* excessive rigidity and formalism,

Fig. 13a   *I Ying Pei* (detail)

and endows the calligrapher with the freedom by which he may turn the characters into vehicles of stylistic expressiveness.

At this point a most confusing element must be injected. It has to do with a script known to the Chinese as *pa fên,* a term the precise meaning of which has never been satisfactorily defined. According to one authority, the first, at least the best known, practitioner of the *pa fên* script was none other than Ts'ai Yung, and Ts'ai Yung's daughter, who presumably ought to know, defined *pa fên* as 'eighty per cent Li Ssǔ's *hsiao chuan* mixed with twenty per cent Ch'êng Miao's *li shu'*. However, a much later writer, the Ming Dynasty critic Ho Liang-chün, asserted that Ts'ai Yung's *pa fên* script as revealed by a tablet attributed to him, the *Hsia Ch'êng Pei,* was 'twenty per cent *hsiao chuan* and eighty per cent *li shu'*. We have seen rubbings of the *Hsia Ch'êng Pei,* and we must agree with Ho Liang-chün that the characters have only the faintest traces of features associated with *hsiao chuan.* In both theories, the character *pa* was interpreted literally as meaning 'eight' and the term *pa fên* meaning 'eighty per cent'. However, some other writers, including the Ch'ing Dynasty critic Pao Shih-ch'ên, claimed that the character *pa* in the term *pa fên* had nothing to do with the concept of 'eight' at all. Basing themselves on etymological explanations, they advanced the proposition that *pa* used in this connotation should be taken to mean 'back-to-back', and that *pa fên* was really a term used by the ancient writers to describe the spread-out formations of the characters done in the script. This latter theory, it may be said, is favoured by most modern writers, who are also in general agreement that most of the tablets of the Eastern Han Dynasty (25-219 A.D.) were done in the *pa fên* script.

The samples of Han calligraphy we now have are rubbings of stone tablets which the Chinese call *pei.* We have been told that, in the Chou Dynasty, tablets were erected against walls to tell time. The Chou tablets had holes in them, permitting sunlight to shine through on to the walls against which the tablets were erected, thus serving the purpose of the sundial. During sacrificial ceremonies, the tablets also served as stumps to which animals were tied before slaughter. In the Ch'in Dynasty, as we have seen, tablets with or without inscriptions were used to commemorate the great deeds of the rulers. The Han people believed strongly in providing lavish funerals for the departed. They used to build elaborately decorated chambers to house the remains of the dead. We owe to this custom the good fortune of being able to see now the magnificent stone carvings of Han tombs such as Hsiao T'ang Shan and Wu Liang Tz'ǔ, which inform us so much of the history and art of the period. The custom of lavish funerals is responsible also for the innumerable tablets by the rubbings of which we are enabled to study the evolution of the script and to see samples of ancient calligraphy. When a person dies, it has been the custom for the descendants and relatives to ask a prominent literary figure of the day to compose an epitaph and an outstanding

Fig. 13b   *Shih Ch'ên Pei* (detail)

calligrapher to transcribe it. Sometimes, another calligrapher, particularly one good in *chuan shu,* is asked to write the title of the tablet. The transcription of the epitaph and the title are then engraved on a stone tablet which is erected either in front or on top of the grave. Although lavish funerals have been proscribed from time to time by rulers on the ground that they are a waste of money, the custom of tablet-erecting has persisted down to the present day and has been regarded as a suitable manifestation of filial piety. There are literally millions of tablets in all parts of China. Although the epitaphs are as a rule routine eulogies and are therefore worthless as historical sources, the inscriptions and the rubbings thereof are invaluable samples of the calligraphic styles of the ancient artists, known and unknown, whose original works have been irreparably lost. Whether wasteful or not, the tablets have certainly furnished us with a most important source for the study of calligraphic art.

Few tablets belonging to the Western Han Dynasty (206 B.C. to 25 A.D.) have come down to us. Tablets of the Eastern Han Dynasty (25-219 A.D.), however, are legion: *I Ying Pei, Shih Ch'ên Pei* and *Ts'ao Ch'üan Pei* are good examples (Fig. 13). Oddly enough, these three tablets were not made to honour the dead. The first one, *I Ying Pei,* is dated 153 A.D. In that year, the Minister of Lu petitioned the Han Emperor Huan-ti to appoint an official to supervise the ceremonies conducted at the Temple of Confucius as a measure of respect for the sage. The petition was accepted. The text of the inscription consists of the petition submitted by the Minister of Lu, a man named I Ying, and related documents. The second tablet, *Shih Ch'ên Pei,* consists of two parts, both erected in 169 A.D., during the reign of Emperor Ling-ti of the Eastern Han Dynasty. The inscription of the first part consists of the text of a petition submitted by the Minister of Lu at the time, Shih Ch'ên, to make offerings to the Temple of Confucius. The text of the inscription of the second part records the ceremonies during the offering. Both parts contain many superstitious references to Confucius and the meaning is not entirely clear. The third tablet, *Ts'ao Ch'üan Pei,* erected in 185 A.D., recounts the good deeds of the magistrate of Ko-yang (Shensi), a man by the name of Ts'ao Ch'üan. All three tablets belong to the category of what the Chinese call *chi kung pei,* 'tablets recording good and noble deeds', to which Li Ssŭ's *I Shan Pei* (Fig. 11) also belongs.

Eastern Han tablets were usually done in the *pa fên* script, and the three tablets we have seen are good samples of it. The most distinguishing features are the wavy strokes and the heavy flick of the terminations (what the Chinese call *po cheh*), features which bring out the full pliability of the brush. As we can see, there are great similarities between *li shu* and *pa fên* (compare the samples in Fig. 12 and Fig. 13), and it is not easy to tell them apart.

Besides tablets, the Han people have also left for us a large number of bricks and tiles bearing inscriptions. Characters on Han bricks are generally

Fig. 13c *Ts'ao Ch'üan Pei* (detail)

in *li shu* or *pa fên*. Those on tiles are often in a script which the Chinese call *mou chuan* and which has been defined as 'simpler than *chuan shu* and more complicated than *li shu*'. For some reason, the *mou chuan* has become the favoured script for the carving of seals and, according to some authorities, it should be considered a script in its own right, a sort of halfway house between *chuan shu* and *li shu,* certainly more so than *pa fên.*

It used to be believed that no Han calligraphy in the original had come down to us. Then, at the beginning of the twentieth century, an enormous number of wood and bamboo slips were discovered at Tun-huang and Chü-yen (Edsin Gol). All the samples of ancient calligraphy we had seen so far were second-hand in the sense that the characters appeared to us engraved on shells and bones, bronze utensils and chunks of stone. The Han slips, known as *Han chien,* for the first time enabled us to see the result of the original application of the brush to the writing surface. The Han slips are, therefore, original manuscripts in the true sense of the term.

The slips are government records made by minor officials. Tun-huang and Chü-yen were outposts of the Han Empire. The texts tell us little concerning either historical events or administrative procedure. The characters on the slips were done by clerks who had no pretensions to calligraphic proficiency. But they are invaluable as source materials for the study of the evolution of the Chinese script. The earliest slip discovered was dated 94 B.C., during the reign of the great Han Emperor Wu-ti. In presenting a photographic reproduction of one of the slips to the public, the custodian of the slips in the Academia Sinica wrote: 'The remarkable thing about this authentic manuscript is not its considerable age (about 2,000 years) but the fact that any present-day Chinese with a good secondary or even primary education can read it' (Fig. 14).

The formal script of the Han Dynasty was the *li shu* or *pa fên.* However, some people apparently became impatient with the act of writing the script and decided to devise 'a quick version' of it. The Chinese, as we have seen, have always been in the habit of crediting a particular individual with the inauguration of something new. In this case, the lucky man was Shih Yu, who was an official in the court of the Han Emperor Yüan-ti (reign 48-33 B.C.). According to classical literature, Shih Yu transcribed the text of an essay entitled *Chi Chiu Chang* in a script which was totally different from *li shu* or *pa fên.* In doing the characters, many strokes and elements were boldly eliminated. The individual strokes, though executed one by one, were of uneven width and the flick was always grossly exaggerated. One old writer defined Shih Yu's writing in these words: 'Keep the basic structure of the character in *li shu,* compromise on its formality, allow it to run wild and free, in order to meet the demands of time.' This type of writing soon acquired the appellation *ts'ao shu,* and Shih Yu's own style was labelled *chang ts'ao.* The original manuscript done by Shih Yu has long been lost.

[46]

Fig. 14   Han Slip

But calligraphers in later days have been copying his style with very pleasing effect (Fig. 15). There are several living calligraphers who are specialists in *chang ts'ao.*

Here again we run into questions of nomenclature which seem to plague the study of Chinese calligraphy throughout. The authoritative *Hsüan-ho Shu P'u,* the encyclopaedia of calligraphy compiled by order of the Sung Emperor Hui-tsung in 1120 A.D., flatly stated: 'The parentage of *ts'ao shu* is the subject of much controversy', and left it at that. Although the terms *ts'ao shu* and *chang ts'ao* have been used freely by Chinese art historians and critics, there has been no agreement at all as to why they have been so called. Parenthetically, it may be mentioned that the term *ts'ao shu* has been translated as 'the grass script'. This is definitely wrong, for the character *ts'ao* used in this connection has nothing whatsoever to do with what grows on the lawn. In common Chinese usage, the character *ts'ao,* used as a verb, may mean either 'to draft' (as in the phrase 'to draft a document') or 'to originate' (as in the phrase 'to originate a reform'). Both meanings of the character have been applied to the use of the character *ts'ao* in the term *ts'ao shu.* Thus, we may either say that *ts'ao shu* was a script devised for the purpose of drafting documents or that it was a script originated by Shih Yu. The origin of the term *chang ts'ao* is equally confusing. One theory is that the script Shih Yu devised has come to be known as *chang ts'ao* because he first used it to transcribe the essay *Chi Chiu Chang,* in other words, *ts'ao shu* in the style of Shih Yu's *Chi Chiu Chang.* Another theory is that in the Han Dynasty the script was extensively used in writing memorials which were known as *chang.* A third theory, which has been totally discredited, is that the script was particularly favoured by the Han Emperor Chang-ti. Whatever its origin, *chang ts'ao* has become a script in its own right, and many Han slips were done in it.

The Han calligrapher Ts'ai Yung, a specialist in *li shu,* was also noted for a type of writing known to the Chinese as *fei po,* a term which has been translated as 'flying white'. The *fei po* is done by dragging the brush over the writing surface at such high speed that the hairs of the brush do not consistently touch the surface, thus leaving irregular white streaks within the black strokes. Thus the *fei po* is really not a separate script but a peculiar effect achieved by the swift movement of the brush. Such effect can best be achieved by the use of a very large brush to write very large characters.

The *chang ts'ao,* as we have seen, is done with the strokes individually and separately executed. A calligrapher in the Later Han Dynasty, Chang Chih, did his *ts'ao shu* characters by having the strokes forming them linked together, even linking the last stroke of the preceding character with the first stroke of the succeeding character; thus a whole line composed of many characters may be written with one continuous application of the brush. This style of writing is, of course, a form of *ts'ao shu,* and has come to be known as

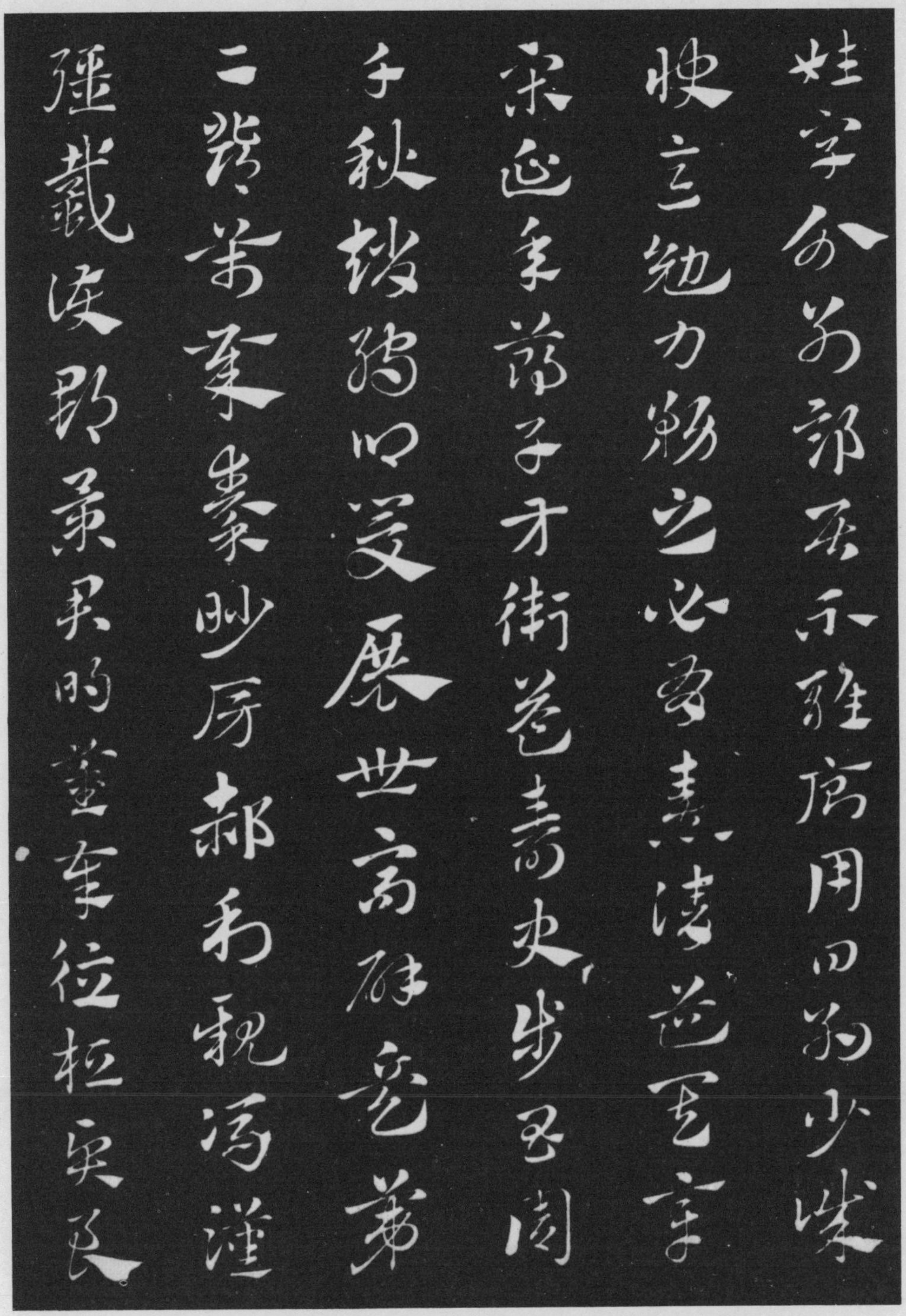

姓字分為部不雅底用四聲少嗟
映言勉力煩之必要壽淩邑至字
承延牢節子才衛卷壽央步邑圖
于秋越狗四受展世高輝宅弟
二裝柔耄眇辱郝利親馮灌
殭戟凌邵柔艮眇董奎位柾吳氏

Fig. 15 *Chang Ts'ao*. Copy of the *Chi Chiu Chang* made by
Chao Mêng-fu, dated 1303 (detail)

chin ts'ao, 'modern *ts'ao shu*', to distinguish it from the *chang ts'ao* originated by Shih Yu. In modern usage, *ts'ao shu* has become a generic term which embraces *chang ts'ao* (Shih Yu), *fei po* (Ts'ai Yung) and *chin ts'ao* (Chang Chih).

Ts'ao shu, in whatever form, was a big jump from the formality of the *li shu* and *pa fên,* perhaps too big to answer everyday needs. One of the great drawbacks of *ts'ao shu* is that the characters written in it are too abbreviated to be easily legible. Some way must therefore be found to bridge the gap. In the third quarter of the first century A.D., a man by the name of Wang Tz'ŭ-chung, of whose life and career we know nothing, was said to have worked out a script which was a modification of the *li shu* with an eye to its general adaptability to ordinary requirements. The script Wang Tz'ŭ-chung allegedly devised soon came to be known as *chên shu* (also known as *k'ai shu and chêng shu*). In its earlier form, the *chên shu* still retained a great deal of *li shu* and *pa fên* features. Gradually these features were shed by the calligraphers until *chên shu* became towards the end of the Han Dynasty a script in its own right, and many *chên shu* characters are found on the Han slips. From that time on, *chên shu* has become standard for formal purposes. In the hands of the great calligraphers of the T'ang Dynasty, *chên shu* rose to be *the* script of the Chinese written language and we shall have much to say about it in the subsequent chapters. In the past two thousand years, it has been the first thing the schoolboy encounters when he begins to learn to write.

Han inventiveness seemed to be truly limitless. Towards the end of the period, a need was felt for a script somewhere between *chên shu* and *ts'ao shu,* some sort of a compromise between the formality of the former and the cursoriness of the latter. This has come to be known as *hsing shu* and is traditionally attributed to one Liu Tê-shêng who lived in the second century A.D. Because of its obvious advantages as a script for everyday purposes, being easily executed and readily legible, the *hsing shu* reached its zenith of perfection in the hands of the great calligraphers of the Sung Dynasty and since then has become the most widely used script of the Chinese written language.

By the end of the Han Dynasty in 219 A.D., the evolutionary process of the Chinese script had completed itself. We cannot help admiring the Han people for their extraordinary courage and sustained vitality in undertaking such ceaseless and daring experimentation to provide the Chinese written language with all the scripts it needs for artistic and practical purposes. The dominant driving force has been to make the characters easy to execute without sacrificing their aesthetic potentialities. The T'ang art historian, Chang Huai-kuan, has explained the evolutionary process as the search for what he calls 'quicker versions', the idea being to make the Chinese written language more serviceable as the demands on it increase with the wider and wider diffusion of culture. At the same time, the calligraphers have been keeping all the scripts in use as vehicles of creative expression. The ancient scripts, though superseded by later ones for everyday purposes, are by no means obsolete. It is therefore proper for us to cast our eyes over the terrain we have traversed and to recapitulate the various scripts we have described:

1. *Chuan shu,* a generic term embracing all the ancient scripts from the characters found on the ancient bronzes and oracle bones (collectively known as *ta chuan*) down to and including Li Ssǔ's *hsiao chuan*;

2. *Li shu,* the prevailing script of the Han Dynasty, including the controversial *pa fên* (the *mou chuan* found on Han bricks, tiles and seals may be regarded as a variation of *li shu*);

3. *Ts'ao shu,* a generic term embracing *chang ts'ao, fei po* and *chin ts'ao*;

4. *Chên shu,* the formal script evolved out of *li shu* and *pa fên*; and

5. *Hsing shu,* a compromise between the formality of *chên shu* and the cursoriness of *ts'ao shu.*

Chapter Five

Wang Hsi-chih: The Master

All the bold experimentation and breath-taking inventiveness of the preceding centuries, it seems, were to set the stage for the appearance of Wang Hsi-chih, honoured and worshipped as the greatest calligraphic genius of all time, 'the master', 'the sage'. His stature in Chinese calligraphy is on the same plane as Michelangelo in sculpture, Beethoven in music, Shakespeare in English literature.

Born in 307 A.D.* to the chaotic and turbulent but gay and light-hearted world of the Period of South and North Dynasties, an age of stunning versatility and charm, Wang Hsi-chih came from one of the most distinguished families of the land. His father, a high official of the Tsin Dynasty, was an accomplished calligrapher, as was one of his uncles who rose to the Prime Ministership. Another uncle, Wang I, was not only a famed calligrapher but also a painter and a connoisseur of art. The aristocratic families of the day took the young Wang Hsi-chih under their wings. He soon earned a national reputation as a precocious and promising child. The lad was allowed to join the gatherings of the eminent scholars and a story was freely circulated that the old and venerable scholars even allowed the lad to eat at the same table with them. When Wang Hsi-chih was seventeen, Hsi Chien, a powerful political figure of the Eastern Tsin Dynasty, was looking for a son-in-law. The

---

* The date of Wang Hsi-chih's birth is traditionally given as 321 A.D. The date does not tally with some of the events in his life, including his artistic career. After painstaking research, Lu I-t'ung, a modern scholar, established the date at 307. The date of Wang Hsi-chih's death is traditionally 379. Lu I-t'ung moved it up to 365. Wang Hsi-chih's life span remains the same for both sets of dates—58 years.

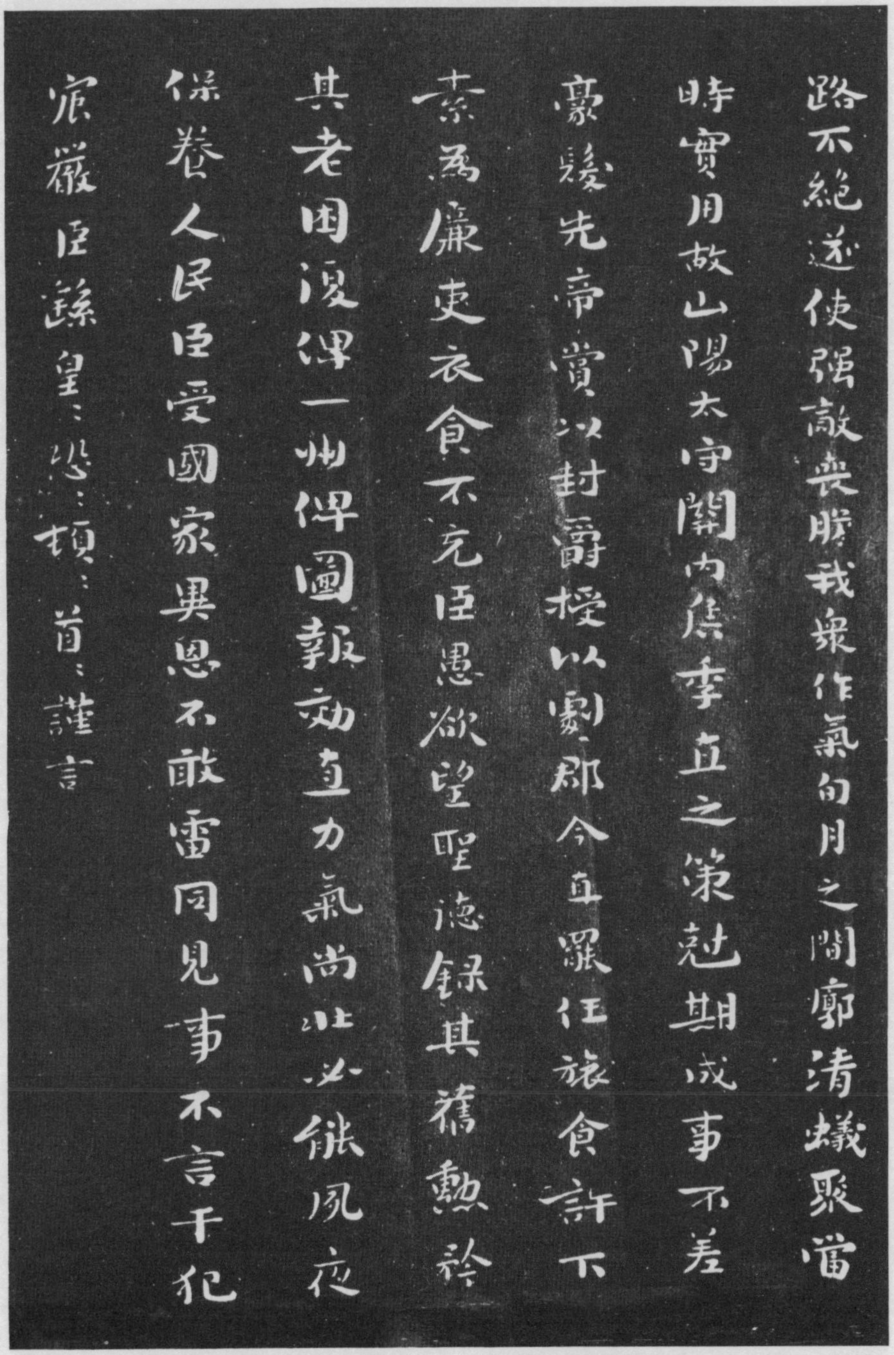

路不絕遂使強敵喪膽我眾作氣旬月之間廓清蟻聚當

時實用故山陽太守關內侯李直之策赴期成事不差

豪矣先帝賞以封爵授以劇郡今尚書僕射任旅食許下

蒙為廉吏衣食不充臣愚欲望聖德錄其舊勳矜

其老困復俾一州倖圖報効盡力氣尚此必徼風夜

保卷人民臣受國家異恩不敢雷同見事不言干犯

宸嚴臣繇惶恐頓首謹言

Fig. 16　Chung Yu: *Chien Chi Chih Piao* (detail)

eligible young men in town, so the story goes, were all dressed up for the selection. Wang Hsi-chih, however, elected to ignore the whole affair. On the fateful day, he was seen lying on a couch on the east porch of his house, his chest and belly fully exposed, nonchalantly munching a biscuit. Inevitably, as Chinese stories go, Wang Hsi-chih got the girl. In Chinese usage, the term 'east couch' (*tung ch'uang*) still means 'son-in-law'. Hsi Chien, Wang Hsi-chih's father-in-law, was also a calligrapher, as were his two sons. The girl Wang Hsi-chih married, with such a background, just could not help but be a calligrapher also. The marriage, it may be added, was a successful one, out of which came seven sons and at least one daughter. The seventh and youngest son, Wang Hsien-chih, became such a renowned calligrapher that he is always mentioned in the same breath with his father.

Wang Hsi-chih began his calligraphic training under the watchful eye of his uncle Wang I. At sixteen, his uncle became convinced that the lad would bring glory and fame to the already illustrious family. Wang Hsi-chih was able, according to his uncle, to imitate a style at first glance, both in painting and in calligraphy. His uncle had laid down the principle that 'a picture is my own picture, a calligraphic piece is my own calligraphic piece'. This rather obscure statement, quoted often in art histories, apparently meant that in painting and in calligraphy one must always try to develop one's own style. The uncle emphasized to Wang Hsi-chih the great importance of ceaseless cultivation of the art. To drive the point home, he did a group portrait of Confucius and his disciples to remind the lad of tutorship and education. 'Add endlessly to your store of knowledge and you will go far', he told Wang Hsi-chih.

Besides his uncle, Wang Hsi-chih had other tutors. One of them was Wei Shuo, a lady commonly known as Wei Fu-jên, who also came from a long line of calligraphers. No sample of Wei Shuo's work has survived and accounts of her calligraphic style differ considerably. It is generally supposed that she was particularly good in *li shu* and *pa fên*. This should occasion no surprise since the scripts were most popular at the time. She is also given credit for writing a manual on calligraphy called *Pi Chên T'u* in which she compared the art of calligraphy to the art of war. The manual may be found in anthologies but it is probably a forgery. In spite of the lady's military analogy, her own calligraphic style, according to a T'ang critic, was like 'a fairy playing with her shadows, a red lotus flower reflected on the pond'. Wang Hsi-chih, in his youthful enthusiasm, thought highly of Wei Shuo's style and worked hard to emulate it. When he became more mature, he turned to other models.

Chinese students of calligraphy are firmly of the belief that the making of a great calligrapher is built on the mastery of the techniques of all the scripts, old as well as new. This theory may be splendidly illustrated by Wang Hsi-chih's programme of training. After going through the early tutorship

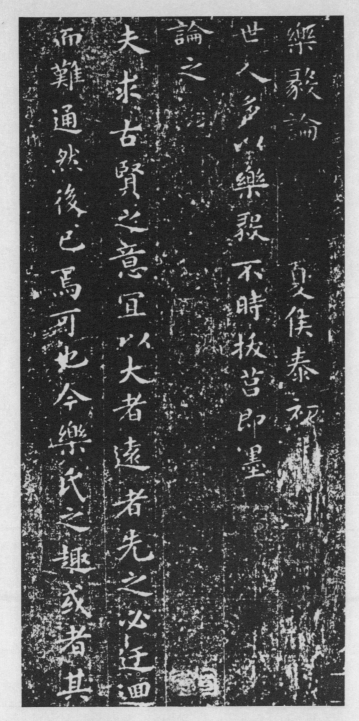

Fig. 17a Wang Hsi-chih: *Yüeh I Lun* (first portion)

of Wei Shuo, Wang Hsi-chih became convinced that he must delve much deeper into the mysteries of the art by learning the different scripts and by modelling after the works of the old masters. To train himself in *chuan shu,* he began to study the Ch'in and Han tablets, going as far back as Li Ssǔ. The rigid discipline in doing the *hsiao chuan* taught him the physical technique of gaining complete control of the brush, while modelling after the Han tablets in *li shu* and *pa fên* helped him to execute modulating strokes and experiment with formal structures. Wang Hsi-chih also admired Ts'ai Yung's *fei po* and Chang Chih's *ts'ao shu.*

The man who probably exerted more influence on Wang Hsi-chih than any other was Chung Yu (151-230 A.D.), a statesman and a scholar who was one of the star pupils of Liu Tê-shêng, traditionally regarded as the father of *hsing shu.* In his long and crowded life, Chung Yu somehow managed to practise calligraphy for thirty years. For a period of ten years he lived alone on a mountain called Pao Tu Shan, scribbling on every surface near at hand, including trees and stones. He even exhumed his friend's grave in search of Ts'ai Yung's calligraphic specimens. Chung Yu was of course proficient in *chuan shu* and *li shu,* and quite a number of late Han tablets, including the *I Ying Pei* (Fig. 13a) have been attributed to him. However, his enormous reputation was built on the fact that he was the first known master of the *chên shu,* a script which was just beginning to gain popularity at the end of the Han Dynasty. From the specimens of Chung Yu's calligraphy we now have (Fig. 16), we can see that the critics were right in describing Chung Yu's style as 'a subtle balance of strength and pliability, the dots and strokes manifesting a peculiar appeal, limitless in its depth, archaically elegant beyond words, verily the greatest master up to his time'. The characters he executed, according to his admirers, were like 'wild geese playing over the waters, storks dancing in the sky'. Wang Hsi-chih was born too late to receive Chung Yu's personal instruction but he was full of praise for the Han master's artistry: 'After studying the works of all the famous calligraphers, I am fully convinced that Chung Yu's and Chang Chih's are the very best and that those of other calligraphers do not deserve attention.'

Because of the family's great prominence and his own achievements in art and letters, it was inevitable that Wang Hsi-chih should join the public service. In the early years of his life, he moved from post to post and was not particularly distinguished for his administrative abilities. After middle age, he began to tire of official life and declined many attractive offers for office, including one that would have made him a Minister of State. He chose for himself a wandering life in Chekiang, moving aimlessly among the hills and waters south of the Yangtse and indulging himself in the pleasures of food and wine. But he never for a moment forgot his calligraphic practice, washing his ink-stone so often that the water of the pond in front of his house, which may still be seen, turned permanently black. In his more relaxed

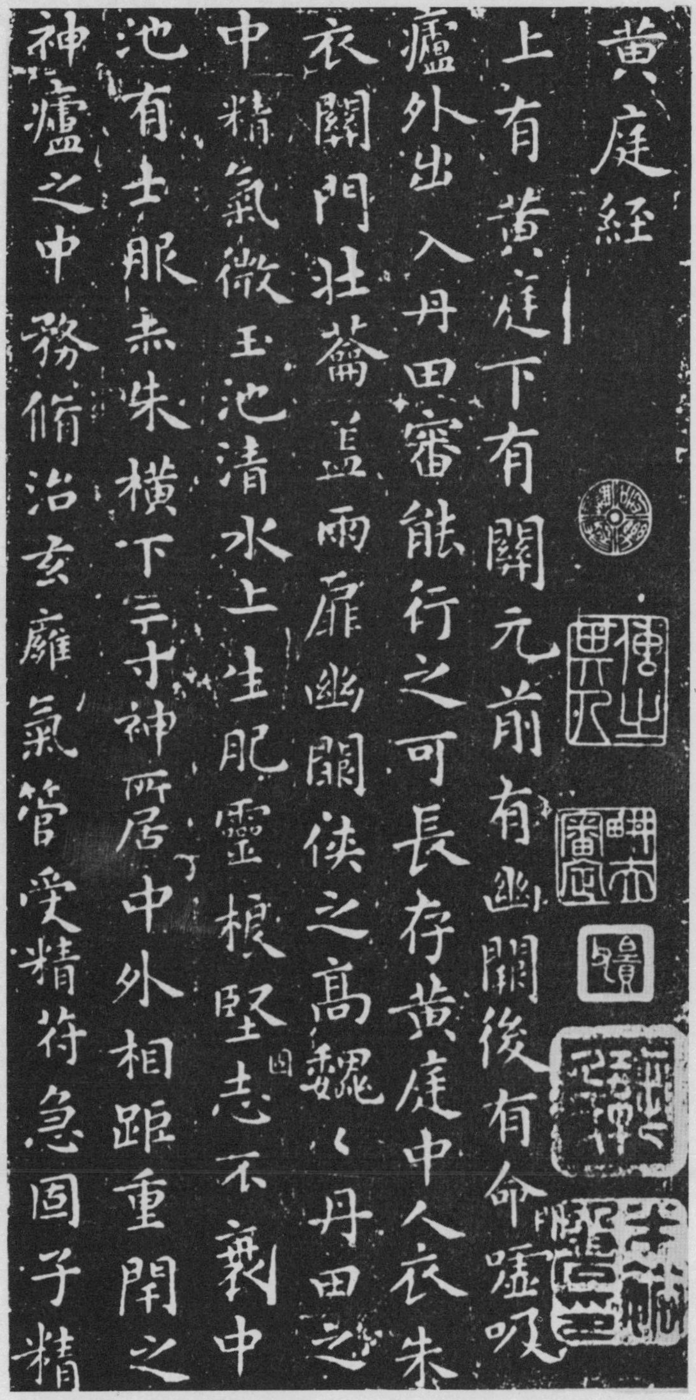

Fig. 17b Wang Hsi-chih: *Huang T'ing Ching* (first portion)

moments, he painted a little, doing his self-portrait by looking at his reflection in the mirror and adorning his fans with small scenes. Wang Hsi-chih, therefore, gained some reputation as a painter. His fondness for the goose was proverbial, although it was never clear whether he liked the goose as a pet or as a delicacy. He would travel for miles to inspect a particularly well-raised bird. He would even offer his calligraphic work in exchange for it. Inevitably the critics asserted that his calligraphic style was inspired by the graceful turn of the goose's neck.

In his early years, Wang Hsi-chih's genius was indeed at work but not in its full range. It was only after middle age that his art came to its full flowering. No sample of his work in *chuan shu* and *li shu* has survived. Even his works in *chên shu* are transmitted to us through stone engravings, of which four are particularly well known—*Yüeh I Lun, Tung-fang So Hua Chan, Huang T'ing Ching,* and *Ts'ao Ngo Pei.* These engravings have gone through many editions and there are countless copies thereof, so that we are not at all sure whether the engravings were made from the originals or the copies. Nevertheless, these engravings have been used as models of *chên shu* by all aspiring calligraphers in the past sixteen centuries. They have become essential elements in the folklore of Chinese calligraphy. Untold numbers of monographs and colophons has been written on them. They most certainly deserve our careful scrutiny.

Yüeh I Lun (Fig. 17a), a biographical essay on the warrior-statesman Yüeh I of the Period of Warring States, was transcribed by Wang Hsi-chih in small *chên shu* in 348 at the age of forty-one. The transcription is rich in vignettes. According to a calligraphic manual called *Pi Shih Lun,* allegedly written by Wang Hsi-chih himself, Wang Hsi-chih intended his transcription of the *Yüeh I Lun* to be a training model for his sons, a sort of family secret, which was not to be shown to outsiders. So when his schoolmate Chang Chih asked to see it, Wang Hsi-chih pretended that it was lost. He also admonished his sons never to say anything about it beyond the family circle. The story is, of course, preposterous, and has been emphatically and convincingly refuted by the T'ang calligrapher-critic Sun Ch'ien-li in his classical essay on the art of calligraphy, *Shu P'u.* To begin with, the manual *Pi Shih Lun,* the text of which has been included in anthologies, is a composition of very inferior literary quality. It could not have been the work of a literary figure such as Wang Hsi-chih. Whoever fabricated the manual also made a fatal chronological slip. Chang Chih, as we have seen, was a *ts'ao shu* specialist of the latter part of the Han Dynasty. He most certainly could not have been Wang Hsi-chih's schoolmate. Above all, Wang Hsi-chih, a gentleman of great personal charm who used to give away his calligraphic works freely to all sorts of people, could not possibly be so narrow-minded as to pass on his artistic secrets only to his sons. As it happened so often in Chinese art history, the man who fabricated the *Pi Shih Lun* was only

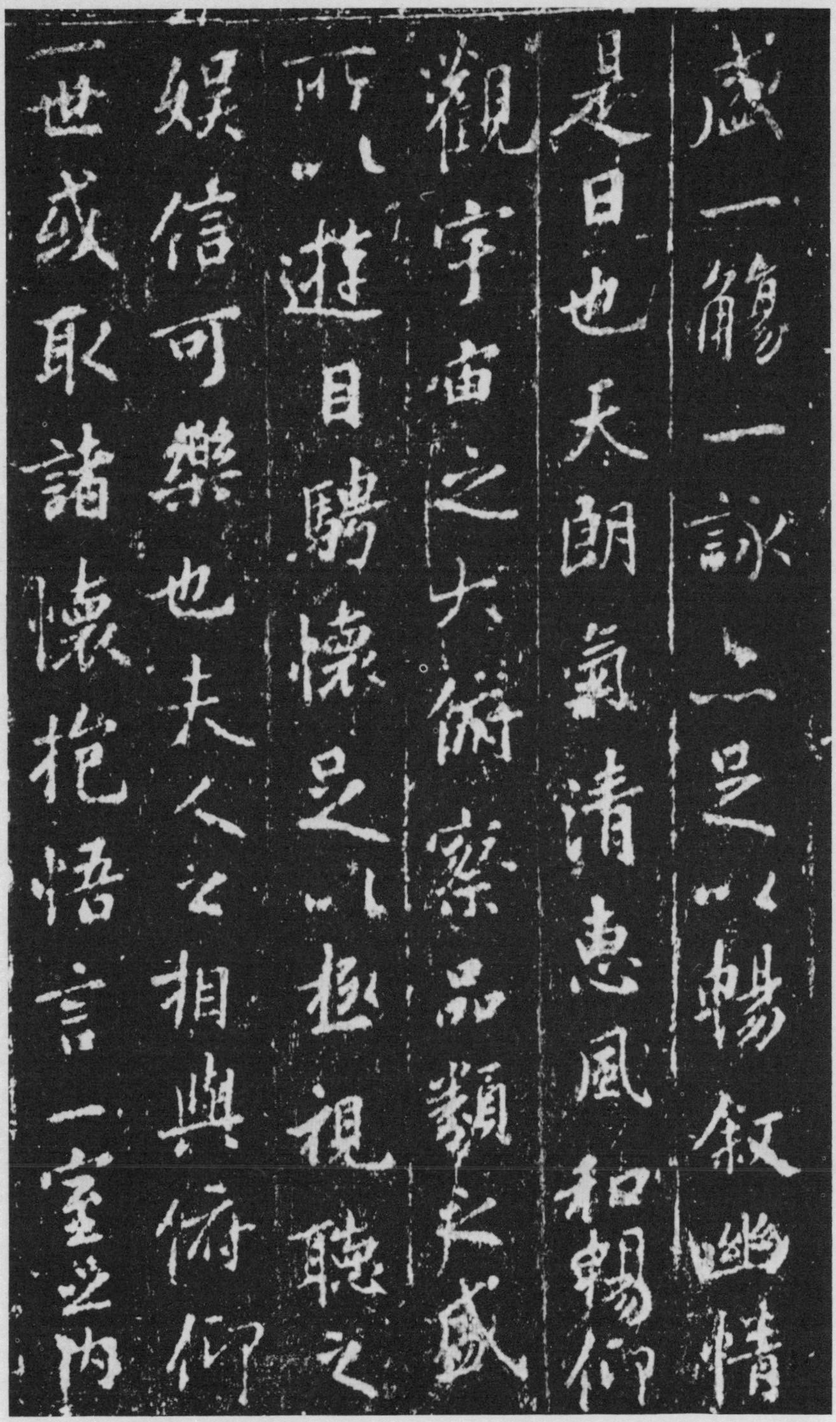

Fig. 18a *Lan T'ing Hsü*. Copy by Ou-yang Hsün (detail)

trying to underline the artistic merits of Wang Hsi-chih's transcription of the *Yüeh I Lun,* with no malice intended. However, his ignorance and his lack of literary merit were inexcusable.

The original manuscript of Wang Hsi-chih's transcription of the *Yüeh I Lun* was lost not long after the master's death. Fortunately, an unknown calligrapher in the Liang Dynasty (502-556) made a copy of it. The Liang copy was later acquired by the T'ang Princess T'ai-p'ing (daughter of Emperor Kao-tsung and Empress Wu Tsê-t'ien), a lady who was deeply involved in T'ang palace politics. A lover of Wang Hsi-chih's calligraphy, the Princess treasured the *Yüeh I Lun* copy dearly, carefully placing it in a brocade sack and locking it up in a trunk. The Princess, however, soon got into political trouble and her possessions were all confiscated. Somehow an old woman managed to smuggle the copy out. As the police chased after the old woman, she left the copy under a kitchen stove. According to the T'ang calligrapher Hsü Hao, 'although a strange fragrance hung over the place all around for many miles, the copy was never found again'. Therefore, the *Yüeh I Lun* we now see is really the engraved version of the copy made in the Liang Dynasty, and even as such it has long been regarded as a great masterpiece in small *chên shu,* so highly is anything associated with Wang Hsi-chih treasured by the lovers of Chinese calligraphy.

Tung-fang So Hua Chan, an essay attached to a portrait of the early Han humourist Tung-fang So, was transcribed by Wang Hsi-chih in small *chên shu* in 356 as a gift to one Wang Ching-jên. Although it has been considered as a worthy sample of the Tsin master's calligraphy, the Sung calligrapher-critic, Mi Fu, was of the opinion that artistically it was below Wang Hsi-chih's standards.

Huang T'ing Ching (Fig. 17b), a Taoist scripture, was supposedly transcribed by Wang Hsi-chih in small *chên shu* in 356. We have been told that Wang Hsi-chih, while living in Shanyin, heard of a flock of good geese raised by a Taoist priest. He forthwith called on the priest who readily offered him the whole flock in exchange for his transcription of the *Huang T'ing Ching.* Wang Hsi-chih was delighted with the transaction and merrily took the birds away with him. Like so many Chinese anecdotes, this one is full of discrepancies. According to Wang Hsi-chih's official biography in the *Tsin Shu,* 'History of the Tsin Dynasty', the master gave the Taoist priest his transcription of Laotzŭ's *Tao Tê Ching*, not his transcription of the *Huang T'ing Ching,* in exchange for the geese. It was also pointed out by some writers that, since the *Huang T'ing Ching* was formally proclaimed as a scripture in 361, Wang Hsi-chih could not have transcribed it in 356. Notwithstanding these discrepancies, Wang Hsi-chih's transcription of the *Huang T'ing Ching* has been regarded as one of his greatest masterpieces in small *chên shu* and has exerted an enormous influence on Chinese calligraphic styles. Many great calligraphers, among them the monk Chih-yung of the Ch'ên Dynasty, Yü

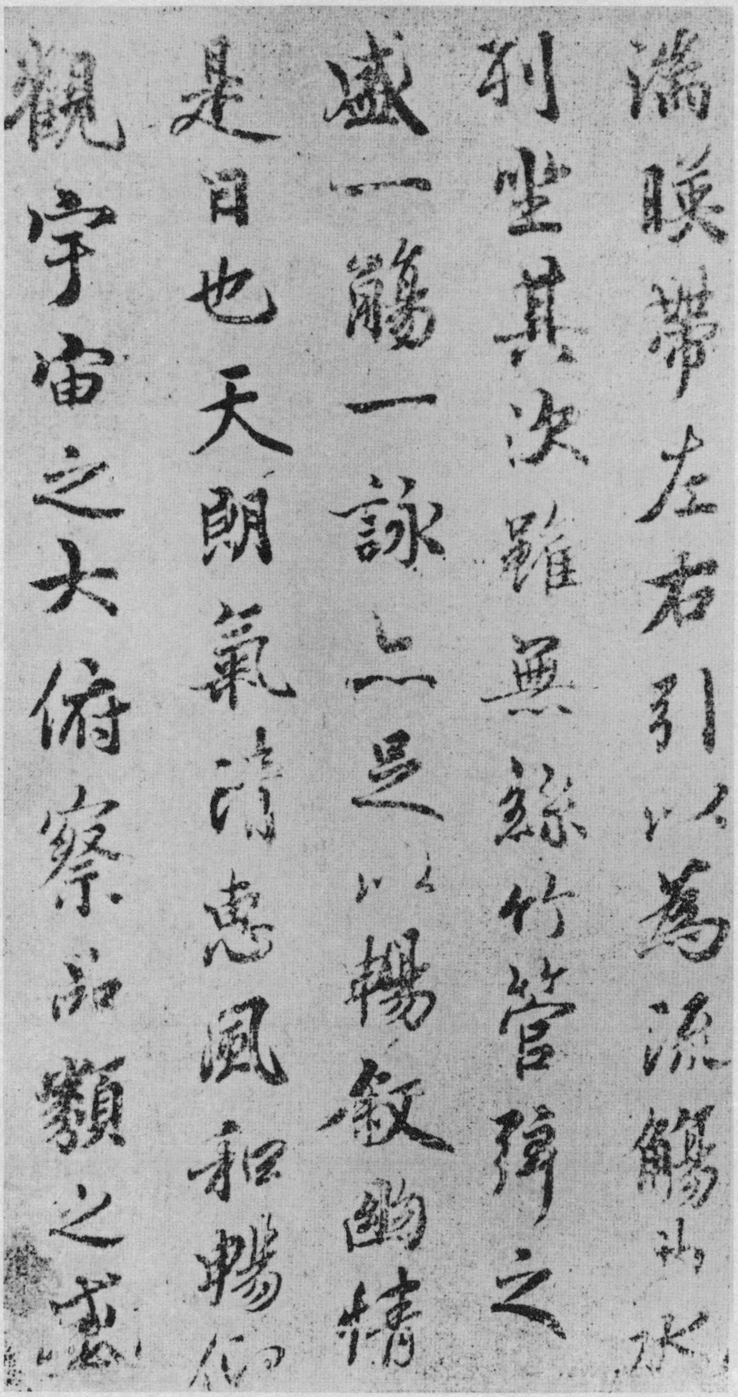

観宇宙之大俯察品類之盛

是日也天朗氣清惠風和暢仰

盛一觴一詠亦足以暢敘幽情

列坐其次雖無絲竹管弦之

湍映帶左右引以為流觴曲水

Fig. 18b *Lan T'ing Hsü*. Copy by Ch'u Shui-liang (detail)

Shih-nan, Ou-yang Hsün and Ch'u Shui-liang of the T'ang Dynasty, made copies of it, so that it is now impossible to tell which is the original, if it still exists, and which are the copies. However, in spite of the doubts surrounding it, Wang Hsi-chih's transcription of the *Huang T'ing Ching* has been one of the indispensable models for calligraphic training throughout the ages.

Ts'ao Ngo Pei, a tablet in memory of the girl Ts'ao Ngo of the Eastern Han Dynasty, was transcribed by Wang Hsi-chih in small *chên shu* in 358. Ts'ao Ngo's father was drowned in the river and his body was not found. Ts'ao Ngo, only 13, was overcome with grief and remained along the river for seven days waiting for her father's body to appear. Finally, she jumped into the river to join her father. Her manifestation of supreme filial piety inspired the Han statesman Tu Shang to erect a tablet in her memory. The Han calligrapher Ts'ai Yung once visited the tablet in the night and 'read' the engraved inscription by feeling the characters with his hand. Wang Hsi-chih's transcription of the text of the tablet passed through many hands and was authenticated by a number of discerning connoisseurs, including the Sung Emperor Hui-tsung and the Yüan calligrapher Chao Mêng-fu. It was also included in the Ch'ing Emperor Ch'ien-lung's *San Hsi T'ang Fa T'ieh.* However, there has been persistent doubt about its authenticity and it is rated lower than the *Yüeh I Lun* and the *Huang T'ing Ching* as a sample of Wang Hsi-chih's small *chên shu.*

A timeless moment in Chinese art history arrived in April 353, when Wang Hsi-chih, at the age of forty-six, joined a gathering of forty-one friends and relatives, including some of his sons, at a place called Lan T'ing (Orchid Pavilion) near Shaohsing in Chekiang. According to Wang Hsi-chih, the place was surrounded by lofty mountains and steep slopes, lush forests and bamboo groves, with a clear brook gushing through, giving reflections to the left and the right. It was a fine day in early Spring. The air was clear and the breeze was soft. After a few rounds of drinks, Wang Hsi-chih composed an essay commemorating the occasion which he wrote down 'on paper made of the silk cocoon with a brush made of mouse-whiskers'. Consisting of three hundred and twenty-four words in twenty-eight lines, the essay, entitled *Lan T'ing Hsü,* is a charming and relaxed philosophical discourse on the past and the present, on the meaning of life and death. It was a moment of supreme inspiration and the calligraphy was a demonstration of the extraordinary power which was all the more impressive for being so spontaneous. The manuscript, which even Wang Hsi-chih tried but failed to duplicate, is the greatest masterpiece of Chinese calligraphy in history. In the past sixteen centuries no calligraphic work has even come near to its Olympian station.

The *Lan T'ing Hsü* went through many vicissitudes. For seven generations it remained in the possession of Wang Hsi-chih's descendants, jealously guarded as a priceless heirloom. In the latter part of the sixth century, it was in the hands of the monk Chih-yung, Wang Hsi-chih's seventh generation

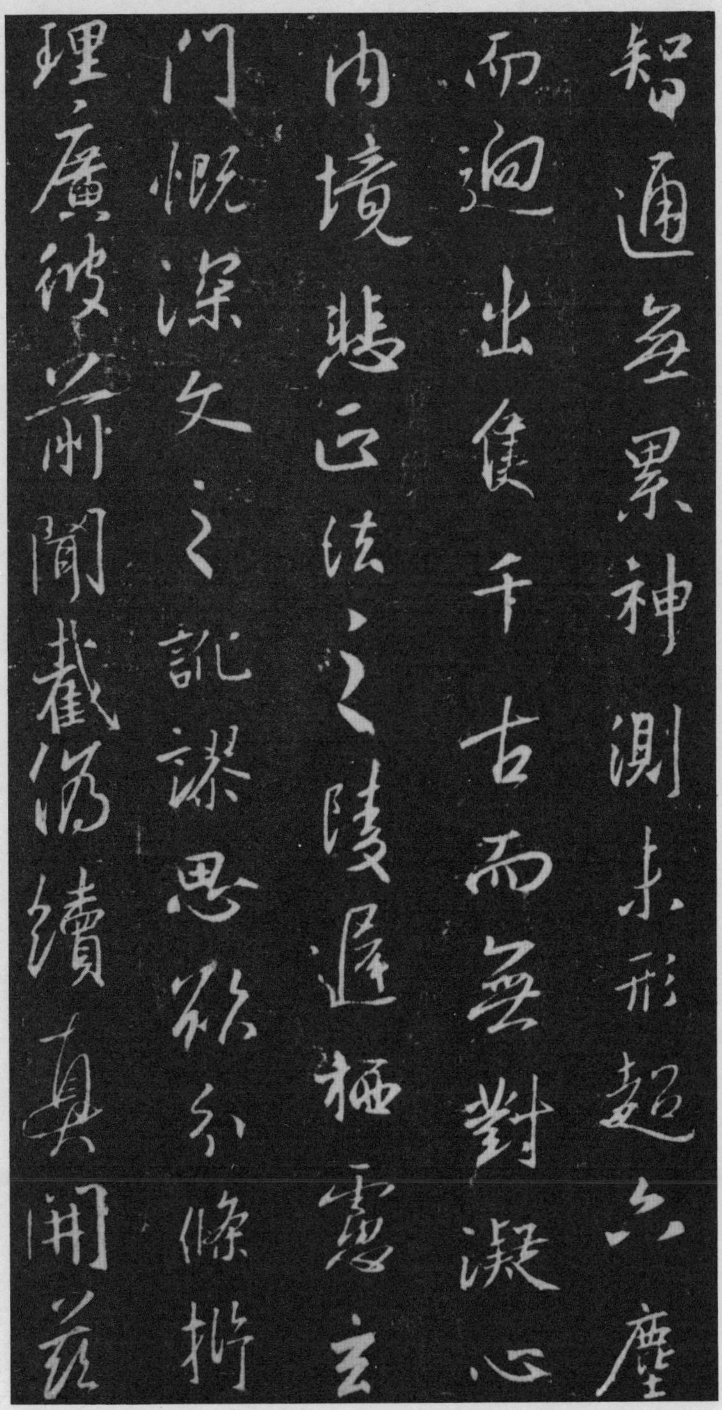

智通無累神測未形超六塵
而迥出隻千古而無對凝心
内境悲正法之陵遲栖慮
門恍深文之訛謀思於分條析
理廣彼前聞截偽續真開茲

Fig. 19 *Shêng Chiao Hsü* (detail)

descendant. He had it engraved on stone. According to a well-circulated story, probably untrue, when Chih-yung died in ripe old age, and as monk he had no heir, he left the manuscript to the care of one of his disciples, the monk Pien-ts'ai, who secreted it in the beam of his cottage. Meanwhile, the great T'ang Emperor T'ai-tsung, who had a special fondness for Wang Hsi-chih's calligraphy, had ascended the throne. In 636, an order went out to gather all the specimens of Wang Hsi-chih's calligraphy for the imperial collection. It was recorded that, as the result of a nationwide search backed by the full authority of the court, 2,290 Wang Hsi-chih manuscripts were found. These were elaborately mounted and grouped into thirteen volumes divided into 128 sections. Of this vast collection, 50 pieces were in *chên shu,* 240 in *hsing shu,* and some 2,000 in *ts'ao shu.* But, alas, the *Lan T'ing Hsü* was not among them. The Emperor, so the story goes, heard rumours that the great masterpiece was at Pien-ts'ai's place. Three times emissaries were despatched to ask the monk for it, and each time the monk answered that it was lost in the war. The Emperor, in desperation, sent the censor Hsiao I to make a last attempt. Pretending that he was just an ordinary admirer of Wang Hsi-chih, Hsiao I gradually worked himself into the monk's confidence. For days and weeks the two men discussed the merits of the various Wang Hsi-chih manuscripts they had seen, Hsiao I lamenting all the time that he had not seen the *Lan T'ing Hsü* itself. The monk was overcome with sympathy and unsuspectingly produced the masterpiece from its hiding place. Thereupon Hsiao I revealed his identity as an emissary of the sovereign and took the manuscript away to the Emperor. The story, whether spurious or not, was told in blow-by-blow detail by a T'ang Dynasty writer and was the subject of a number of historical novels and plays. It was also depicted in paintings by some great T'ang and Sung masters.

Upon getting the manuscript, the first thing the overjoyed Emperor T'ai-tsung did was to have it traced and copied by the most capable calligraphers of his court, among them Ou-yang Hsün and Ch'u Shui-liang. It was generally believed that, when Emperor T'ai-tsung died in 649, the manuscript, in accordance with his testament, was buried with him in his tomb at Chao-ling. However, like the story of all art treasures of such stature, the matter was permeated with mysteries. For instance, one of the minor calligraphers asked by the Emperor T'ai-tsung to copy the manuscript, a man named T'ang P'u-ts'ê, was said to have kept the original for himself and substituted his own copy for it. A story was also circulated to the effect that Emperor T'ai-tsung's son, later Emperor Kao-tsung, did not actually carry out his father's will and that the copy which went into the tomb was one made by Ou-yang Hsün. However, these stories, though intriguing, cannot be believed for the simple reason that since 649 no one has ever claimed that he has seen the original. The *Lan T'ing Hsü,* as we now know it, is definitely not from Wang Hsi-chih's hand. A sharp argument has been raging for centuries

[64]

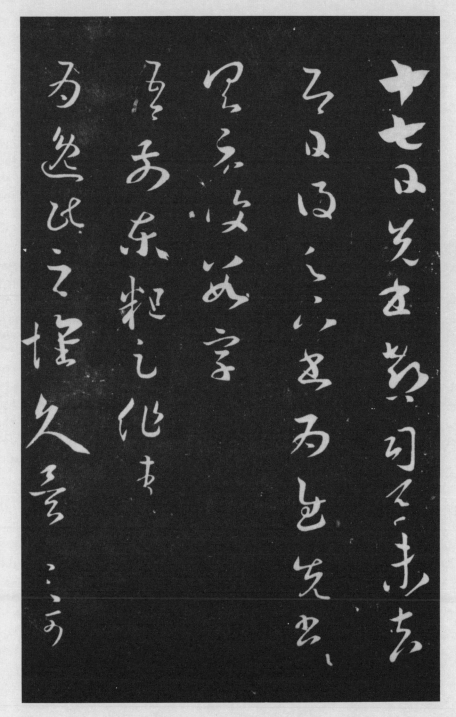

Fig. 20   Wang Hsi-chih: *Shih Ch'i T'ieh* (detail)

regarding the relative merits of the various copies extant, among which that made by Ou-yang Hsün, known as the Ting-wu version (Fig. 18a), and that made by Ch'u Shui-liang, known as the Shên-lung version (Fig. 18b), are the principal contenders.

The various tracings and copies made by the T'ang calligraphers, if not the original, have appeared a million times over in tracings, copies, rubbings, woodcuts, lithographs and photographs. At least 117 versions now exist, all claiming to bear some resemblance to the original. The better versions and the older rubbings are worth a small fortune. Even the stones on which the *Lan T'ing Hsü* was engraved have become prized treasures. For instance, in 1129, as the Tartars drove the Sung court to the South, the Sung Emperor Kao-tsung, in a desperate effort to save a *Lan T'ing Hsü* stone from falling into the hands of the barbarians, had it hidden in a well in a monastery. The stone remained there for exactly three hundred years before it was accidentally discovered by a monk, a discovery which sent a wave of excitement throughout the art world of China. Countless treatises have been written on the *Lang T'ing Hsü*, singing its praise, collating its many versions, telling stories about its trials and tribulations, tracing its peregrinations, all of which bear testimony to the high regard it commands among the lovers of Chinese calligraphy. The study of *Lan T'ing Hsü* has become a discipline in itself.

One of the most exciting exploits of the T'ang Dynasty was the monk Hsüan-chuang's visit to India in search of Buddhist scriptures. Hsüan-chuang left China in 629, following the Silk Route through Turfan, Karashar, Kucha, Kapisa and Gandhara to India. He stayed in Benares for many years. He returned to China via Kashgar, Yarkand, Khotan, Lop-Nor, Lou-lan and Tun-huang, arriving in the Chinese capital Changan in 644. Upon his return, Hsüan-chuang, assisted by Indian missionaries, undertook to translate the numerous Buddhist scriptures he brought back into the Chinese language. The Buddhist faith spread like wildfire throughout the T'ang Empire.

In commemoration of this extraordinary event, the T'ang Emperor T'ai-tsung personally composed an essay in 648 to which he gave the title *Shêng Chiao Hsü*. The essay was transcribed by a number of calligraphers in the T'ang court, among whom was Ch'u Shui-liang, who did it in formal *chên shu* in 653. Meanwhile, the monk Huai-jên of the Buddhist temple Hung Fu Ssŭ of Changan, one of Wang Hsi-chih's descendants, spent more than twenty years cutting out characters written by Wang Hsi-chih and reassembling the characters into literary compositions. In reassembling the Wang Hsi-chih characters, Huai-jên chose as his text Emperor T'ai-tsung's *Shêng Chiao Hsü*, to which he appended an essay on Buddhism written by the T'ang Emperor Kao-tsung when he was the Crown Prince, entitled *Shu Shêng Chi,* and a Buddhist scripture called *Hsin Ching* translated from Sanskrit by Hsüan-chuang. The remarkable thing about Huai-jên's work was that, although the texts were composed three hundred years after Wang Hsi-chih's time, the

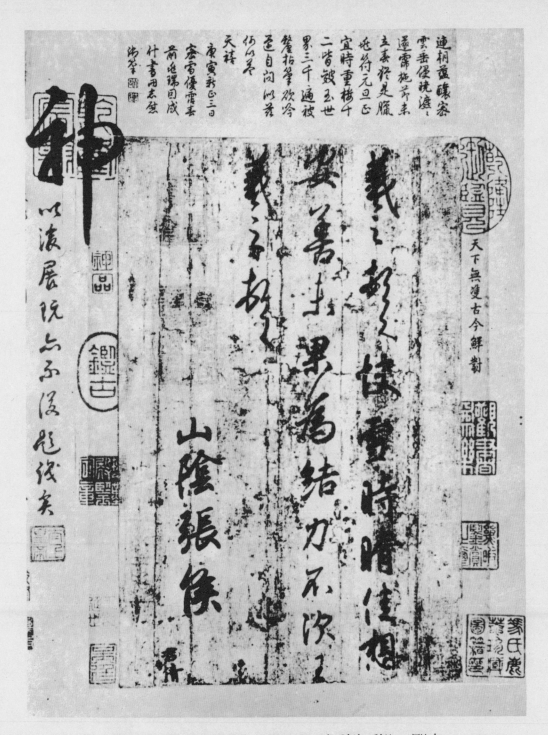

Fig. 21 Wang Hsi-chih: *K'uai Hsüeh Shih Ch'ing T'ieh*
(full text). Colophons surrounding it are by the
Ch'ing Emperor Ch'ien-lung

transcription of the texts was done entirely with characters taken out from Wang Hsi-chih's works. Huai-jên's monumental work was engraved on stone by the best craftsmen of the day in 672, and the tablet was erected with appropriate ceremony in the Buddhist temple Ta Tz'ŭ En Ssŭ of Changan in the same year. Known as Huai-jên's *Shêng Chiao Hsü* (Fig. 19) to distinguish it from transcriptions of the same essay by the other calligraphers, it is a splendid example of Wang Hsi-chih's calligraphy and has been used as a standard model for calligraphic exercises in Emperor T'ai-tsung's Academy of Calligraphy (Hung Wên Kuan) and in subsequent centuries. It may be mentioned in this connection that the practice of reassembling characters, known to the Chinese as *chi tzŭ,* so auspiciously initiated by Huai-jên, has become a favourite pastime of calligraphy-lovers down to the present day. The task was painstaking in the old days before the invention of photography. Nowadays, the craftsman, aided by modern technology, can reassemble characters from any calligrapher to meet your every wish, from epitaphs to Christmas cards.

Both the *Lan T'ing Hsü* and the *Shêng Chiao Hsü* are in *hsing shu,* while the *Yüeh I Lun* and *Huang T'ing Ching* are in *chên shu.* The T'ang Emperor T'ai-tsung, easily Wang Hsi-chih's most august and ardent admirer, also put together a collection of Wang Hsi-chih's calligraphy in *ts'ao shu* as a model for calligraphic exercises. The collection consists of twenty-four (in some editions as many as twenty-eight) letters and notes written by the Tsin master in *ts'ao shu,* each one identified by the initial or the key words of the text. The collection has come to be known as *Shih Ch'i T'ieh* (Fig. 20), the two characters *shih ch'i,* literally 'seventeen', being the first two characters of the first item of the collection and not designating the number of items in the collection. Like the *Shêng Chiao Hsü,* the *Shih Ch'i T'ieh* has become a standard model for calligraphic training since the T'ang Dynasty. According to Emperor T'ai-tsung, the best samples of Wang Hsi-chih calligraphy were: *Yüeh I Lun* in *chên shu, Lan T'ing Hsü* in *hsing shu* and *Shih Ch'i T'ieh* in *ts'ao shu.*

All the specimens of Wang Hsi-chih's calligraphy we have been looking at and discussing so far are second-hand in the sense that they are either engravings or tracings and copies. Wang Hsi-chih's originals are understandably rare, and they have been traced and copied so often, and by such competent hands, that it is not always possible to tell the difference. One of the few Wang Hsi-chih originals extant, as far as we can determine, is a short letter now in the Chinese National Palace Museum identified as the *K'uai Hsüeh Shih Ch'ing T'ieh* (Fig. 21), which may be translated as 'Letter After Snowfall'. Written partly in *hsing shu* and partly in *ts'ao shu,* the manuscript consists of only twenty-four characters arranged in two and a half lines. It is a casual note the master addressed to one of his friends after a snowfall. Included in the *San Hsi T'ang Fa T'ieh,* the manuscript seemed to be a particular favourite of the Ch'ing Emperor Ch'ien-lung who inscribed countless

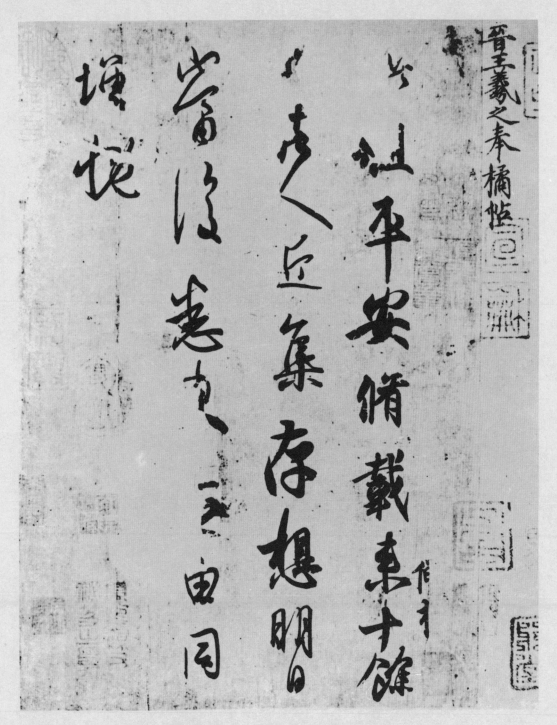

Fig. 22   Wang Hsi-chih: *Fêng Chü T'ieh* (portion). Title
on upper right-hand corner is by the Sung Emperor
Hui-tsung

colophons on it and spattered it with his seals. It was Emperor Ch'ien-lung's habit to inspect the manuscript every time it snowed in Peking during his long reign. On one occasion he even painted a small snow scene after the style of the Yüan Dynasty painter Ni Tsan as a colophon to the manuscript. The manuscript as it now stands also carries many colophons by other collectors and connoisseurs, including one by the great Yüan Dynasty calligrapher-painter Chao Mêng-fu (Fig. 69). All these testimonies indicate that, in the opinion of the best qualified judges, the letter is genuinely by Wang Hsi-chih's hand.

Letters and notes by Wang Hsi-chih have been collected into anthologies, of which there are many, many editions. One of the most frequently reproduced letters is the *Fêng Chü T'ieh* (Fig. 22), which may be translated as 'Letter Offering Oranges'. Although the calligraphy of this letter is breathtakingly beautiful, the experts are in general agreement that it is a copy made by an unidentified calligrapher of the T'ang Dynasty. As we see it now, the manuscript also bears a title in seven characters undoubtedly by the hand of the Sung Emperor Hui-tsung. We shall be introducing two other notes attributed to Wang Hsi-chih in the following pages, the *Hsiang Han T'ieh* (Fig. 65) and the *Hsing Jang T'ieh* (Fig. 67) as illustrations of other aspects of Chinese calligraphic art.

Critical acclaim of Wang Hsi-chih's calligraphy has always been in the superlative. The most widely quoted dictum is that his hand is 'as light as the passing cloud, as vigorous as the startled dragon'. The T'ang Emperor T'ai-tsung, besides honouring Wang Hsi-chih in a number of ways, also personally wrote a eulogy following the master's official biography in the *Tsin Shu,* describing Wang Hsi-chih's art in these immortal words:

After surveying the past and the present and studying all that is worthwhile in calligraphic art, who but Wang Hsi-chih stands out as the embodiment of the highest achievement in both goodness and beauty. The dots and lines he executed so ably, as well as the structure and composition he created so exquisitely, remind me of the clouds and mists which appear isolated and yet linked, or of the soaring phoenix and curling dragon which appear reclining and yet upright.

An outstanding mark of Wang Hsi-chih's calligraphic style is the incredible vitality of the characters he executed, each one seemingly bursting with life, each a moving architecture of grace and balance, of strength mixed with beauty. Although he dealt with characters which must conform to their basic structure in order that they may be legible, he was, however, breaking the characters down, exploring form and probing possibilities. In his *chên shu* and *hsing shu* characters, he showed himself to be an artist who gave new movement to static form. In the *ts'ao shu* characters he executed, he allowed himself the utmost freedom to manipulate them with a kind of explicit symbolism, exaggerating their shapes and twisting their patterns with almost

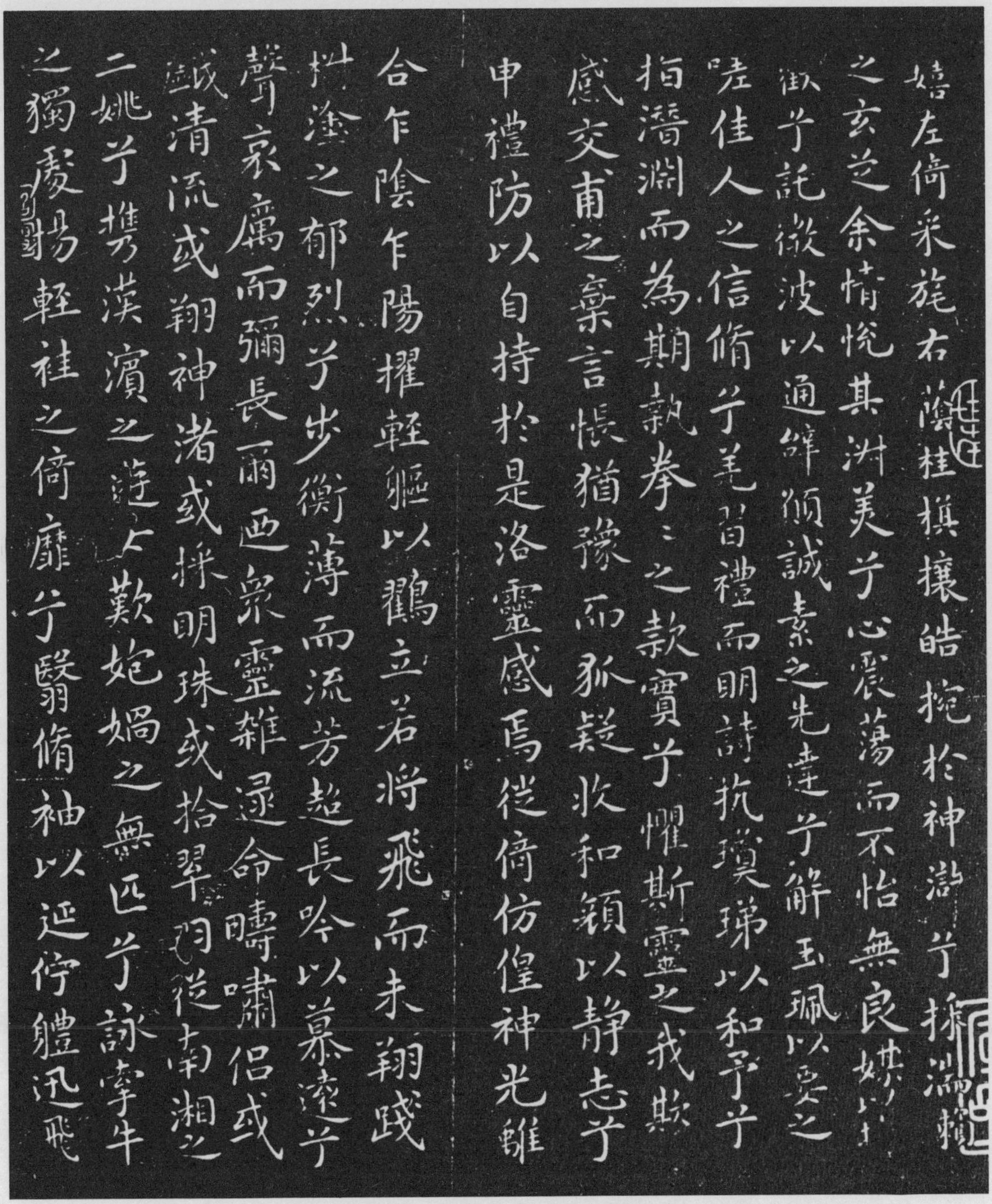

嬉左倚采旄右蔭桂旗攘皓腕於神滸兮采湍瀨
之玄芝余情悅其淑美兮心振蕩而不怡無良媒以
接歡託微波以通辭願誠素之先達兮解玉佩以要之
嗟佳人之信脩羌習禮而明詩抗瓊珶以和予兮
指潛淵而為期執眷眷之款實兮懼斯靈之我欺
感交甫之棄言悵猶豫而狐疑收和顏以靜志兮
申禮防以自持於是洛靈感焉徙倚彷徨神光離
合乍陰乍陽擢輕軀以鶴立若將飛而未翔踐
椒塗之郁烈步蘅薄而流芳超長吟以慕遠兮
聲哀厲而彌長爾乃眾靈雜遝命儔嘯侶或
戲清流或翔神渚或採明珠或拾翠羽從南湘之
二妃攜漢濱之遊女歎匏瓜之無匹兮詠牽牛
之獨處揚輕袿之猗靡兮翳脩袖以延佇體迅飛

Fig 23　Wang Hsien-chih: *Shih San Hang* ('Thirteen Lines')

mannerist intent. He boldly devised symbols for the elements of the characters, even turning entire characters into symbolic images. And yet he was always able to keep his hand under a measure of restraint. Unlike the *ts'ao shu* of the Han calligrapher Chang Chih, whose characters were frequently illegible, Wang Hsi-chih never allowed himself to run wild, and if he employed symbols to represent elements, they were symbols that were clearly understood. In all the modern scripts, he was the supreme master of all time because the harmony and balance by which he gave a lovable perfection to the characters was never the product of calculation or conscious refinement. It was his power of grasping the ideal through the senses, a part of his physical apprehension.

Wang Hsi-chih was blessed with talented descendants, among whom his seventh and youngest son, Wang Hsien-chih, is particularly famed. When the lad was seven or eight, as he was practising calligraphy, his father sneaked behind him and tried to snatch the brush from his tiny hand. This was to test how firmly he was holding the brush. To Wang Hsi-chih's amazement, the brush was held so tightly that he could not take it away. The proud father thereby exclaimed: 'This son of mine will enjoy great fame!' Under the exacting tutorship of his illustrious father, Wang Hsien-chih worked hard on his art. Crowds of several hundred people would gather to watch the young man do characters ten feet square on the white walls of his house. Early in his life, Wang Hsien-chih's reputation spread far and wide.

Wang Hsien-chih has left us with a sample of his small *chên shu*. It is his transcription of the *Lo Shên Fu,* the prose-poem written by Ts'ao Chih in 222 recounting his dream encounter with the nymph of the Lo River, the legendary daughter of Fu Hsi, a prose-poem which Wang Hsien-chih's contemporary, the great painter Ku K'ai-chih, also illustrated in a scroll. Wang Hsien-chih's transcription of the *Lo Shên Fu* was engraved on jade. Soon afterwards, both the original manuscript and the jade engraving were lost. In the Sung Dynasty, first nine and then four lines of the engraved version were discovered. Hence the term *Shih San Hang,* literally 'Thirteen Lines' (Fig. 23). It is the only sample of Wang Hsien-chih's *chên shu* we now have.

Wang Hsien-chih, however, is more admired for his *ts'ao shu* in which he often wrote a whole line of many characters with the twist and turn of a single, continuous swoop of the brush, creating writhing images, as the critics said, 'suggesting the forward movement of dragons and serpents'. One of Wang Hsien-chih's original *ts'ao shu* manuscripts, the *Chung Ch'iu T'ieh* (Fig. 24), which may be translated as 'Mid-autumn Letter', was one of 'three rarities' of the Ch'ing Emperor Ch'ien-lung's San Hsi T'ang. It consists of only twenty-two characters, but is fully illustrative of the 'one brush writing' (*i pi shu*) for which Wang Hsien-chih is justly famed.

The Chinese critics, in deference to the monumental achievements of the father and son, often mention their names in the same breath, *erh Wang*, 'the two Wangs'. However, a discerning critic may detect quite a bit of difference

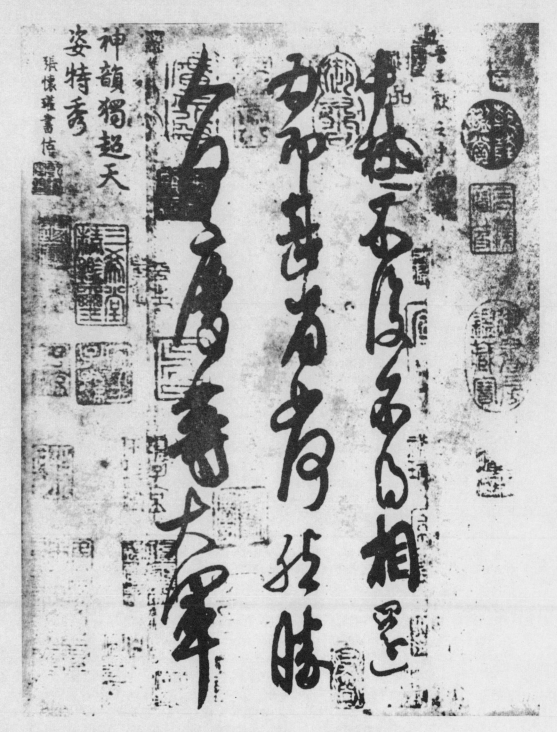

Fig. 24   Wang Hsien-chih: *Chung Ch'iu T'ieh*

between the style of the father and that of the son. When Hsieh An, a powerful figure of the Tsin Dynasty, asked Wang Hsien-chih: 'How does your calligraphy compare with your father's?' Wang Hsien-chih replied: 'There is a difference.' This was as far as a son would go in traditional China to claim equality with his father, especially a father of such outstanding achievements. However, the T'ang Emperor T'ai-tsung was not impressed by Wang Hsien-chih's accomplishments, comparing the younger Wang's character-structures to 'dead trees in deep winter' and his brush-traces to 'hungry slaves of a parsimonious family'. In fairness, it may be said that Wang Hsien-chih's accomplishments must be judged only in the script in which he is most proficient, namely *ts'ao shu* in the Chang Chih school, sometimes known as *k'uang ts'ao, 'ts'ao shu* in the wild form', and if one likes that kind of calligraphy, as the T'ang critic Chang Huai-kuan undoubtedly did, the son would be rated as high if not higher than the father. In terms of brushmanship, the son also manifests a kind of controlled power, a demonstration of innate strength, which is in contrast to the glint and suavity of the father's style. Verily it has been said: 'If the father were not born, the son would be the king of calligraphy.' Even with the father's presence, the son has not been overshadowed, not by any means.

Wang Hsi-chih's seventh generation descendant, the monk Chih-yung, whom we recall was the custodian of the *Lan T'ing Hsü,* was in many ways a most worthy upholder of the family tradition. For forty years he kept himself upstairs practising calligraphy and modelling after his illustrious ancestors indefatigably. In this time he made eight hundred transcriptions of the *Ch'ien Tzǔ Wên* (a chant composed of one thousand characters with no duplicates, a favourite text for calligraphic exercises) and had them distributed to the Buddhist temples and monasteries of East China. In this Herculean task, he used up five full barrels of top quality brushes which he solemnly buried as retired heroes, complete with epitaphs composed and transcribed by himself. There were so many demands for his calligraphy that he had to cover his threshold with iron sheets. Hence his nickname, 'the iron threshold'. The Ch'ing Emperor K'ang-hsi, following the precedent of the T'ang Emperor T'ai-tsung, had a copy of Chih-yung's *Ch'ien Tzǔ Wên* buried with him in his mausoleum.

Wang Hsi-chih and his descendants lived in an age when China was divided into the South and the North Dynasties. As far back as 199, the ambitious warrior-politician Ts'ao Ts'ao had succeeded in persuading the Han government to decree the prohibition of erecting tablets before graves. Ts'ao Ts'ao's son, Ts'ao P'i, who became Emperor Wên-ti of the Wei Dynasty, also favoured simple funerals. The prohibition was reiterated in 278 by Emperor Wu-ti of the Tsin Dynasty. As a result of such emphatic and repeated proscription, we have only a few samples of tablet writing from the Southern Dynasties. One of them is the *Ch'üan Lung Yen Pei* erected in 458, done by

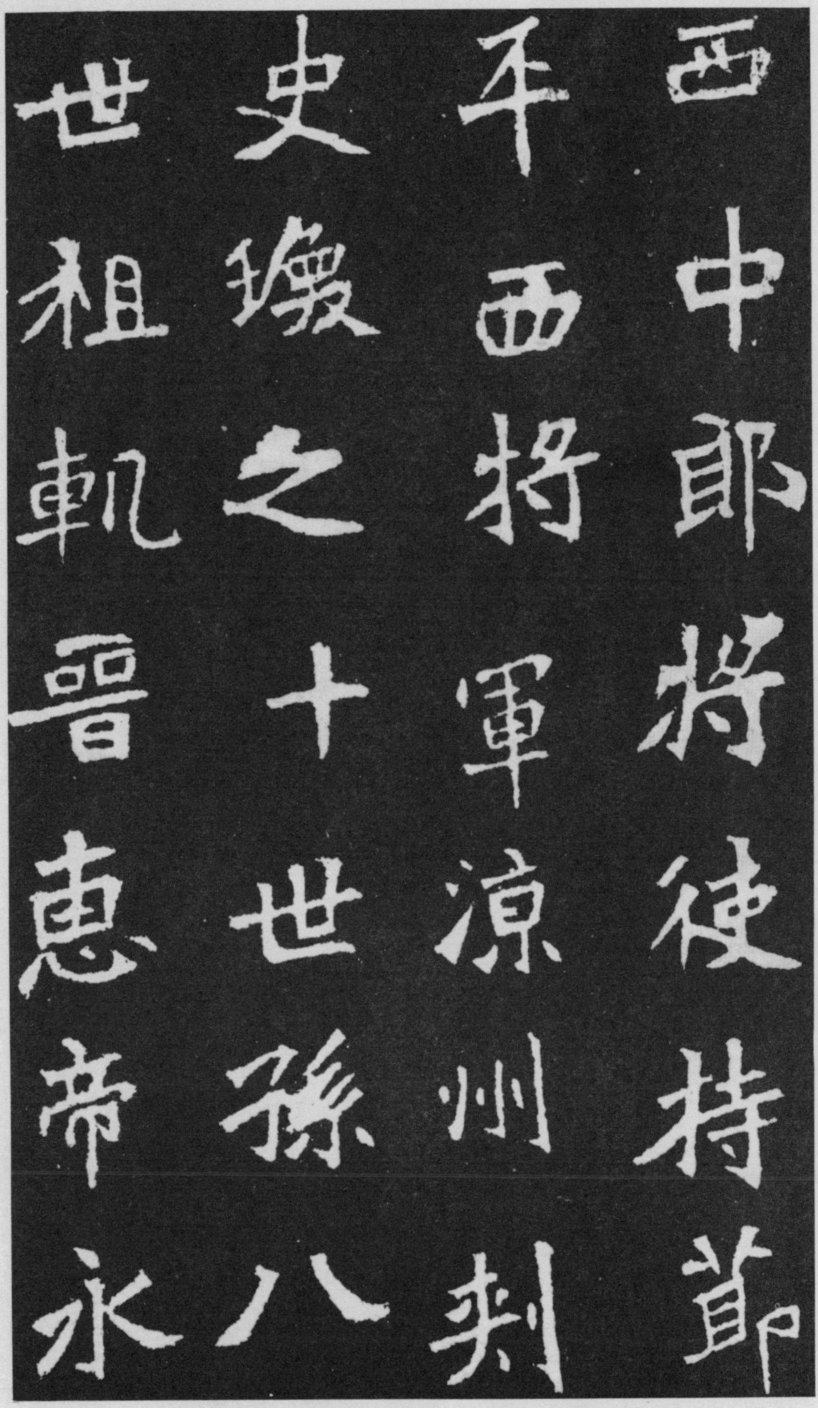

Fig. 25 *Chang Mêng-lung Pei* (detail)

an unknown calligrapher in *chên shu* which still carries a strong flavour of *li shu* and *pa fên*. Another is the *I Ho Ming* erected in 514, done by an unknown calligrapher in *chên shu* which, according to the Ch'ing Dynasty critic K'ang Yu-wei, 'follows the style of Chung Yu and upholds the tradition of Ts'ai Yung'. An odd feature of the *I Ho Ming* is that its text, written in vertical lines, reads from left to right instead of from right to left in the traditional Chinese fashion.

Even as Wang Hsi-chih, Wang Hsien-chih and their school of calligraphy was exercising almost complete dominance in the South, calligraphers in the succeeding dynasties in the North, especially the Wei Dynasty (386-556), were developing a calligraphic school of their own. Although the ruling houses of the North were originally nomads, they were second to none in their enthusiasm for cultural pursuits. Except for a very brief interlude, the Northern rulers were devout Buddhists. There was no prohibition of tablet-erecting. The peoples of the North have left us with thousands of tablets, all done by unknown calligraphers, displaying a style which is as aesthetically satisfying as it is archaically delicious. One of the best examples is the *Chang Mêng-lung Pei,* erected around 523, in memory of a man named Chang Mêng-lung (Fig. 25). Another is the *Chang Hei-nü Mu Chih,* erected around 593, in memory of a man named Chang Hsüan whose honourable name was Hei-nü, literally 'black girl' (Fig. 26). From these two samples, we can readily see that *chên shu* done by the Wei calligraphers was still under a great deal of *li shu* influence and was quite different in style and flavour from that of Wang Hsi-chih and his followers.

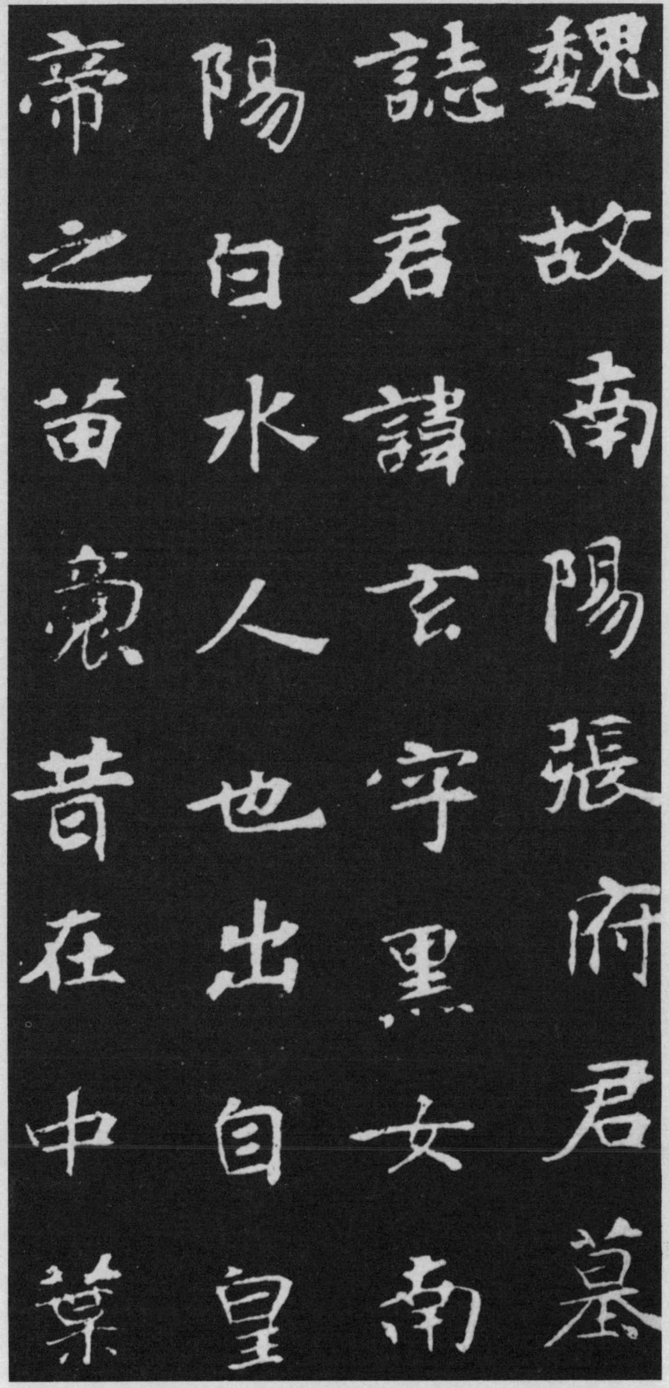

魏故南陽張府君墓誌君諱玄字黑女南陽白水人也出自皇帝之苗裔昔在中葉

Fig. 26　*Chang Hei-nü Mu Chih* (detail)

Chapter Six

T'ang: The Age of Chen Shu

The first part of the T'ang Dynasty, from the complete unification of the realm in 623 to the outbreak of the An Lu-shan rebellion in 755, was a period of prolonged peace and prosperity during which Chinese art came into full maturity, blossomed and bore fruit. Following the shining example of Emperor T'ai-tsung, the early T'ang rulers were not only ardent patrons of the arts but were artists in their own right. The T'ang court was graced by a blinding coruscation of variously talented men unrivalled in any other period of Chinese history. It was served by a group of ministers who were pillars of the State, among whom were found the calligraphers whose styles reflected the potency and health, the grace and majesty of their age.

One of them was Yü Shih-nan, a towering figure in Emperor T'ai-tsung's court, who was noted for his profound scholarship, impeccable conduct, deep loyalty, elegant prose and superb calligraphy—'the five superlatives'. In his calligraphy he was a follower of his fellow provincial, the monk Chih-yung, and was therefore in the mainstream of the Wang Hsi-chih tradition. However, the times had changed, and the emphasis was to make calligraphy the vehicle to transport the lofty moral ideals of Confucian philosophy. It was a solemn matter for him to be asked by Emperor T'ai-tsung to transcribe a composition which was to be engraved on stone as a tablet commemorating the building of a temple of Confucius. This Yü Shih-nan did in 616 at the age of 69. Of course, for a work of this nature, the characters must be done in *chên shu* with all the dignity and formality the occasion demanded. Known as the *K'ung Tzŭ Miao T'ang Pei* (Fig. 27), it was Yü Shih-nan's master-

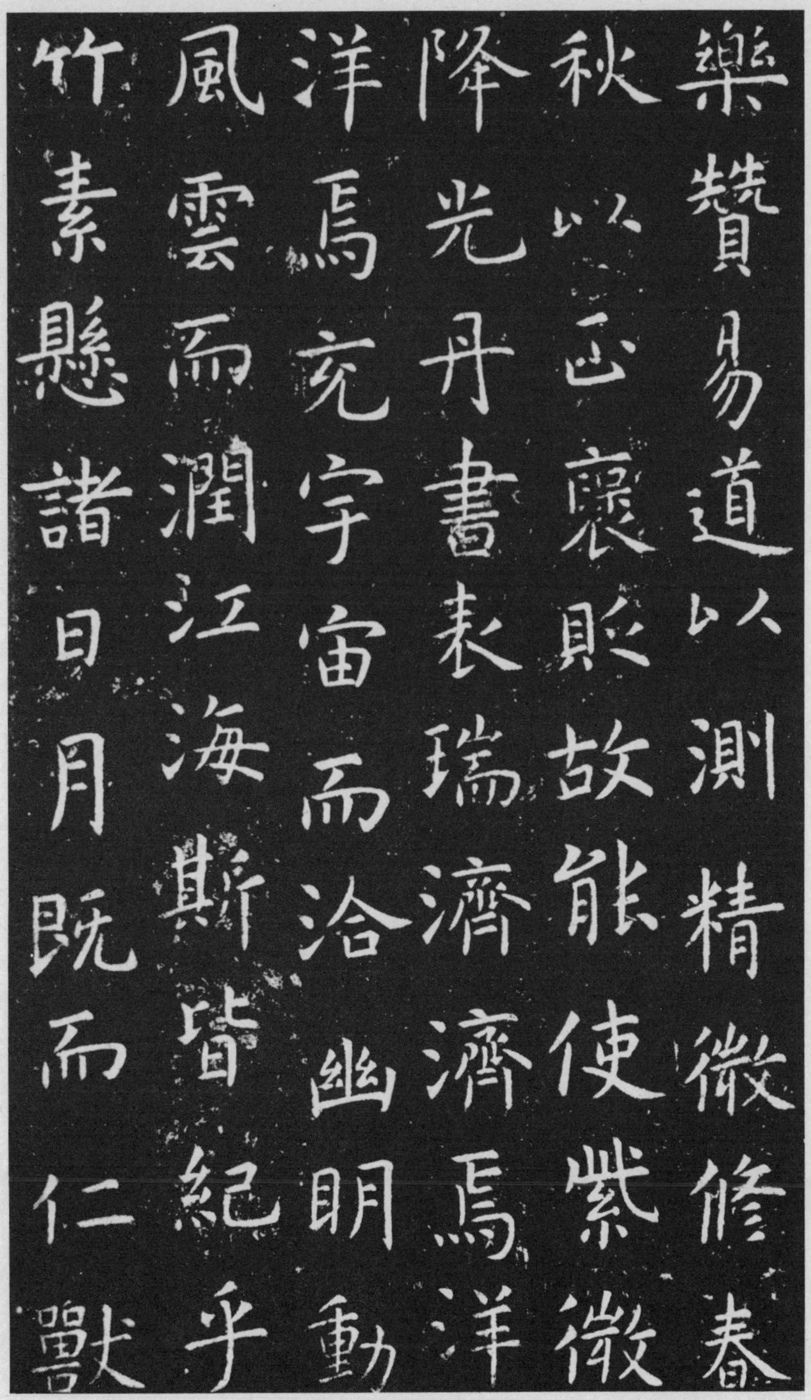

樂贊易道以測精微修養
秋以正襄敗故能使縈微
降光丹書表瑞濟濟焉洋
洋馬而充宇宙而洽幽明動
風雲而潤江海斯皆紀乎
竹素懸諸日月既而仁獸

Fig. 27　Yü Shih-nan: *K'ung Tzŭ Miao T'ang Pei* (detail)

piece and one of the most celebrated tablets of the T'ang period. Upon completion of this great work, the Emperor rewarded Yü Shih-nan with a yellow silver seal commending him as 'a true son of Wang Hsi-chih'. Coming from Emperor T'ai-tsung, this was no routine praise. It indicated that Yü Shih-nan's style, elegant and expansive, was still in the Tsin tradition, although traces that were to be indelibly T'ang were beginning to make their appearances.

Emperor T'ai-tsung, while building his far-flung empire and attending to the multifarious affairs of state, always found time to indulge in the study and practice of calligraphy. His idol, of course, was Wang Hsi-chih. He once inscribed two screens, one in *chên shu* and one *ts'ao shu*, after the style of the Tsin master. When he gave a banquet to his court, he used to do a number of scrolls in *fei po* as souvenirs to his senior ministers. He also did a tablet, *Tsin Tz'ŭ Chih Ming,* in *hsing shu* after Wang Hsi-chih's style. However, Yü Shih-nan was his tutor in *li shu.* On one occasion the Emperor did a large scroll in *li shu* and left out the element *kuo* in the character *chien* because he felt he could not do it well. Yü Shih-nan noticed the missing element and filled it in himself. When the Emperor asked his minister Wei Chêng for comments on the scroll, Wei Chêng reported: 'Characters done by Your Majesty excel in formal beauty all that is in the universe, and it is not for Your Majesty's humble servant to offer any opinion concerning them. However, since I am now looking at Your Majesty's work, I should like to say that the way the character *chien* is done manifests the highest approximation to perfect technique.'

The true spirit of T'ang calligraphy was embodied in what may be regarded as the Big Four—Ou-yang Hsün (557-645), Ch'u Shui-liang (596-658), Yen Chên-ch'ing (709-785) and Liu Kung-ch'üan (776-865). Unlike the poets, painters, musicians, sculptors and dancers who made the T'ang court so gay and sensuous, these men were steeped in classical philosophy and learning and took it upon themselves to play the role of the jealous guardians of the Confucian code of ethics and the defenders of the nation's morality. As such they risked their lives to uphold the high standards of government, to chart the course of right conduct for their sovereigns to follow. To them the practice of calligraphy was not so much an artistic pursuit as a revelation of personal character, a noble endeavour in which only men of sterling qualities were fit to engage. Some of them, as we have noted, were asked by Emperor T'ai-tsung to trace and copy Wang Hsi-chih's *Lan T'ing Hsü,* and to all intents and purposes they accounted for themselves wonderfully well. They were also avid students of the *Huang T'ing Ching*. But their own calligraphy was correct and formal, as befitting their high station in life. 'When the heart is upright, the hand will be upright,' Liu Kung-ch'üan solemnly reminded his sovereign.

Ou-yang Hsün, a precocious child who led a full life, took his calligraphy as seriously as the duties of his high official positions. He was most fastidious

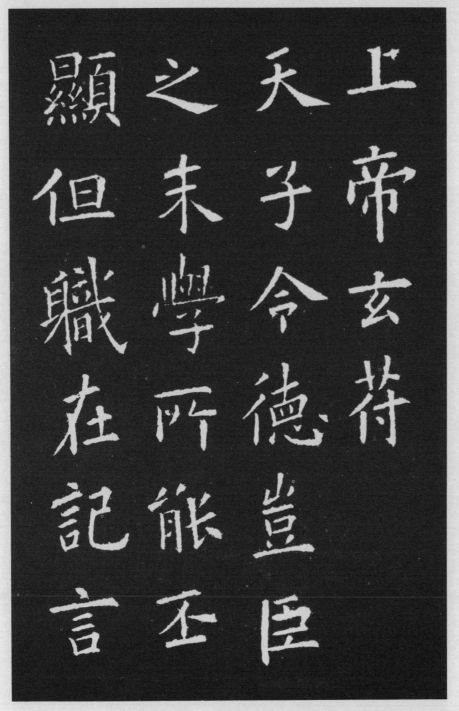

Fig. 28a   Ou-yang Hsün: *Chiu Ch'êng Kung, Li Ch'üan Ming* (detail)

about the instruments he used. His brush was made with fox-hair as the core (kernel) of the tuft covered by a mantle made of rabbit-hair plucked in autumn, to which a stem made of ivory or rhinoceros-horn was attached. His ink was a mixture of high quality pine-soot and musk. He wrote only on paper that was 'firm, thin, white and smooth'. Ou-yang Hsün began his training by modelling after the ancient tablets and the works of the Tsin masters. The exercises he took in *chuan shu* and *li shu* gave him mastery of the brush with which he developed a style in *chên shu* which was to be his main claim to fame. He took great care in trying to make every character he wrote a graphic reflection of his moral personality. The strokes forming the characters he executed have been compared to straight wooden beams and bent iron girders. The forms he created were square and erect, strong and angular, like a suit of armour, austere and forbidding, symbolizing his uncompromising approach to the problems of life. Every character was made to stand rigidly and solidly by itself, like a solitary peak of granite highlighted against the horizon.

This type of calligraphy, it goes without saying, was best suited for tablets and he did many of them in the course of his long life. One of them, *Chiu Ch'êng Kung, Li Ch'üan Ming,* has been regarded as his masterpiece (Fig. 28a). The story behind the tablet is rather interesting. In 592, the Sui Emperor Wên-ti built a palace at T'ien T'ai Shan and named it Jên Shou Kung. In 631, the T'ang Emperor T'ai-tsung, having taken over the palace, renamed it Chiu Ch'êng Kung. In 632, he spent his summer in the palace and found to his chagrin that there was a shortage of water. He struck his cane on the ground and miraculously a sweet spring was discovered. He thereupon called the place Li Ch'üan, 'sweet spring'. To commemorate the good omen, the minister Wei Chêng composed an essay which Emperor T'ai-tsung asked Ou-yang Hsün to transcribe for engraving as a tablet. We can see from this sample of his calligraphy why his style appealed particularly to those involved in formal writing, especially to young men taking part in civil service examinations. Those who like Ou-yang Hsün's style praise it for 'combining the grace of the serpent and the vigour of the warrior'. To his detractors, among them the Sung savant Mi Fu, his style suffers from being too austere and unadorned, 'like a man who has just recovered from a serious illness, colourless and lacking the sap of life'. Although Ou-yang Hsün's specialty was undoubtedly the *chên shu,* he was equally at home in the other scripts—*hsing shu, ts'ao shu,* even *fei po.* The *San Hsi T'ang* collection includes one of his manuscripts in *hsing shu,* known as *Chang Han T'ieh* (Fig. 28b), a brief account of the recluse Chang Han who voiced his contempt for urban life and longed for the green vegetables and fresh fish in his native place. Even in his lifetime, Ou-yang Hsün's fame was enormous. The Kingdom of Chi-lin (now Korea) once despatched a special envoy to China to seek his calligraphy. Because

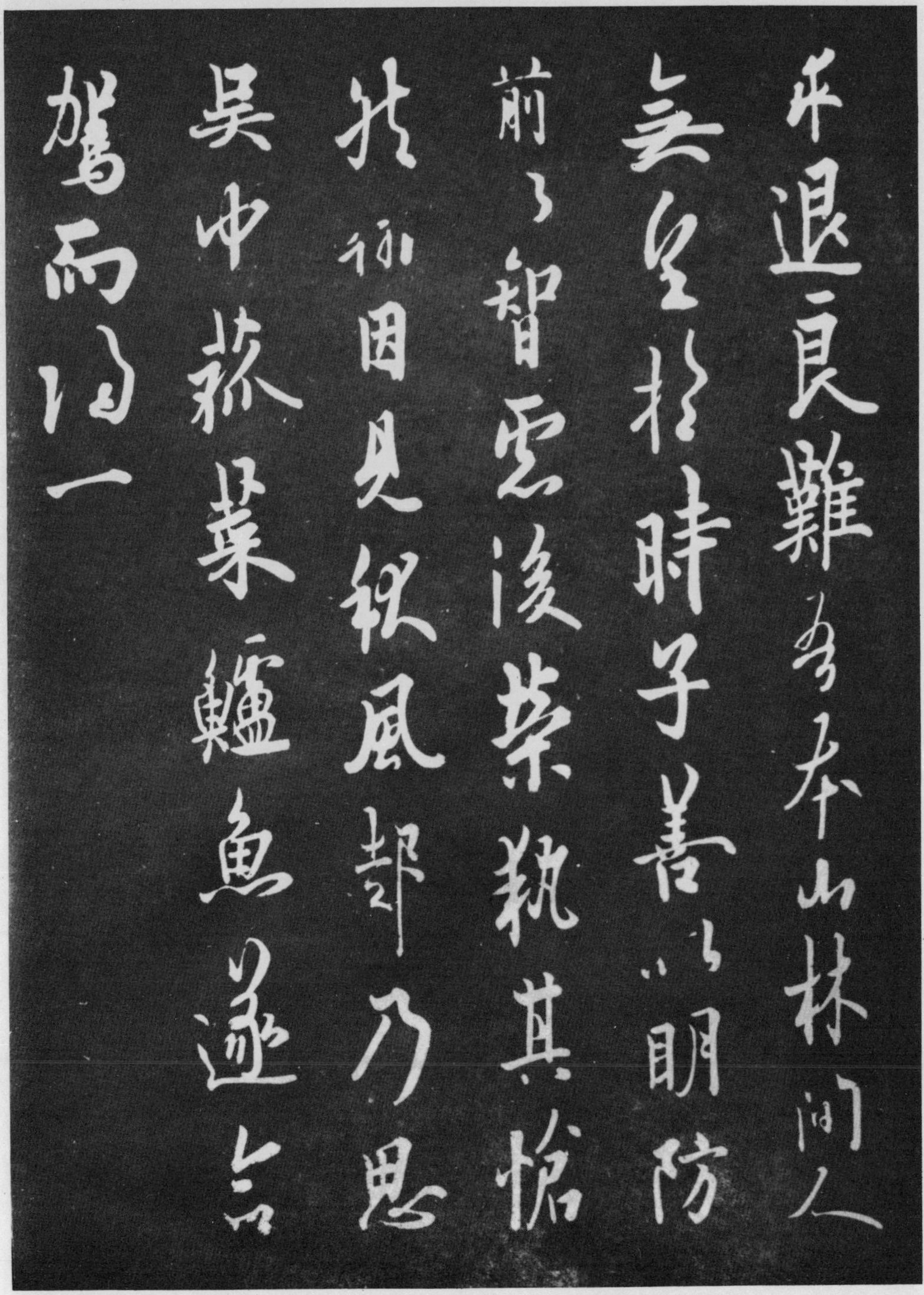

平退良難為本山林間人無至於時子善以期防前々智雲後葉執其悦北孫因見積風部乃思吳中蒜菜鱸魚遂言駑而馮一

Fig. 28b Ou-yang Hsün: *Chang Han T'ieh* (detail)

his *chên shu* has been used as models for schools, his style has exerted a tremendous influence on the common man.

Ch'u Shui-liang, a scholar who was good in *li shu* and *chên shu,* was recommended to Emperor T'ai-tsung as a man qualified to discuss the art of calligraphy after Yü Shih-nan's death. The Emperor gave him the office of court recorder. The Emperor once asked him: 'If I do something wrong, would you record it also?' Ch'u Shui-liang replied: 'Your Majesty's humble servant is charged with the duty of recording all that Your Majesty does.' Known as an upright and loyal official, Ch'u Shui-liang rose rapidly in the favourable climate of Emperor T'ai-tsung's reign and was made the Duke of Honan by Emperor Kao-tsung. However, during the turmoil attending Empress Wu Tsê-t'ien's usurpation, Ch'u Shui-liang fought valiantly but vainly for the principle of legitimacy. He even went so far as to return the symbol of his office to the Emperor and asked to be retired. In the palace revolution that followed, Ch'u Shui-liang's life was spared by the tempestuous Empress only because of his enormous stature as a veteran statesman, although he died in obscurity and disgrace.

We have departed from the usual practice and interjected this bit of biographical data because Ch'u Shui-liang has been as much honoured for his moral integrity as for his achievements as a calligrapher. As the Sung savant Su Shih said: 'Those who discuss Ch'u Shui-liang's calligraphy should always take into account his towering personality; if not for the man, his calligraphy would not be so highly rated.' This is not to say that Ch'u Shui-liang's calligraphy is in any way inferior to that of his contemporaries. Thoroughly grounded in *li shu* and *pa fên,* Ch'u Shui-liang's *chên shu,* done with sinuous and taut lines balanced by heavy terminations, is full of grace and charm, concealing his inner strength behind an exterior of jade-like smoothness. His style is indeed a subtle combination, a delicate derivative, of the very best in the Tsin tradition.

As we have noted, in 653 Ch'u Shui-liang did a transcription of the *Shêng Chiao Hsü,* which was engraved on stone. We have now in the collection of the Chinese National Palace Museum what is undoubtedly an original manuscript of Ch'u Shui-liang, known as *Han Ming Ch'ên Chuan Chan* (also known as *Ni K'uan Chan*) done in formal, middle-sized *chên shu* (Fig. 29). The essay transcribed by Ch'u Shui-liang consists of 344 characters, all carefully and exquisitely done, giving an account of the great figures in all walks of life serving the court of the Han Dynasty in an effort to show that the assembling of true talents is the guarantee of political success. It is not hard to see in the manuscript that Ch'u Shui-liang's *chên shu* contains an unusually large amount of *li shu* features. His deliberate effort to effect a balance between slender and heavy strokes is not only extremely pleasant to the eye but is also a stunning demonstration of his complete mastery over the brush. Quite apart from his stature as a man of principles in politics, Ch'u Shui-liang

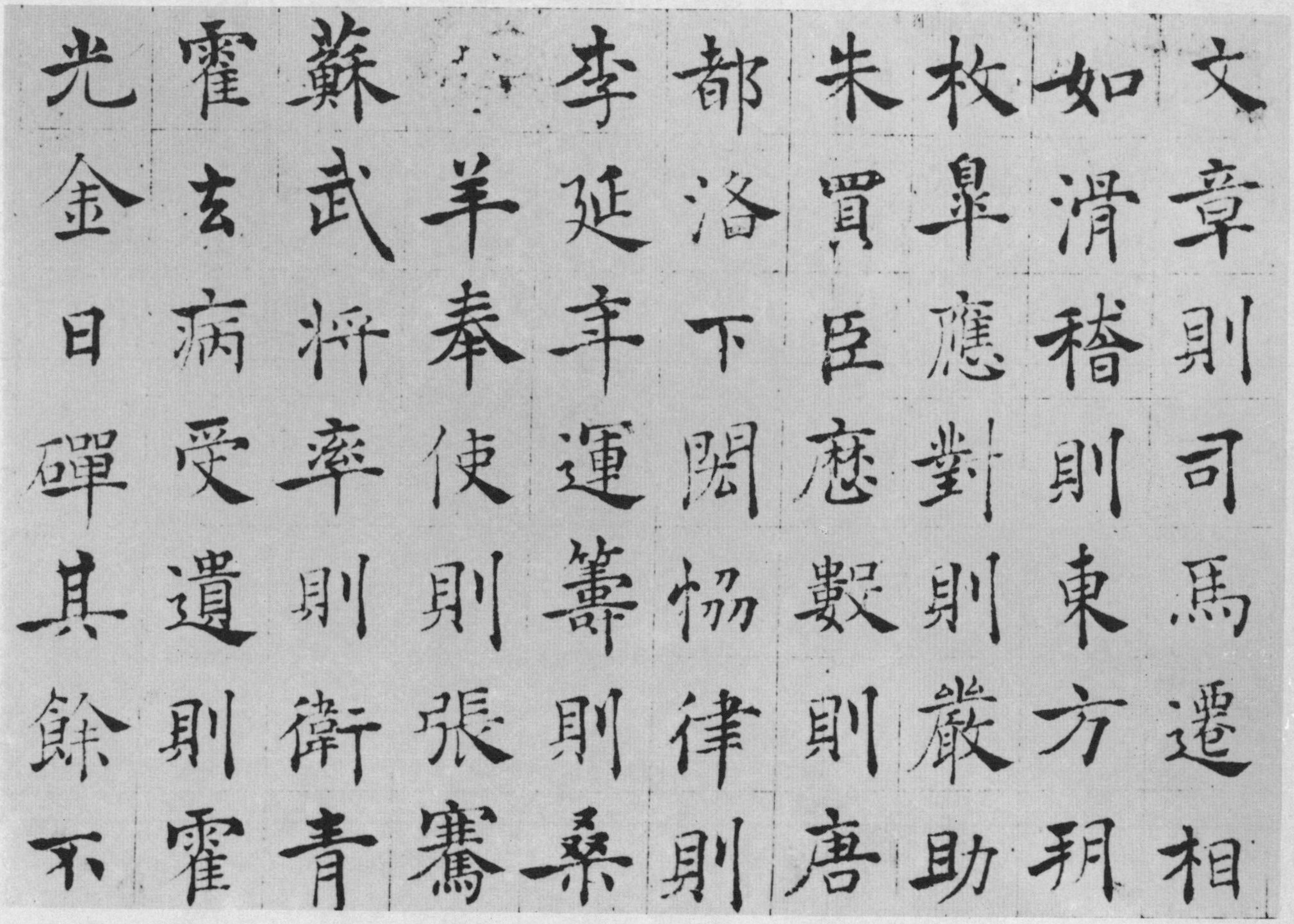

文章則司馬遷相
如滑稽則東方朔
枚皋應對則嚴助
朱買臣奏議則唐
都洛下閎協律則
李延年運籌則桑
羊奉使則張騫
蘇武將率則衛青
霍去病受遺則霍
光金日磾其餘不

Fig. 29　Ch'u Shui-liang: *Han Ming Ch'ên Chüan Chan* (detail)

deserves in every way the niche he occupies in the hierarchy of merit in the art of calligraphy.

The most widely respected calligrapher of the T'ang Dynasty was Yen Chên-ch'ing, a man who was also highly revered for his great courage and moral fibre in defending what he considered to be the best interests of the State. Although he was a descendant of a very famous family, his early life was plagued by poverty, and his parents could not even afford to provide him with a brush and paper to learn writing. His early training in calligraphy was therefore done by smearing mud on blank walls. Like all calligraphers he began his exercises by modelling after the old masters. His distinction was his ability to absorb what he learned and to put it to his own use. Of all the T'ang calligraphers, Yen Chên-ch'ing's style was the most original. Like the poetry of his contemporary Tu Fu, his style was a form of liberation from the dead weight of the past. His overriding desire was to impart the maximum power into his strokes—'dots like falling stones, horizontals like rain clouds, corners like bent metal, curves like extended bows'. The characters he executed were full of weight, achieved by enclosed forms which had the ideal solidity of the block or the cylinder. In this way he hoped to gain a greater fullness and a more pervasive movement. At the same time, he endowed his characters with an invigorating lustre—the brightness that is so essential to beauty.

Yen Chên-ch'ing's style has always been surrounded with an aura of cool majesty and a general impression has grown up that his calligraphic pieces were neatly planned segments in a mosaic of form and morality rather than spontaneous acts of artistic creativeness. Indeed, upon initial contact, his style does appear ponderous and heavy, even somewhat frightening, as if he were overwhelmed by the thought of his own importance. This may be illustrated by one of his original manuscripts in the collection of the Chinese National Palace Museum known as *Kao Shên* (Fig. 30a). In the T'ang Dynasty, *kao shên* was a formal document of appointment to office. In 780, Yen Chên-ch'ing was promoted to a high office and a *kao shên* was issued him. He undertook to transcribe in his own calligraphy, the *kao shên,* a document praising him highly for his profound learning, his scholastic distinctions, his deep sense of loyalty and his many achievements in the management of the affairs of State, all in justification of his appointment to an even higher office. The document must have pleased Yen Chên-ch'ing very much, and the calligraphic style in which he transcribed it was fully commensurate with its contents, truly a most remarkable revelation of personal pride and self-congratulation. It informs us that Yen Chên-ch'ing was a man who took himself very seriously, humourless and somewhat pontifical.

A specialist in *chên shu* and an important political figure of the day, Yen Chên-ch'ing was naturally very much in demand for the transcription of tablets. It was his habit to do tablets only in the most formal *chên shu*. One of the best examples is the *To Pao T'a* (Fig. 30b), a tablet erected in 752

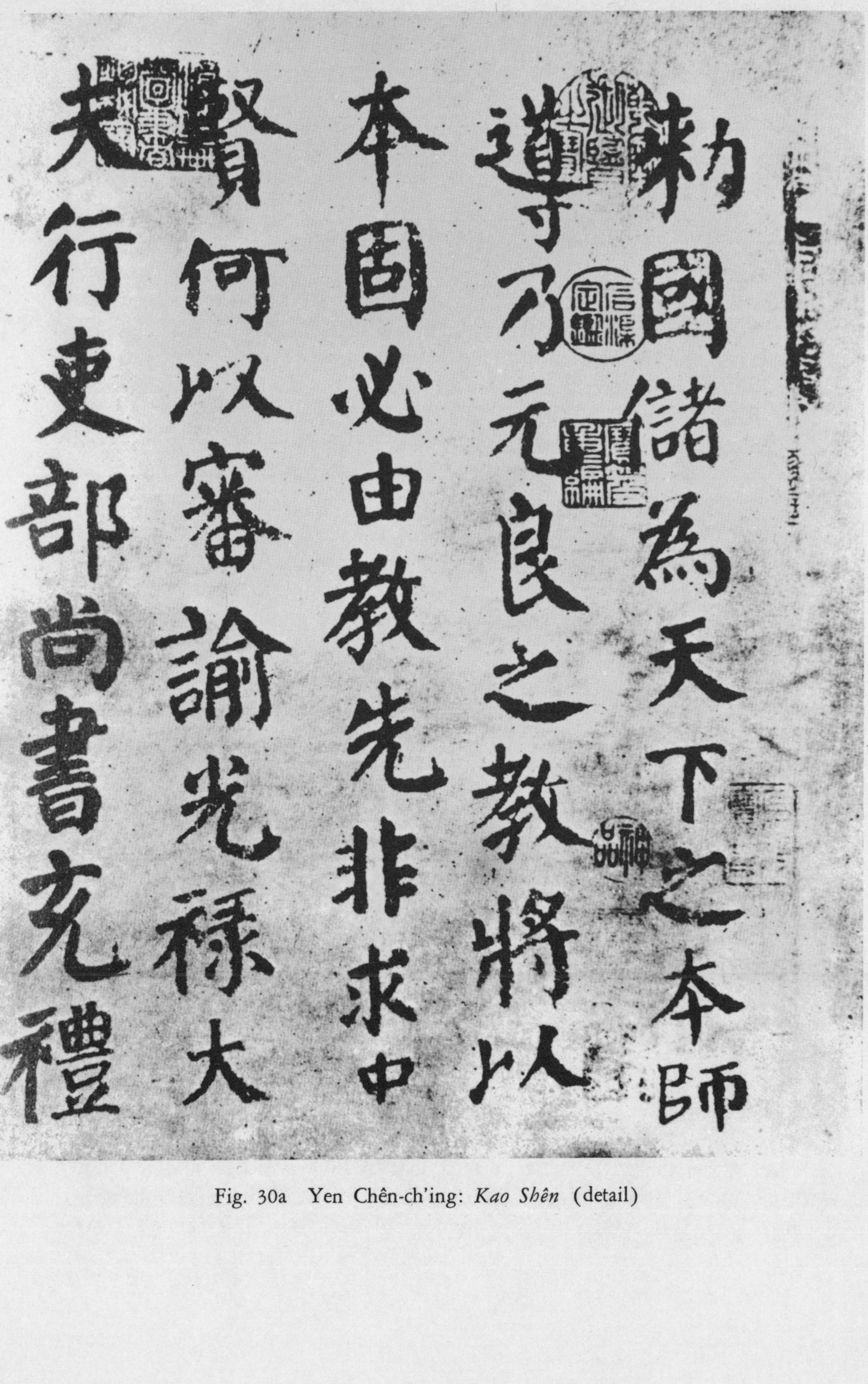

勑國諸為天下之本師
導乃元良之教將以
本固必由教先非求中
賢何以審諭光祿大
夫行吏部尚書充禮

Fig. 30a   Yen Chên-ch'ing: *Kao Shên* (detail)

at the Buddhist temple Ch'ien Fu Ssŭ in Changan. From the calligraphic style of the tablet, we detect that Yen Chên-ch'ing had, at least for the time being, forgotten his role as a statesman and had assumed the status of a devout Buddhist making offerings to his deity. Gone was the arrogance and self-confidence which permeated his transcription of the *kao shên*. Instead, we have in the *To Pao T'a* a subdued manifestation of piety, reverence and humility befitting the occasion.

One of China's calligraphic treasures is the draft of 'An Obituary of My Nephew', *Chi Chih Wên,* done by Yen Chên-ch'ing in 758 (Fig. 31), a document with a rich historical background. In 755, An Lu-shan staged a rebellion against the House of T'ang, a rebellion Yen Chên-ch'ing anticipated. As the Emperor Hsüan-tsung fled from the capital, Yen Chên-ch'ing joined with his brother to fight the rebels. In the ensuing battle, Yen Chên-ch'ing's brother and his brother's son were killed. In 758, as his nephew's remains were passing through the city in which he was stationed, Yen Chên-ch'ing drafted an obituary in his own hand. The draft, done in *hsing shu* mixed with *ts'ao shu* with many corrections, has miraculously been preserved. Although in the form of a draft and written in a moment of distress, it is a remarkable specimen of Yen Chên-ch'ing's calligraphy. A modern critic said: 'Having seen the *Chi Chih Wên,* we may well forget the *Lan T'ing Hsü* and the *Shêng Chiao Hsü*!' It may be mentioned in this connection that another Yen Chên-ch'ing draft, *Tsêng Tso Wei,* recounting a protocol fight in 764, is equally renowned.

With Yen Chên-ch'ing we have reached, in the view of most critics, the unchallenged master of calligraphy of the T'ang Dynasty, and all the familiar words stand ready to flow from the pen—power, exuberance, dignity, mastery of technique. But they are not enough. One of the most exciting features of Yen Chên-ch'ing's calligraphy is its variousness, its chameleon-like quality, which enabled him to put on a different face each time he applied his brush to the paper, as the three samples we have seen amply demonstrate, and if we were to survey the entire field of his work, we would find that even in the same category, such as tablets, his versatility was wellnigh limitless, so that in our study of Yen Chên-ch'ing we have to treat each one of his works as a separate and distinct entity to be evaluated on its own merits. But in the eyes of the Chinese art historian, Yen Chên-ch'ing's calligraphy, masterful as it undoubtedly is, should also be considered, even more so than Ch'u Shui-liang's, as the product of a man of sterling qualities—qualities which found expression both in his political conduct and in his art.

Liu Kung-ch'üan was born to the sombre world of T'ang China after the An Lu-shan catastrophe. Like the previous T'ang calligraphers, Liu Kung-ch'üan served the government in a number of high positions and was noted for his honesty and courage in the conduct of public affairs, including openly contradicting his sovereign on a number of occasions. His famous remark

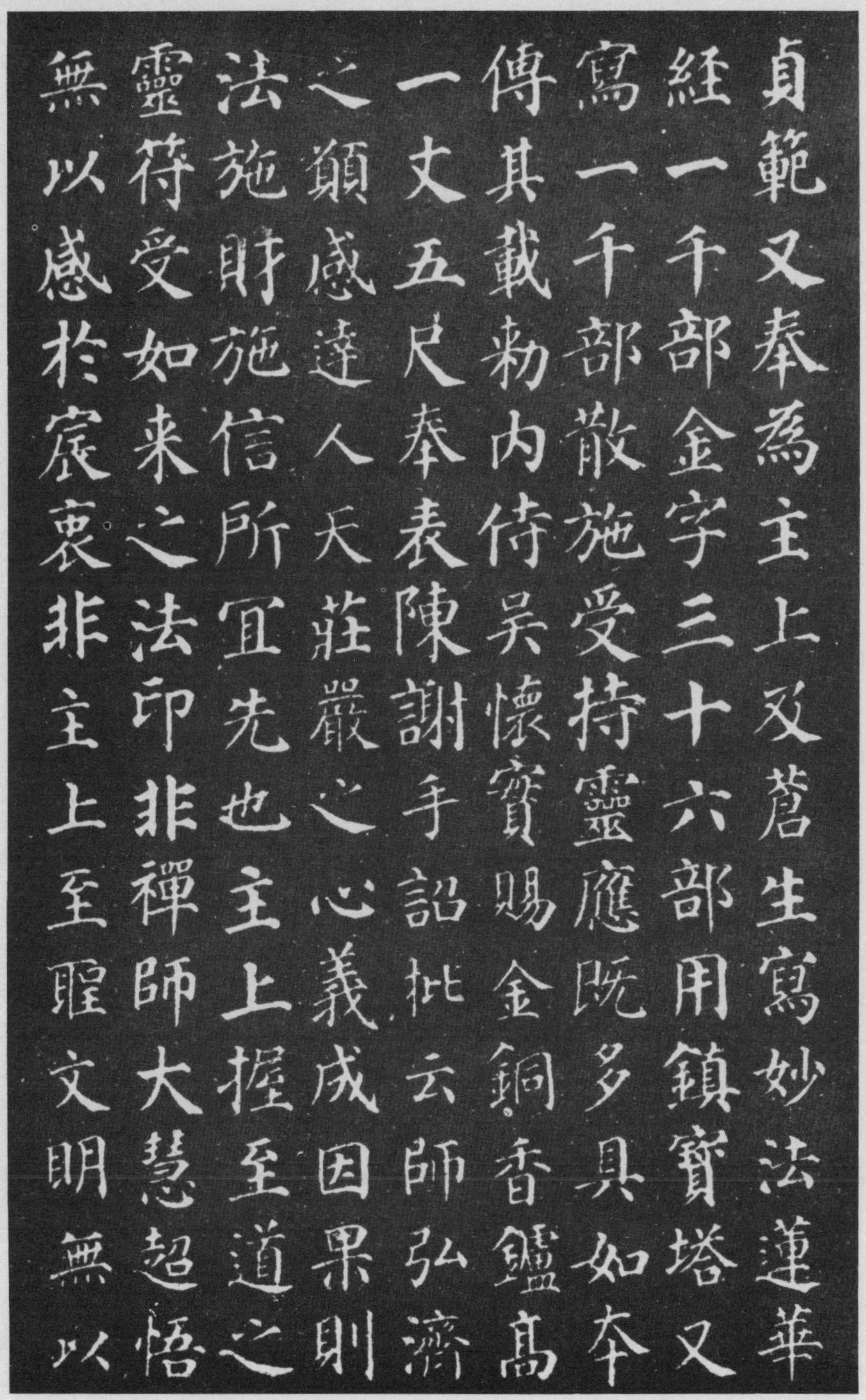

貞範又奉爲主上及蒼生寫妙法蓮華
經一千部金字三十六部用鎮寶塔又
寫一千部散施受持靈應既多具如本
傳其載勒內侍吳懷寶賜金銅香鑪高
一丈五尺奉表陳謝手詔批云師弘濟
之顙感達人天莊嚴之心義成因果則
法施財施信所宜先也主上握至道之
靈符受如來之法印非禪師大慧超悟
無以感於宸衷非主上至眞文明無以

Fig. 30b　Yen Chên-ch'ing: *To Pao T'a* (detail)

'when the heart is upright, the hand will be upright', was meant to be an admonition to the Emperor who innocently asked him a question about the technique of brushmanship. But in supplying the answer, which must have stunned the Emperor, Liu Kung-ch'üan was making a statement which reflected succinctly the mentality of the T'ang calligraphers, that calligraphy was essentially a manifestation of the morality of man, and by morality they meant more than anything else the sense of duty towards the best interests of the State.

An official of the T'ang government, he was recommended to Emperor Mu-tsung (reign 821-825) as a good calligrapher. The Emperor was delighted because he had seen Liu Kung-ch'üan's work in the temples of the capital city. A specialist in *chên shu*, Liu Kung-ch'üan first modelled after Yen Chên-ch'in, to whom he bore a superficial resemblance. But his effort was directed towards the elimination of all traces of mannerism and affectation. The strokes he executed are like branches of an old tree, sinewy and gnarled. The forms he created are bony and lean, suggesting a Taoist priest in the deep mountain who has through long meditation shed the cares of everyday existence. The dominant quality of Liu Kung-ch'üan's style is its clarity, like the cool air of an autumn moonlit night, or the rarified atmosphere on top of a high mountain. One of his masterpieces is the tablet *Hsüan Mi T'a Ming* (Fig. 32), which he transcribed in 841 at the age of 65. In the course of his long life, he did many others. His style caught the imagination of his contemporaries, who besieged him with requests to do epitaphs. The offspring of the aristocratic and well-to-do families of the day considered it a breach of filial piety if they could not get Liu Kung-ch'üan to do the tablets in memory of their elders. Like Ou-yang Hsün, Liu Kung-ch'üan was popular beyond the borders of China. From his calligraphy he amassed a huge fortune. Generous to a fault, he allowed it to be squandered by members of his family and his attendants, but he himself kept the key to the boxes containing his brushes and books.

T'ang calligraphy, fortunately, was not all as solemn and sombre as the styles of the Big Four. After all, T'ang China in its full glory, particularly in the reign of Hsüan-tsung, was full of fun. In some ways we may say that a man such as Yen Chên-ch'ing was somewhat out of step with his age. Even as he was doing the tablets in *chên shu* with all their formality and dignity, other people were enjoying themselves and producing works of art that were as enduring as his tablets. In calligraphy the medium was the *ts'ao shu,* and the artists were the drunken geniuses Chang Hsü and Huai-su.

Like so many of their contemporaries—Li Po the poet, Wu Tao-tzŭ the painter, Li Kuei-nien the musician, Yang Hui-chih the sculptor—the *ts'ao shu* calligraphers Chang Hsü and Huai-su drew inspiration from Emperor Hsüan-tsung's court dancer, the fabulous Kung-sun Ta Niang (Lady Kung-sun), whose graceful movement was the rage of the age. According to the poet Tu Fu, when the dancing lady was darting forward, it was like the crack of

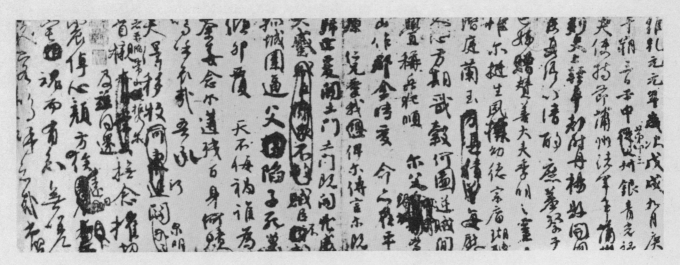

Fig. 31   Yen Chên-ch'ing: *Chi Chih Wên* (detail)

thunder under imposed restraint; when she concluded a number, it was like an angry wave subsiding in a blaze of blue light. Her swiftness was like the arrow of Hou Yi who shot down nine suns in the sky to leave us with the one we now have; her rhythm was like the gods cruising in the clouds on the back of dragons.

Chang Hsü, a man about town, was fascinated by the rhythm of movement and sought to apply it to his calligraphy. He was often drunk, and in that state he wielded his brush in frenzied speed, yelling and laughing as he went along. In moments of extreme wildness, he even tried to write with his head, soaking his hair in a basin of ink, twisting and turning his neck against the blank wall. It was only natural that he should specialize in that type of *ts'ao shu* known as *k'uang ts'ao,* linking the strokes and characters in any way he saw fit, more or less in the manner of Wang Hsien-chih. All this about Chang Hsü we read in art histories. But we have good reason to believe that he was a most accomplished artist, even when he was sober. For instance, he once did a tablet in *chên shu* showing us that he was well grounded in the script. Following the *ts'ao shu* tradition handed down by the Tsin masters, Chang Hsü endeavoured to apply the brushmanship of *chuan shu* to *ts'ao shu* with striking effect. This amazing ability on his part to maintain a link with the past, however tenuous, while blazing a path on his own, was very much admired by his contemporaries who affectionately called him 'Mad Chang' on the one hand and 'the sage of *ts'ao shu*' on the other.

Ts'ao shu in the T'ang Dynasty was probably better represented by Huai-su, a boy from a very poor family who entered a Buddhist monastery in his youth. Passionately devoted to the art of calligraphy, he was so destitute that he could not afford to buy paper and had to use banana leaves to practise his brushmanship. He was also troubled, he told us in his autobiographical essay, by not being able to see and model after the manuscripts of the old masters. Somehow, in his more mature years, he managed to go to the capital where he took lessons under the famous calligraphers of the day, among them Chang Hsü. Huai-su shared many of the eccentricities of his teacher. He, too, was intoxicated most of the time and when drunk used to soak his cap with ink and write on the temple walls. Like the monk Chih-yung, the monk Huai-su also buried his used brushes in solemn ceremonies, honouring them as old soldiers. Appropriately he was nicknamed 'the drunken monk'.

Huai-su, like his teacher Chang Hsü, admired Wang Hsien-chih's *ts'ao shu.* In many ways the styles of the three men were strikingly similar. In doing characters in *k'uang ts'ao,* the emphasis was all on the sense of movement in space and time. This quality Huai-su undoubtedly possessed in full measure. Looking at his works, we seem to see and feel his brush dashing and dancing in total abandon on the writing surface, as if he were watching, as one eye-witness told us, 'the sudden outbreak of a violent storm when the birds fly out of the woods and the startled serpent seeks shelter in tall grass'.

[92]

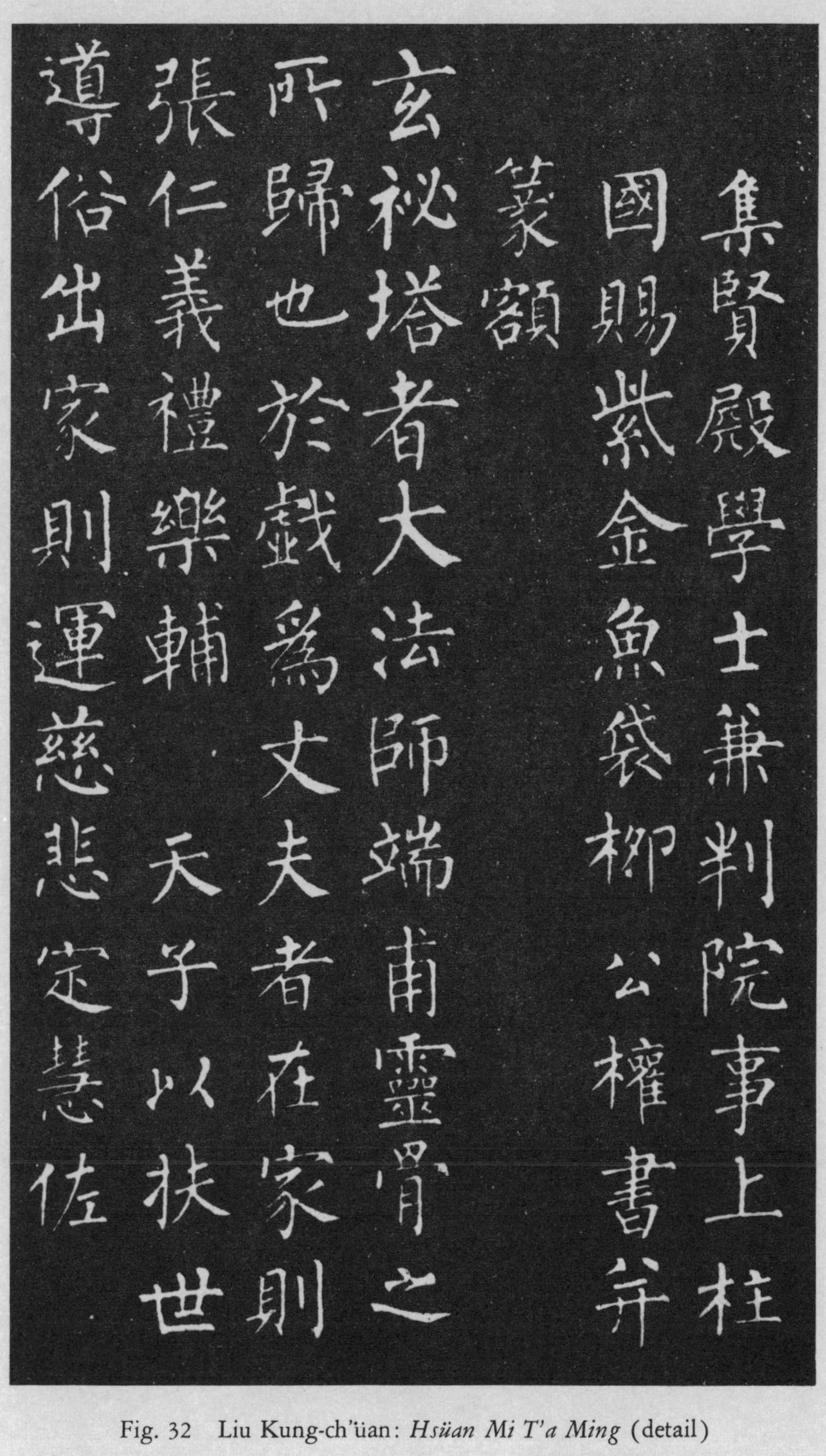

集賢殿學士兼判院事上柱
國賜紫金魚袋柳公權書并
篆額
玄祕塔者大法師端甫靈骨之
所歸也於戲為丈夫者在家則
張仁義禮樂輔天子以扶世
導俗出家則運慈悲定慧佐

Fig. 32　Liu Kung-ch'üan: *Hsüan Mi T'a Ming* (detail)

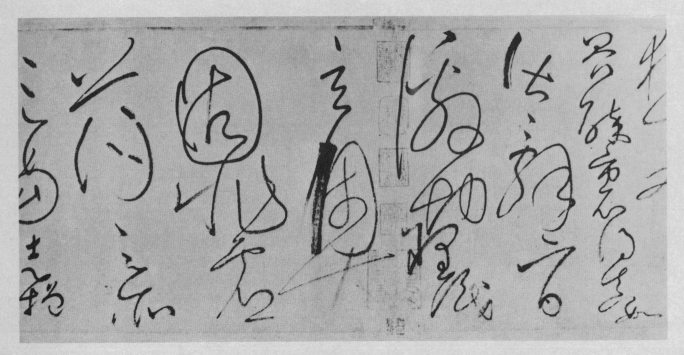

Fig. 33a   Huai-su: *Tzŭ Hsü T'ieh* (detail)

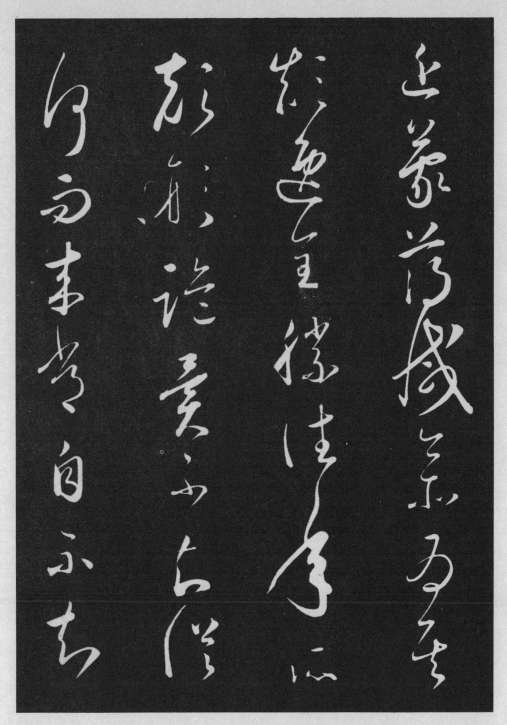

Fig. 33b   Huai-su: *Shan Kao Shui Shên T'ieh* (detail)

In his lifetime Huai-su was showered with praise, including a long poem by the celebrated poet Li Po and a laudatory essay by the calligrapher Yen Chên-ch'ing. In 777, at the age of 41, Huai-su composed an autobiographical essay called *Tzŭ Hsü T'ieh*, which he transcribed himself in *k'uang ts'ao* (Fig. 33a). In the essay Huai-su, quite immodestly, sang the praise of his own calligraphic achievements by quoting liberally from the eulogies he had received from his friends and admirers, including the full text of the essay by Yen Chên-ch'ing. The Sung poet-calligrapher Su Shih was certainly right in saying that Huai-su's vanity would be quite insufferable if he did not fully deserve the accolade lavished on him. Huai-su's *Tzŭ Hsü T'ieh*, the original of which is now in the Chinese National Palace Museum, is in many ways his representative work. The concept of *k'uang* (wildness) in his *ts'ao shu* was given dramatic emphasis by the extremely uneven size of the characters as well as by the random, even wanton, placement of the characters forming a line, most notably in the third line from the right. The particularly heavy stroke in the middle, however, was an accidental slip of the brush and should not be regarded as an integral part of the composition. The entire piece was done in *chung fêng* with lines like iron wires. This lack of linear expressiveness was compensated for by Huai-su's extraordinary sensitivity to form and movement, and if we like this type of *ts'ao shu* (quite a number of people detest it), we would consider the writhing forms he created things of enchanting abstract beauty.

That Huai-su was indeed a most accomplished calligrapher was attested by his ability to do *ts'ao shu* in the more conventional style with remarkable effect. This may be seen in a short note in the *San Hsi T'ang* collection known as the *Shan Kao Shui Shên T'ieh* (Fig. 33b) wherein the 'drunken monk' seemed to be much soberer than he was prepared to admit. In a colophon (dated 1318) to the manuscript, the Yüan Dynasty calligrapher-painter Chao Mêng-fu said:

What makes Huai-su's calligraphy so wonderful is that, with all his talk about wild and spontaneous creation and the multiple metamorphosis of his style, he was always able to abide by the standards of the Wei and Tsin masters. People in recent times are fond of breaking the old rules in pursuit of new fashions. Those who do not know calligraphy are often amazed by their feats. To the knowledgeable such feats are not even laughable. This scroll (*Shan Kao Shui Shên T'ieh*) comes straight out of Huai-su's heart. It is head and shoulders above the other Huai-su works we have seen.

In our account of T'ang calligraphers we have tried hard to limit ourselves only to the truly great. But the age was so prolific that we are compelled to mention, however briefly, some of the others who have undoubtedly left their marks in history. Inspired by the shining example of Emperor T'ai-tsung, most of the rulers of the early T'ang Dynasty were not only avid patrons of art but were accomplished artists in their own right. Even the Empress

[96]

朕以為常鳥爰所
志懷左清道率府
長史魏光乘才雄白
鳳鞘壯碧雞以其宏
達博識名王軒檻
預觀其事以獻其
頌夫頌者所以褕楊
德業襃讚成功顧
湑盧睞誠有負美美
其彬蔚俯同頌云
伊我軒宮奇樹青

Fig. 34 Emperor Hsüan-tsung: *Chi Ling Sung* (detail)

Wu Tsê-t'ien was able to emulate the calligraphic style of the monk Chih-yung with remarkable proficiency. Emperor Hsüan-tsung, in particular, was talented in the arts. In calligraphy he was good both in *pa fên* and *chang ts'ao*. Regrettably the only original manuscript of his now extant is his transcription of an essay entitled *Chi Ling Sung* (Eulogy of the Pied Wagtail) done in *hsing shu* (Fig. 34) now in the Chinese National Palace Museum.

In an age in which calligraphy was so much in fashion, it was inevitable that someone should write in praise of its abstract and recondite beauty. Such a man was Sun Ch'ien-li whose prose-poem *Shu P'u* has become a classic from which we shall quote at some length in subsequent chapters. An ardent admirer of the *ts'ao shu* of the Tsin masters, Sun Ch'ien-li transcribed his essay in his own hand in 687, a breath-taking display of a *ts'ao shu* style which many critics are inclined to regard as more superb than that of Chang Hsü and Huai-su (Fig. 35).

When Empress Wu Tsê-t'ien was on the throne, one of her favourite calligraphers was Chung Shao-ching, a tenth generation descendant of the late Han calligrapher Chung Yu. A passionate lover of calligraphy, Chung Shao-ching spent a fortune, aggregating several million units of currency, to scour the country for original manuscripts of the great calligraphers of the past, particularly those of Wang Hsi-chih. His position as a court calligrapher also gave him the rare privilege of studying and modelling after the treasures in the fabulous collection amassed by Emperor T'ai-tsung. During Empress Wu Tsê-t'ien's reign, most of the calligraphic decorations of the palace were done by his hand. In 738, Chung Shao-ching was asked by the Princess Yü-chên to transcribe the *Ling Fei Ching,* a Taoist treatise, as a present to the Emperor Hsüan-tsung. Done in small *chên shu* very much in the style of Wang Hsi-chih, Chung Shao-ching's *Ling Fei Ching* (Fig. 36) has become a standard model for elementary calligraphic exercises and has exerted a tremendous influence on subsequent generations. It has been lavishly praised by discerning critics as a work embodying the essence of small *chên shu* of the Tsin masters, most notably Wang Hsi-chih's *Huang T'ing Ching* and Wang Hsien-chih's *Lo Shên Fu* (Thirteen Lines). Other critics, however, are inclined to the opinion that Chung Shao-ching's style is weak and somewhat effeminate and therefore unworthy of the high place it has occupied over the ages. In any case, Chung Shao-ching's calligraphy is the end result of a tradition, not the beginning of a new approach.

T'ang China, following in the Han tradition, was an age of lavish funerals and all calligraphers were besieged with requests to do tablets in memory of the dead. Li Yung, a calligrapher in the time of Emperor Hsüan-tsung, did no less than eight hundred tablets in his lifetime, amassing a huge fortune in the process. For forty years, until his death at the hands of his political enemies in 747, he was the most popular calligrapher of the land. A specialist in *chên shu,* Li Yung's style was slightly mannerist and affected. Even in

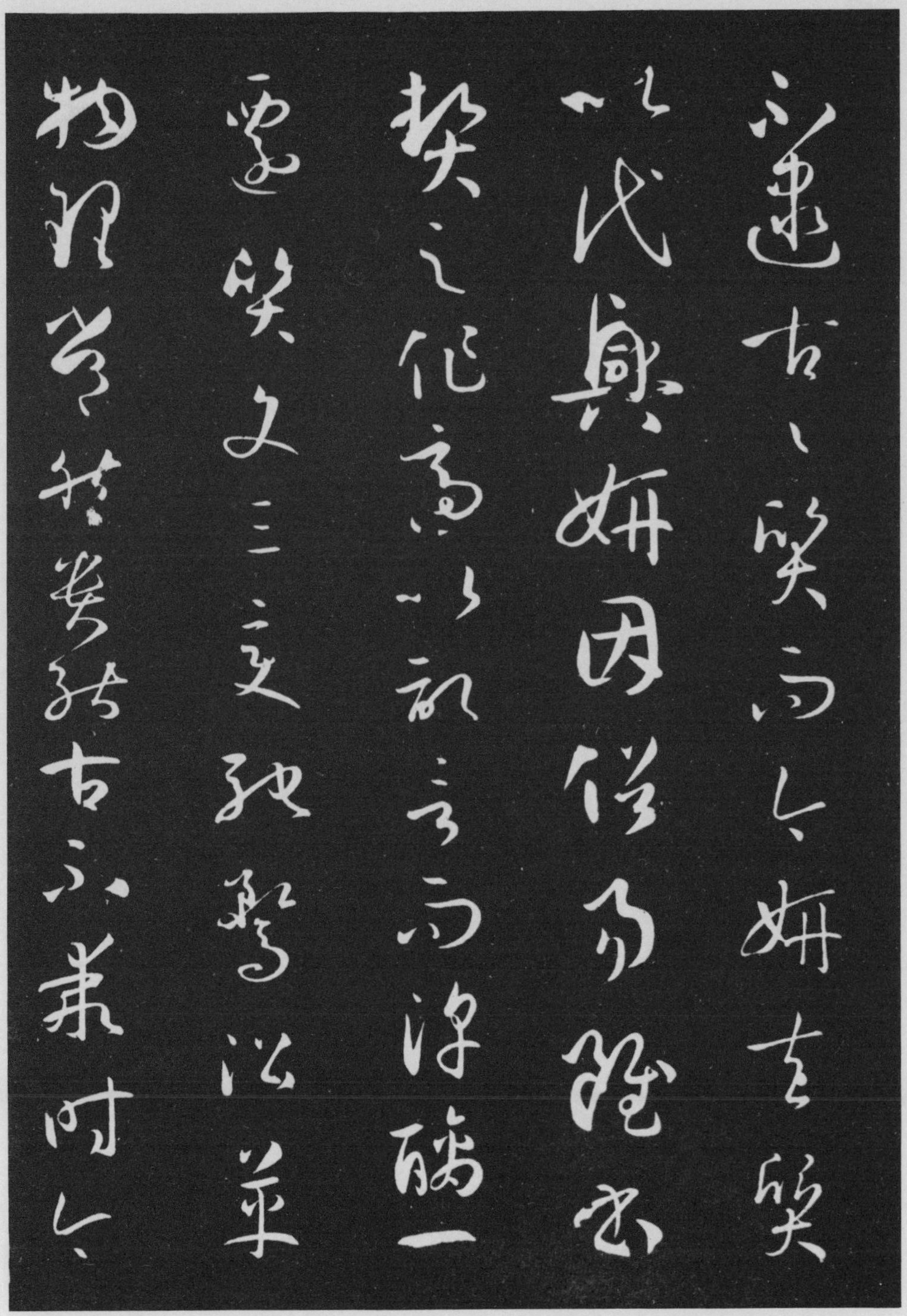

Fig. 35   Sun Ch'ien-li: *Shu P'u* (detail)

doing characters in *chên shu,* he was fond of linking some of his strokes with lobes which to some eyes appear to be rather annoying. He was also prone to exaggerating the strength of his strokes.

Another calligrapher of the period, Hsü Hao, was the favourite of Emperor Su-tsung, who entrusted him with the transcription of practically all the important royal proclamations of the period. A descendant of a long line of calligraphers, Hsü Hao tried his hand in all the scripts. He once demonstrated his versatility by doing forty-two screens in eight different scripts. Although he enjoyed great fame in his lifetime, Hsü Hao was primarily an accomplished craftsman and was honoured as such by his contemporaries. The fact that both his grandfather and father were accomplished calligraphers also helped in building up his reputation.

A tablet, as we have seen, was usually accompanied by a heading, a title, done by a different calligrapher and in a different script. Since most of the T'ang tablets were either in *chên shu* or *hsing shu,* the heading therefore was either in *chuan shu* or *li shu.* The most honoured *chuan shu* calligrapher of the T'ang Dynasty was Li Yang-ping whose *hsiao chuan* was considered the best after the great Li Ssŭ, although he also did several tablets in *ta chuan* (stone drums and bronze inscriptions). A tablet transcribed by Yen Chên-ch'ing in *chên shu* with a heading by Li Yang-ping in *chuan shu* would delight the heart of any lover of calligraphy and was about the best thing a son could offer in memory of his departed father.

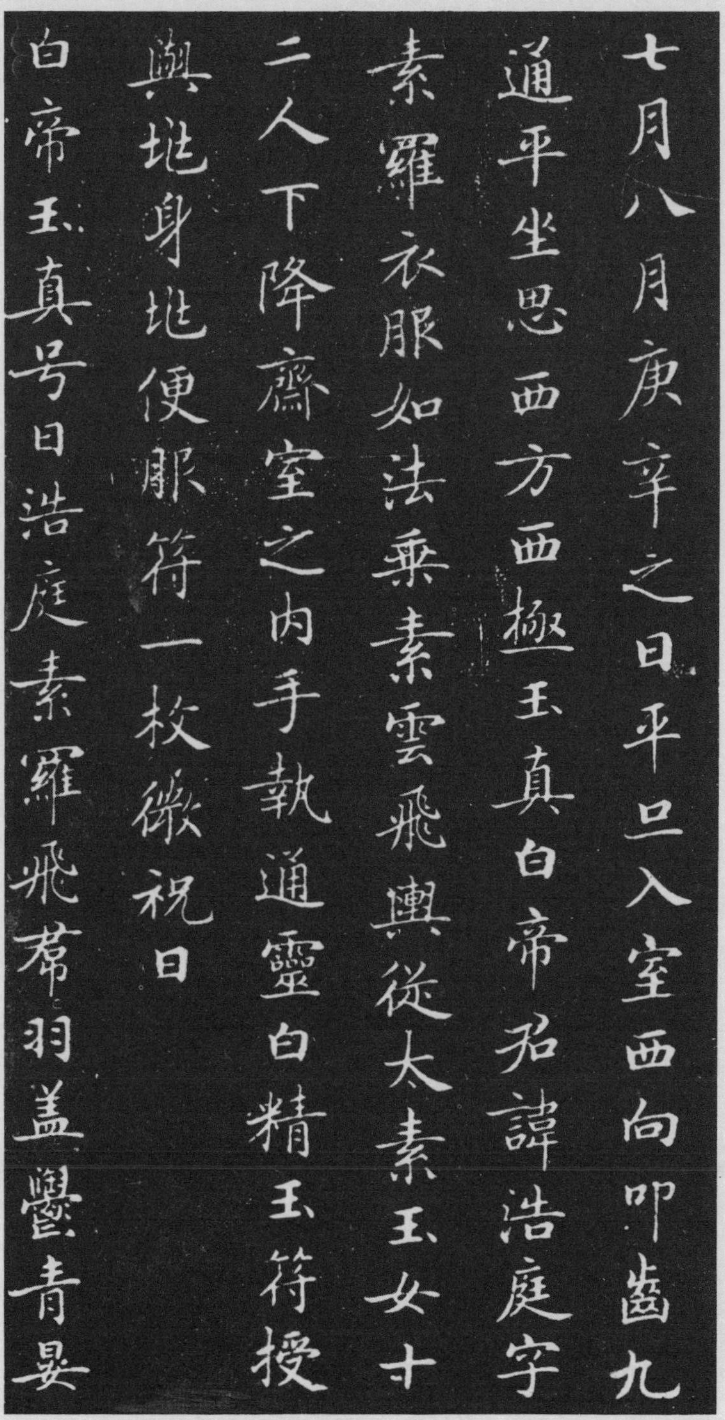

七月八月庚辛之日平旦入室西向叩齒九

通平坐思西方西極玉真白帝君諱浩庭字

素羅衣服如法乘素雲飛輿從太素玉女十

二人下降齋室之內手執通靈白精玉符授

興坤身坤便服符一枚微祝日

白帝玉真号日浩庭素羅飛帬羽盖鬱青晏

Fig. 36　Chung Shao-ching: *Ling Fei Ching* (detail)

Chapter Seven

Sung: The Age of Hsing Shu

Between the T'ang and Sung Dynasties there was a sharp division, though it would be difficult to define its precise nature. All one can say is that the weighty, conscientious, though often romantic seriousness which pervaded T'ang calligraphy seemed to give way to a lightheartedness and playfulness in the Sung period. The Sung Dynasty was an age of refinement with an overtone of intellectualism. The Sung calligraphers were first and foremost men of letters who dabbled in the arts. Among them Ts'ai Hsiang (1011-1066), Su Shih (1036-1101), Huang T'ing-chien (1050-1110) and Mi Fu (1051-1107) were easily the most prominent. Their calligraphic styles, even in *chên shu,* appeared to be casual and even careless, permitting their hand great liberty, like the landscape painters of the period, to follow the dictates of their heart, sometimes in reckless disregard of established conventions. Reminiscent of the Tsin tradition, they felt perfectly free to make innovations in individual strokes and in the overall formation of the characters, abbreviating and eliminating lines and dots, exaggerating and distorting basic forms, substituting symbols for radicals and elements. In their writing, vertical strokes may appear somewhat curved, the squares may be rounded, the hooks may shed their customary terminal flicks. The characters are far from uniform in size and the lines are not of the same length. Some strokes are slender and long, others heavy and stubby.

The progenitor of this exciting movement was Yang Ning-shih of the Period of Five Dynasties, the interregum of disunion and strife in the first half of the tenth century which proved to be so fabulously productive in the

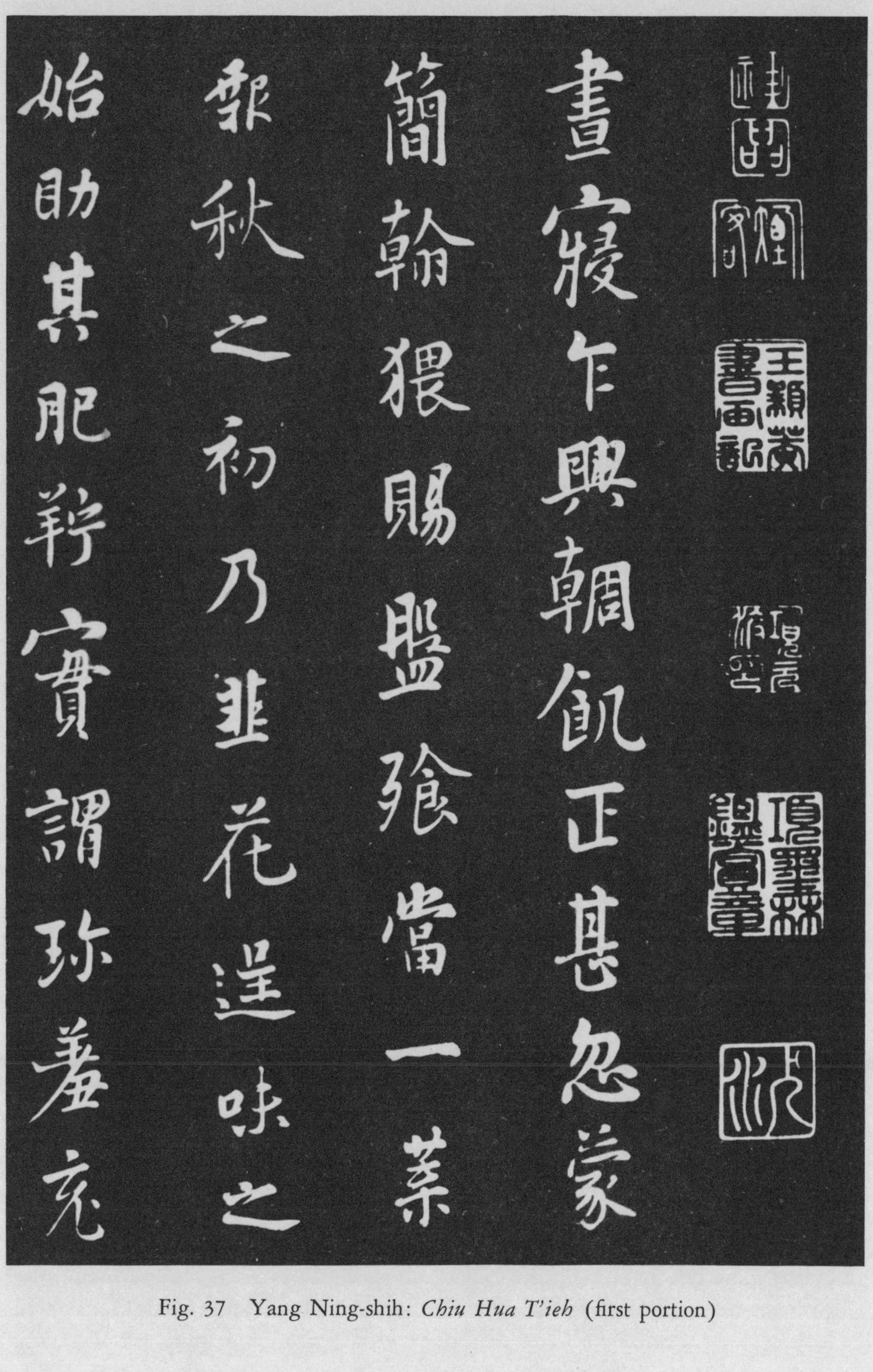

Fig. 37   Yang Ning-shih: *Chiu Hua T'ieh* (first portion)

field of the creative arts. An ugly boy whose 'waist was broader than the body', Yang Ning-shih was the son of a Prime Minister of the last Emperor of the T'ang Dynasty. When the succeeding Liang Dynasty was established in 907, his father, in violation of the Confucian code of loyalty, turned over the T'ang imperial seal to the new ruler. Yang Ning-shih admonished his father against the move, but to no avail. In the next half century, Yang Ning-shih himself was drafted into the service of one succeeding dynasty after another, but he was most unhappy over the turn of events. His behaviour was wilfully strange, which was his way of dodging public service. He soon came to be known as 'Yang the Lunatic' and spent his time spattering the walls and screens of temples and shrines in the capital city of Loyang with his calligraphy. Although he was good at *ts'ao shu* in the manner of Chang Hsü and Huai-su, his greatest contribution was in *chên shu*. His justly renowned work, *Chiu Hua T'ieh* (Fig. 37), is in the form of a letter to one of his friends who sent him some delicacies. Yang Ning-shih, in expressing his appreciation, told his friend in a carefully written note that the delicacies arrived just as he woke up from his nap and he was very hungry at the time. The delicacies he received included some *chiu hua,* a Chinese vegetable noted for its pungency. Hence the appellation of the manuscript *Chiu Hua T'ieh.*

The calligraphic style of Yang Ning-shih's *Chiu Hua T'ieh* showed that he was making a conscious departure from the solemn dignity of the early T'ang masters and a return to the grace and elegance of the Tsin period. Some critics have commended him for having captured the essence of the *Lan T'ing Hsü* by 'leading the tip of the brush into the paper'. Others have compared him to Wang Hsien-chih because of his ability to rid his characters of all traces of vulgar preoccupations. Although the *Chiu Hua T'ieh* is the only original Yang Ning-shih extant, we can well see that his style is a bridge between the T'ang and the Sung periods.

Ts'ai Hsiang, a high official of the Sung court, found time to write treatises on tea and on litchi, both products of his native province. His calligraphy was regarded by his contemporaries as the very best in the Northern Sung Dynasty. A marked feature of his calligraphic art is its infinite variety—*chên shu* which is calm and restrained, *hsing shu* which is full of grace and elegance, and *ts'ao shu* which dances like dragons and serpents. In a moment of ecstasy, Ts'ai Hsiang would dash off his *ts'ao shu* with a split brush in frenzied speed, thus leaving irregular white streaks in the strokes, a reminder of the *fei po* for which his namesake, Ts'ai Yung, was justly famous. Sometimes a character he executed appears like a dignified gentleman coolly contemplating the affairs of state; another appears like a maiden just coming out of puberty, shy but slightly eager. All these styles Ts'ai Hsiang manifested with an accomplished proficiency to the amazement and admiration of his friends, including Su Shih and Mi Fu. His sovereign, Sung Emperor Jên-tsung,

[104]

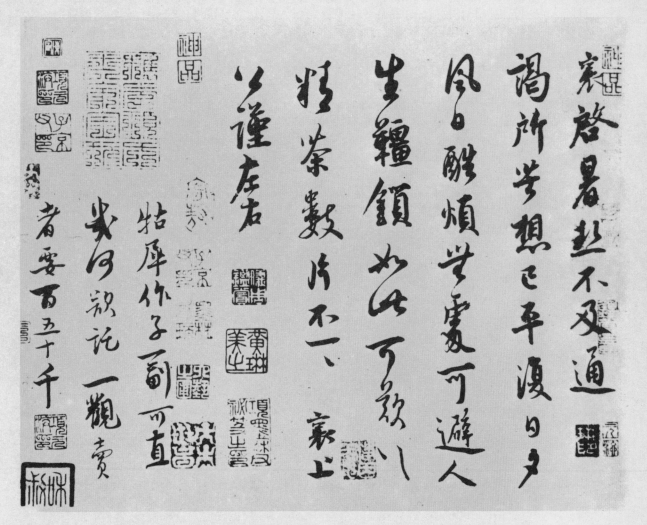

Fig. 38a Ts'ai Hsiang: *Letter to Li Tuan-yüan*. In this informal note, Ts'ai Hsiang complained of the oppressive heat and offered his friend some fine quality tea

repeatedly asked Ts'ai Hsiang to do tablets for the noble and the great. He often declined such royal commissions because he felt *chên shu,* which had to be used on tablets out of respect for the dead, was not the script in which he could distinguish himself. The manuscripts he did in *hsing shu* and *ts'ao shu,* a draft of a poem, a note to his friend, a receipt for a gift of edibles, came to be much more highly treasured for their casualness and spontaneity (Fig. 38). Like the tea he was so fond of, Ts'ai Hsiang's calligraphy leaves in our mouth a delicate flavour which seems to linger on and which can be fully savoured only after the effect of the initial contact has worn off. His style tells us in unmistakable terms that we are entering the world of Sung art, a world quite apart from the previous one, featuring the music of the poetry in the form of *tz'ŭ,* the sublime and enchanting landscape painting of the Sung masters, the delicate and artfully simple porcelains of the Ting kiln, the Neo-Confucianism of the philosophers, the meditation of Taoism, the mysticism of Ch'an (Zen) Buddhism. We have indeed arrived at a high plateau of Chinese culture, an era whose splendour is to be measured not in flashes of light but in the glow of good taste.

Su Shih, affectionately known to his admirers as Su Tung-po, was a scholar and an official who was on occasion attracted to the practice of alchemy with the dual purpose of transmuting metal into gold and of rejuvenation of old age. The elixir of life, according to the Taoists, was a pill (*tan*) which was to be extracted by purification through burning various rare elements until only their essence was retained. Su Shih never succeeded in producing the pill, but almost everything else he laid his hand on bore the indelible mark of immortality. In poetry and prose, in calligraphy and painting, he reigns as one of the greatest masters of all time.

In going over his life, one gets the impression that he was a gay sort of a fellow, singing, versifying and drinking his way through life. Like his friend Ts'ai Hsiang, he was fond of the fruit litchi and ate hundreds of them a day. But the tangible troubles that attended his life were formidable indeed. On the strength of sheer intellectual conviction he got himself involved in a titanic political struggle in which he was alternately honoured with high office and humiliatingly sent into prolonged exile. On several occasions he was poverty-stricken and had to keep himself alive by tilling the land with his own hands. But he kept on making fun of his physical labours which he must have loathed. To these concrete instances of suffering and sorrow there must be added the great travail of spirit involved in the intellectual ordeal he passed through in fighting his political enemies. It was an ordeal that brought him great agony. But thoroughly convinced of the nobility of his cause, and reinforced by his practice of the Taoist religion, including yoga, he was able to conquer his woes, learned to transcend suffering, and came to terms with the society into which he was thrown. At moments Su Shih was

[106]

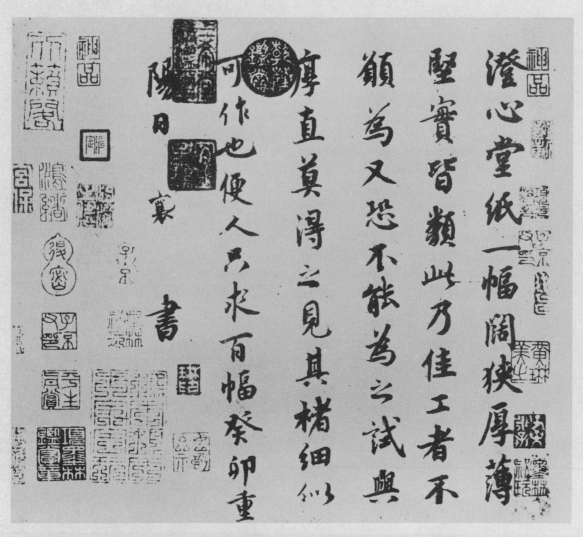

Fig. 38b Ts'ai Hsiang: *Letter Seeking Good Paper*. In this informal
note dated 1063, Ts'ai Hsiang discussed the qualities of
good paper and said one hundred sheets were needed

driven to compulsive satire. When his concubine, the famous Chao-yün, gave birth to a son, he wrote:

> All people wish their children to be brilliant,
> But I have suffered from brilliance all my life.
> May you, my son, grow up dumb and stupid,
> And, free from calamities, end up as a premier.*

But soon enough he became his gay self again, as if no troubles were too much to bear.

Besides being a great poet, Su Shih is better known for his calligraphy than his painting. He himself paid more attention to his calligraphy and wrote extensively on the subject. He began his calligraphic training first by modelling after Wang Hsi-chih's *Lan T'ing Hsü* and later by emulating the style of Yen Chên-ch'ing and Yang Ning-shih. It was his habit to hang manuscripts of the old masters on the walls of his dwelling and to study them 'with the heart and the hand' until it was no longer possible for him to tell what aspects belonged to himself. But he refused to be a slave of any particular style. He once said: 'Although I am not an accomplished calligrapher, no one understands the art better than I do. If one acquires a true grasp of its meaning, I would say that one needs no teacher to model after.' He confessed that he was not to be compared to the Tsin masters, but he considered himself the equal of the T'ang calligraphers, including Yen Chên-ch'ing. The real achievement of Su Shih's calligraphy, it may be said, consists in its wholesomeness. The characters he executed appear heavy and squat, somewhat reminiscent of the *pa fên* of the late Han period. But they radiate a great deal of charm. To use an analogy, a character by Su Shih bears the appearance of a well-nourished gentleman, but somehow he is not a profit-chasing merchant stuffed with wine and pork. The character forms he created quietly and simply take place, but they also take us, and it is only after the first delightful experience that we look back and recognize the conscious art that has gone into them. His style is strikingly original because it is delicately balanced on the razor-edge between what is called 'ink pig' on the one hand and 'unbridled horse' on the other.

Even in his lifetime Su Shih's calligraphic specimens were eagerly collected. When he was in disgrace at the court, many of his manuscripts were deliberately destroyed by their owners in fear of political implications. Fortunately a substantial quantity has survived. One of the best samples of Su Shih's *chên shu* is the *Ch'ih Pi Fu* (Fig. 39) composed and transcribed by the man himself. The essay is a prose-poem which all Chinese school children have been required to learn by heart. It describes a trip Su Shih took with his friend in a small boat along the Yangtse River on an autumn, moonlit night. As the boat drifted by Ch'ih Pi (Red Cliff), his friend began to play a sad

* Translation by Lin Yutang.

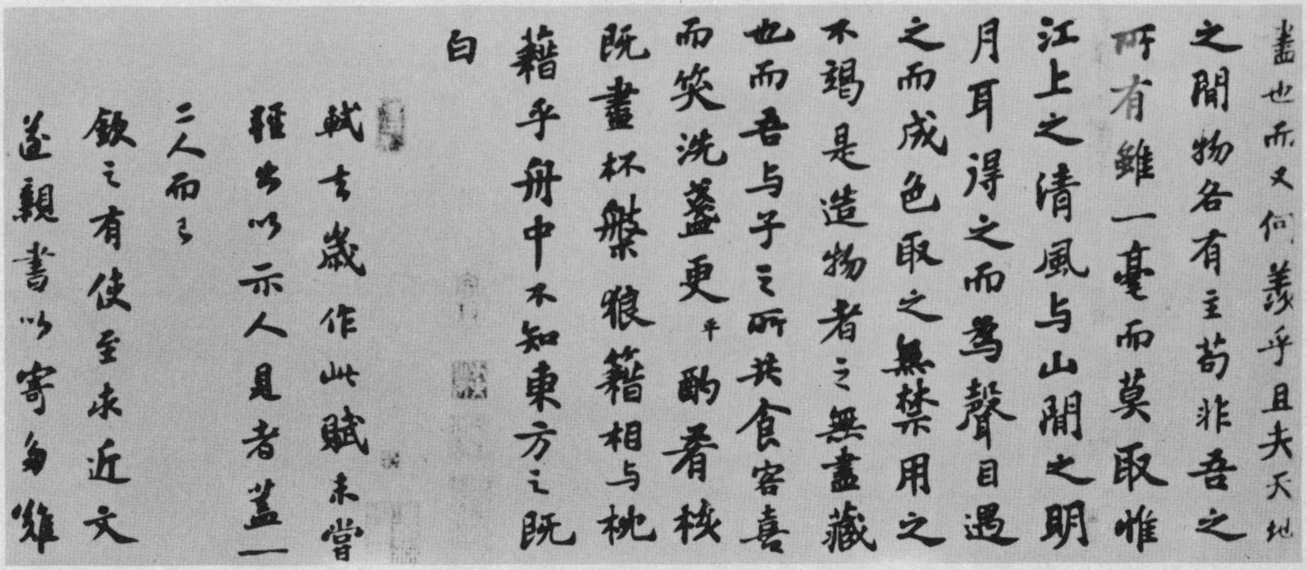

盖也而又何羨乎且夫天地
之間物各有主苟非吾之
所有雖一毫而莫取惟
江上之清風與山間之明
月耳得之而為聲目遇
之而成色取之無禁用之
不竭是造物者之無盡藏
也而吾與子之所共食客喜
而笑洗盞更酌肴核
既盡杯盤狼籍相與枕
藉乎舟中不知東方之既
白

軾去歲作此賦未嘗
輕出以示人見者蓋一
二人而已
欽之有使至求近文
遂親書以寄舉之

Fig. 39 Su Shih: *Ch'ih Pi Fu* (last portion)

and melancholy tune on the flute while Su Shih followed by humming the lyrics. The melody was so depressing that a woman in a nearby boat began to weep and even 'the fish in the water were disturbed'. Why did his friend choose to play the melody? A thousand years ago, at Ch'ih Pi, a momentous battle was fought which decided the destiny of the Three Kingdoms following the dissolution of the Han Dynasty. One of the principals of the battle, Ts'ao Ts'ao of the Kingdom of Wei, crossed his spear over the boat and sang of the fleeting and ephemeral nature of life in these immortal lines:

> When the moon is bright,
>   The stars are sparse . . .
> Man's life is short
>   Like the morning dew,
> Its best days lamentably few.

Su Shih, overcome by the pathos of the recollection, was driven to ask: 'And where are the heroes of yester year now?' He answered: 'Only the cool breeze over the river and the bright moon in the mountains are here to fill our ears with music and our eyes with colour, things we can partake of without limit and use without end—such is the beauty of Nature, so let you and I feast on them!'

After writing the prose-poem, Su Shih kept it to himself because 'in these days of troubles and complications' it might be used against him. In 1083, one of his friends sent a messenger to ask for his latest literary composition. In response, he transcribed the *Ch'ih Pi Fu* in his own hand and sent it along, still entreating his friend to keep it from others. The manuscript (Fig. 39), like Wang Hsi-chih's *Lan T'ing Hsü,* is doubly treasured because it is a great calligrapher's transcription of his own literary masterpiece. It is in the form of a horizontal scroll (*shou chüen*), the body of the prose-poem done in *chên shu* with a postface done in *hsing shu.* It is a splendid example of Su Shih's calligraphy, each individual character written with great care, full-bodied and sure, and yet there is nothing deliberate about it. The whole piece is permeated with an air of naturalness and spontaneity with a touch of artlessness, an expression of a true genius at work, uninhibited by convention and artificiality. Wang Hsi-chih purposely wrote the same character differently in the *Lan T'ing Hsü* as a demonstration of virtuosity. Su Shih did not resort to such a device in the *Ch'ih Pi Fu.* Academics have discovered that the Ch'ih Pi which inspired Su Shih was not the actual location of the famous battle in the Period of the Three Kingdoms. Notwithstanding, most Chinese critics are in agreement with the Ming Dynasty calligrapher-painter Tung Ch'i-ch'ang (in a colophon dated 1601) that Su Shih's transcription of his own *Ch'ih Pi Fu,* in literary composition as well as in calligraphic art, represents the optimum of Sung art.

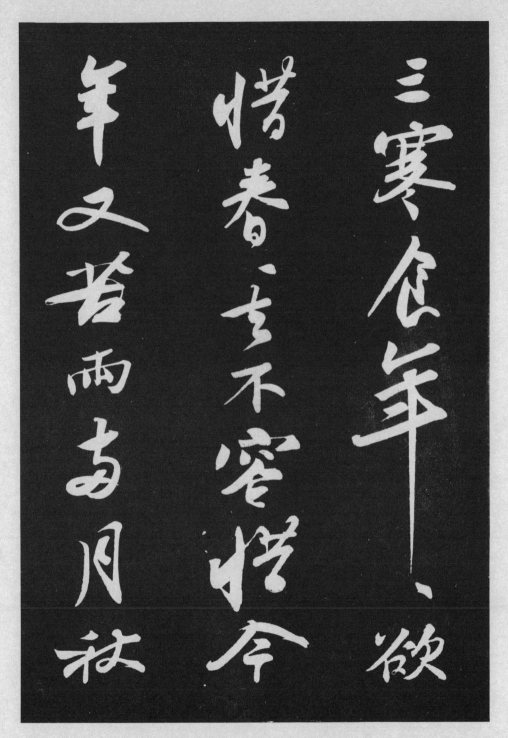

Fig. 40 Su Shih: *Han Shih T'ieh* (detail)

After passing through the hands of many collectors, the first three lines of the manuscript were damaged. In 1558, the Ming Dynasty calligrapher-painter Wên Chêng-ming, at the advanced age of eighty-eight, was asked to replace the missing lines totalling thirty-three characters in his own writing. Although Wên Chêng-ming's calligraphic style is very different from Su Shih's, this conjunction of two great artists is a matter of great delight to the connoisseurs and enhances the value of the scroll, as if a Michelangelo were to be touched up by a Monet or Cézanne. Quite a number of Su Shih manuscripts have come down to us, copies of his poems, notes to his friends, mostly done in *hsing shu,* of which the *Han Shih T'ieh* (Fig. 40), transcribing some of the poems he composed in Huangchou, is generally regarded as one of the best.

As every Chinese schoolboy knows, Huang T'ing-chien is a supreme example of filial piety. When his mother was afflicted with a long illness, he devoted himself so wholeheartedly to her care that he remained by her bedside for a whole year without ever undressing himself. For this manifestation of one of the cardinal virtues of the Confucian code of ethics, Huang T'ing-chien's story was included as one of the twenty-four exemplary cases of filial piety. Early in his life, Huang T'ing-chien presented to Su Shih samples of his prose compositions and poetry. The old master was impressed and predicted that the lad would go far. In his mature years, Huang T'ing-chien was a high official of the Sung court. He was deeply involved in politics. But never for a moment did he neglect his pursuit of poetry and calligraphy. Although he admired Su Shih profoundly, Huang T'ing-chien tried to develop a literary and calligraphic style of his own. For thirty years he worked with devouring diligence. He trained his hand indefatigably on all the scripts, ancient and modern. Finally he was able to claim that he had established communion with Wang Hsi-chih, whom he called his 'friend across the centuries'. However, what he eventually evolved was entirely personal to him.

One of the better known Huang T'ing-chien manuscripts is his transcription in *chên shu* of some of his own poems, one of them being the *Sung Fêng Ko Shih* (Fig. 41). The poems, composed in 1102, deal with a tower or pavilion built on a hill slope in Huichou, Kwangtung Province. They describe the old pines in front of the structure and the sound of the wind blowing through the trees. There is a reference to Su Shih, who visited the place before. Huang T'ing-chien tells us that he feasted and took a nap in the tower, and woke up saddened by the thought of Su Shih's death. He ends by expressing his wish that he could sail on the water below with his friends. We call the script used by Huang T'ing-chien to transcribe these poems *chên shu* because as a rule this is as far as he would go towards formality. We have seen tablets done by Huang T'ing-chien in formal *chên shu* but we are inclined to regard them as unrepresentative of his calligraphic style. The shape of his characters, as we can see, are purposely elongated, sometimes

[112]

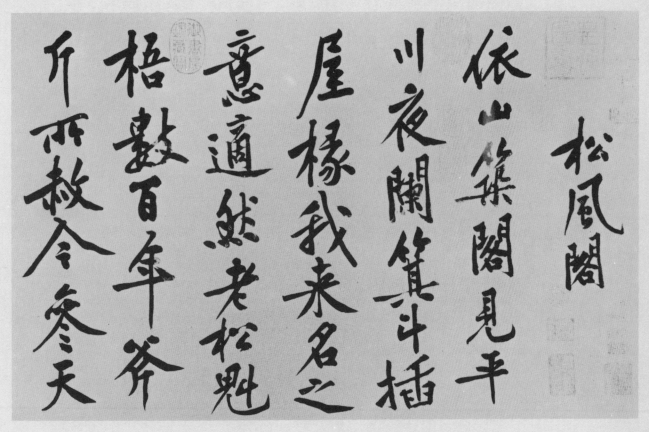

Fig. 41　Huang T'ing-chien: *Sung Fêng Ko Shih* (first portion)

gaunt and fumbling by design, occasionally merely awkward and childlike, then by fits and starts strikingly brilliant. Little effort is directed towards concealing the conscious display of brushmanship, and the strokes manifest the application of nervous energy. The excitement is intense and the distortions are consequently more noticeable. There is no doubt that the whole purpose is to extract from the characters new convolutions of form, new textures, new rhythms in composition. These features may be even more clearly seen in Huang T'ing-chien's *ts'ao shu* manuscripts, of which the *Hua Ch'i Shih* (Fig. 42) is one of the finest examples. The short poem (totalling twenty-eight characters in four lines of seven characters each) records Huang T'ing-chien's feelings as he was enveloped by the fragrance of flowers, telling us that after middle age sailing in spring waters was what he wanted most to do. In this transcription we can see that there is no attempt whatsoever to achieve any degree of regularity. The whole thing is a grandstand display of mature, if somewhat reckless brushmanship. This type of calligraphy is Huang T'ing-chien at his very best.

In the Northern Sung capital Pienching, a man might be seen wandering aimlessly along the river followed by a mocking crowd whispering and giggling behind his back. This man would be Mi Fu,* one of the most variously gifted artists in the history of China. A passionately sensitive man, an irrepressible rebel against stuffy conventions, full of exaggerated attitudes, his was a decisive experimental voice in both calligraphy and painting. Mi Fu was gifted with deep perceptions and, at his fervent best, with a remarkable power of expression. A living legend in his time, he knew the legend and fostered it. The above-mentioned crowd in Pienching was following him because he was known around town as 'Mi the Eccentric', capable of all sorts of strange behaviour, always good for a hearty laugh. For one thing, he liked to wear robes in the fashion of the T'ang Dynasty, loosely fitted with sweeping sleeves. He had a fixation on cleanliness, a phobia of dirt and filth, which kept him constantly washing himself and all the things with which he came in contact. He would not allow himself to be touched, nor would he share towels and basins with others. Like Emperor Hui-tsung, whom Mi Fu briefly served, he had a passion for eroded and grotesquely shaped rocks. When confronted with a particularly good piece, he was likely to prostrate himself before it, addressing it as either his brother or his father-in-law. No wonder he was the favourite of the idle people of the metropolis. The children just loved him.

Mi Fu did and said a lot of very funny things—the stuff of anecdote— and he has taken the game away from many earnest students seeking to study the serious business of his career. But few artists have ever made such a prolonged, laborious and fruitful study of his predecessors' work. At the early

---

* According to one authority, the man called himself Mi Fu before the year 1091 and Mi Fei after that date. His manuscripts bear both names.

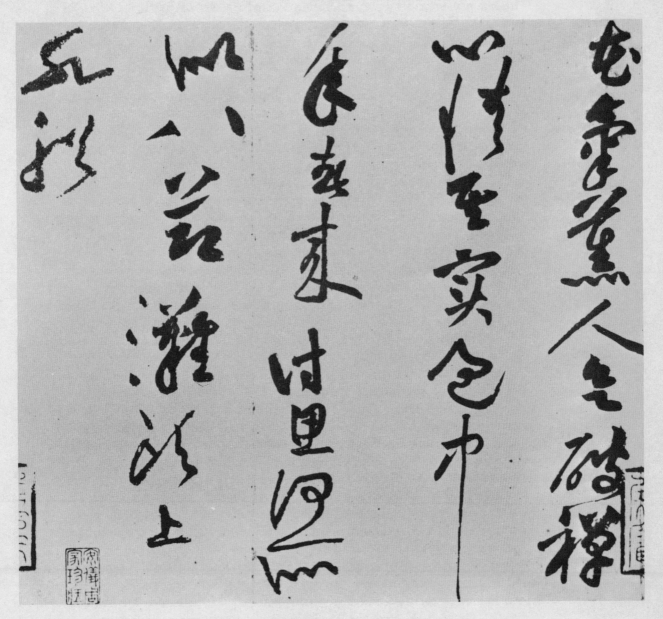

Fig. 42   Huang T'ing-chien: *Hua Ch'i Shih*

age of twenty-two, he journeyed to Tungpo to pay his respects to Su Shih. The old master and the young man discussed the art of painting. Later Su Shih, in a moment of extravagance, praised Mi Fu for having reached the ultimate in the art, as Tu Fu in poetry and Yen Chên-ch'ing in calligraphy. However, Su Shih always considered Mi Fu a junior, a disciple, a protégé. They were sometimes in literary collation sessions as on the famous occasion in the garden of the painter Prince Wang Shen, an occasion immortalized by the picture, a sort of group portrait, done by one of the participants, the painter Li Kung-lin. In the picture Su Shih, in his black cap and yellow gown, is depicted leaning over a table writing a poem, while Mi Fu is shown standing and inscribing something on an upright slab of stone. When Su Shih was taken ill and was almost on his deathbed, he addressed a stream of letters to his friend Mi Fu. In one letter Su Shih complained that he was being consumed by mosquitoes. Mi Fu sent a repellent. In another letter, Su Shih longed to read Mi Fu's literary compositions and see his calligraphic pieces as a cure for the poison (presumably malaria) he was getting in steaming Hainan Island. Su Shih and Mi Fu were close friends for twenty years, although Su Shih's frequent exiles kept them from being together as often as they would have liked. There was much in common between these two towering figures.

Inevitably in those days even a man like Mi Fu must be given governmental posts. Just as inevitably his many eccentricities, his extraordinary nonconformity and his caustic tongue prevented him from making a success of any one of his administrative assignments. The post he liked most must have been that of Adviser on Calligraphy and Painting to the court. His passion was the collection and study of ancient art objects—bronzes, porcelains, inkstones, and of course painting and calligraphic pieces. He equipped himself with a boat called 'Shu Hua Fang', literally 'the boat of calligraphy and painting', and sailed it up and down the waterways of East China collecting and exhibiting art objects, a sort of a floating museum. He jotted down for his own use fragmentary notations and observations of various kinds which were later published as art commentaries euphemistically entitled 'histories'. At first reading, they may seem disappointing to students of art, but they will appeal to those who, already familiar with the subject, have the sensitivity and interest to read between the lines, to disentangle the paradoxes, and then to reconstruct from a wealth of disconnected and heterogeneous remarks some of the many-faceted moods, doubts and preoccupations that eventually reached their full expression in Mi Fu's own works. Many of the entries were personal views and fleeting impressions, sometimes cantankerous, often penetrating, of the enormous volume of painting and calligraphic pieces that had come under his expert scrutiny. Mi Fu's critical opinions are unpredictable, full of quirks, strange intuitions, irreverent theories to the point of impudence. He castigated Chang Hsü's *ts'ao shu* for 'violating ancient norms'; he regarded

[116]

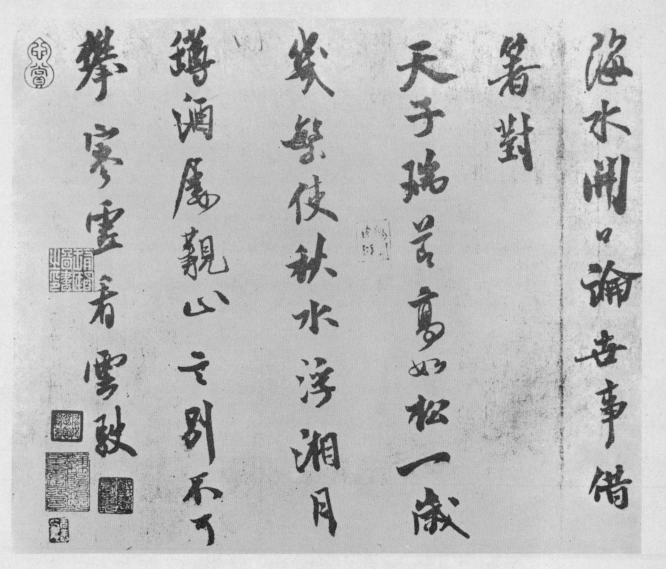

Fig. 43a   Mi Fu: *Valedictory Poem* (last portion).   One of Mi Fu's friends was going to Kiangsi and Mi Fu wrote a poem to bid him farewell.   The first part of the poem relates his friend's qualities.   The last part describes his own feelings at parting

Yen Chên-ch'ing's calligraphy as 'ugly and bad'; he considered Liu Kung-ch'üan 'a poor imitator' of Ou-yang Hsün; he thought Huai-su was 'grossly over-rated'. His views are not shared by most critics but they are always magnificently and unfailingly stimulating, and often inspired attacks from others. All these haphazard opinions delineated the kingdom of Mi Fu, a man endowed with a sharp eye and a sharp tongue determined to lay down the basic norms of artistic worth for his age and for all ages to come. To him it was above all a matter of taste, of standards, which in the nature of things he considered absolute and eternal.

Mi Fu's calligraphic style was derived from practically everything which could conceivably add to his already overflowing resources. According to his own account, he began with the T'ang calligraphers, from Yen Chên-ch'ing to Liu Kung-ch'üan to Ou-yang Hsün and finally to Ch'u Shui-liang. After modelling after Ch'u Shui-liang for some time, he acted upon Su Shih's advice and turned to the Tsin masters, especially Wang Hsi-chih's *Lan T'ing Hsü,* and made remarkable progress. Tracing the sources of the Tsin masters, he went back to Chung Yu and the *li shu* of the Han calligrapher Ssǔ I-kuan. His developing interest in archaeology later took him to the inscriptions on the stone drums and ancient bronzes. He was, however, not enthusiastic about engraved calligraphy, believing that only original manuscripts could enable him to capture the true spirit of a style. In undergoing such a severe formal discipline, he acquired an extraordinary ability to copy the old masters so faithfully that even the top connoisseurs were often confounded. He was particularly good at copying Wang Hsi-chih and Wang Hsien-chih, even fooling as high an authority as the Sung connoisseur Shen Kua. Among the manuscripts of the Ch'ing Imperial Collection was a short note in *ts'ao shu* bearing Wang Hsi-chih's signature. For generations it was considered a Wang Hsi-chih original until an expert ascertained that it was a Mi Fu copy. All this copying, of course, was not to make forgeries for profit. It was his way of training his hand in search of a style of his own. His detractors said that his calligraphic style is nothing but a collection of characters written by the old masters and that his skill consists only in his ability to pick out the best from the past. They called him 'a character assembler'. Mi Fu was proud of his copies and imitations but he was naturally annoyed by the attack. 'In my old age, I do have a style of my own, and nobody is able to trace my sources.' Once Mi Fu was asked by Emperor Hui-tsung to do a transcription on a palace screen. After he finished the task, he threw the brush on the ground and exclaimed: 'I have in this transcription done away with all the bad habits of Wang Hsi-chih and Wang Hsien-chih and achieved an excellence that will shine through the eternal age of Imperial Sung!' Emperor Hui-tsung, who was standing behind the screen, was amused by the boast, and bestowed upon Mi Fu the ink-stone he used. Overjoyed by the royal approval, Mi Fu took the ink-stone and put it inside his gown, spilling ink all over the place.

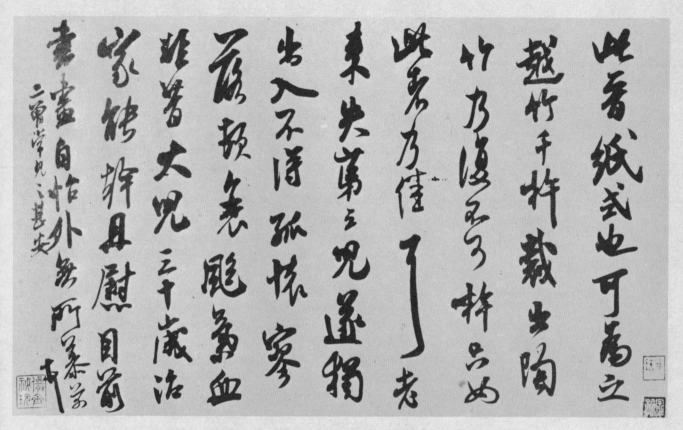

Fig. 43b Mi Fu: *Letter on Paper-making*. In this short note, Mi Fu first gave us some hints on paper-making. In the latter part, he told his friend that since the death of his third son, he was unable to go out and that he felt lonesome and old. He ended by saying that his eldest son fortunately had reached thirty and was quite able to run his household

It is difficult for us to agree with Mi Fu's detractors that his calligraphic style is no better than a derivative of the old masters. But it is equally true that Mi Fu, like all revolutionary artists, was far more tied to tradition than he was willing to admit, or than his admirers, confused by the cataract of his talk, were able to recognize.

Mi Fu's specialty is *hsing shu,* the script of his age. We shall be showing many samples of his work in the subsequent chapters. In this connection we have chosen from the collection of the Chinese National Palace Museum three specimens of his *hsing shu* (Fig. 43) which we consider to be representative of his style. From these illustrations we can readily see that the most striking quality of Mi·Fu's calligraphy is its effortlessness and unconventionality. The strokes are full of unpredictable decisions. They pulsate with their own adventurous progress—daring dashes, unexpected stops, rhythmic turns and soaring runs. The forms of his characters are distorted in a deliberate effort to achieve a balance of spatial relationships. The surfaces of his pieces are inexhaustibly accented, never static, always moving immediately from one climax to another, executed with a grand display of restless energy. The perfectionists may sometimes be annoyed by the occasional lapses of his brush, the faults and flaws and false notes which have inadvertently crept in, known in Chinese as *pai pi* (faulty brush). These shortcomings, however, are far outweighed by the enchanting beauty of the over-all effect, the power and lyricism of his work. Looking at Mi Fu's calligraphy, one will admire skill, dexterity, the brilliant and the unexpected; but still that is the surface. In the man himself one's admiration will give way to that love we feel for artists and for art that is really great.

Mi Fu tells us that he began his training by modelling after Yen Chên-ch'ing. But the styles of the two men could not be more different, and in his maturity Mi Fu detested Yen Chên-ch'ing's style. If we may be permitted an analogy with Western art, we would say that, if a Yen Chên-ch'ing character reminds us of a Greek temple, solid, static, clear-cut and noble, then a Mi Fu character is like a Gothic cathedral, fretted, restless, dynamic, mysterious and even playful. After some practice, one can emulate at least the outward appearance of Yen Chên-ch'ing's style, and quite a number of later calligraphers, especially in the Ch'ing Dynasty and the Republic, were good Yen Chên-ch'ing followers. It is almost impossible to emulate Mi Fu with any measure of success.* Only his son, Mi Yu-jên, who also painted after his father's style, was able to approach him, as may be seen in one of his letters (Fig. 44). Mi Fu, in his clearly recognizable self, is certainly a child of tradition. One of the later critics, Chu Ho-kêng, has accused him of secretly copying the work of Lu Chien-chih, who was the nephew of Yü Shih-nan

---

* Among Yen Chên-ch'ing's followers were Ch'ien Li, Ho Shao-chi, Wêng Fang-kang of the Ch'ing Dynasty and T'an Yen-k'ai of the Republic. Among Mi Fu's followers, only Ch'ên Li, the author's great grandfather, deserves mention.

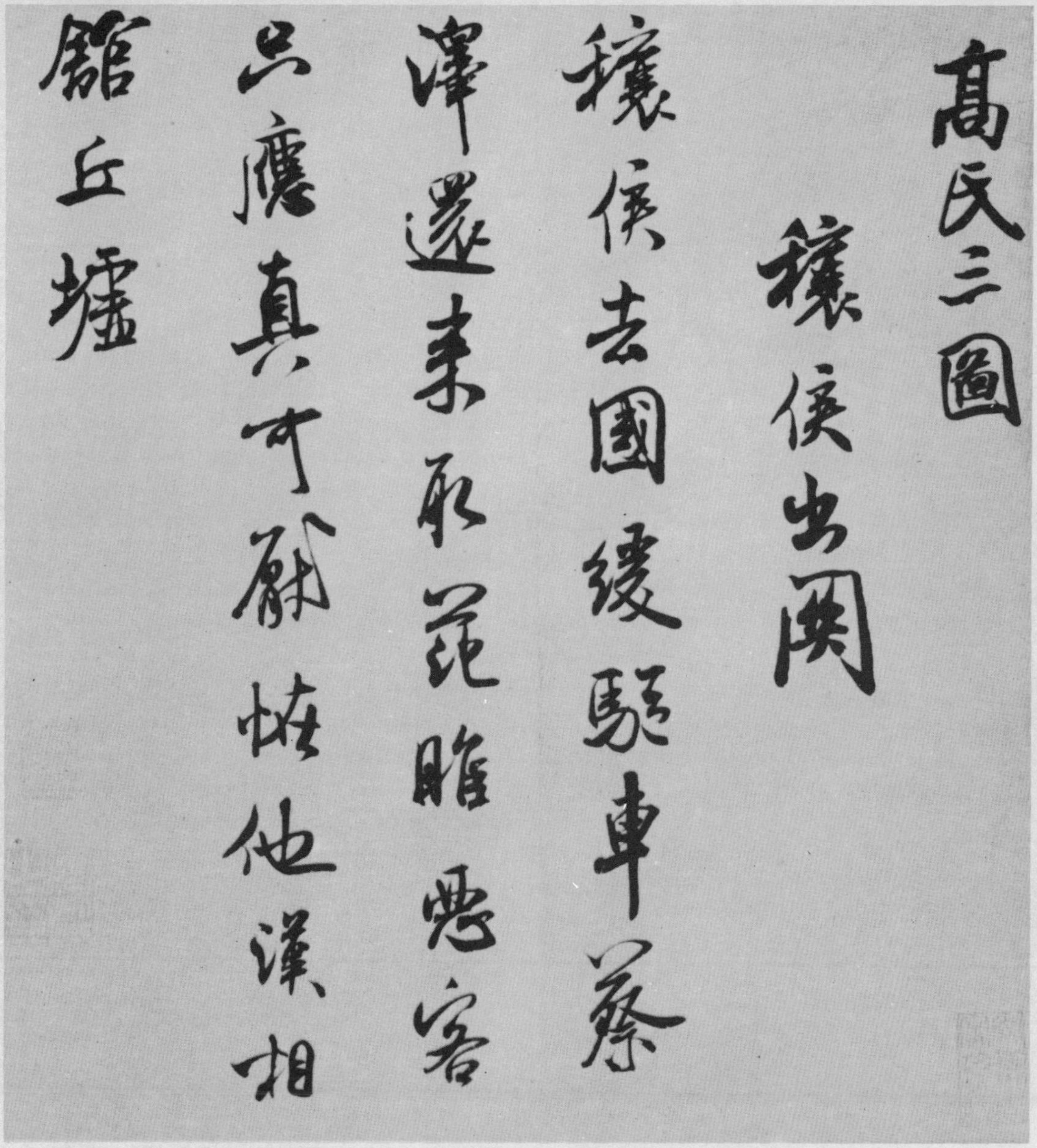

高氏三圖

穰侯出關

穰侯去國緩驅車蔡
津遂素承范睢惡客
吳應真可獻姹他漢相
韶丘墟

Fig. 43c Mi Fu: *Jang Hou Shih*. A poem transcribed by Mi Fu as
a colophon to a painting depicting the exploits of Jang
Hou, a warrior of the Period of the Warring States

of the T'ang Dynasty. This charge is patently unjustified, even malicious. Whether we like Mi Fu's style or not, he seems to be strangely without ancestors or descendants. That, it appears, is the true measure of his originality.

The Sung Emperor Hui-tsung (1082-1135) is justly renowned not only as an avid patron of art but an accomplished artist as well. The whole world now knows about his colourful and meticulously detailed studies of birds and flowers. It was his passion for painting that brought him to the company of the painters Wang Shen and Chao Ling-jang, both members of the royal family. Chao Ling-jang was an admirer of Huang T'ing-chien's calligraphy and persuaded the Emperor to emulate it. Later the Emperor took the advice of the painter Wu Yüan-yü and tried to model after the style of the T'ang calligrapher Hsüeh Chi. All the while the Emperor was painting birds and flowers and was applying his painting technique to calligraphy. In due course he evolved his own calligraphic style which he labelled *shou chin shu,* 'slender gold script', which was used both for *chên shu* and *hsing shu.* Using a brush with a long and slender tuft, suitable for the Emperor's own style of painting, he made the strokes of his characters thin and attenuated, the hooks and turns exaggerated, the terminals accented by diagonal thrusts. One of the best examples of Emperor Hui-tsung's calligraphy is his transcription of his own poems on the peonies, *Mu Tan Shih* (Fig. 45), accompanied by a short preface explaining the poems. The Emperor tells us that one of his peony trees bore two flowers on the same branch but the red colour of the flowers was slightly different in shade. A proverbially meticulous observer of Nature, he ventures the opinion that the two flowers should be differentiated by name. Amazed by the vagary of Nature, he versifies on the flowers' beauty, comparing them to all sorts of things that grow together. The poems themselves are indifferent but the calligraphy is Hui-tsung at his very best. Speaking of the scroll, a Ch'ing Dynasty critic said:

The scroll is an example of the application of the technique of painting to calligraphy, and therefore should not be judged by the normal considerations of brushmanship and inkmanship. The lines remind us of orchids and bamboos, and we seem to hear the sound of wind and rain in them. A divine creation indeed!

Originating from such a high place, Hui-tsung's *shou chin shu,* though somewhat mannerist and affected, soon became a style, even a script, in its own right. Even the coins of the period bore characters executed in the style. Be that as it may, we must say that, like the Academy style of painting over which he presided, Hui-tsung's calligraphy, however delicate and elegant, cannot be placed on the same pedestal as that of the other Sung masters.

In the year 1127 the Tartars captured the capital city Pienching. Emperor Hui-tsung was carried off to the North where he died in captivity nine years later. The Sung court was driven to the South and set itself up in the city of

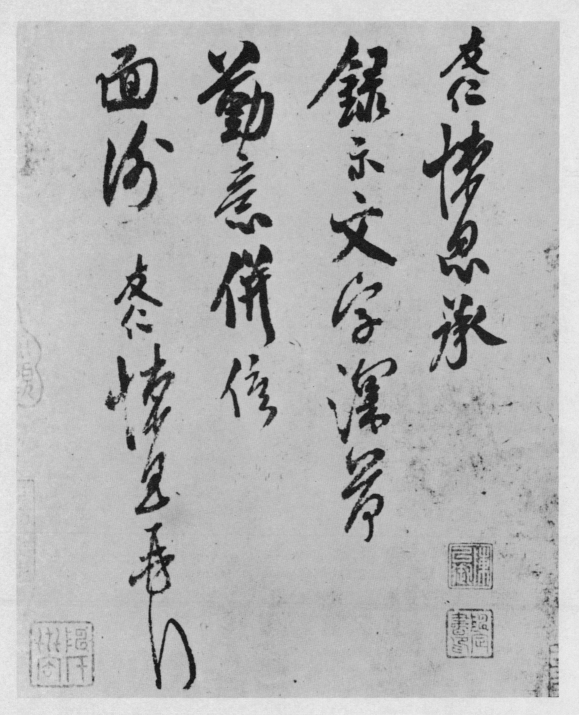

Fig. 44   Mi Yu-jên: *Letter Thanking Friend for Showing Him Literary Compositions*

Hangchow, which later gained world renown through the pen of the Venetian traveller Marco Polo as the city of Quinsay. There on the banks of the Ch'ien-t'ang River and the shores of Hsi-hu (West Lake), one of the most scenic spots of China, the artists gathered. The Academy of Painting of the Southern Sung Dynasty included such brilliant painters as Li T'ang, Ma Yüan, Hsia Kuei, Liang K'ai and Liu Sung-nien, to mention only the best known, with achievements which were in many ways as glittering as those of Pienching. But for reasons which will forever remain obscure, the fire of creativeness in calligraphy seemed to have become a faint flicker. Here and there were a few calligraphers whom we may regard as good and competent imitators. The poet Chiang K'uei wrote an essay on the art of calligraphy which was meant to be an elaboration of Sun Ch'ien-li's *Shu P'u*. But there was nobody who could stand on the same level with Ts'ai Hsiang, Su Shih, Huang T'ing-chien and Mi Fu. For calligraphic works of the Southern Sung Dynasty we have to go to the great scholars such as Chu Hsi and Lu Hsiang-shan, great poets such as Lu Yu and Chiang K'uei, great patriots such as Yüeh Fei and Wên T'ien-hsiang, men who were most distinguished in their respective fields but not creative calligraphers in the true sense of the term.

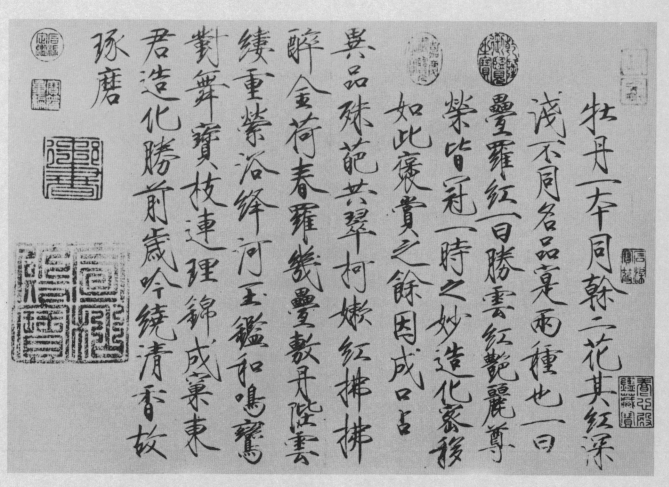

牡丹一本同榦二花其紅深

淺不同名品寔兩種也一曰

疊羅紅一曰勝雲紅艷麗尊

榮皆冠一時之妙造化豪後

如此襃賞之餘因成口占

異品殊芳菓翠柯嫩紅拂拂

醉金荷春羅幾疊數丹陛雲

綵重紫浴絳珂玉鑑和鳴鸞

對舞寶枝連理錦成棄東

君造化勝前歲吟繞清香故

琢磨

Fig. 45   Emperor Hui-tsung: *Mu Tan Shih*

Chapter Eight

The Yuan-Ming Eclectics

The dearth of talent in the Southern Sung Dynasty seems to indicate that calligraphy had just about exhausted its artistic possibilities. The stage is thus set for the emergence of the eclectics. In the Chinese conception there is nothing pejorative or condescending in the term 'eclectic'. It is used to describe a talent and a career which, through the exacting discipline of copying and modelling after the old masters, polished, enriched and imperceptibly extended the range and scope of art to embrace all that was good in the past. A prince of the eclectics was the Yüan Dynasty calligrapher-painter Chao Mêng-fu.

A scion of the House of Sung, Chao Mêng-fu was born at a time (1254) when the fortunes of the Southern Sung Dynasty were rapidly sinking. The Mongols had been on the rampage and were destroying the kingdoms of the North one by one. For forty years the Chinese armies engaged the Mongols in battles and large sections of the country were laid waste. In 1279, when Chao Mêng-fu was twenty-five, the last Sung pretender was destroyed. In the stormy years towards the end of the House of Sung, Chao Mêng-fu had occupied some minor official positions. When the Yüan (Mongol) Dynasty was founded, he lost his job. For ten years, he and his talented wife, *née* Kuan Tao-shêng, led a life of want and privation. He was compelled time and again to sell his calligraphic pieces for cash to replenish the empty family coffer. These must have been years of agony and anguish for the young man so tragically torn by his loyalty to the House of Sung and the dire need of an income to go on living and to raise a family. Some of his friends, following the traditional code of conduct, turned into recluses, among them

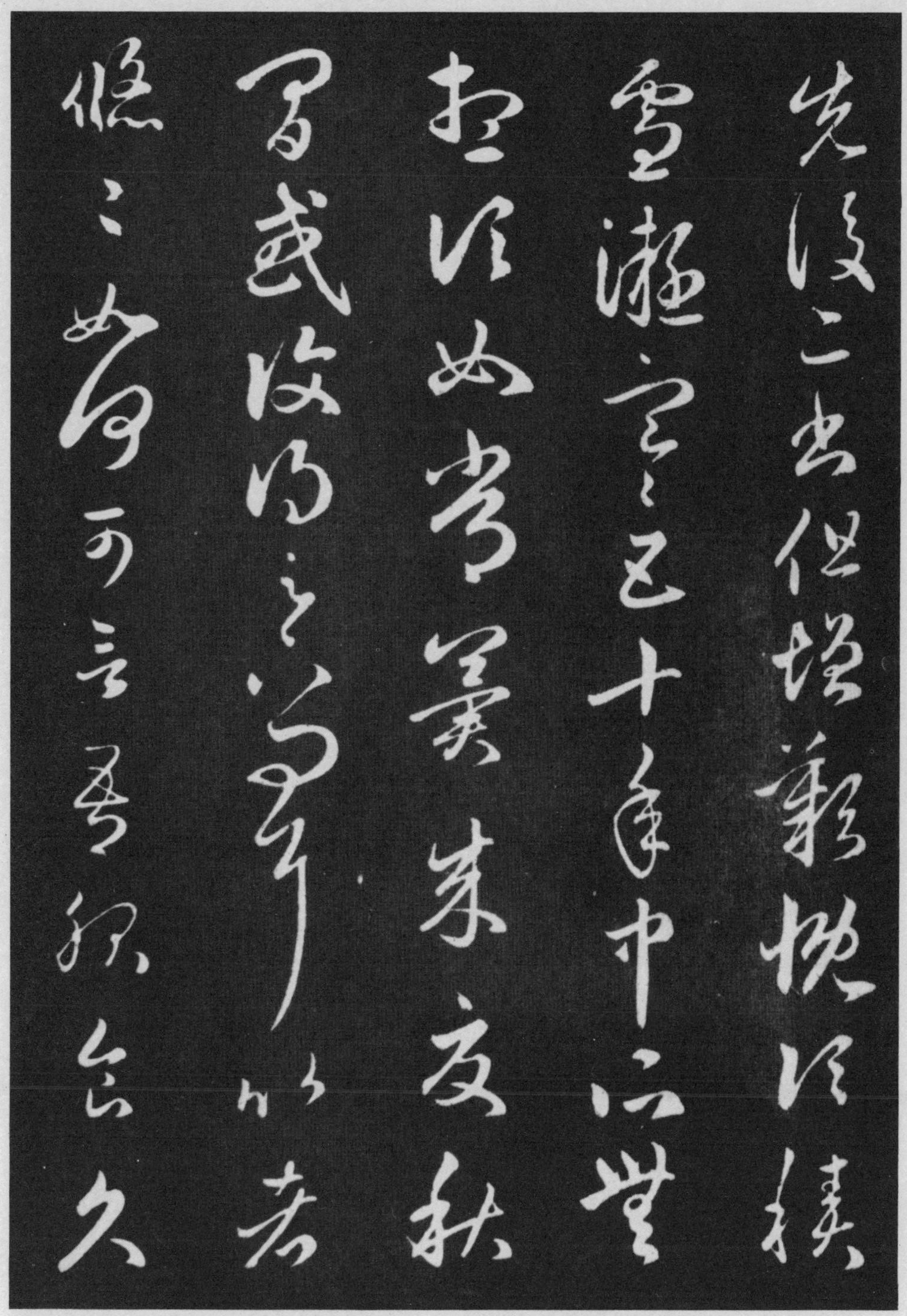

Fig. 46a Chao Mêng-fu: *Ts'ao Shu After Wang Hsi-chih* (detail)

the celebrated painter Ch'ien Hsüan. Chao Mêng-fu, very naturally, was tempted to follow suit. But he was a young man (he was nine years younger than Ch'ien Hsüan) and his whole life was ahead of him. Meanwhile, the Mongol court was offering inducements to attract the intellectuals who were the mainstay of any Chinese government. Finally, in 1286, Chao Mêng-fu, after much soul-searching, took the fateful step of accepting Kublai Khan's offer. He became a court calligrapher, charged with the duty of transcribing memorials and proclamations. The decision was not an easy one to take, and he had to face the scorn of many of his friends, some of whom openly accused him of being a shameless collaborator.

After he took the plunge, he devoted himself wholeheartedly to his job and rose rapidly in the official hierarchy. The Mongol rulers rewarded him heavily, bestowing upon him one honour after another. As the Mongols settled down to rule China, animosity against the regime gradually subsided. But Chao Mêng-fu, who was brought up in the Confucian tradition of loyalty, was uncomfortable, even tormented, in the high office he occupied. He and his wife sought spiritual consolation by becoming devout Buddhists. If they felt uneasy in the company of the intellectuals of the day, they found solace in the friendship of the abbots and monks of the land. In many ways the couple, both extraordinarily gifted, did not seem to belong to this world of mortals. The bad weather they encountered in the early years of their lives must have given them the courage to brave the storm of censure from people of their own class. While making the most of the lucrative positions and earthly pleasures that came their way, they devoted themselves religiously to the cultivation of their art as if it led its own life independently of its creators. One can almost say the couple seemed to be only the earthly vessels of their art. For thirty years they shared the rewards of artistic pursuit seemingly without the sordid world around them. The husband used to do about ten thousand characters a day, day in and day out, in addition to painting numerous pictures—religious figures, landscapes, horses, stones and bamboos. To him calligraphy was not only an art but a 'call' so strong that he could not resist it. Unlike Su Shih and Mi Fu, Chao Mêng-fu had little to offer in the way of theory. He just kept on working and producing and allowed his products to speak for themselves. Nature was generous to him. He remained in full command of his faculties until his death in 1322 at the age of 68. His colophon to Chung Shao-ching's *Ling Fei Ching,* done in 1319 at the age of 65, is in small *chên shu* as controlled and disciplined as the characters of the *Ling Fei Ching* itself. The wife, on her part, paralleled every endeavour in which the husband was engaged. She was one of the few who gained proficiency in the arts—poetry, painting, calligraphy—without having to go through a too rigorous programme of training. Being a devout Buddhist, she transcribed dozens of Buddhist scriptures in her own exquisite hand for distribution among the famous abbots and monks. The Mongol Emperor honoured

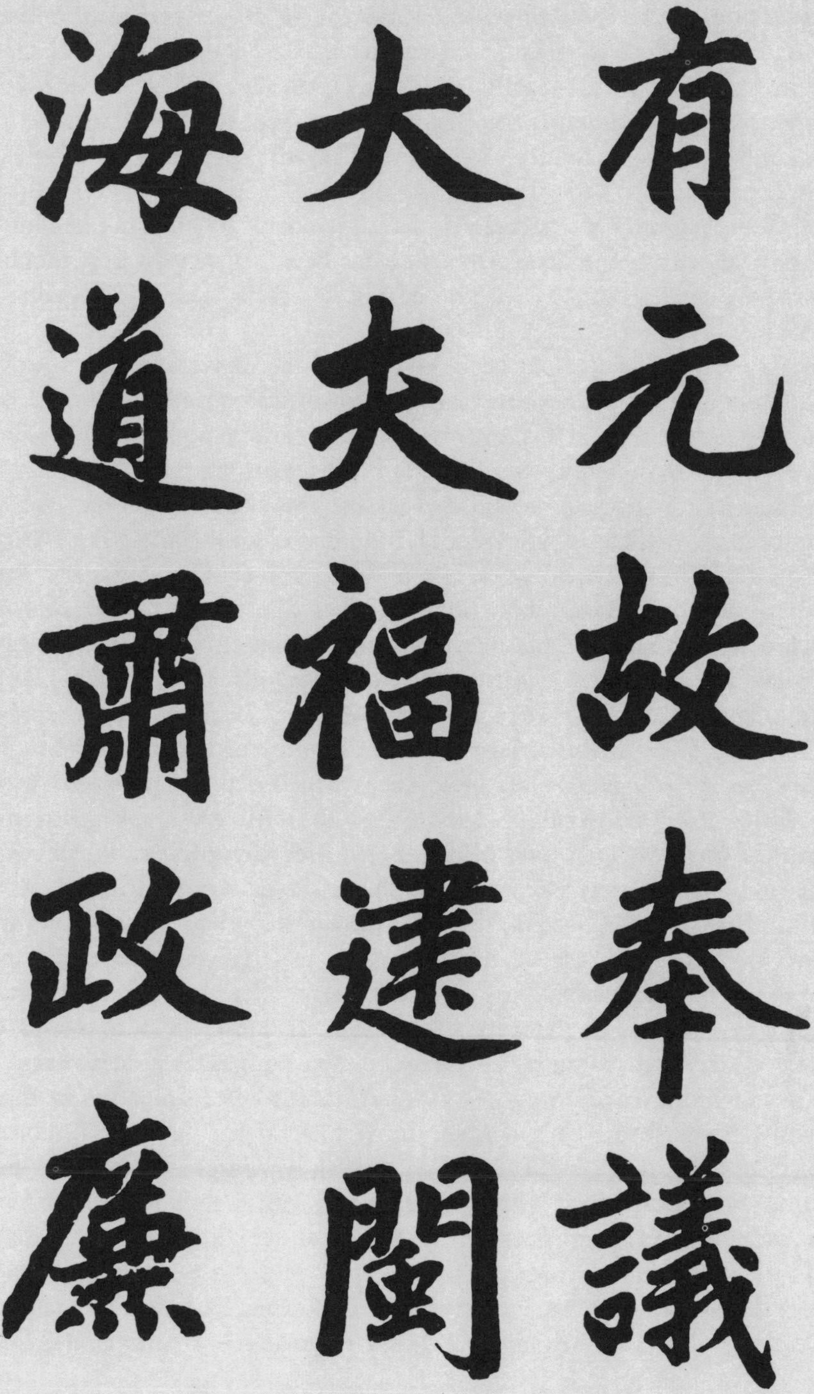

有元故奉議大夫福建閩海道肅政廉

Fig. 46b   Chao Mêng-fu: *Ch'iu Kung Miao Pei* (detail)

her by asking her to transcribe the *Ch'ien Tzǔ Wên* for the royal collection, a transcription which the Emperor caused to be mounted on brocade and made into a scroll with a roller made of jade. Theirs was an idyllic life, prodigious and astoundingly prolific, climaxed repeatedly by soaring fulfilments, individually or jointly. Sometimes the wife dreamed longingly of a life of leisure and seclusion and expressed her sentiments in delightful little poems. She even enlisted the help of sarcastic poetry to dissuade her husband from taking a concubine. Their romance has been written up in a number of novels and plays, illustrated with woodcuts depicting their life together (see Fig. 47b).

Chao Mêng-fu has often been considered a supreme example of the antiquity-minded. His procedure was that which has become the dogma of the eclectics: he copied from his predecessors till certain ideals of formal completeness were absolutely fixed in his mind; then when he wrote he instinctively conformed to the pattern established in his imagination. In his pursuit of calligraphic excellence, it was natural for him to undervalue the T'ang and Sung masters, preferring to go back to Wang Hsi-chih, and further back to the Han and Wei tablets. Like Mi Fu, he was extremely good in copying the manuscripts of the old masters, producing replicas that were indistinguishable from the originals. We have already seen his copy of the *Chi Chiu Chang* in *chang ts'ao* (Fig. 15). The *San Hsi T'ang Fa T'ieh,* which reproduces the *Chi Chiu Chang* in full, also includes a number of Chao Mêng-fu's copies of *ts'ao shu* by Wang Hsi-chih (Fig. 46a), which may be compared with the *ts'ao shu* of the Tsin master himself (Fig. 20). All this copying, of course, was part of Chao Mêng-fu's training as he was searching for a style of his own.

It is not easy to describe a calligraphic style in words. Perhaps we may point out that one of Chao Mêng-fu's trademarks is a somewhat novel distortion of the basic structure of the characters, usually consisting in crowding the upper portion and spreading out the lower portion, sometimes deliberately shifting the component elements slightly out of place, in a conscious effort to effect a precarious balance. This may be seen most clearly in his large *chên shu,* of which the *Ch'iu Kung Miao Pei* (Fig. 46b) is a splendid example. It is a tablet transcribed by Chao Mêng-fu in 1319 at the age of 65. According to the critics, the tablet represents Chao Mêng-fu's large *chên shu* at its very best, done with a big brush with a stiff tuft and with the elbow fully suspended to impart the maximum strength to the strokes, with the result that the characters appear to be formed of 'bent iron bars'. It may be mentioned in passing that the tablet was equipped with a heading in *chuan shu* also done by Chao Mêng-fu, a rare example of the Yüan master's artistry in that ancient script.

In 1319, as Chao Mêng-fu and his wife were travelling home in a boat, the wife unexpectedly took ill and died. Upon arrival, the grief-stricken husband penned a stream of letters to the Buddhist abbot Chung-fêng pouring

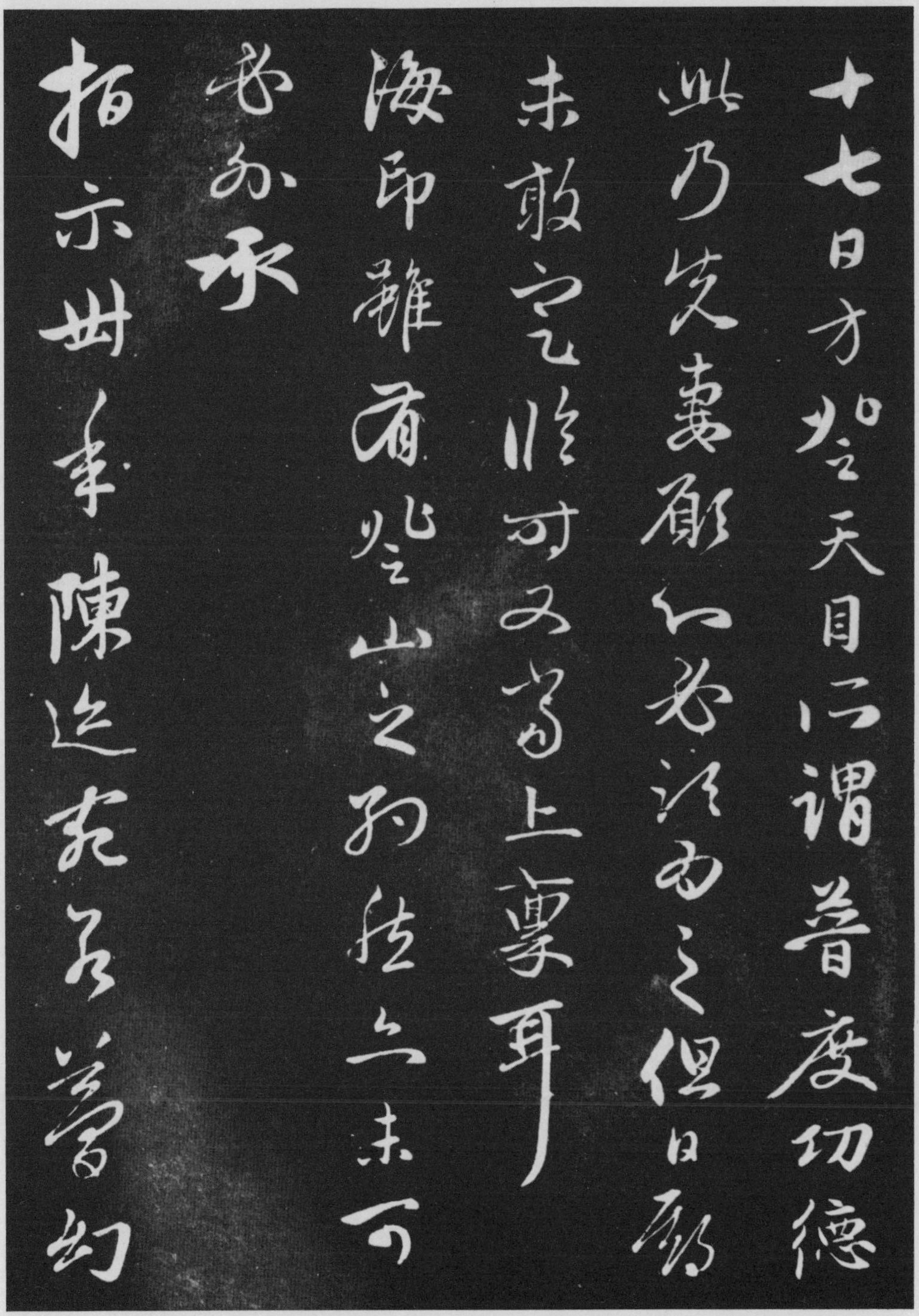

十七日方歇天目二謂普度功德
此乃笑事耳公若許之但日頒
未敢究竟可又當上覆耳
海印雖有普歇山之約恐未可
也勿承
拈示世尊陳迢尧子菩幻

Fig. 46c   Chao Mêng-fu: *Letter to the Monk Chung-fêng* (detail)

out his heart and making arrangements for religious services in his wife's memory. These epistles, full of pathos and piety, were written by Chao Mêng-fu at a stage of his life when his calligraphy was in full maturity. One of the letters (Fig. 46c) was a discussion of the date of an offering in memory of his wife and various related matters, including his own religious experiences, all couched in Buddhist terms. The calligraphy is a charming mixture of *chên shu, hsing shu* and *ts'ao shu,* even with a dash of *chang ts'ao,* truly a most impressive and yet unostentatious display of Chao Mêng-fu's virtuosity in the art of calligraphy. The *San Hsi T'ang Fa T'ieh* includes all Chao Mêng-fu's letters to the abbot as well as some letters written by his wife in her lifetime. From the wife's letters (Fig. 47a) we can see that her calligraphic style is very similar to her husband's. Indeed, never in Chinese art history has there been a couple so devoted to each other, so evenly matched in talent, who have left so many things of true beauty to posterity. It remains only to be said that the couple left seven sons and one daughter of whom at least two sons, Chao Yung and Chao I, were justifiably entitled to carry on the family torch.

To those who like to find manly and heroic qualities in calligraphy, such as the admirers of Yen Chên-ch'ing, Chao Mêng-fu's style may be a bit too pretty and sweet to suit their taste. To his ardent admirers, such as the Ming Dynasty critic Ho Liang-chün, Chao Mêng-fu was 'the greatest calligrapher since Wang Hsi-chih, more proficient than the T'ang and Sung masters, one who synthetized the best of the past in all scripts'. In any case, Chao Mêng-fu's style is not easy to emulate, and those who try are in danger of falling victim to plebeianism, which the Chinese call *shu ch'i.* Auguste Rodin once said that, for the artist, 'it is not thinking with the primitive ingenuity of childhood that is most difficult, but to think with tradition, with its acquired force, and with all the accumulated wealth of its thought'. Here, it may be said, is exactly where Chao Mêng-fu's greatness lies. He may be antiquity-minded, and he may be too zealous in quest of what he called 'archaic elegance'. But the point is that he has made a total success of it.

The eclectic school of calligraphy so brilliantly founded by Chao Mêng-fu was carried on in the Ming Dynasty by a number of men among whom Wên Chêng-ming and Chu Yün-ming are easily the most outstanding.

A descendant of the great Sung patriot Wên T'ien-hsiang, Wên Chêng-ming came from a long line of scholars and artists and was the begetter of an even longer line of artistic talents. From his early youth he devoted himself to learning calligraphy and painting, seeking personal instruction from the leading artists of the day. Like so many other calligraphers, he started with the T'ang and Sung masters, and soon abandoned them for the older ones. Inevitably he found his most rewarding model in Wang Hsi-chih's *Huang T'ing Ching*. Wên Chêng-ming told us that for many months he lived with a copy of the masterpiece, studying and analysing it from morning till

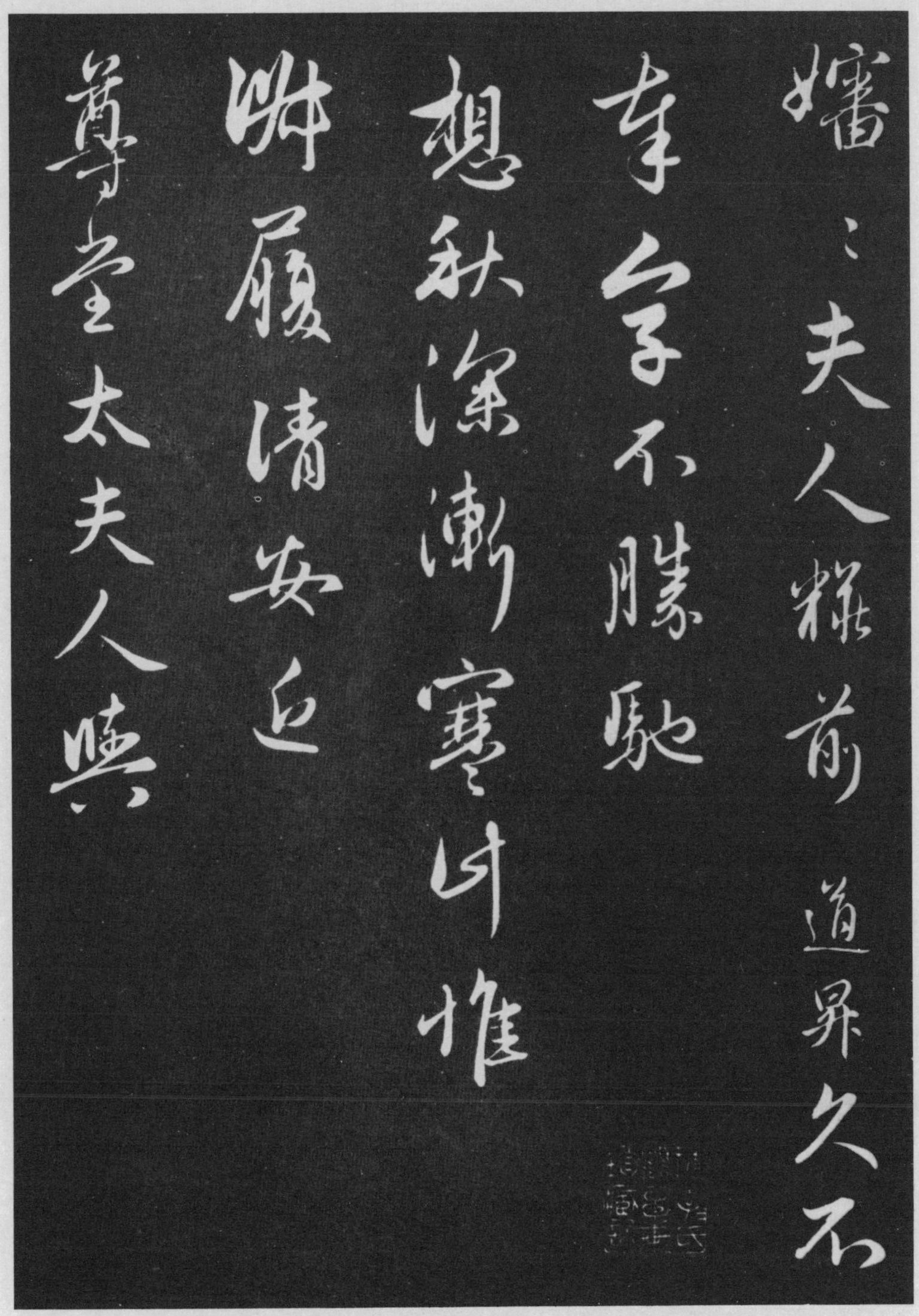

嬸嬸夫人糚前

道昇久不

李字不勝馳

想秋深漸漸寒切惟

州履清安迄

尊堂太夫人興

Fig. 47a　Kuan Tao-shêng: *Letter to Her Aunt* (first portion)

night. His only relief was an occasional cup of tea. Even when he lay down to rest, he still had the *Huang T'ing Ching* in his hand. This went on day after day until he felt that he had captured the true essence of the Tsin master's style. Only then did he pick up his brush to write a few characters, doing them over and over again. To him calligraphy was an art to be perfected with loving care and persistent effort. There was, he tells us, no short cut to excellence.

For a substantial part of his long and rather uneventful life (he lived to be ninety), Wên Chêng-ming made it a routine to transcribe the *Ch'ien Tzǔ Wên* ten times a day. He would rise early in the morning, have his page prepare a huge dish of ink, and before attending to his toilet and taking his breakfast, sit at his desk to transcribe the *Ch'ien Tzǔ Wên* once by the light of the rising sun. Only after he had done the thousand characters would he go downstairs to transact the day's business and receive his callers. He was at home with all the scripts, ancient and modern, and according to his son he was particularly proud of his *li shu* after the style of Chung Yu. One of the most remarkable manuscripts he left us is the *Ch'ien Tzǔ Wên* transcribed in four scripts—*chuan shu, li shu, ts'ao shu* and *chên shu* (Fig. 48a), a phenomenal display of the uncommon skill and technical variousness expected of the true eclectic. Wên Chêng-ming has also left us many manuscripts and scrolls in *chên shu* and *hsing shu,* some of them done in his old age, showing that he was in full command of his brush in the evening of his life. A good example is his transcription of the famous essay *Tsui Wêng T'ing Chi* composed by the Sung scholar Ou-yang Siu. The vertical scroll (Fig. 48b) was dated 1551, when Wên Chêng-ming was 81. It is truly remarkable how a man could do tiny *chên shu* characters with such a sure hand at such an advanced age. It is his particular grace that in such fine pieces there is nothing very striking, nothing unusual or spectacular. They just appear as nothing more than handsomely polished exercises, the product of his professional naturalness.

In view of his avowed admiration of Wang Hsi-chih, it is but natural that echoes of the Tsin master are everywhere in Wên Chêng-ming's calligraphy. From the Tsin master he also inherited that touch of daintiness which in his hands sometimes borders on the weak and the effeminate. As a matter of fact, he himself has compared the *Huang T'ing Ching* characters to 'fairies flying among the clouds and dancing on the waves', thus informing us that he was attracted to those qualities of Wang Hsi-chih's style rather than to its dragon-like and tiger-like qualities so lavishly praised by men such as Emperor T'ai-tsung. Wên Chêng-ming's calligraphy has also been criticized for showing too much the traces of the brush, suggesting 'a country lass wearing too much makeup', thus overshadowing the natural beauty that should be there. Notwithstanding, there should be no doubt that Wên Chêng-ming, tradition-

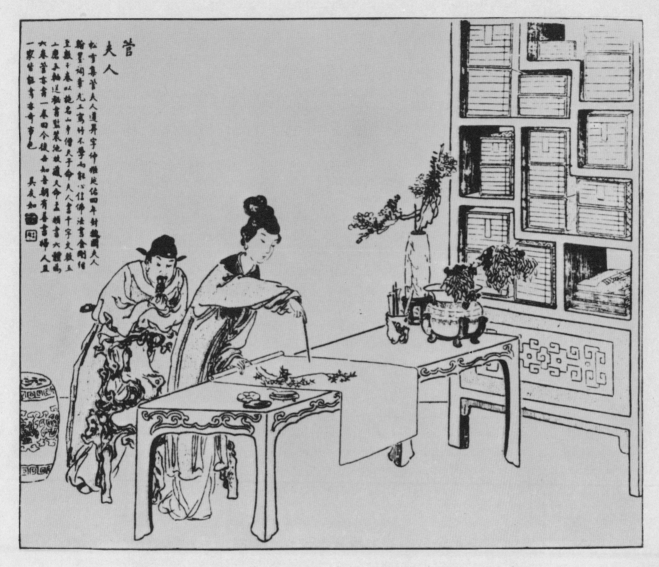

Fig. 47b *Woodcut Illustrating Life of Chao Mêng-fu and Kuan Tao-shêng*

minded and laboriously apprenticed, is a master craftsman fully deserving the accolade given him.

Chu Yün-ming, the other outstanding Ming eclectic, was a child prodigy who was able to do simple characters when he was only four years of age. By the time he was eight, he had learned the major classics by heart. Great expectations attended this precocious child, due note being also taken that he was born with an extra finger on his right hand. Under the persistent encouragement and strict supervision of his elders, he was put through the rigorous programme of training. The list of calligraphers he was called upon to emulate reads like the biographical dictionary of Chinese calligraphy, from Chung Yu of the Han Dynasty, through the Tsin, T'ang and Sung masters, down to and including the Yüan eclectic Chao Mêng-fu. The boy was amazingly responsive and soon became, in the opinion of some critics, the topmost calligrapher of his time.

The boy, unfortunately, was near-sighted. He therefore had difficulty in doing large characters. His specialty was small *chên shu* about half an inch square. One of the specimens in this script that he left us is his transcription of Su Shih's *Ch'ih Pi Fu* (Fig. 49) done in 1515. The transcription was intended to be appended as a postface to a painting by the Ming artist T'ang Yin. It is calligraphic eclecticism of the highest order. Every stroke he executed, every composition he assembled, may be definitely traced and attributed to some ancient masters, readily identifiable by the trained eye. While Chu Yün-ming's calligraphic style may not serve as a model for future styles, he himself certainly will serve as a model for future calligraphers. No one in the entire history of Chinese calligraphy was more unremittingly dedicated than he was to the cultivation of the art. The careers of Wên Chêng-ming and Chu Yün-ming are shining examples of the cult of professional eclecticism in its purest form.

The Ming Dynasty was an age when all eyes were turned in the direction of the past. Most Ming artists, calligraphers and painters alike, were acclaimed by their contemporaries purely on the ground that they were able to inherit the style and proficiency of some old masters, and that was considered more than sufficient as a passport to the hall of fame. The Ming painter, Shen Chou, gained high reputation also as a calligrapher because he was a successful imitator of Huang T'ing-chien's calligraphic style. Shen Chou did not even try to be an eclectic. Chu Yün-ming's calligraphy, in fairness, is of a different order. A calligrapher of fine potentialities, he was nevertheless caught in a web of over-emphasized knowingness and exaggerated sophistication. In his age his reputation, which was considerable, was well deserved.

If one were to accept his own account at face value, Tung Ch'i-ch'ang, the most outstanding artistic personality of the Ming Dynasty, owed his drive to achieve distinction in calligraphy to his failure to win over his cousin in the examination at the prefectural school of his native place, Sungkiang,

[136]

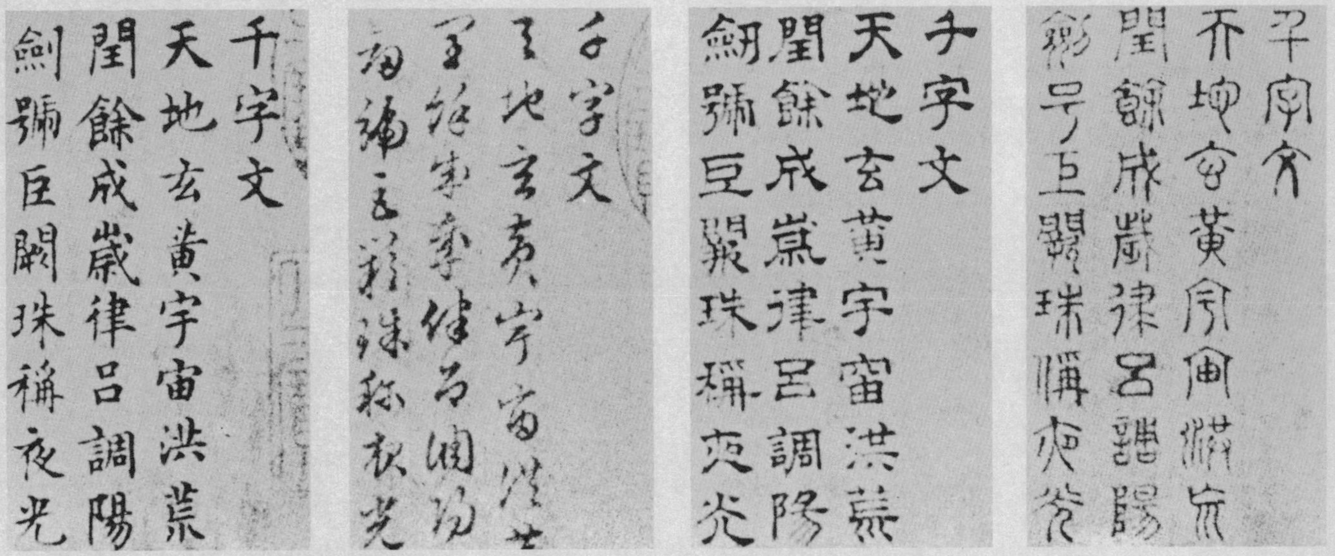

Fig. 48a   Wên Chêng-ming: *Ch'ien Tzŭ Wên in Four Scripts* (first portion)

when he was seventeen. From that disappointment he applied himself for the rest of his life to artistic pursuits. His several contacts with governmental service were interposed by prolonged periods of retirement, which only left him with more time to perfect his calligraphic and painting styles and to sharpen his critical wits. One of his most fortunate and fruitful encounters was his association with the art collector Hsiang Yüan-pien whose vast and fabulous collection he was permitted to explore and examine. In an age when public museums were unknown, this was a rare opportunity indeed. Tung Ch'i-ch'ang was born at a time (1555) when the House of Ming was beset with troubles. In his official career he made a number of narrow escapes. In the midst of almost constant crises, he went on serenely with his artistic pursuits, becoming in due course the dominant artistic figure of his age—the most accomplished calligrapher and painter, the most revered and feared maker of artistic taste. His reputation spread beyond the borders of China, into Japan, Korea and the Ryukyus. His calligraphic style was the fashion for more than two hundred years. There are people who dislike his style and dispute his critical judgment. But he has to be reckoned with in any discussion of Chinese art in the last four hundred years, even though in terms of sheer creativeness the merits of his contributions have always remained a matter of taste.

In an age of rampant eclecticism, it was the duty of an artist to tell his public the sources of his art. Tung Ch'i-ch'ang has told us:

I began to learn calligraphy when I was seventeen. My first calligraphic model was the tablet *To Pao T'a* by the T'ang master Yen Chên-ch'ing (Fig. 30a). Later I changed to Yü Shih-nan (Fig. 27). Then I came to realize that T'ang calligraphy was not as good as that of the Tsin and the Wei period. I therefore started to model after the *Huang T'ing Ching* (Fig. 17b) and also manuscripts by Chung Yu (Fig. 16). After three years, I felt I was able to approach the style of the old masters and I began to belittle Wên Chêng-ming and Chu Yün-ming. However, I really had not captured the essence of the art of calligraphy. All that I was able to do was to emulate the outward appearances. Later I travelled to Chiahsing and was privileged to see the vast collection of originals in Hsiang Yüan-pien's house. I also came across the *Kuan Nu T'ieh* (a manuscript in *chên shu* by Wang Hsi-chih) in Nanking. It was then that I understood how wrong I was in rating myself so highly at first. From that time on, I began to improve bit by bit. It has been twenty-seven years since I first began to learn calligraphy. I am still a run-of-the-mill calligrapher now. Although calligraphy is but a craft, the path is as rough as that!

Has Tung Ch'i-ch'ang told us everything? If not, what are the other sources? Which one is the most dominant? These are questions which have been asked over and over again in the past three hundred years. To the professional Chinese critics, the question of artistic sources is most important to the

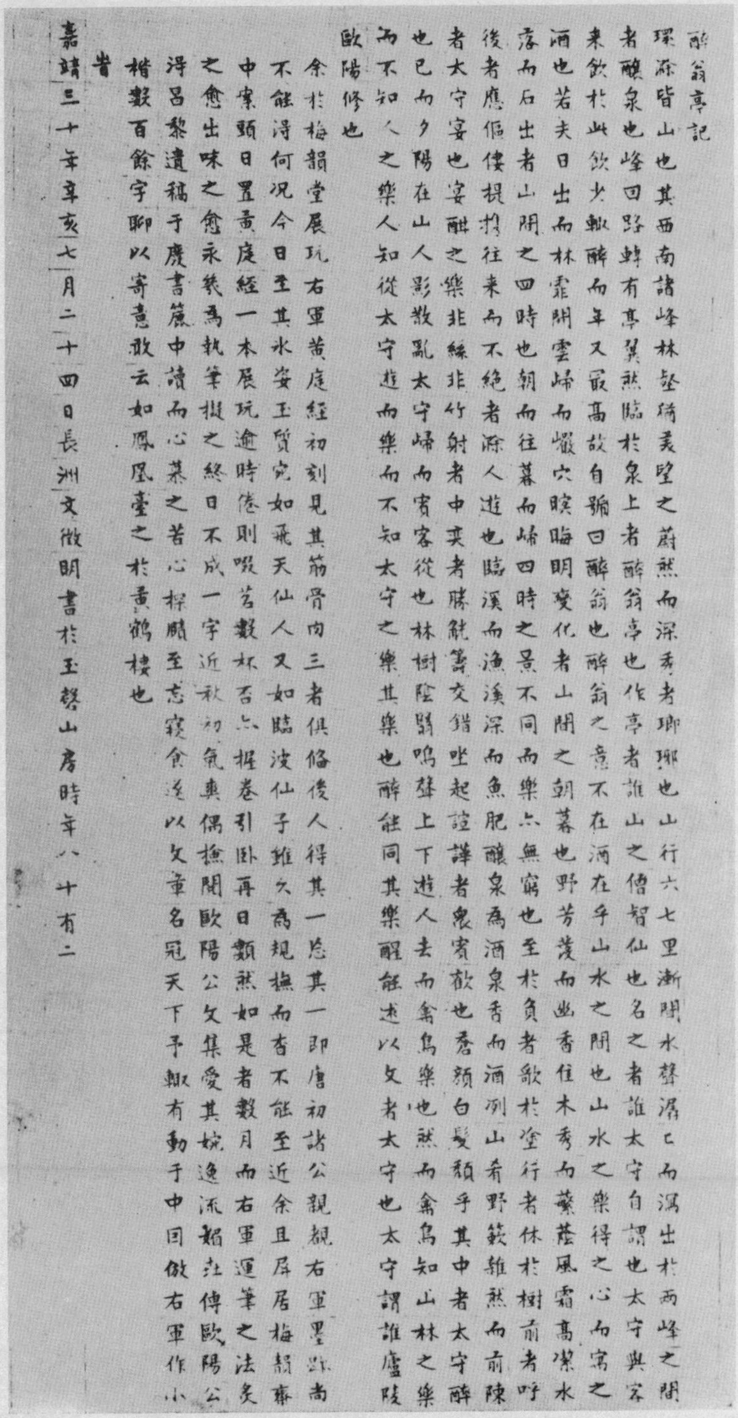

醉翁亭記

環滁皆山也其西南諸峰林壑尤美望之蔚然而深秀者瑯琊也山行六七里漸聞水聲潺潺而瀉出於兩峰之間者釀泉也峰回路轉有亭翼然臨於泉上者醉翁亭也作亭者誰山之僧智仙也名之者誰太守自謂也太守與客來飲於此飲少輒醉而年又最高故自號曰醉翁也醉翁之意不在酒在乎山水之間也山水之樂得之心而寓之酒也

若夫日出而林霏開雲歸而巖穴暝晦明變化者山間之朝暮也野芳發而幽香佳木秀而繁陰風霜高潔水落而石出者山間之四時也朝而往暮而歸四時之景不同而樂亦無窮也

至於負者歌於途行者休於樹前者呼後者應傴僂提攜往來而不絕者滁人遊也臨溪而漁溪深而魚肥釀泉為酒泉香而酒洌山肴野蔌雜然而前陳者太守宴也宴酣之樂非絲非竹射者中弈者勝觥籌交錯起坐而喧譁者眾賓歡也蒼顏白髮頹然乎其間者太守醉也

已而夕陽在山人影散亂太守歸而賓客從也樹林陰翳鳴聲上下遊人去而禽鳥樂也然而禽鳥知山林之樂而不知人之樂人知從太守遊而樂而不知太守之樂其樂也醉能同其樂醒能述以文者太守也太守謂誰廬陵歐陽修也

余於梅韻堂展玩右軍黃庭經初刻見其筋骨肉三者俱備後人得其一即唐宋諸公親覩右軍墨跡尚不能得何況今日主其水姿玉質宛如飛天仙人又如臨波仙子班久為規撫而杳不能至近余且屏居梅韻春中案頭日置黃庭經一本展玩逾時倦則臥引卧再日顏燃如是者數月而右軍運筆之法炙之愈出味之愈永裁為執筆擬之終日不成一字近秋初頗自傷閒歐陽公文集愛其姹逸派稿於傳歐陽公文集中讀而心慕之若心探關至志寢食遂以文章名冠天下予輒有動於中因做右軍作小楷數百餘字聊以寄意敢云如鳳毫之於黃鶴樓也

嘉靖三十年辛亥七月二十四日長洲文徵明書於玉磬山房時年八十有二

Fig. 48b   Wên Chêng-ming: *Tsui Wên T'ing Chi*

understanding of a calligraphic style. They do not believe in original creation. They only believe in parentage. Like a tree, a calligraphic style must have its roots in the ground. It cannot grow from nothing.

It is to Tung Ch'i-ch'ang's glory that he seems to have the critics, the stylistic genealogists, completely confounded, for to the question of the sources of his calligraphic style we have the following answers:

'Mainly Wang Hsi-chih, particularly the style of the manuscript *Kuan Nu T'ieh*'.

'Retaining quite a bit of Yen Chên-ch'ing, especially in *chên shu*'.

'The parentage is Mi Fu' (not mentioned by Tung Ch'i-ch'ang himself).

'Influenced by Li Yung and Hsü Hao' (these two T'ang calligraphers were not mentioned by Tung Ch'i-ch'ang himself).

'Chiefly Hsü Hao, with references to Li Yung and Mi Fu, while in later years dominated by Yen Chên-ch'ing and close to Liu Kung-ch'üan and Yang Ning-shih' (only Yen Chên-ch'ing was mentioned by Tung Ch'i-ch'ang himself as a model in early years).

Such talk is, of course, utter nonsense. It is the product of an age in which eclectic calligraphy had sunk to a level of unparalleled falseness, garnished with so many historical trappings that it had become totally uninspired. Although Tung Ch'i-ch'ang was just as much a worshipper of the past as most of his contemporaries, he nevertheless told us in unmistakable terms that calligraphy modelled strictly after an old master was 'dead' calligraphy and that only an individual, personal style could be considered 'live'. That he tried to practise what he preached is graphically illustrated by an album containing Tung Ch'i-ch'ang's copies of the works of the old masters, including Wang Hsi-chih, Wang Hsien-chih, Yen Chên-ch'ing, Hsü Hao, Chang Hsü, Huai-su, Liu Kung-ch'üan, Su Shih and Mi Fu. We have noted that Mi Fu and Chao Mêng-fu, among others, were able to copy so well that their copies were often indistinguishable from the originals. The most remarkable thing about the Tung Ch'i-ch'ang album is that all the copies, labelled as such, do not resemble the originals at all, indicating that Tung Ch'i-ch'ang, even when copying, insisted upon being Tung Ch'i-ch'ang and nobody else.

But Tung Ch'i-ch'ang, we hasten to add, is still an eclectic. Like Mi Fu, he spent a lifetime studying and analysing the works of the old masters. The Hsiang Yüan-pien collection brought him on intimate terms with some of the greatest masterpieces of all time. He took profuse notes of what he saw and wrote a prodigious number of commentaries and colophons, which made him the leading authority on matters of art for generations to come. He has his strong likes and dislikes, but his own calligraphic style remains derivative and classic in its concentration on formal values.

In the Yüan Dynasty, a type of painting was developed which has come to be known as *wên jên hua*, 'scholar painting', which reached its apex in the works of Huang Kung-wang and Ni Tsan. Tung Ch'i-ch'ang, in his art

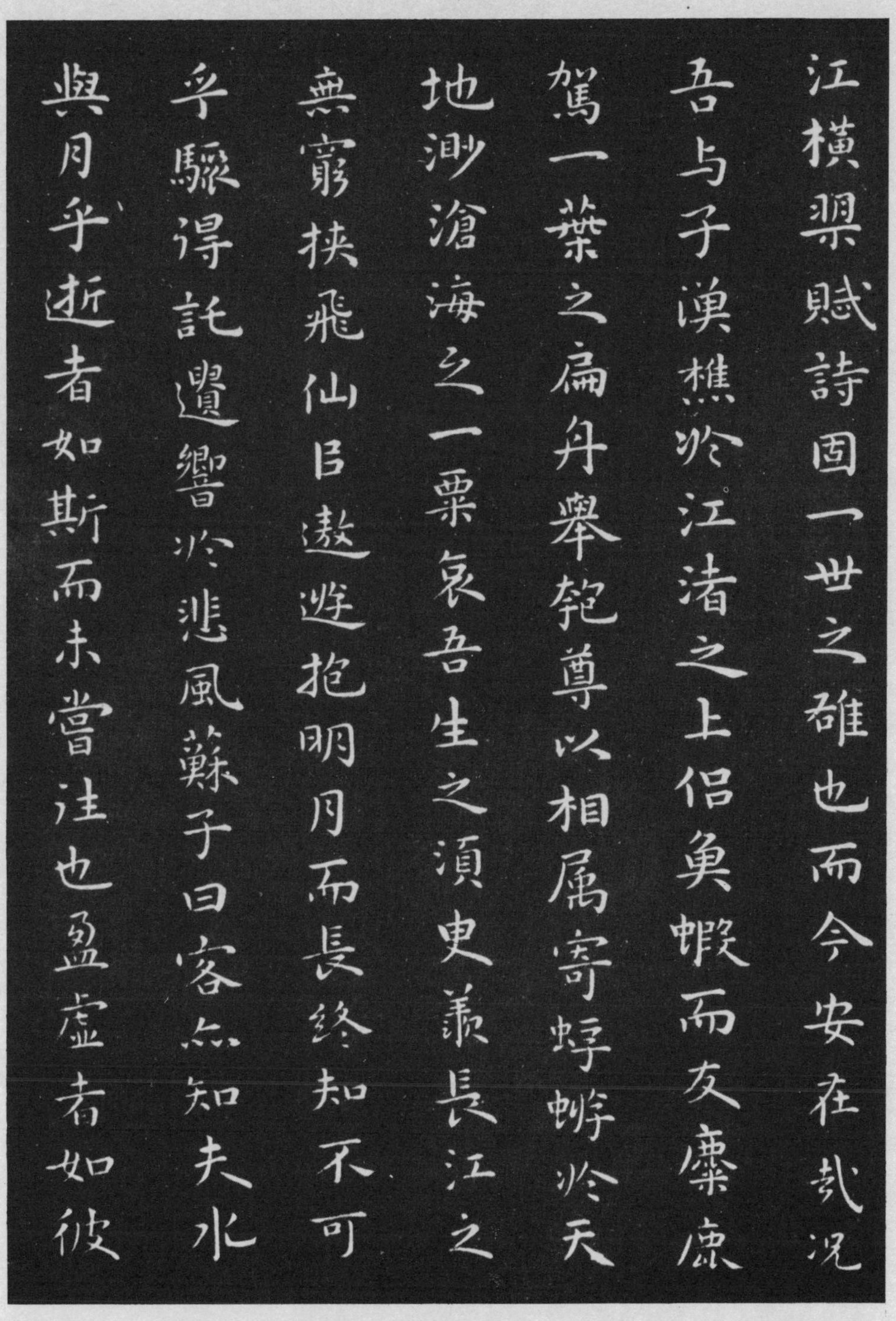

江橫槊賦詩固一世之雄也而今安在哉況
吾与子漁樵於江渚之上侶魚蝦而友麋鹿
駕一葉之扁舟舉匏尊以相屬寄蜉蝣於天
地渺滄海之一粟哀吾生之須臾羨長江之
無窮挾飛仙以遨遊抱明月而長終知不可
乎驟得託遺響於悲風蘇子曰客亦知夫水
與月乎逝者如斯而未嘗往也盈虛者如彼

Fig. 49   Chu Yün-ming: *Ch'ih Pi Fu* (detail)

criticism, is an unqualified admirer of the Yüan landscape painters, particularly their austere simplicity and ruthless elimination of mannerist adornments. Tung Ch'i-ch'ang's own landscapes undoubtedly belong to this school. In terms of technique, the *wên jên hua* features the use of the 'thirsty brush' (*k'o pi*), sometimes known as 'dry brush' (*kan pi*), that is, a brush only partially soaked with ink. We may recall that the Han calligrapher Ts'ai Yung was the master of the *fei po,* an effect achieved by dragging the brush so rapidly over the writing surface that irregular white streaks are left within the strokes. Chao Mêng-fu, in an often quoted poem, advocates the use of the *fei po* technique in the painting of rocks. Other painters have used it to paint weather-beaten tree trunks and large bamboo branches. The *fei po* effect, as we have said, is achieved by the rapid motion of the brush. It is not achieved by soaking the brush only partially with ink. The 'thirsty brush' technique, it seems, is primarily an innovation of the Yüan landscape painters, and because they were in the habit of putting inscriptions on their paintings, the calligraphy was done also with a 'thirsty brush'. Tung Ch'i-ch'ang, in both calligraphy and painting, is a follower of this technique.

Tung Ch'i-ch'ang has left us a prodigious number of his works, some in formal scrolls and more often in the form of colophons on or attached to works of art. All through his long life (he died in 1636 at the age of 81) he wielded his brush ceaselessly and, like Wên Chên-ming, he was in full command of his faculties until the very end. He was generous to a fault in giving away his calligraphic pieces, especially to his many concubines in exchange for their favours. But he refused resolutely to be commissioned by the eunuchs, no matter how powerful they were at court. We shall be looking at some of Tung Ch'i-ch'ang's colophons in the following chapters. One of his scrolls in *chên shu* is his transcription of a passage on the attainment of sagehood from the short, pithy essay entitled *T'ung Shu* (Treatise on Understanding) by the Sung Neo-Confucianist philosopher Chou Tun-i, a transcription which is a splendid example of Tung Ch'i-ch'ang's calligraphic style (Fig. 50).

There is always an air of casualness enveloping Tung Ch'i-ch'ang's works. The admirers of Yen Chên-ch'ing believe that a well executed character should assume the posture of a military hero returning from battle in triumph. These men are Tung Ch'i-ch'ang's detractors who accuse him of approaching the art of calligraphy too light-heartedly. It is true that Tung Ch'i-ch'ang seems to pay little attention to the structural organization of the characters, allowing his highly trained hand the maximum freedom to express his inner moods. He believes that a true artist is not a man who carries the burdens of society on his shoulders but one whose soul has been distilled by learning and meditation. Yen Chên-ch'ing's strokes have been compared to bent iron bars, his dots to tumbling boulders. Tung Ch'i-ch'ang's strokes suggest weather-beaten vines, his dots drops of morning dew. There may be some superficial

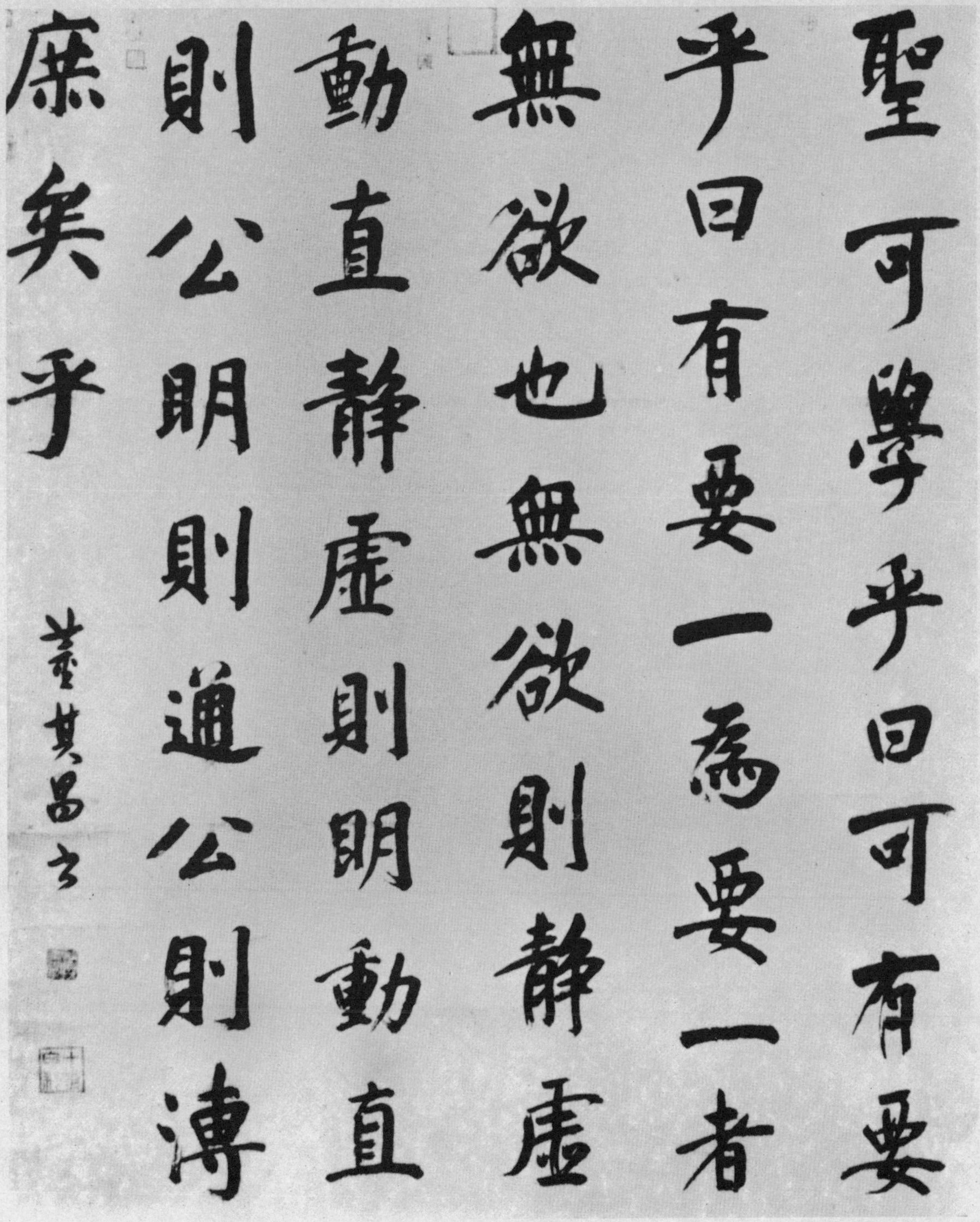

聖可學乎曰可有要
乎曰有要一為要一者
無欲也無欲則靜虛
動直靜虛則明動直
則公明則通公則溥
庶矣乎

董其昌書

Fig. 50　Tung Ch'i-ch'ang: *T'ung Shu*

resemblance between the styles of the two men, but the spirit animating them is totally different. If one reminds us of a conquering hero, the other reminds us of a devotee to Ch'an (Zen) Buddhism. Tung Ch'i-ch'ang's style, it may be said, is a calculated rejection of the formalism and morality of T'ang calligraphy. Whoever tries to make Yen Chên-ch'ing the progenitor of Tung Ch'i-ch'ang is guilty of mixing up the standards of two entirely different worlds. As Tung Ch'i-ch'ang pointed out, a landscape by the T'ang painter Li Ssŭ-hsüan belongs to a school totally different from a landscape by the Yüan painter Ni Tsan. There should be no doubt that Tung Ch'i-ch'ang's calligraphic and painting style is with the latter.

Tung Ch'i-ch'ang's adaptation of the 'thirsty brush' technique of painting to calligraphy has added a new and pleasant image to the restricted repertory of Chinese calligraphy. And it is by an unequalled combination of skill, intelligence and honesty that he has won a place near the summit of that Tsin-T'ang-Sung tradition which has crushed so many of his contemporaries. While his reputation in his lifetime was enormous, the posthumous honours that came his way were formidable. In 1705, sixty-nine years after his death, the Ch'ing Emperor K'ang-hsi paid tribute to him by personally writing an essay praising his artistic achievements, and the redoubtable Emperor Ch'ien-lung flattered him by imitating his calligraphic style, alas with questionable success. With commendation from such high places, Tung Ch'i-ch'ang's calligraphy, coming at such a late date, actually succeeded in overshadowing for a considerable period of time all that had gone before. He is indeed a giant among eclectics.

Chapter Nine

The Ch'ing Renaissance

In China, perhaps more than anywhere else, an artist is never supposed to make a clean break with the past. Critical and popular taste simply will not tolerate such a radical departure. Creativeness in art, to the Chinese, has always been a process of adaptation and assimilation of old and tried forms into something which enriches and energizes them. All innovations, therefore, have been based on an appeal to a perfected state assumed to have been achieved by the old masters. One is entitled and expected to deprecate the present by lamenting how low standards have fallen—a recurring theme in classical criticism. Even as the Sung masters were in their period of great creativeness, Ou-yang Siu complained in a letter to his friend Ts'ai Hsiang that 'modern (Sung) calligraphy has sunk below T'ang standards'. But never is one allowed to question the occupants of the Pantheon of the great. To do so is not only impertinent; it is unacceptable.

For many, many centuries, it was taken for granted that Wang Hsi-chih had reached such a state of perfection that it was neither necessary nor respectful, nor even in good taste, to look beyond him. If we read more than one of the descriptions of Wang Hsi-chih's art at a sitting, we are confronted with so many superlatives, so many florid assertions of greatness, richness and importance that our mind will boggle at them. For a calligrapher even to approach his style was considered a good enough achievement to guarantee a reputation and a steady income. 'Directly pursuing Wang Hsi-chih' was about as high a critical accolade as one could hope to get. The programme of training and practice led inevitably back to Wang Hsi-chih. If an aspiring

[145]

calligrapher had talent, after many years of painstaking labour, he would get somewhere, and he would be receiving the acclaim of having captured the Tsin master's style, an acclaim not easy to come by and an unmistakable sign that he had arrived. There he would rest on his laurels. He would be asked to write scrolls and epitaphs and shop-signs. That would be as far as he could go, because he would be considered to have reached the top, and there was no higher place beyond. This has been the success story of practically all latter-day calligraphers.

An Emperor, however Philistine, must somehow pretend to be a Wang Hsi-chih admirer if he wanted the support of the intellectuals. Consequently, Wang Hsi-chih manuscripts, including good copies and rubbings, had nearly all found their way into royal collections. If the Emperor happened to be a connoisseur, he would append endless colophons to the manuscripts. If the Emperor did not consider himself good enough for that, he could at least have the manuscripts mounted and remounted with the most expensive materials and order his court calligraphers to do the colophons on his behalf. Palace buildings with high-sounding names were designated to house these treasures which were seldom if ever shown to the public. Under such circumstances, all that were available to the youngsters learning calligraphy were rubbings or woodcuts of the masterpieces. After centuries of pounding on the stones to make rubbings, plus the natural process of disintegration and decay as well as the ravages of wars and rebellions, what passed as Wang Hsi-chih calligraphy really bore very little resemblance to the originals. This situation led some people to ask: 'Is it worthwhile to spend a lifetime modelling after such deteriorated specimens? Since the original *Lan T'ing Hsü* was buried, is it worthwhile to model after the copies made by Ou-yang Hsün and Ch'u Shui-liang? If calligraphy is to remain a living art, can one not find some other things to model after than the corrupted rubbings?'

These were the questions asked by a group of calligraphers of the Ch'ing Dynasty. By asking such questions and doing something about the situation, they wrote a new chapter in the history of Chinese calligraphy.

The Ch'ing calligraphers boldly held forth the proposition that fifteen centuries of unadulterated veneration and slavish imitation of Wang Hsi-chih was just about enough. The eclecticism of Chao Mêng-fu and Tung Ch'i-ch'ang, a miracle in itself, was about the most that could be expected under the old system. If calligraphy were to be saved from dying of starvation, new nourishment had to be found.

Never before, as in the Ch'ing Dynasty, had calligraphy been pursued with such ant-like industry. The landscape was strewn with names of men known as calligraphers in their day. Yet their work, when taken together, was unexciting. But across the rolling country, a few peaks appeared. They were the men, according to a modern critic, who 'threw Wang Hsi-chih away like a pair of old shoes'. These men, oddly enough, were professional

Fig. 51a Chin Nung: *Calligraphy in Li Shu* (detail)

antiquarians. They began their careers by studying the ancient artifacts—the bronzes and tablets of remote antiquity. Some of them were pioneers in the study of the oracle bones. Known as *chin shih hsüeh,* the study of ancient artifacts had been the province of archaeologists and epigraphers since the Sung Dynasty. However, the early explorers of this rich and fascinating mine were primarily interested in the identification, authentication and description of the articles rather than in their evaluation as works of art. Men such as Ou-yang Siu and Li Kung-lin were concerned with deciphering the characters in the inscriptions. Although some of the *chin shih hsüeh* experts were artists, their artistic styles were not appreciably influenced by the subjects of their archaeological research. One of the explanations for this strange neglect was that almost all of the bewildering mass of ancient artifacts were made by individuals to whom it had not occurred to have their names recorded. To them, what we now regard as great works of art were either objects of use or symbols of authority. Ancient artifacts, therefore, were almost always anonymous. It was not until the late Han Dynasty, confining ourselves to calligraphy in this connection, that the calligrapher Chung Yu saw fit to tell us who he was.

The great contribution of the Ch'ing Dynasty calligraphers was to recognize the artistic merits of the ancient artifacts, even though the men who made them were unknown. As antiquarians, the Ch'ing calligraphers collected the stones and rubbings of the ancient artifacts and studied them as intensively as their predecessors compared and commented upon the various versions of the *Lan T'ing Hsü.* They spent time and money looking for the oldest and the best-preserved stones and rubbings. The T'ang essayist Han Yü, with all his eloquence, pleaded in vain with the government to preserve the stone drums. In the Ch'ing Dynasty, the stone drums were considered national treasures. Ch'ing scholars were known for their meticulous research. They applied their technique to the study of the ancient artifacts with equal fervour. Those who were artistically inclined modelled after the calligraphic styles of the ancient artifacts in the same way the T'ang-Sung-Yüan-Ming calligraphers modelled after the *Huang T'ing Ching* and *Lan T'ing Hsü.* Those among them who were talented eventually evolved calligraphic styles distinctly different from the old masters, as refreshing as a cool breeze on a stuffy summer day. In a way, the movement they started was typically Chinese in that it was an attempt to open new vistas by references to the very old. It was in this sense a renaissance.

One of the pioneers of the movement was Chin Nung (1687-1763), more popularly known as Chin Tung-hsin. An eccentric included in the group known as the 'Eight Oddities of Yangchow' (*Yangchow Pa Kuai*), Chin Nung was widely acclaimed by his contemporaries as a versatile artist in poetry, painting and calligraphy. The first part of his life was spent in archaeological research, not in the sense of doing field work in the modern way, but in searching for

[148]

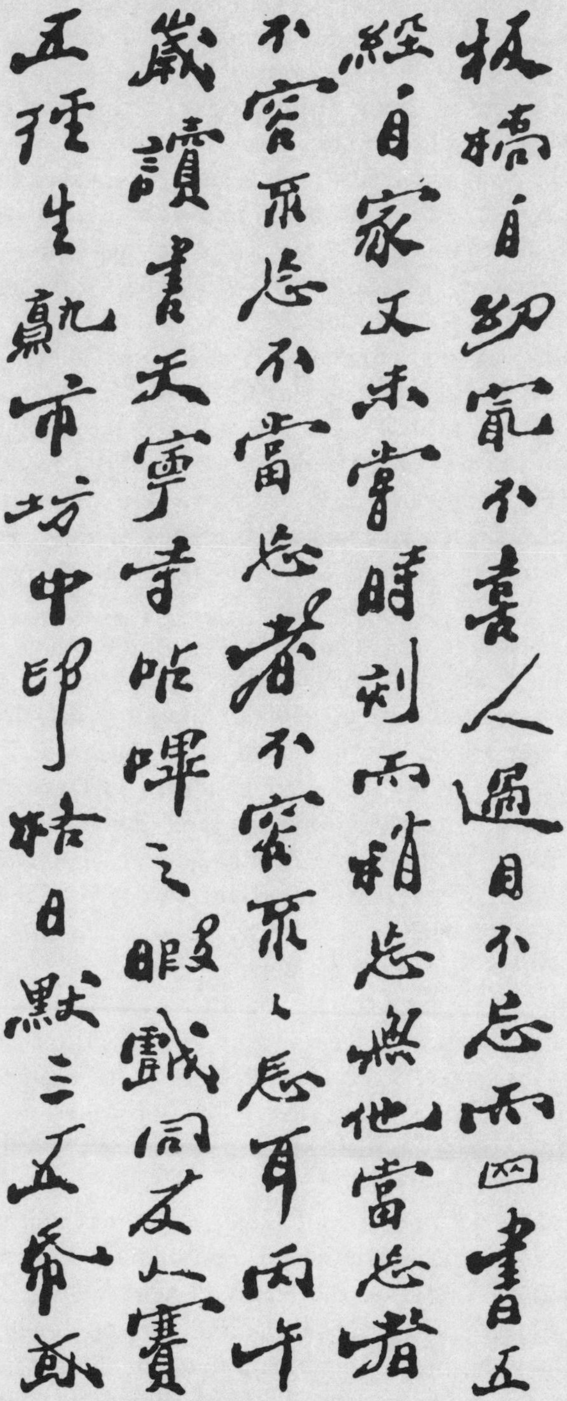

板橋自幼寄不喜人過目不忘而四書五

經自家又未嘗時刻而誦忘然他當忘者

不窮亦不當忘者不窮亦忘之耳兩午

歲讀書天寧寺咊嗶之眼戲同友人賣

五經生魁市坊中印稿日默三五次蘇

Fig 51b Chêng Hsieh: *Calligraphy in Hsing Shu* (detail)

textual references to the artifacts that were extant. It was not until he was fifty that he began to devote himself to artistic creations. In calligraphy his contribution was to simulate on paper the characters he found engraved on metal and stone, even to the extent of clipping off the tip of the brush to give it knife-like qualities, something unheard of in the past.

There should be no question that Chin Nung was engaged in a bold experiment seeking to create new calligraphic forms. The appearance of the characters he executed, as we can see from a sample of his writing (Fig. 51a), is most unusual indeed. However, if we are familiar with some of the old tablets, we will not be greatly astonished by it.

Another member of the group known as the 'Eight Oddities of Yangchow', Chêng Hsieh, more popularly known as Chêng Pan-ch'iao, was also an avid student of the ancient artifacts and had adopted the calligraphic style he found on them to his calligraphy and bamboo painting. From a specimen of his calligraphy (Fig. 51b), we can see that he was inclined to be too mannerist. The deliberate use of the two lobes at both ends of the diagonal stroke of the eighth character in the third line from the right, for instance, is ugly and offensive.

While we have nothing but admiration for the ingenuity and courage of such men as Chin Nung and Chêng Hsieh, we are constrained to say that their struggle is a bit too obvious and the effect too contrived, so that we are driven, however reluctantly, to regard their endeavour as one of those bitter footnotes in the history of art reminding us that experimentation and advancement are not necessarily always the same thing.

Writers on Chinese calligraphy generally go into superlatives over Têng Shih-ju (1743-1805), often regarded as the prince of Ch'ing calligraphy. Early in his life, Têng Shih-ju, a poor boy, learned to carve seals. This is important information because it presupposes that the boy had gone through the discipline of learning the various types of *chuan shu,* the script for seals. Driven by a burning desire to see as many ancient artifacts as possible, he led a wandering life, travelling for hundreds of miles equipped with only a bamboo hat and a bamboo cane. He called on collector after collector, begging to see the treasures in their possession. One of the collectors, Mei Liu by name, took him in and supported him for eight years. Freed from the drudgeries of making a living, Têng Shih-ju worked day and night modelling after the bronze and stone inscriptions to perfect his calligraphy, from those on the stone drums to those on the Han and Wei tablets, doing at least a hundred copies of each. He spent about five years on *chuan shu* and three on *pa fên.* Significantly, he paid no attention to the Tsin masters, not to say those of a later age. In due course his fame spread far and wide. Always poor, he lived on his patrons. His biography, by his disciple and admirer Pao Shih-ch'ên, is a seemingly unending account of how this uncouth and

Fig. 52a Têng Shih-ju: *Calligraphy in Chuan Shu*

ill-clad man was received by the rich and the powerful with the utmost courtesy and respect purely on the strength of his calligraphic and seal-carving accomplishments.

As a professional calligrapher, Têng Shih-ju was proficient in all the major scripts—*chuan shu, li shu, chên shu* and *hsing shu* (Fig. 52). According to Pao Shih-ch'ên, Têng Shih-ju's *chuan shu* was built on the foundation of Li Ssŭ and Li Yang-ping but mixed with certain features taken from the *ta chuan* of Shih Chou and the *ta chuan* characters found on the Ch'in and Han bricks and tiles. His *chên shu* was grounded not on the Tsin-T'ang-Sung-Yüan-Ming masters but on his mastery of the brushmanship of *chuan shu* and *pa fên.* Although his *hsing shu* and *ts'ao shu* were not as good as the other scripts, he was somehow able to divest himself of the plebeianism (*shu ch'i*) of the post-T'ang period.

Another Ch'ing calligrapher of note is the eminent scholar in philosophy and philology Chao Chih-ch'ien (1829-1884) who took to calligraphy as a result of his interest in deciphering the inscriptions on the ancient artifacts. His calligraphic style in *chên shu* and *hsing shu* (Fig. 53) is a subtle combination of the styles of many tablets and ancient artifacts, creating forms which are as archaic as they are aesthetically satisfying. The same may be said of our contemporary, Wu Chün-ch'ing, more popularly known as Wu Ch'ang-shih, whose calligraphic style, though radically different from Têng Shih-ju's and Chao Chih-ch'ien's, was nevertheless derived from the same sources (Fig. 54).

In their calligraphic styles, these men—Têng Shih-ju, Chao Chih-ch'ien and Wu Chün-ch'ing—are of course enamoured with classicism. However, classicism was not to them an end in itself, but a lamp to guide them to explore new and exciting forms. It is important to note that these men, besides developing their own styles in *chên shu* and *hsing shu,* also developed their own styles in *chuan shu* and *li shu,* thus adding new dimensions to the old scripts and reviving them as vehicles of artistic expression. They have taught us that, in doing characters in *hsiao chuan,* we do not have to do them in exactly the same way as Li Ssŭ and Li Yang-ping. To them, *chuan shu,* like all other scripts, may be made into a subject of stylistic interpretations. They have thus resuscitated *chuan shu* and *li shu* and made them into living scripts, which may be used in calligraphy as well as in seal-carving. They were archaeologists turned artists. Chao Chih-ch'ien, it was said, wielded his seal-carving knife like a brush and treated the stone seal like a sheet of paper. In their hands calligraphy and seal-carving became allied arts, and their proficiency in the old scripts served them well on both counts.

The Ch'ing archaeologists, palaeographers, epigraphers and calligraphers were expectedly avid collectors of the rubbings of the old artifacts. They scoured the country for good rubbings generally on the assumption that the earlier the rubbing the more faithful it was to the original. A manuscript

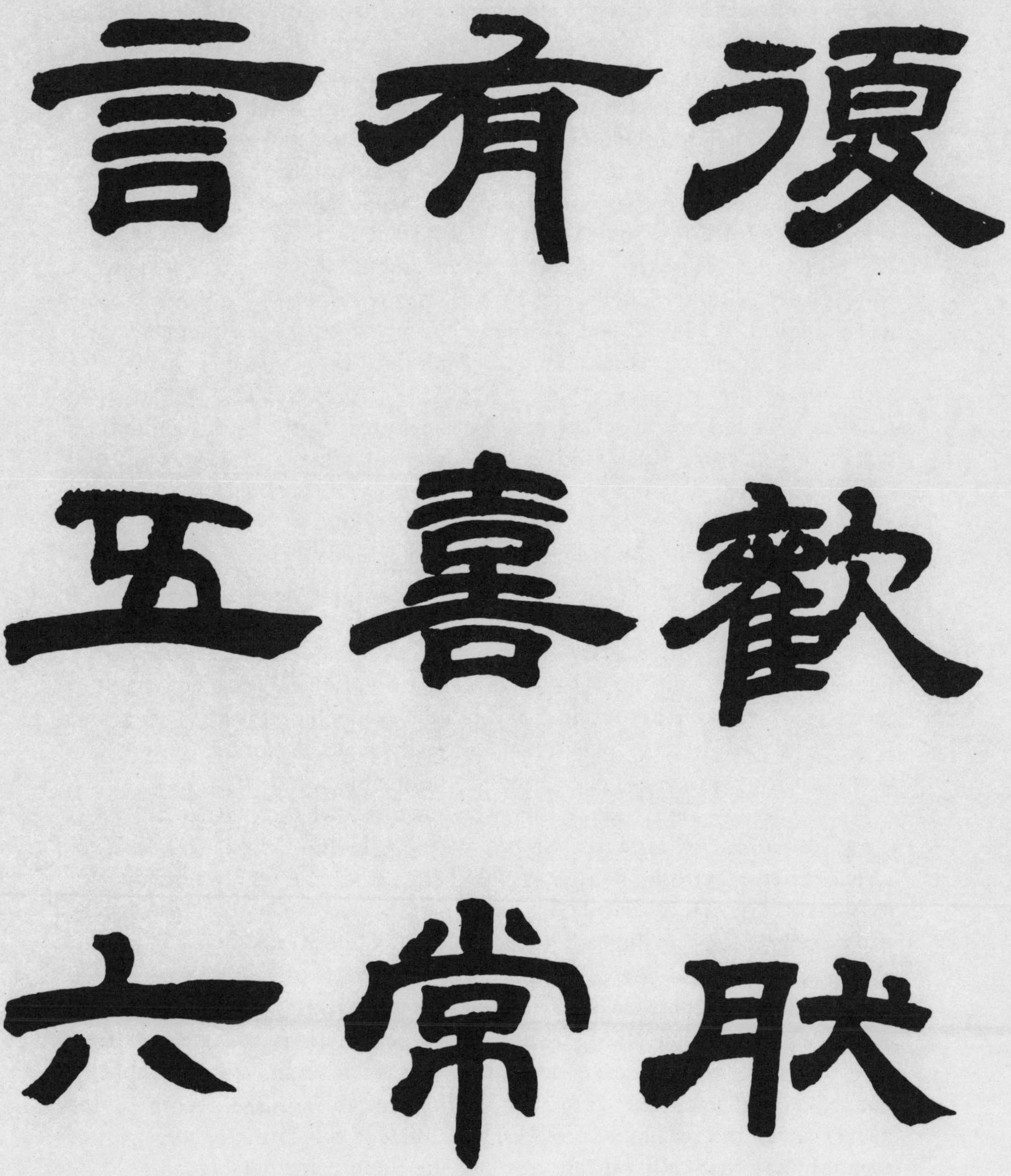

言 肴 復

五 喜 歡

六 常 朕

Fig. 52b Têng Shih-ju: *Calligraphy in Li Shu*

might be engraved many times. The practice was to have an expert craftsman trace the manuscript and commit the tracing to the stone, leaving the original intact. A good deal therefore depended upon the expertise of the tracer. And, of course, there were good engravers and bad ones. All these were the concern of the scholars and collectors who wrote voluminous commentaries on their discoveries, comparing the different versions detail by detail and grading them according to their merits. Rubbings thus became almost as eagerly sought after as the manuscripts of the Tsin, T'ang and Sung masters. One of the most comprehensive treatises on calligraphy is the book *I Chou Shuang Chi* by Pao Shih-ch'ên. This was followed by an amplification written by another Ch'ing lover of calligraphy, K'ang Yu-wei. Entitled *Kuang I Chou Shuang Chi* and published in 1889, K'ang Yu-wei's book is not only an assessment of the artistic merits of the various tablets extant but also a passionate plea for their importance as calligraphic models. K'ang Yu-wei was a reformist in politics. Wielding his eloquent pen, he submitted a stream of petitions to the Ch'ing Emperor Kuang-hsü urging sweeping constitutional reforms and the establishment of a limited monarchy. His pleas in favour of the Han and Wei tablets were in every way as ardent as his political tracts and certainly had more appreciable effect. Putting his prodigious knowledge of the tablets to the best advantage, he informs and instructs us regarding their relative artistic worth, all the time urging us to forget the Tsin-T'ang-Sung-Yüan-Ming masters and focus our eyes entirely on the anonymous Han and Wei scribes. Quite naturally K'ang Yu-wei was an ardent admirer of Têng Shih-ju. In a moment of extravagance, K'ang Yu-wei said: 'Têng Shih-ju is to *chuan shu* as Mencius is to Confucian philosophy.' It really takes a political reformer, a man with ironclad convictions, to be so thoroughly iconoclastic.

K'ang Yu-wei was certainly one who practised what he preached. After many years of modelling after the Han and Wei tablets, he was able to forge a style which is startlingly original and at the same time highly revelatory of its sources. His rather unorthodox style may be seen in a short passage he wrote commenting on the calligraphy of Chao Chih-ch'ien (Fig. 55), which shows up the formal graces of the tablet characters and what they can do in the hands of someone who understands and feels their true uses and selects with discretion among their endless permutations and combinations. The characters K'ang Yu-wei executed move in a clean, classic simplicity, unadorned and unaffected, and without that quickly tarnished sheen of the merely novel, the fetchingly precious, the different, which marks the styles of some of the other calligraphers treading the same path, notably Chin Nung and Chêng Hsieh. K'ang Yu-wei is particularly good in large characters, sometimes so large that they had to be done with a broom instead of a brush. His style is less good when he is entirely serious; it is when abandon, wild calculation and seriousness meet that his style really soars.

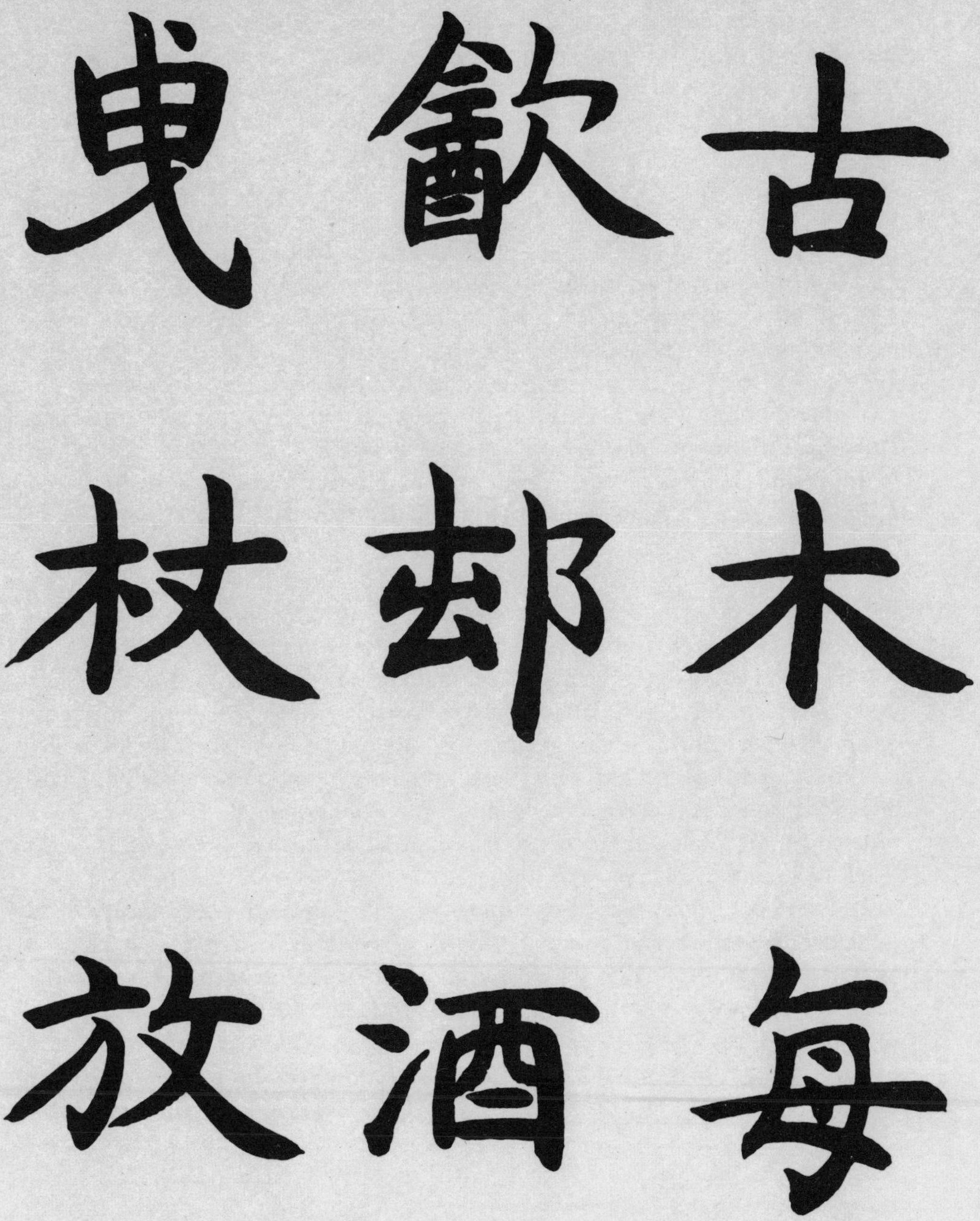

古歡曳

木郊杖

每酒放

Fig. 52c   Têng Shih-ju: *Calligraphy in Chên Shu*

The intense interest generated by the Han and Wei tablets has given rise to a school of calligraphy broadly identified as *pei hsüeh* (the study of tablets) in contrast to the traditional preoccupation with manuscripts known as *t'ieh hsüeh* (the study of manuscripts). Like so many generic terms in Chinese art, the distinction between *pei hsüeh* and *t'ieh hsüeh* is unclear and rather confusing. For one thing, *t'ieh* in the sense of an original manuscript by an acknowledged master has long been a rarity secluded behind palace gates and in modern times preserved in air-conditioned museum vaults. Only on the rarest of occasions is it seen by the general public, and modelling after it as a calligraphic exercise is completely out of the question. As a measure to encourage the practice of calligraphy, the T'ang and Sung Emperors inaugurated the practice of engraving the manuscripts in their possession for wide distribution. Early in the Sung Dynasty, around the year 990, the Sung Emperor T'ai-tsung committed a number of manuscripts in the royal collection to engraving. Known as the *Shun Hua Ko T'ieh,* the manuscripts engraved included those by Chung Yu, Wang Hsi-chih, Wang Hsien-chih, the T'ang Emperor T'ai-tsung, the T'ang Emperor Hsüan-tsung, Ou-yang Hsün, Yen Chên-ch'ing, Huai-jên, Huai-su, Liu Kung-ch'üan, and some others. In 1109, Emperor Hui-tsung issued the *Ta Kuan T'ieh* comprising items in his own collection. In 1185, Emperor Hsiao-tsung had the entire body of the *Shun Hua Ko T'ieh* re-engraved together with manuscripts acquired after the Sung court moved to the South. Known as the *Shun Hsi Ko T'ieh,* it was the most comprehensive collection of manuscripts up to that time. In the following centuries, these manuscript collections were re-engraved innumerable times, and other collections were issued, most notably the *San Hsi T'ang Fa T'ieh* ordered by the Ch'ing Emperor Ch'ien-lung, who also had the *Shun Hua Ko T'ieh* re-engraved.

The repeated engraving of the manuscripts naturally gives rise to the question as to which is *t'ieh* and which is *pei* for the simple reason that a Han or Wei tablet was originally a manuscript which was engraved in exactly the same manner as a Wang Hsi-chih letter was engraved. Furthermore, most calligraphers have left us with both tablets and manuscripts. The question may be asked: Why should we draw a sharp line of distinction between a tablet and a manuscript, particularly when both were done by the same calligrapher? Is there really an essential difference between Yen Chên-ch'ing's *Kao Shên* and his *To Pao T'a* (Fig. 30)? Or between Chao Mêng-fu's *Ch'iu Kung Miao Pei* and his letter to the monk Chung-fêng (Fig. 46)? Mi Fu, who included in his floating museum many original manuscripts, and Tung Ch'i-ch'ang, who was privileged to examine the Hsiang Yüan-pien collection, could afford to indulge in a bit of snobbery by saying that one should model only after originals. Few others are so fortunate.

We have chosen to label the Yüan and Ming calligraphers—Chao Mêng-fu, Wên Chêng-ming, Chu Yün-ming, Tung Ch'i-ch'ang—the eclectics. In a sense,

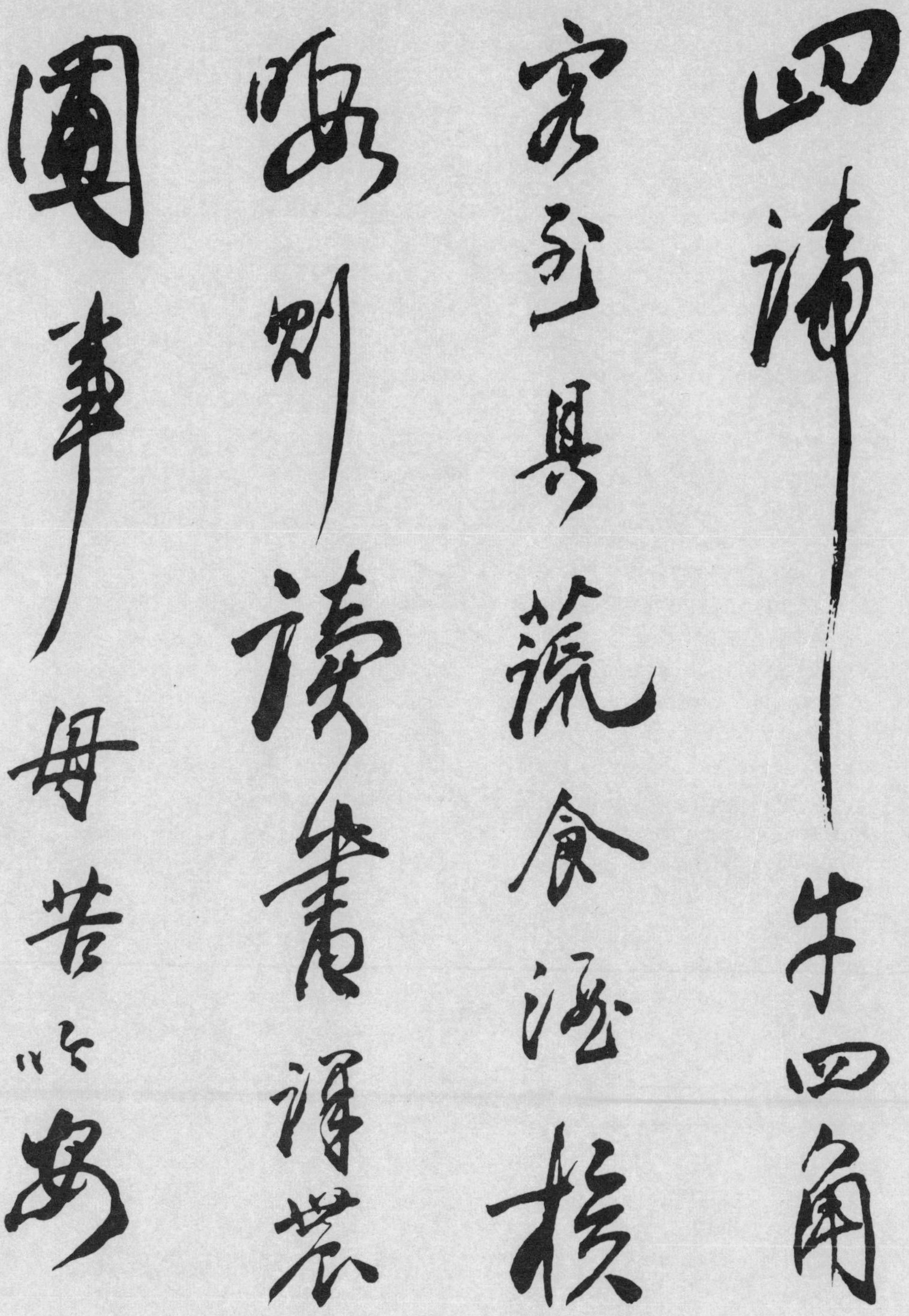

Fig. 52d   Têng Shih-ju: *Calligraphy in Hsing Shu*

the Ch'ing calligraphers may also be so labelled. Eclecticism, in Chinese art at least, is not something that can be lightly brushed aside as unworthy of our serious attention. An eclectic begins his training by studying, analysing and modelling after the best that the past has to offer. In Chinese calligraphy, he has a choice between the old masters' manuscripts on the one hand and the ancient tablets on the other. Whatever his decision, he proceeds to eliminate what he considers to be the undesirable elements of the past. His is essentially the task of purge and purification. If he is gifted, he will in due course come up with something worthwhile, even a style distinctly his own. However, to the true eclectic, that is not enough, for he is also compelled to demonstrate at every opportunity his stylistic virtuosity and discerning taste. He feels obliged to show off his proficiency in all scripts and styles, old and new. He wants to tell us that he is a master thief able to transmute influence and style from almost any source. His work is often a frame of reference that embraces all artistic periods and stylistic vocabularies. This is why Chao Mêng-fu did the *Chi Chiu Chang* in *chang ts'ao* (Fig. 15) and Wên Chêng-ming the *Ch'ien Tzŭ Wên* in four scripts (Fig. 48a). This is a form of pedantry the eclectic just cannot resist.

Like thieves, there are good eclectics and bad ones. A good eclectic is quite capable of producing works which represent a high degree of aesthetic sophistication, an acquaintance and concern with the history of style. Speaking of Chinese painting of this type, James Cahill, the American student of Chinese painting, has called it 'art based on art based on art' and has compared it to evocative allusion in the fashion of 'Stravinsky playing upon Tchaikowsky or the Baroque, T. S. Eliot shifting into a Spenserian language, Picasso referring to primitive or Hellenic styles'. Whatever Cahill may think of this type of art, it is something which the Chinese love and cherish. A bad eclectic, of course, is like a dwarf who recklessly borrows a giant's robe and collapses under its weight. Fortunately we do not have to be bothered with him at all.

But in our study of Chinese calligraphy we do have to concern ourselves with a number of calligraphers who unashamedly admit that they are doing their pieces after the style of this and that old master or this and that tablet. They do not make any pretence at eclecticism. And yet their works are accepted as deserving serious attention. The catalogue of a Chinese calligraphy exhibition may contain as many names of old masters and ancient tablets as there are exhibitors. This sort of thing is of course scandalous, moribund and self-defeating. But the argument has been advanced in its defence that what these calligraphers are trying to do is not to innovate or originate but to refine their inheritance, which is rich and wondrous enough without any ambition to widen its scope. A more convincing argument is the analogy of music. Speaking of this sort of thing in Chinese painting, Fritz van Briessen, the German student of Chinese and Japanese art, said:

Fig 53a   Chao Chih-ch'ien: *Calligraphy in Chên Shu*

A Chinese painting is like a piece of music brought to life again by a brilliant pianist or violinist—coaxed out of an orchestra by the conductor's baton, as splendid and beautiful as ever, but in clumsy hands painfully bad. Chinese painting is often nothing more than a new rendering of a well-known piece, a variation on a theme, or even simply an *étude*. The important thing is the quality of the performance.

And at this point there is a second analogy between Chinese art and music: only when the technical problems have been mastered will the artist be able to express himself lucidly, for only then will the material differences which hinder pure expression have vanished. Of course, original compositions have also been produced in Chinese art at all times, but once created, they become part of the repertoire of all painters, to be reproduced again and again with new variations.

In other words, when we ask a pianist to perform for us at a party, we do not expect him to compose an original piece for the occasion. We only expect him to play an old masterpiece, and if he plays it well, we are quite prepared to applaud him and call him an artist. It is on the basis that they are 'performing' rather than 'creative' artists that we give recognition to this kind of calligrapher whose ranks are legion today.

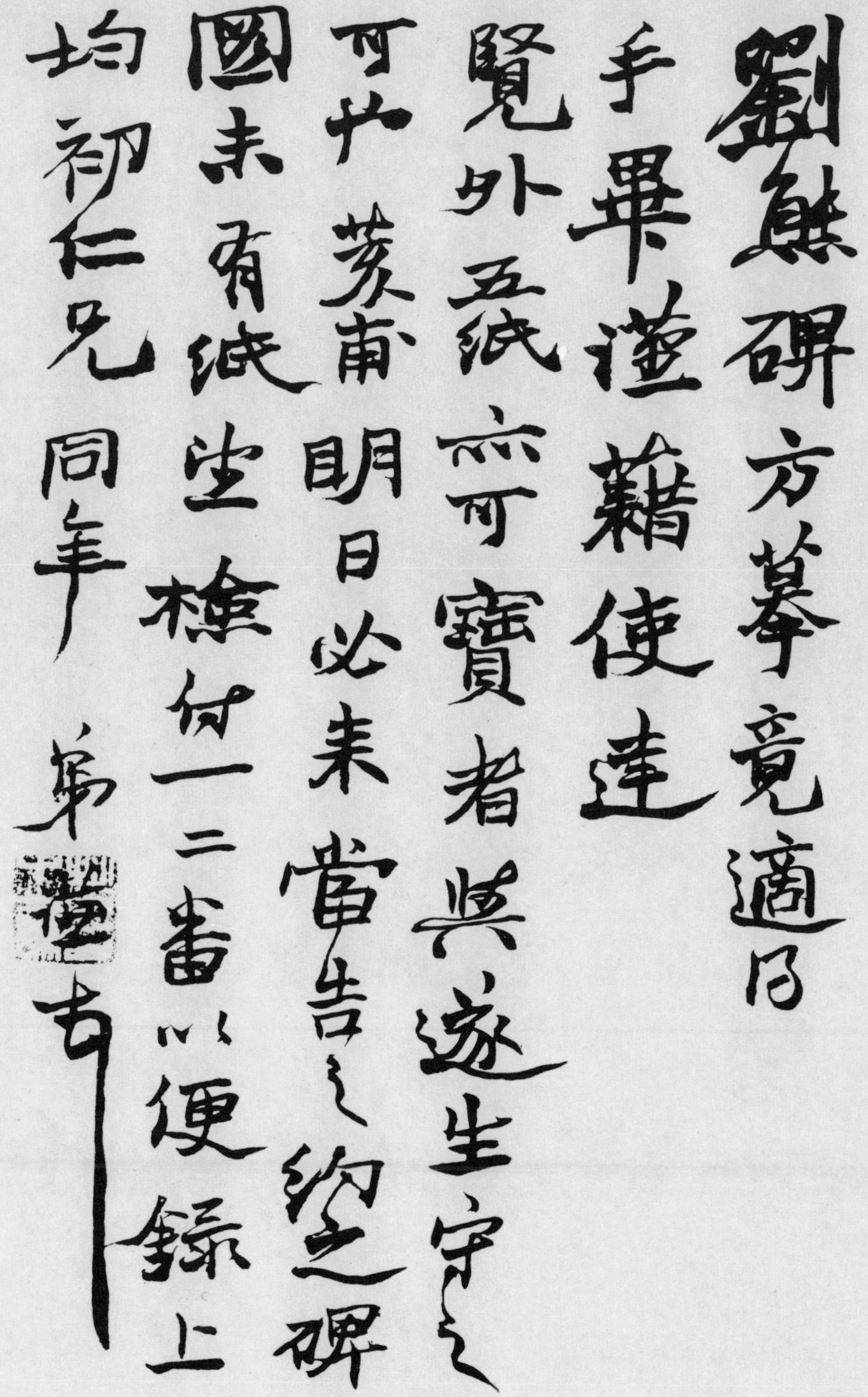

劉熊碑方募竟適日
手畢謹籍使連
覽外五紙乃寶者與遂生守ㄥ
可廿荔南明日必未當告ㄥ絕之碑
國未有彼坐檢付一二畫以便錄上
均初仁兄同年第撝古

Fig. 53b Chao Chih-ch'ien: *Calligraphy in Hsing Shu*. An informal letter to a fellow calligrapher

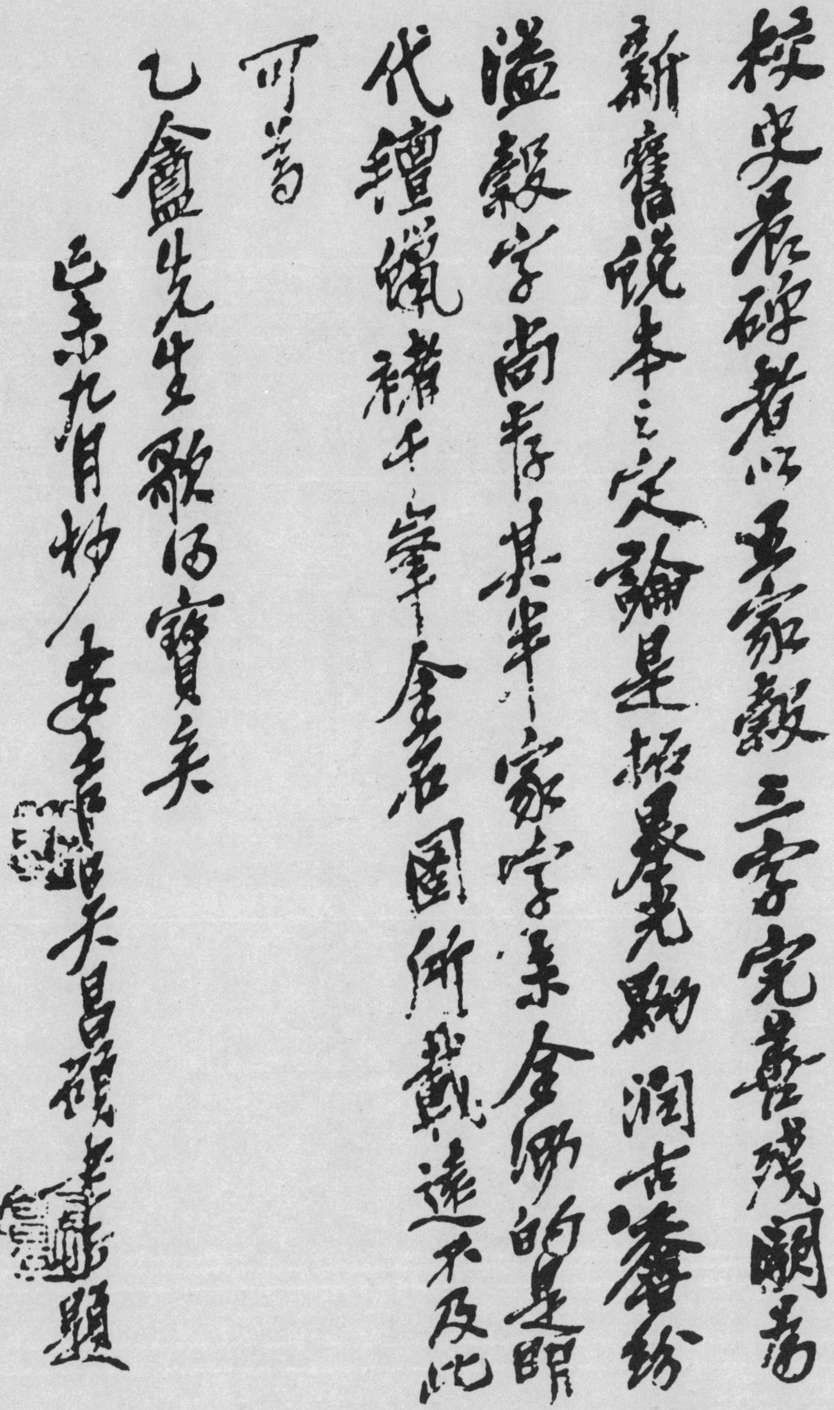

校史晨碑者以王家毅三字完整殘闕為
新舊說本之定論是矯枉過甚之談潤古塗紛
溢毅字尚存其半一家字皆金鄉的是明
代鐘鼎補千筆金石圖所載遠不及此
可若
乙盦先生歌泊寶美
己未九月杪 吳昌碩題

Fig. 54 Wu Chün-ch'ing: *Colophon to the Shih Ch'ên Pei*

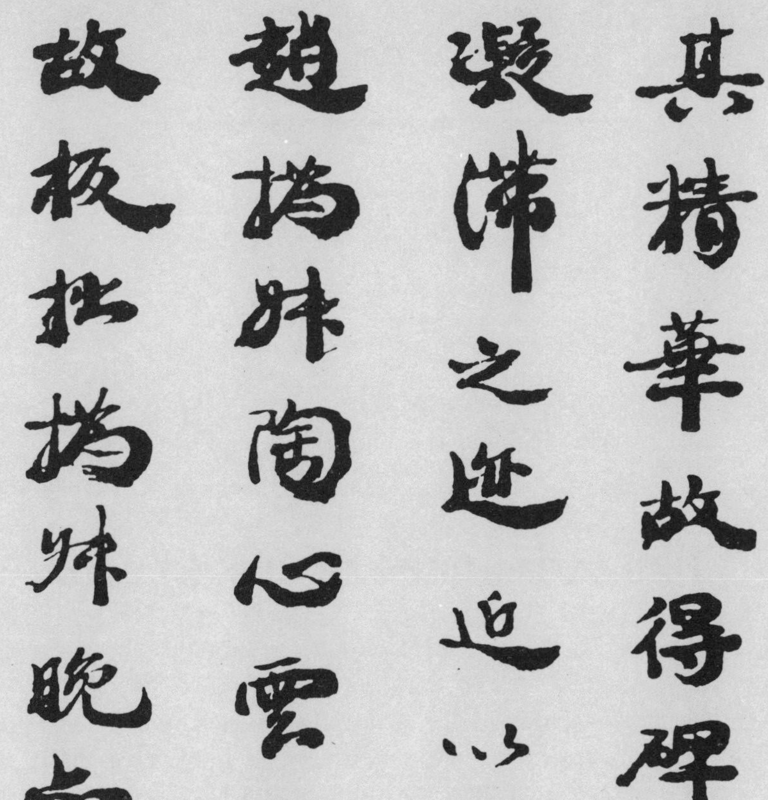

其精華故得碑意之厚而善

變沸之延追以篤北碑得者

趙撝叔陶心雲然誤法龍門

故板扡撝叔晚出篤鄭文公乃

Fig. 55 K'ang Yu-wei: *Calligraphy in Hsing Shu*

Chapter Ten

The Advances of Ts'ao Shu

Of the three modern scripts of the Chinese written language, *ts'ao shu* was the first to make its appearance. We would be in grave error if we were to regard it as a 'quick version' of *hsing shu*. In the Han Dynasty, the type of *ts'ao shu* known as *chang ts'ao*, supposedly innovated by Shih Yu in his transcription of the *Chi Chiu Chang*, was often used for the drafting of public documents, as we have seen on the Han wood and bamboo slips. Modern archaeology has discovered an even earlier form of *ts'ao shu* on the public documents of the Kingdom of Ch'u in the Period of the Warring States, which appears to be some sort of a cursory version of the *chuan shu*. Surprisingly this type of *ts'ao shu* was also used by the great literary figure of the Tsin Dynasty, Lu Chi (261-303), best known as the author of the immortal prose-poem on literature, *Wên Fu*. Lu Chi's *P'ing Fu T'ieh* (Fig. 56) is the earliest original calligraphic manuscript extant. In this miraculously preserved though badly deteriorated manuscript, we can see what may be regarded as a 'quick version' of *chuan shu*. However, the *chang ts'ao* of the Han Dynasty had shed all traces of *chuan shu* and had become a 'quick version' of *li shu*. Although in *chang ts'ao* characters the individual strokes were still separately executed, many of the elements making up the characters were boldly abbreviated or turned into symbols.

Chang Chih of the late Han Dynasty, and more particularly Wang Hsi-chih and his son Wang Hsien-chih, brought about a revolution in the *ts'ao shu* script. For one thing, they undertook to eliminate practically all the *li shu*, not to say the *chuan shu* features, from the *ts'ao shu*. In a way, *ts'ao shu* as

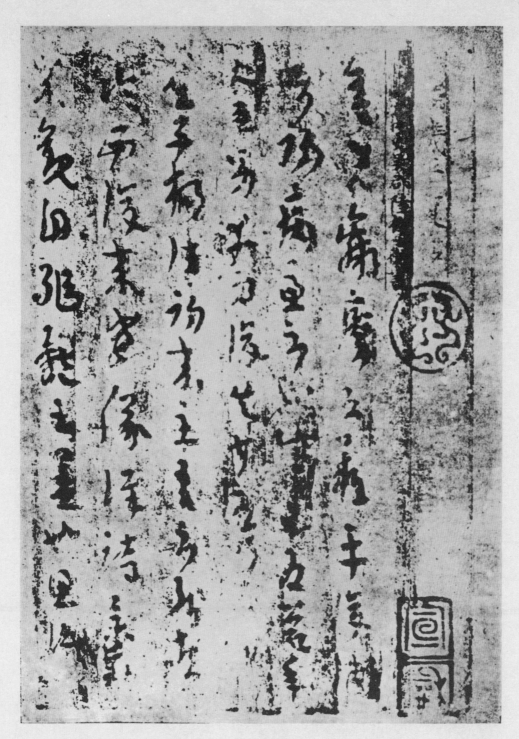

Fig. 56   Lu Chi: *P'ing Fu T'ieh*

executed by Chang Chih, Wang Hsi-chih and Wang Hsien-chih has become a form of non-representational art in the sense that the *ts'ao shu* characters they executed bear very little resemblance to the structural organization of the characters. Except for characters with a minimum of strokes, they have turned nearly all the elements into symbols, and it is for the connoisseur to learn the symbols before he can read the text. This line of development has deprived *ts'ao shu* of its place as a script for the transaction of everyday business and has turned it into an art form intelligible only to the thoroughly initiated.

Chang Chih and Wang Hsien-chih have generally been considered the innovators of the wild form of *ts'ao shu* known as *k'uang ts'ao*, which seems to have reached its culmination in the T'ang calligraphers Chang Hsü and Huai-su. Besides making more and more symbols for the various elements composing the characters, the addicts of *k'uang ts'ao* were in the habit of working at terrific speed, and in the case of Chang Hsü and Huai-su, often under the influence of liquor. They were prone to allow the brush the maximum freedom and to cast all conventions to the wind, with the result that many of the characters are completely illegible. Furthermore, in their mad drive for dramatic appeal, they chose to write the characters in any way they pleased so that the same character appeared in a variety of forms in the same text. Chang Hsü and Huai-su were both guilty of this practice, although the latter was regarded as less unbridled. The two men have had many admirers and imitators in subsequent periods, and *k'uang ts'ao* has become an established form of Chinese calligraphy and has exerted an enormous influence upon Japanese calligraphy.

The T'ang and Sung masters, taken as a whole, were not devotees of *k'uang ts'ao*. The manuscripts they did in *ts'ao shu* may be regarded as conventional in the sense that they tried to conform as far as possible with the acknowledged symbols, especially those created by Wang Hsi-chih. This is certainly true with Sun Ch'ien-li (Fig. 35) whose style is strikingly similar to that of Wang Hsi-chih (Fig. 20). The same applies to the *ts'ao shu* of the Yüan master Chao Mêng-fu and the Ming master Chu Yün-ming.

One of Chao Mêng-fu's contemporaries, Hsien-yü Shu, was probably the best *ts'ao shu* calligrapher since the end of the T'ang Dynasty. An official of the Mongol court with an indifferent record as an administrator, Hsien-yü Shu was a brilliant antiquarian, a poet of genius, versed in every branch of knowledge, and endowed with a stimulatingly daring mind. Fame was not slow in taking him under her wing, and he soon became almost as admired as the great Chao Mêng-fu. There was an ugly rumour to the effect that Chao Mêng-fu was jealous of Hsien-yü Shu's calligraphic achievements and secretly bought up the latter's work to be destroyed. This story appears to be a fabrication deliberately circulated by Hsien-yü Shu's admirers to underline the extent of his artistic merits.

[166]

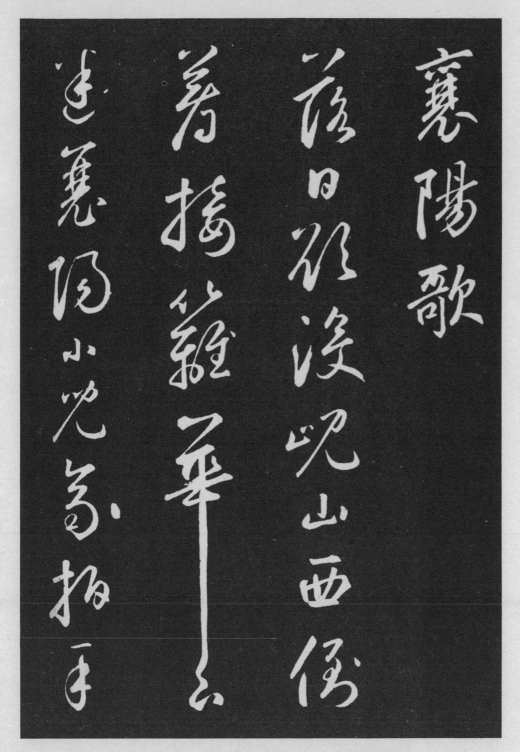

Fig. 57   Hsien-yü Shu: *Hsiang Yang Ko* (detail)

Hsien-yü Shu's specialty is in *ts'ao shu* of the more conventional type. In fact, his best work is a script which is halfway between *hsing shu* and *ts'ao shu,* as may be seen in his transcription of the *Hsiang Yang Ko* done in 1300 (Fig. 57). It is quite evident that he was in no haste. His characters were done slowly and deliberately, creating calligraphic forms that are at once readily legible and appealing. As far as *ts'ao shu* is concerned, Chao Mêng-fu had good reason to be jealous of him. It has been said that, although Wang Hsien-chih's *ts'ao shu* is justly renowned, he always did his characters with an eye to their structural organization in *chên shu.* Hsien-yü Shu, it may be said, belongs to the same school.

The question of *k'uang ts'ao* has given rise to a sharp difference of opinion among calligraphers and critics alike. Su Shih, in a colophon on one of Chang Hsü's manuscripts, castigated the *ts'ao shu* specialists in these words:

Some calligraphers specializing in *ts'ao shu* claim that they do not know how to do *chên shu* and *hsing shu* well. This is all wrong! *Chên shu* gives rise to *hsing shu* which in turn gives rise to *ts'ao shu.* To do *chên shu* is like a child learning to stand on his feet, *hsing shu* to walk and *ts'ao shu* to run. I have never heard of a child who could run before he could stand up and walk.

In this statement Su Shih is guilty of historical inaccuracy because in point of time *ts'ao shu* antedated *chên shu* and *hsing shu* by quite a few centuries and cannot therefore be regarded as their derivative. However, Su Shih does have a point in saying that, when all the scripts are there, one should train one's hand first in *chên shu* in order to gain mastery over the stroke execution and structural organization so fundamental to good calligraphy before plunging into the more difficult and sophisticated *ts'ao shu.* It is really a matter of commonsense.

A standing criticism of *ts'ao shu,* particularly *k'uang ts'ao,* is that characters written in it are often illegible to the laymen, sometimes even to the experts. For this reason it is common practice for *ts'ao shu* manuscripts to be accompanied by a text in *chên shu* unless the text is something which most people have learned by heart, such as the *Ch'ien Tzǔ Wên.* To some people, the whole thing is utterly ridiculous. For instance, the great Ming scholar Ku Yen-wu, whose views are always entitled to the utmost respect, is of the belief that it is nonsensical if not insulting to address a communication to someone in a script which the recipient cannot read. 'If you do not respect others, you are not showing any respect for yourself,' he said. Besides, for persons to be corresponding in an illegible script may lead to disastrous consequences. Ku Yen-wu tells the story of a T'ang official who upon receiving an edict in *ts'ao shu* which he could not read became panic-stricken and fled from his post. After all, what is the idea of leaving a note to your servant in characters which he cannot decipher? Ku Yen-wu's question appears unanswerable.

To the calligraphers, however, *ts'ao shu* is too good an art form to be abandoned. One way to overcome the question of illegibility is to standardize

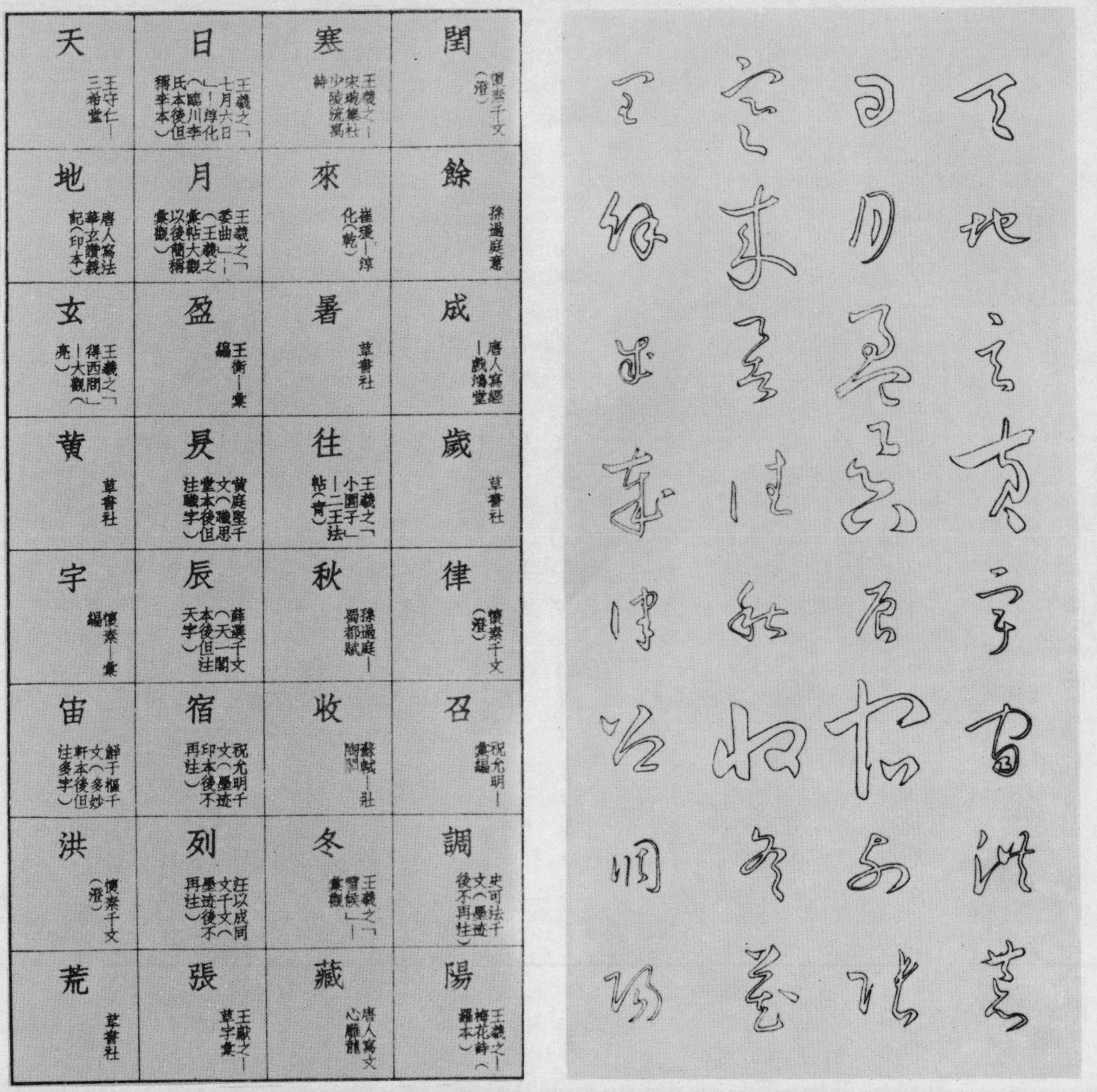

Fig. 58 Yü Yu-jên: *Piao Chun Ts'ao Shu*. Reproduction of the first page consisting of 32 characters. Notation in *chên shu* on the left indicates that the *ts'ao shu* characters are taken from Wang Hsi-chih, Wang Hsien-chih, Sun Ch'ien-li, Huai-su, Su Shih, Huang T'ing-chien, Hsien-yü Shu and Chu Yün-ming, in addition to four devised by Yü Yu-jên himself, to name only those calligraphers we have known

the way each character is written. Suppose a good *ts'ao shu* calligrapher were to transcribe some well-known literary piece such as the *Ch'ien Tzŭ Wên* and have it widely distributed as a model for all to emulate. After a while, all the *ts'ao shu* characters would become standardized and legible to those who take the trouble to learn them. This was exactly what the monk Chih-yung (Wang Hsi-chih's descendant) had in mind when he spent thirty years transcribing the *Ch'ien Tzŭ Wên* eight hundred times for wide distribution. Chih-yung had two purposes in mind: to try to standardize the *ts'ao shu* characters and at the same time to propagate the calligraphic style of his illustrious ancestor. However commendable such an effort might be, Chih-yung's purposes were destined to be unfulfilled. All through the subsequent centuries, new styles of *ts'ao shu* kept appearing and *k'uang ts'ao* was as wild as ever, as we have seen in the case of Chang Hsü and Huai-su.

More than thirteen centuries later, another man took up where Chih-yung left off. He is our contemporary Yü Yu-jên, one of the revolutionaries who helped found the Chinese Republic. Born in Shensi in 1878, Yü Yu-jên found time in his eventful political career to collect and study thousands of tablets and manuscripts in *ts'ao shu*. In a book first published in 1936 under the title *Piao Chun Ts'ao Shu,* which has become a classic, Yü Yu-jên and his associates make a careful comparison of the many ways a character has been written in *ts'ao shu* by the old masters and select one of the ways as the standard. In making the selection, Yü Yu-jên tries his best to conform to four tests he has set up himself, namely (1) easily legible, (2) easy to write, (3) accurate, and (4) aesthetically appealing. Following the age-old practice, he adopts the *Ch'ien Tzŭ Wên* as the text. The general rule is to choose from the old masters as far as possible. Only when nothing staisfactory can be found in the tablets and manuscripts does Yü Yu-jên resort to devising a character-structure of his own, which is decided upon after careful consideration by a panel of specialists over which he presides. The result is a composite vocabulary of one thousand characters in *ts'ao shu* which embraces the best the past has to offer. Each character is presented in outline form and *chên shu* notations indicating the source are found on the opposite page (Fig. 58). All through the years, Yü Yu-jên and his associates have kept up their labours, revising the book over and over again as new sources are found.

Yü Yu-jên spreads his net wide, from characters found on the Han slips to those by some of the Ch'ing calligraphers such as Fu Shan. A rough tabulation shows that, of the one thousand characters of the *Ch'ien Tzŭ Wên,* by far the largest number (215) comes from Wang Hsi-chih, still the un-challenged master of all time. The second largest selection (128) is from Huai-su, followed by Sun Ch'ien-li with 61. Surprisingly, Wang Hsien-chih, so highly renowned for his *ts'ao shu,* is represented by only 19 characters, while Chih-yung has 26 to offer. Yü Yu-jên has taken some characters from the Han calligraphers Chang Chih (6) and Chung Yu (7). Chang Hsü,

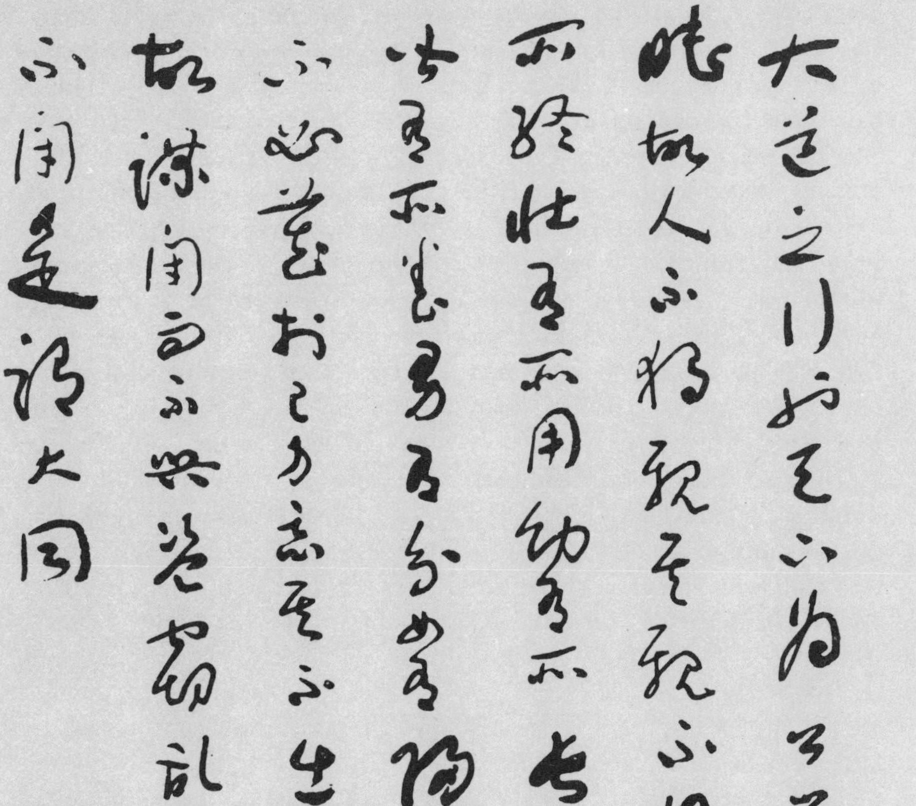

大道之行也，天下為公，選賢與能，講信修睦，故人不獨親其親，不獨子其子，使老有所終，壯有所用，幼有所長，矜寡孤獨廢疾者皆有所養，男有分，女有歸，貨惡其棄於地也，不必藏於己，力惡其不出於身也，不必為己，是故謀閉而不興，盜竊亂賊而不作，故外戶而不閉，是謂大同

于右任

Fig. 59 Yü Yu-jên: *Ta T'ung P'ien*

despite his fame as 'the sage of *ts'ao shu*', has only one single character to contribute, presumably because his *k'uang ts'ao* characters are not conducive to isolated presentation. Most of the *chên shu* and *hsing shu* calligraphers have their contributions to make: Ou-yang Hsün (6), Ch'u Shui-liang (3), Yen Chên-ch'ing (5), Liu Kung-ch'üan (3), Ts'ai Hsiang (2), Su Shih (10), Huang T'ing-chien (6), and Mi Fu (18). In the Yüan and Ming period, the contributors are: Hsien-yü Shu (6), Wên Chêng-ming (12), Chu Yün-ming (13), and Tung Ch'i-ch'ang (17). Although Yü Yu-jên would undoubtedly like to base his entire vocabulary on the old masters, he was compelled to devise no less than 72 characters to fill the gaps.

It is as yet too early to say whether Yü Yu-jên has succeeded in bringing some order into the chaotic situation of *ts'ao shu* and whether his ambition to make the script one for general practical use has been fulfilled. On the occasion of Yü Yu-jên's eighty-sixth birthday in April 1964, there was in Taipei a mammoth exhibition of *ts'ao shu* done in his style, indicating that calligraphers in modern China are supporting his cause. Whether or not the trend will prevail in the future, there should be no doubt at all that Yü Yu-jên himself is easily the most outstanding and most conspicuously successful calligrapher in the Republican period with incalculable influence on the calligraphy of our time. Like the Ch'ing calligraphers, Yü Yu-jên began his training by modelling after the ancient tablets, particularly those of the Northern Wei Dynasty. His *chên shu,* as seen by the epitaphs he did for the parents of some of his friends, including the mother of Chiang Kai-shek, is deceptively simple and hauntingly elegant. Since 1931, Yü Yu-jên has been devoting himself wholeheartedly to the perfection of his *ts'ao shu.* We can take any one of his scrolls, such as his transcription of the *Ta T'ung P'ien* from the ancient classics (Fig. 59), and check each character against the characters in his book *Piao Chun Ts'ao Shu* and we will find that he has adhered strictly to the forms he has chosen. It is a most remarkable performance indeed.

In his book Yü Yu-jên has also laid down a number of basic principles on calligraphy which are a tremendous improvement upon the abstract and abstruse terms habitually used in the manuals and commentaries. Quoting from the old masters, especially Wang Hsi-chih, Yü Yu-jên formulates the following points to guide calligraphers:

(a) Conceive of an image of the finished character in the mind before applying the brush to the writing surface. (We have often seen a Chinese calligrapher working at great speed. While speed is not necessarily a mark of good calligraphy, the Chinese calligrapher is able to achieve it because he has a pre-conceived notion of what he is doing. With a trained hand, he can transmit his mental image to the writing surface seemingly without much effort.)

[172]

(b) Make full use of every hair at the tip of the brush. (We shall have more to say on this point when we come to discuss the technique of brushmanship.)

(c) Introduce as many variations into the strokes and structures as possible.

(d) The dots and strokes forming a character should be made to bear integral relationship one with another as if they are linked together like the circulatory system of the human body.

(e) Avoid making a stroke cross another stroke unnecessarily. (Some strokes in a Chinese character are meant to cross each other. The character *shih*, 'ten', for instance, is a simple cross of a horizontal line by a vertical line. But when the character-structure does not call for crossing, it is wise to avoid it.)

(f) Avoid causing strokes and elements to touch or collide with one another. (This means that the visual effect of the strokes and elements should not be spoiled or deformed by other strokes or elements which have no integral relationship with them.)

(g) Avoid making too many 'eyes'. (*Ts'ao shu* permits the use of circles and lobes as elements of a character. For instance, a horizontal stroke may be linked with a vertical stroke without lifting the brush from the writing surface. The connection may take the appearance of a circle or lobe which is technically known as an 'eye'. One 'eye' in a character may be pleasing, but it should not be overdone. In the mental image mentioned in (a) above, the calligrapher should first plan the character in his mind so that if he wishes to make an 'eye' in the element to the left, he should try to avoid making another one in the element to the right.)

(h) Avoid drawing parallel lines and making symmetrical elements. (It has been said. 'The virtue of an equilibrium is that it is easily upset: the thrill it communicates comes from its delicate tension.' Yü Yu-jên is applying the same idea to calligraphy.)

These are principles which Yü Yu-jên tells us he has derived from his life-long study of calligraphy. He has followed them scrupulously in his own works. With the possible exception of (g) above concerning 'eyes' (the T'ang calligrapher Li Yung employs the 'eye' even in *chên shu* and the Ch'ing calligrapher Chêng Hsieh employs it in *hsing shu*—Fig. 51b), all the principles enunciated are equally applicable to *chên shu* and *hsing shu*. It would be most profitable for us to check these principles, except (a), against the calligraphic specimens we have seen. We will find that even some of the greatest artists, such as Wang Hsien-chih and Su Shih, are guilty of violating some of the principles, as Yü Yu-jên himself has pointed out. Yü Yu-jên has made a great contribution to the art of calligraphy by defining the structural principles in such clearcut and unmistakable terms.

Chapter Eleven

The Learning Process

A poet, it has been said, is born, not made. A calligrapher, like a painter, requires a long apprenticeship and gets off to a tardy start. The full command of the brush comes only after years, even decades, of intensive training and practice and extensive study of the works of the acknowledged masters. Even Wang Hsi-chih, who showed great promise while a boy, did not come to full flowering until middle age. A child prodigy in calligraphy is at best an oddity, not an artist.

In learning calligraphy, as in learning golf, the first lesson begins with the grip, the proper way to hold the stem of the brush. The beginner is supplied with a diagram (Fig. 60) showing the respective positions of the several fingers. It should be made perfectly clear that all Chinese are expected to write with the right hand. No consideration whatsoever is given to the person who happens to be left-handed. A diagram of the grip in an elementary manual carries instructions which may be summarized as follows:

1. Remember that all five fingers have their separate roles to play in the grip of the brush. No finger is superfluous. Wrap the first section of the index finger on the brush-stem from the outside and back it up with the thumb on the inside, holding the brush in an upright position perpendicular to the writing surface. Then wrap the first section of the middle finger on the brush-stem immediately under the index finger and balance it with the foremost knuckle of the ring finger on the inside. The brush is now in firm control. The little finger is placed back of the ring finger as a support.

2. Keep the wrist parallel to the desk surface as much as possible. In writing small characters (*chên shu* characters as small as the fly's head), the elbow may rest on the desk. In writing large characters the elbow should be suspended, while the forearm should be almost parallel to the desk surface.

3. Keep the palm hollow. The finger-tips should not touch the palm. The hollow space in the palm should be large enough to hold an egg.

4. Keep the brush upright all the time. Do not tip or slant it.

These are the most elementary principles. Some manuals go into considerably more detail concerning the grip and, as in golf, there are several variations of the grip. The grip shown in the diagram and described above, with both the index and middle fingers wrapping the brush-stem from the outside, is technically known as *shuang kou*, i.e. double wrap.* It is the most common grip. However, some calligraphers prefer to have only the index finger wrapping the brush-stem from the outside, leaving the middle, the ring and the little finger on the inside. This grip is known as *tan kou*, i.e., single wrap. Generally speaking, these are the two main grips used by the calligraphers. We have been told that the double wrap is preferred for doing characters in *chên shu*, *hsing shu* and *ts'ao shu,* while the single wrap is more suitable for doing characters in *chuan shu* and *pa fên*. However, not all calligraphers are in agreement on this point.

Wei Shuo, Wang Hsi-chih's tutor, has laid down some rules on the position of the hand in relation to the brush-pen. We do not propose to go into her rules because opinion differs considerably about them. Broadly speaking, a brush-stem may be divided into three sections—upper, middle and lower. The general practice is to hold the brush-stem lower when doing small characters in *chên shu* and to hold it in the middle section when doing large characters in *hsing shu*. It has also been said that one should hold the brush-stem in the upper section when doing characters in *ts'ao shu*. When the brush-stem is held at the very top, it is sometimes known as *hsüan chên*, 'suspended needle'.† Some calligraphers use all five fingers to hold the brush-stem at the top, while others use only three fingers, leaving the ring and the little fingers idle (Fig. 47b). The 'suspended needle' grip is generally employed when writing large characters.

Su Shih once said: 'There are no established rules governing the grip; the basic technique is to keep the fingers firm and the palm hollow.' Different calligraphers have different grips and they may change the grip to do the

---

* In the technical language of Chinese calligraphy, the term *shuang kou,* in exactly the same two characters, has also been used to describe the process of drawing the outline of the characters as in the case of the characters in Yü Yu-jên's *Piao Chun Ts'ao Shu* (Fig. 58). *Shuang kou* in this sense is a technique used for tracing manuscripts for stone- or wood-carving.

† Like so many terms relating to Chinese calligraphy, the term *hsüan chên*, besides applying to the grip, has been applied to other aspects of the art. In doing *hsing shu* and *ts'ao shu,* some calligraphers like to over-extend the middle, vertical stroke of some characters as a demonstration of controlled brushmanship, as may be seen in Fig. 40 (Su Shih) and Fig. 42 (Huang T'ing-chien). This practice is also known as *hsüan chên*.

different scripts. For the novice, however, it is advisable to adopt the standard grip at least at the initial stage, namely the *shuang kou* (Fig. 60).

When doing calligraphy on a desk, the left elbow should be extended outward to allow the right hand holding the brush to occupy a position directly under the nose, the idea being to keep the brush action in full view of both eyes. This is the most natural position, so no further explanation is necessary. The question of the right elbow, however, is complicated and controversial. As a rule, the fingers are used to do small characters, the wrist to do middle-sized characters, and the elbow to do large characters. To achieve the best effect, some manuals suggest that in doing small *chên shu* characters the left hand may be placed under the right wrist to serve as a support, and that in doing middle-sized *chên shu* characters the elbow may rest on the desk while the wrist is suspended. In doing large characters in all scripts, the whole arm should be suspended.

From this brief description, we can see that the brush grip, like the golf grip, is unnatural and requires a great deal of practice. At first the fingers will be quite sore and the whole hand will tremble, making it very difficult to do even a smooth, straight stroke. The suspended elbow or arm is the hardest part of the exercise and the muscles will be strained and painful. It is wise to begin writing very large characters with the suspended elbow and then gradually working down to smaller and smaller characters. To be able to write small *chên shu* characters with the elbow suspended has always been considered a supreme achievement. And yet, according to Huang T'ing-chien, his good friend Su Shih never suspended his elbow in doing his wonderful calligraphy!

The normal and natural way for the beginner to practise the grip is for him to do the basic strokes forming the Chinese characters. Over the centuries, literally hundreds of manuals, some of which were written by great calligraphers such as Wei Shuo, Wang Hsi-chih, Ou-yang Hsün and Yen Chên-ch'ing, instructed the novice how to begin his lessons. Since *chên shu* is the script to begin, the manuals by and large are confined to characters in this script to the neglect of others, and the first step is to break down the Chinese characters into their basic strokes.

What are the basic strokes? According to a widely accepted theory, the Chinese characters may be broken down into eight basic strokes, all of which are to be found in the character *yung,* 'perpetual' (Fig. 61). The character *yung* is the first character in Wang Hsi-chih's *Lan T'ing Hsü.* The great master, according to one story, laboured for fifteen years to get that character exactly right. Carrying on the Wang family tradition, the monk Chih-yung, whose name happens to contain the character *yung,* went on to develop the theory of the eight basic strokes, known as the *yung tzŭ pa fa,* 'the eight methods of the character *yung',* which is in essence the definition of the correct and proper way to do the basic strokes of the Chinese characters.

[176]

Fig. 60 *The Brush Grip*

As a result, the term *pa fa,* 'eight methods', has for the sake of semantic convenience become identified with the art of calligraphy on the same basis that the *lu fa,* 'six methods', as stated by the Southern Ch'i Dynasty art historian and critic Hsieh Ho, has come to represent the summation of the art of painting. It has been contended that 'the character *yung* embodies the structure of all characters' and that the eight strokes composing it are basic to all calligraphic exercises. The Sui-T'ang calligrapher Yü Shih-nan studied the art under Chih-yung and inherited the *pa fa* from his teacher. Yü Shih-nan's contemporary, Ou-yang Hsün, made some modifications of the theory and Yen Chên-ch'ing wrote a song in eight lines in its praise.

Although backed by such high authorities, to break down all Chinese characters into the eight basic strokes of the character *yung* leaves many vexing problems unresolved. For one thing, it is rather arbitrary to divide the mainly vertical element in the centre of the character *yung* into three separate strokes. In modern practice, such as in the dictionary (consulting a Chinese dictionary involves counting the number of strokes forming the character), the whole element, i.e. strokes 2, 3 and 4 as indicated in the diagram (Fig. 61), is counted as one continuous stroke. The same is true with the sharply angular element to the left, i.e. the element formed by strokes 5 and 6 according to the diagram. The result is that, in the standard dictionary, the character *yung* consists only of five, and not eight strokes. Such a situation is bound to confuse the child beginning to learn to write. Furthermore, the horizontal stroke, which is found in a large number of characters, is represented in the character *yung* by a short bar near the top, i.e. stroke 2 in the diagram. This is quite unsatisfactory since the horizontal stroke done in considerable length is often the principal stroke serving the purpose of unifying the various parts of a character. A child who has learned how to do the short horizontal bar in the character *yung* is, therefore, in no position to do the extended horizontal stroke. In addition, the right-angled stroke which normally forms the upper right-hand corner of a rectangle found so often in Chinese characters is in the diagram broken up into two separate strokes (strokes 2 and 3 in the diagram) with the result that the child is not given the opportunity to learn how to turn a right-angular corner. Finally, the central vertical stroke in the character *yung* ends up in a hook (strokes 3 and 4 in the diagram) instead of making a termination by itself, which is the case of most vertical strokes in Chinese characters. All these objections, it may be said, are perfectly valid, and we are at a loss as to why the *pa fa* has won so much support in the past.

The Chinese artists and scholars have been paying lip service to the *pa fa* out of respect for its distinguished originators. It is bad taste if not sacrilegious to question the validity of a system derived from such high authorities. However, the child must be taught to write well and the *pa fa* is patently inadequate for the purpose. In subsequent centuries, other manuals of instruction have appeared from time to time, and the modern ones are equipped with motion

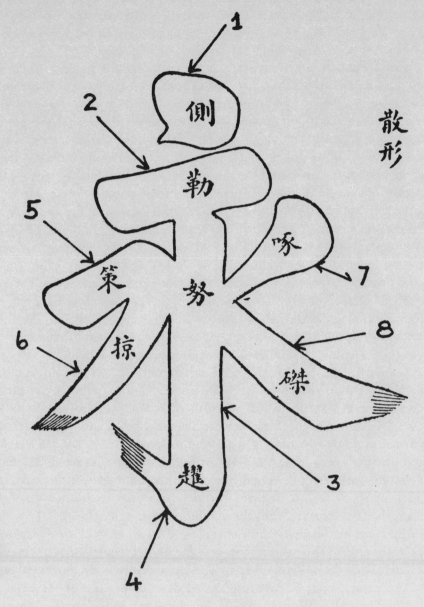

散形

Fig. 61 *Yung Tzŭ Pa Fa* (The Eight Basic Strokes)

pictures and sound tracks. The literature on the subject is vast and often highly technical. For the purpose of this book, it seems wise for us to give a summary of one of the most comprehensive manuals published—*Shu Fa Chêng Chuan* (The Standard Book of Calligraphy) by the Ch'ing Dynasty writer Fêng Wu —which is also an anthology of writings on the subject.

Fêng Wu, of course, was too much of a classical scholar to denounce the *pa fa* or to discard it altogether. He still retained the concept that the strokes forming the Chinese characters could be reduced to eight basic ones. However, without specifically saying so, he very subtly dissociated the *pa fa* from the character *yung* (although several diagrams of the character *yung* were still included in his book) and undertook to turn the eight basic strokes into entities in their own right. He then went on to elaborate on the eight basic strokes, dividing each one of them into several possible forms. He ended up with a list of thirty-two basic strokes, which he called the *san shih erh fa,* 'thirty-two methods'. It was Fêng Wu's contention that, instead of having only eight basic strokes, there should be eight basic groups of strokes. He further taught us that, for the sake of variety and aesthetic appeal, the same stroke should be done slightly differently when closely juxtaposed. For instance, quite a number of characters consist of the element formed by a row of four dots. It is obvious that each one of the dots should be done slightly differently so that they do not appear as a string of identical beads. The same principle applies to parallel horizontals or verticals. In other words, Fêng Wu tried to tell us that, in good calligraphy, strokes should not be done uniformly in the same manner, while at the same time the novice should not be allowed to innovate at his free will. After studying the subject thoroughly over a lifetime (he lived to be more than eighty), it was his belief that his scheme of thirty-two basic strokes would cover most if not all the varieties to be desired. Fêng Wu's thirty-two strokes are shown on pages 182 to 186.

Besides instructing the pupil how to do the basic strokes, the manuals also teach him how not to do them. Further labouring on the number eight, the manuals have come up with the concept of the eight 'diseases' (*pa ping*) of calligraphy, each one of which is explained by an analogy to the shape of an ordinary object. The instructor in calligraphy is expected to help his pupils to avoid making the unsightly shapes. The eight 'diseases' are shown on page 187.

The point cannot be over-emphasized that the practice of the basic strokes outlined above applies only to *chên shu* characters and is intended for the rank beginner, such as a child below ten years of age. It is a process of acquiring the rudimentary techniques of writing Chinese characters in which the question of artistic presentation is too early to be involved.

After gaining the proper grip of the brush and familiarity with the basic strokes, the beginner is in a position to do the individual characters. His introduction to the subject is the all-important question of what may be called

Fig. 62 *Squared Practice Sheet*. Characters by Chao Mêng-fu

1 THE DOT — eight varieties

Standard, as in

Suspended pearl, as in

Pearl drop, as in

Dragon claw, as in

Melon seed, as in

Almond, as in

Plum nut, as in

Stone bar, as in

立
系
寸
シ
火
一
公
且

2   THE HORIZONTAL — two varieties

Standard, as in

Extended, as in

3   THE VERTICAL — four varieties

Standard, as in

Suspended needle, as in

Ivory slab, as in

Right angle, as in

4   THE HOOK — seven varieties

亅   Standard, as in   求

乚   Flying geese, as in   成

乚   Dragon tail, as in   也

乁   Phoenix wing, as in   風

乛   Lion mouth, as in   句

乚   Double, as in   長

乚   Canopy, as in   冗

[184]

5   THE SLANTED UPWARD STROKE — two varieties

Standard, as in 孔

Extended, as in 耳

6   THE SLANTED DOWNWARD STROKE — three varieties

Standard, as in 孝

Suspended spear, as in 月

Fluttering ribbon, as in 列

7　THE SLANTED HORIZONTAL TO THE LEFT — four varieties

Standard, as in

Fluttering butterfly, as in

Coiled dragon, as in

Singing locust, as in

8　THE SLANTED HORIZONTAL TO THE RIGHT — two varieties

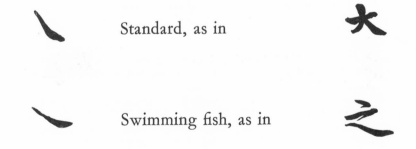

Standard, as in

Swimming fish, as in

Ox head

Mouse tail

Wasp waist

Stork knee

Bamboo joint

Water-chestnut

Broken branch

Loaded pole

stroke-sequence, that is, which stroke should be done first and which follows. There are general rules governing stroke-sequence with only very minor exceptions. The normal procedure is to start with the part or parts of the character on the left side and following with those on the right. In doing the different parts, the customary practice is to commence with the topmost part and work downwards. However, in doing the cross, the horizontal stroke should be done first. In doing the square, the vertical stroke to the left should be done first. Practice models provided for the beginner usually have numerals indicating the stroke-sequence. The first elements he learns are the radicals. Since most characters consist of one or more radicals, it does not take long for the novice to get used to the stroke-sequence. The ability to do the characters in accordance with stroke-sequence is the foundation of writing. Wrong stroke-sequence is an unpardonable offence, a mark of the illiterate. Besides, it will make the finished character look odd and unsightly.

The practice of stroke-sequence begins with the radicals. The pupil is expected to do them over and over again until the process comes naturally to him. The next step is to put the radicals together to form characters. Whether a character is well composed or not depends largely on how the character is constructed—the formal arrangement of strokes and elements. At this stage the pupil is provided with practice sheets consisting of squares each one of which is subdivided into nine small squares. The novice is called upon to write the characters in the large squares, using the sub-divisions as guides to help him place the component parts of the characters in their correct relationship with other parts. Of course the beginner cannot be expected to know where to place what. He is therefore given a model to copy (Fig. 62). Practising with squared sheets and squared models is fundamental to the learning process and should be undertaken for a lengthy period of time. The teacher usually advises the pupil to do the same character over and over again. A practice sheet consisting of fifty or so characters may be used for many years.

When the pupil has acquired a reasonable measure of proficiency, he is encouraged to abandon the squared practice sheet and to model after the manuscripts of the masters. The process is known as *lin* more or less on the same principle of the art student copying the pictures in the gallery. The manuscript is placed either in front or to the left of the student who does his copying stroke by stroke and character by character. The number of models at his choice is wellnigh limitless. The most popular ones are the works in large *chên shu* characters of some of the T'ang masters, especially Ou-yang Hsün (Fig. 28a), Yen Chên-ch'ing (Fig. 30b) and Liu Kung-ch'üan (Fig. 32). Wang Hsi-chih's *Huang T'ing Ching* (Fig. 17b) and Chung Shao-ching's *Ling Fei Ching* (Fig. 36) are excellent models from which to learn small *chên shu* characters. The works of the Sung masters, being unconventional, are seldom used at the initial stage. In more recent times, the works of the

Yüan master Chao Mêng-fu (Fig. 46b) and the Ming master Tung Ch'i-ch'ang (Fig. 50) have gained considerable popularity, and tablets in *chên shu,* such as the *Chang Mêng-lung Pei* (Fig. 25), are sometimes used. After practising *chên shu* for some time, working from the larger to the smaller characters, the pupil is in a position to try his hand at *hsing shu,* of which Wang Hsi-chih's *Shêng Chiao Hsü* (Fig. 19) and *Lan T'ing Hsü* (Fig. 18a and Fig. 18b) are the basic texts. Only at an advanced stage is the pupil permitted to learn *ts'ao shu,* and the standard model is Wang Hsi-chih's *Shih Ch'i T'ieh* (Fig. 20).

Good calligraphy begins with the ability to control, manipulate and master the brush. Yü Yu-jên was voicing a well-established principle when he told us to make full use of every hair of the tip of the brush. This is technically known as *chung fêng,* an effect achieved by holding the brush in a perfectly upright position, perpendicular to the writing surface. This will enable the hair of the brush-tip to spread out evenly in all directions. Whether a stroke is done in *chung fêng* or not may be tested by watching the way the ink dries on the paper. If the fringes dry first, leaving momentarily a wet streak in the middle, the brush is held in the correct position. It is generally agreed among experts that, when a manuscript done in *chung fêng* is held up against the light, a thin line of thick ink should be seen running in the middle of the stroke, even when the stroke turns at sharp angles or in curves. Mi Fu told us that one of the best examples of *chung fêng* is Su Shih's transcription of the *Ch'ih Pi Fu* (Fig. 39). Unfortunately the effect cannot be discerned in photographic reproductions. 'The entire piece is done in *chung fêng*' remains to this day a standard phrase of critical acclaim.

Like all good principles, some exceptions are allowed, provided that they are done in moderation and in good taste. Most good calligraphers have attempted to introduce a certain measure of variation into their characters, and one of the variations is the use of the slanted brush (*ts'ê fêng*) at some strategic points, with the purpose of achieving a more graceful posture in the characters. This practice may be seen in the works of such great calligraphers as Wang Hsi-chih, Wang Hsien-chih, Su Shih, Huang T'ing-chien, Chao Mêng-fu, Tung Ch'i-ch'ang, among others. An accomplished calligrapher, it seems, is one who follows the *chung fêng* as a matter of principle but who also allows himself the luxury of occasional departures here and there as a device to enhance the aesthetic appeal.

When applying the brush to the writing surface, the natural impulse is simply to drag it across, leaving the two ends pointed. The oldest character done with the brush we have discovered, written on a shard found among the oracle bones, was done precisely in this manner. Sophistication in brush-writing calls for hiding the marks of the brush-tip, a technique known as *ts'ang fêng,* which came into being with the general use of the brush and the adoption of *chuan shu* as the script. The *chuan shu* strokes, as we have seen, are done with all terminations carefully and symmetrically rounded. This must have appeared rather monotonous to the artistically inclined Han people who forthwith introduced the wavy lines and pointed flicks in *li shu* and *pa fên*. From that time on, a character is done with two types of strokes —the blunted terminations of some strokes and the pointed ones of others. In doing the rounded terminations of all scripts, the normal procedure is to make the brush-tip contact the writing surface slightly behind the point where the stroke is intended to begin, and then push it gently forward before carrying it in the opposite direction. This delicate manoeuvre will make the initial part of the stroke rounded with the traces of the brush-tip hidden. This manoeuvre is accompanied by pressing the brush-tip just a bit harder on the writing surface. The same manoeuvre in reverse order is made at the termination of the stroke. Since the brush is held upright throughout (*chung fêng*), the fringes of the stroke will hide the traces of the brush-tip within the stroke. The principle of *ts'ang fêng,* however, is applied only to some of the strokes forming the Chinese characters. The calligrapher, in fact, is quite free to forego the terminal manoeuvres and leave the traces of the brush-tip exposed. It is up to the calligrapher to work out the combination of the two types of strokes which constitutes an element of his personal style.

Whether the traces of the brush-tip are hidden or exposed, the calligrapher is always obliged to see the stroke through. When we make a check mark with a pencil, we normally do the second part of it with a flip. This flip action is absolutely taboo in Chinese writing. The calligrapher must try to bring each and every stroke to its desired end without the slightest slackening in the process. To the Chinese, writing is a consistent and controlled motion throughout. Nothing casual or careless is allowed.

The first major goal the learner strives for is the ability to do the characters evenly and on a level, what the Chinese call *p'ing chêng.* In the old days, books were copied by hand and scriptures were transcribed as religious offerings. The copyist is a highly trained scribe in *chên shu,* able to write each character in an upright manner and in good balance as well as in uniform size. He takes pride, for instance, in being able to make the character *i* (one), consisting of only one single horizontal stroke, appear in perfect harmony with the character *tou* (to fight), consisting of twenty-four intricately arranged strokes, on the same page and in close proximity. Since the characters are arranged in vertical lines with an equal number of square or rectangular spaces, the space allocated to one character is of the same size as that allocated to another character, irrespective of the number of strokes of which the characters are composed. The craftsmanship of the professional copyist is to fill up the prescribed spaces in such a way that the contrast resulting from the disparity of the number of strokes does not stare us in the eye. Anyone who has tried his hand at writing Chinese characters knows that this is no mean task. The copyist belongs to a profession of exacting standards. Some

[190]

books printed in woodblock in the T'ang and Sung period are wonderful specimens of the copyist's skill. The same may be said of some of the earlier editions of Chinese books printed in Korea.

In learning character-construction, the aspiring calligrapher is advised to abide by certain formal rules laid down for his guidance. Wang Hsi-chih's much-quoted advice is as follows:

The shape of the character should not be too wide at the top and too narrow at the base. The strokes should not be crowded together or the character will look as though it is plagued by a hundred ailments. The strokes should not be too far apart or the character will look like a bird soaked in water. The character should not be too elongated or it will look like a dead snake hanging from a tree. It should not be too squat or it will look like a frog floating on a pond.

Although Wang Hsi-chih's analogies appear to be rather incongruous, what he said about character-construction is the counsel of sensible arrangement. Wang Hsi-chih's principles were later elaborated by Ou-yang Hsün into thirty-six rules and by a Ming student of calligraphy, Li Shun, into eighty-four. Li Shun was so proud of his work that he submitted it to his sovereign, the Ming Emperor Ching-tsung, in a memorial to the throne dated 1451. Li Shun's main contention is that, since the radicals and elements of the Chinese characters come in a great variety, there should be certain rules to help the novice in arranging them in order to make the finished characters look even and on a level, *p'ing chêng*. By analysing all the characters in the Chinese written language, he discovered that the radicals and elements composing them could be reduced to eighty-four combinations. He then listed the combinations and illustrated each one of them with four characters.

In the old days when calligraphy was considered a prerequisite to literary success, which in turn would open the gates to official honours and private fortunes, calligraphic training included all the major scripts. In modern times, if one aspires to be a calligrapher instead of merely a man who knows how to write, training in the major scripts is also essential. Following the pattern set as far back as the Han Dynasty, a programme has been laid down some-what as follows:

From 11 to 13, practise 100 characters in middle-sized *chên shu.*
From 14 to 16, practise small *chên shu.*
From 17 to 20, practise *hsing shu.*
From 21 to 25, practise *ts'ao shu.*
From 13 to 23, practise in addition *chuan shu.*
From 24 to 25, practise also *li shu.*

The only reliable way one can learn to know what is good calligraphy is through the intensive study of the works that have stood the time and the

[191]

exacting appraisal of the connoisseurs. Sun Ch'ien-li, author of the *Shu P'u,* told us:

The first lesson the novice should learn is to look attentively at the peculiar traits of each style. For works of the same style by different artists usually show marked divergences and different pieces done by the same artist are by no means identical. Sometimes strength and sinuosity are coiled in one stroke, sometimes they are boiled forth separately; an apparent smoothness may disguise the bones and sinews, or a burly vigour beat and throb on the surface. In any case the student should delve deep into his subject; and if he starts by copying, he should copy his model without equivocation. When he fails in this—when, from absence of mind or reluctance to copy faithfully, the distribution of the strokes falls out of order and the structure of the body is loosely shaped—then, to what is splendid *and* to what are the pitfalls in this art, he is equally a stranger, and such he will remain.*

In his early years, the aspiring calligrapher has been modelling after rubbings of tablets and reproductions of manuscripts. If he is really ambitious, he may like to see and model after some originals. To do so he would have to visit the famous collectors scattered all over the land, begging them for permission to see their treasures. It is customary for him to keep a journal of his travels and to note carefully the priceless manuscripts he is privileged to see, the ecstatic joy he experiences when he comes face to face for the first time with the works of the immortals. If he happens to be a high official at court, he may have access to the royal collection. His is an unending search. The learning process is a life-long pursuit which terminates only with the grave. This has been the story of most of the calligraphers of the past, and their journals are the stuff from which art histories are written.

Although in the Chinese mind to copy (*lin*) is to enter into the creative spirit and therefore to inherit rather than to imitate the genius of the original artist, and many works in the great collections are copies made by one artist of the work of another artist, mere competence in copying does not make a good calligrapher. It is at best what Mi Fu called 'slave calligraphy'. As the Ch'ing Dynasty critic Chou Hsing-lien said:

The student should try to study and to be inspired by the old masters, to learn their similarities and differences, to examine their merits and deficiencies, and finally to absorb and adapt the different styles. After going through the process for some time, one may hope to develop a style with a face of its own.

Every Chinese schoolboy is impregnated with calligraphic appreciation from childhood. From the first day in school, he has learned to use the brush to write and has been exposed to calligraphic specimens of the old masters. His eyes are trained and he has gone through the process of trying to transmit the images before his eyes to the paper on his desk. He has tried to gain

* Translation by Sun Ta-yü.

[192]

command of the brush—to make it serve his purpose. Thus the age-old struggle between opportunity and limitation begins. He has experienced how the simple instrument he holds in his hand stubbornly tries to impose its will on him, while he valiantly struggles to turn its stubbornness into account, making the brush work for him instead of allowing himself to be its slave. This is what the manuals tell him: to use the brush instead of being used by it.

Somewhere in the long and arduous process, he will find to his benefit that calligraphic excellence does not come easily. He will try hard to go through the learning process and he will be encouraged by his progress. But to develop a style with a face of its own, a face that is not only personal but also artistically worthy, is an achievement only the highly gifted can hope to make.

As an example of the learning process, we should like to quote in abbreviated translation the autobiographical account of the Ch'ing Dynasty calligrapher Pao Shih-ch'ên, author of the previously mentioned book *I Chou Shuang Chi,* as follows:

In 1789, I was fifteen years old. I had been practising calligraphy for ten years. Since my family did not have any good examples of the old masters for me to model after, I was compelled to rely on reproductions I obtained at the bookshops. After ten years I was still unable to make an even, straight line. People in my district thought I would never become a calligrapher.

Then I happened to notice that an old relative of mine, contrary to the usual practice, was modelling after rubbings of T'ang tablets. I went to seek his advice. He gave me some manuals which taught me first how to hold the brush, to maintain the proper grip on the stem, and to keep my elbow suspended. I tried to do accordingly. The task was so arduous that I found I had trouble breathing. My hand quivered under the strain. But I kept relentlessly on, even tracing strokes on my bed-sheet with my bare fingers. After a long while my hand became steadier. That was in 1794. I felt then that I was ready to tackle the works of Huai-su. I copied Huai-su's *Ch'ien Tzŭ Wên* for three years. I got nowhere and I gave up.

In the winter of 1799, I approached my fellow townsman Ts'ai Tung-fu for help. He advised me to model after Su Shih on the ground that the Sung master's characters, fleshy and heavy-set, might conceal my weakness. In two months I made remarkable progress!

In the next year, I borrowed many manuscripts from my friends and began to copy the *Lan T'ing Hsü* (by Wang Hsi-chih). I did four characters a day, doing each over and over again a few hundred times. In one hundred days I finished the whole text and I went on to the *Lo Shên Fu* (by Wang Hsien-chih) for another hundred days.

By this time I was fortunate enough to be able to travel all over the country. Wherever I went I looked for good manuscripts in private collections. I studied them intensively.

In 1802, I met Ch'ien Lu-ssŭ who advised me to use brushes made of rabbit-hair instead of sheep-hair. He confessed that he learned the trick after practising calligraphy for fifty years. In the same year, I took lessons with the great Têng Shih-ju who suggested that I model after Yen Chên-ch'ing and Ou-yang Hsün in order to get back to the mainstream of T'ang calligraphy.

In 1806, I came into possession of a few Yü Shih-nan manuscripts. I learned from them how Wang Hsi-chih and Wang Hsien-chih reached such dizzy heights and how the styles of the father and the son differed from one another.

In 1815, I met Huang Hsiao-chung, a good and devoted calligrapher. We were together in Yangchow for three months, all the time talking about calligraphy. From him I finally learned the secret of the grip.

In the autumn of 1816, I met Chou Ong-chih who gave me many valuable tips. In the same year, I also met Wang Liang-ssŭ who told me that his wife had dreamed of a god who imparted to her the mysteries of brushman-ship which boiled down to the maintenance of a proper grip. Then I met Wu Yü who taught me the correct way to apply the brush to the paper.

Now, after twenty years of uninterrupted application, I am in a position to claim that I have digested the essence of what I have learned. My hand and my mind are now one!

There are many points in Pao Shih-ch'ên's own account of his trials and tribulations that strike us as singularly odd. It appears that he was quite wrong in trying to tackle Huai-su's *Ch'ien Tzŭ Wên* done in *ts'ao shu* so early in the game. Su Shih would scold him severely for trying to run before he was able to walk. The proposition of modelling after Su Shih's works in an attempt to 'conceal weaknesses' is preposterous and unpardonable. Su Shih had no weaknesses to conceal. How could Pao Shih-ch'ên conceal his own weaknesses by modelling after the great Sung master? How could he make 'remarkable progress' by taking such a devious and dubious route? Pao Shih-ch'ên was also guilty of erroneous procedure when he modelled after the *Lan T'ing Hsü,* which is in *hsing shu,* before he tackled the *Lo Shên Fu,* which is in small *chên shu.* Why did he begin his practice with brushes made of sheep-hair instead of rabbit-hair is beyond comprehension. Têng Shih-ju was certainly right in guiding him back to the *chên shu* of the T'ang masters. He should have started with them in the first place, as all school children have been doing for centuries.

Pao Shih-ch'ên's own programme of training, it appears, was all wrong. No wonder, despite his lifelong devotion to the art, he never became a first-rate calligrapher. His reputation in the world of calligraphy, which is considerable, rests mainly on his exuberant loquacity and declaratory judg-ments. His knowledge of tablets and manuscripts is prodigious, and some of his critical assessments are sharp and on occasion penetrating. After reading about his labours in the passage quoted above, one really does not have the heart to judge his work too harshly. But we are compelled to say that he is not a good calligrapher, not by any means. We can see from his work (Fig. 63) that his hand is clumsy and heavy and his style far from distin-guished. Instead of applying his brush dexterously on the paper, he seems to be pulling and dragging the brush across in an obvious attempt to simulate

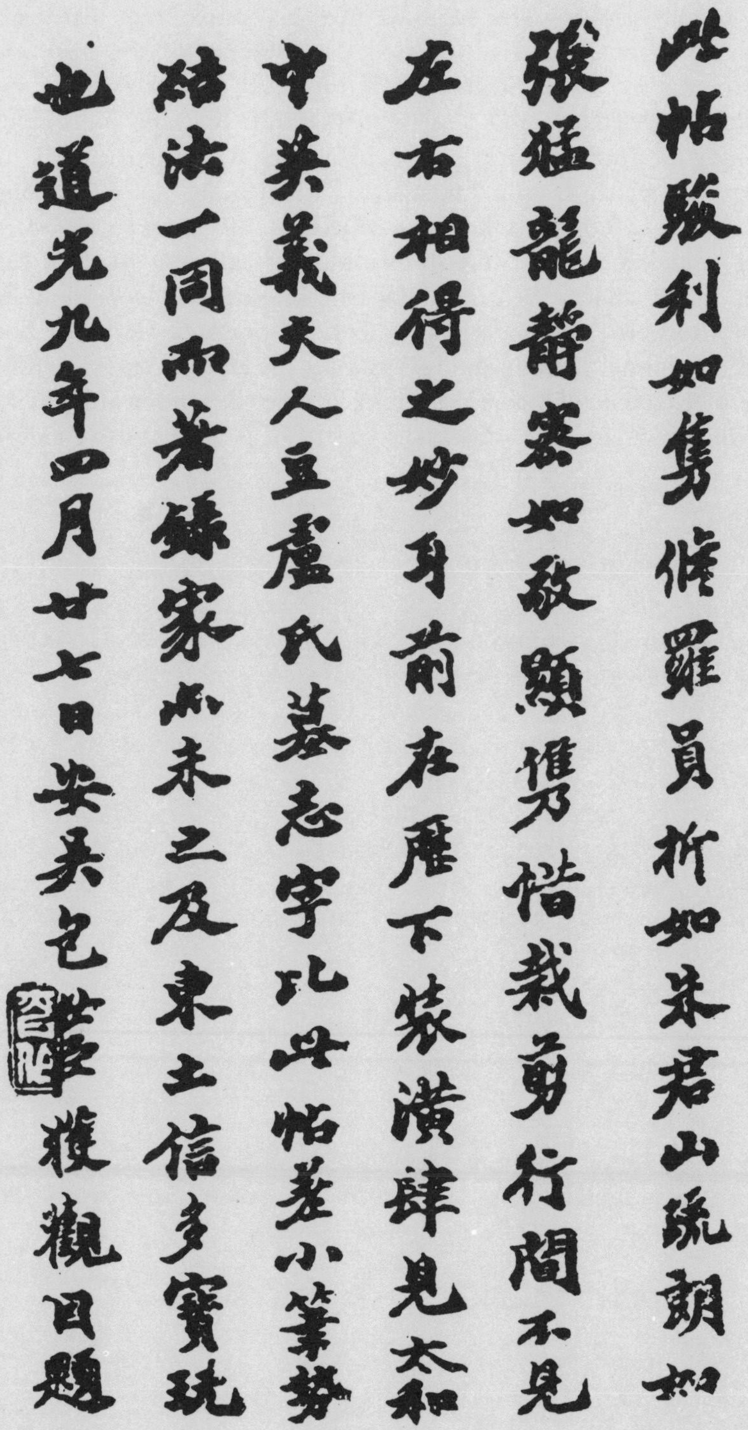

此帖駿利如隼修羅員析如朱君山琉朗如
張猛龍靜密如敬顯儁乃惜裁剪行間不見
左右相得之妙身前在雁下裝潢肆見太和
中英義天人豆盧氏墓志字此母帖差小筆勢
結法一同而著錄家如未之及東土信多寶玩
也道光九年四月廿七日安吳包〔印〕獲觀因題

Fig. 63　Pao Shih-ch'ên: *Colophon to Chang Hei-nü Mu Chih* (Fig. 26), dated 1829

strength in the strokes. The result is that his strokes are often shapeless. Although he claimed to have mastered the mysteries of the grip, too much of his strokes were done with a slanted brush. He is also guilty of crowding his strokes and elements too closely so that they become indistinguishable, thus spoiling the formal appeal of the characters. This is particularly true with his *hsing shu* which is quite repulsive. Commenting on a Pao Shih-ch'ên scroll in *hsing shu* now in a Japanese collection, Lü Fu-t'ing, a modern critic, says that 'it makes one feel like throwing up'. It all goes to show that calligraphy is an art, and as such, it cannot be mastered only by reading manuals, seeking instructions and undergoing laborious practice. Had Pao Shih-ch'ên followed the normal learning process and set his aim lower, he could at least have the satisfaction of having acquired a trained hand which, in a nation where calligraphic art is so universally regarded, is a great asset indeed.

Chapter Twelve

Calligraphy as an Art (1)

The appreciation of Chinese art in all its many and varied manifestations must begin with calligraphy. It is China's basic aesthetics.

Over the centuries innumerable books and tracts have been written on the subject—manuals, commentaries, biographies, histories, records of great works seen, catalogues of large collections, stylistic analyses. Persons deserving mention number in the thousands. From these voluminous materials we try to find the answer to the question: Wherein lies the artistic worth of Chinese calligraphy?

We discover at the outset that we have given ourselves an almost impossible assignment. It is here that the normal methods of art criticism break down. We find to our dismay that there is really no means of demonstrating that the world of lines and shapes created by generations of Chinese calligraphers is one of exceptional beauty, or even that the underlying structures of the characters are based on an unusually satisfying set of tensions and resolutions. To return to our analogy to music, as Eric Newton said of the paintings of Ben Nicholson, 'one can no more analyse such tensions than one can explain why a melody has its own inevitability by analysing the length of the notes or measuring the intervals between them'. Only familiarity with the great works and experience in trying to emulate them will enable us to tell between mediocrity and mastery in any given instance of the difficult process of creation. There are no set rules to go by.

The Chinese character, in all the scripts, is a graphic composition the elements of which are not haphazardly thrown together but are structurally integrated with all the component parts maintaining an organic relationship with one another. 'It is,' as the modern critic Yao Mêng-ku said, 'a life-unit consisting of bones and muscles, flesh and blood, a pattern in which the upper and lower portions are balanced, the left and right sides juxtaposed, the four corners interrelated, the relative sides of the different elements harmonized, although its length and width are left to the discretion of the artist—in short, a work of art with a life of its own.'

From the earliest time, Chinese critics have tried to compare the beauty of calligraphy to that of natural objects. Sun Ch'ien-li wrote:

Of the wonders of *shu fa* (art of writing) I have seen many and many a one. Here a drop of crystal dew hangs its ear on the tip of a needle; there, the rumbling of thunder hails down a shower of stones. I have seen flocks of queen-swans floating on their stately wings, or a frantic stampede rushing off at terrific speed. Sometimes in the lines a flaming phoenix dances a lordly dance, or a sinuous serpent wriggles in speckled fright. And I have seen sunken peaks plunging headlong down the precipices, or a person clinging on a dry vine while the whole silent valley yawns below. Some strokes seem as heavy as the falling banks of clouds, others as light as the wings of the cicada. A little conducting and a fountain bubbles forth, a little halting and a mountain settles down in peace. Tenderly a new moon beams on the horizon; or, as the styles becomes solemn, a river of stars, luminous and large, descends down the solitary expanse of night. All these seem as wonderful as Nature herself and almost beyond the power of man.*

Such analogies to natural objects have led some to believe that the inspiration and aesthetic appeal of Chinese calligraphy lies in the principle of animism. There are ample historical grounds to support such a view. Since Ts'ang Chieh, the legendary father of the Chinese written language was said to have derived the idea of forming characters by observing the patterns and designs of natural objects and phenomena, the scripts of remote antiquity were named after such things as clouds and plants, birds and tadpoles. And in a later age, many calligraphers, in discussing their art, have told us that its essence has suddenly and unexpectedly come to them through accidental encounter with natural phenomena or everyday happenings—a sort of revelatory flash such as that experienced by the Ch'an (Zen) devotee. Chang Hsü told us that his *ts'ao shu* style was inspired by the dance of Lady Kung-sun and the agitation of two carriers disputing their right of way on a narrow mountain path; Huai-su was said to have perfected his style by observing the multifarious changes of summer clouds blown by the wind; Huang T'ing-chien, who loved sailing, claimed to have acquired his sense of rhythm by following the motion of the paddle; Wên T'ung, the ink bamboo painter, asserted that he found the secret of *ts'ao shu* by watching two snakes in mortal combat. Many others captured the secret of innate strength, so basic to good calligraphy, from the massive paws of

* Translation by Sun Ta-yü.

[198]

the tiger, the sinewy legs of the deer, the gnarled vines of the wistaria, not to say all the qualities of the bamboo. Tabulating some of the analogies of natural objects to *ts'ao shu,* we have the following: 'floating clouds', 'thirsty horse', 'angry lion', 'startled dragon', 'the serpent wriggling through grass in spring', 'the wild geese alighting on reedy banks at dusk', 'the dragon dancing at the heavenly gate', 'the tiger resting at the phoenix pavilion', 'withered vines encircling an old tree', 'frosty skin embracing a bamboo branch'. Some T'ang and Sung calligraphers used to compare the dots in a character to drops of water leaking through the ceiling, the corners to bent hairpins. When they discussed the structural formation of the characters, they compared it to the cracks of the plaster on the wall. When they tried to describe the application of strength in executing the characters, they resorted to the analogy of drawing with awl on sand or of impressing a seal on mud. These T'ang and Sung analogies, originated and applied by such calligraphers as Yen Chên-ch'ing, Huai-su, Mi Fu and Chiang K'uei, have all become highly technical terms in the vocabulary of Chinese calligraphy, and their meaning has been subjected to different and often obscure interpretations. Indeed, the propensity to equate calligraphy with natural objects and phenomena has been such that as soon as a Chinese sees a European writing in horizontal lines he says that the European languages 'crawl like a crab'. Sir Herbert Read said:

The artist . . . is a man who is gifted with the most direct perception of natural form. It is not necessarily a conscious perception: he may unconsciously reveal his perceptions in his works of art. Artists are to a considerable degree automata—that is to say, they unwittingly transmit in their works a sense of scale, proportion, symmetry, balance and other abstract qualities which they have acquired through their purely visual and therefore physical response to their natural environment.

As far as Chinese calligraphy is concerned, the critics as well as the artists themselves have long since found such words as 'elegant', 'exquisite', 'sublime', 'vigorous', 'graceful', all of which have been so much abused, altogether inadequate to describe the abstract and recondite beauty they see and feel in good calligraphy, still less to tell the styles of the different calligraphers apart. By finding analogies to natural objects they think they can more clearly convey what is in their mind, although 'the dragon dancing at the heavenly gate' is a concept we find very hard to conceive. But the natural references, however ingenuous, really do not explain fully wherein calligraphic beauty lies. We have to delve a bit deeper to find its true meaning.

The eight and the thirty-two types of calligraphic strokes which go to form the Chinese characters are lines of different varieties. Calligraphy in essence is an art of lines. A line has the quality of arousing certain reactions from us. Different kinds of lines awake in us different sensations. The Western painters do their drawings with the hard and sharp tips of the silver point, pen, quill, charcoal, chalk or pencil. The Chinese calligraphers employ the medium of the pliable brush whose range of stylistic expressiveness is almost limitless. It has been emphasized over and over again that the strokes forming a character should above all be the embodiment of innate strength, the latent force of all natural movement, which is no more or less than to affirm Blake's saying that 'energy is eternal delight'. Wang Hsi-chih, inevitably resorting to natural analogies, said:

Every horizontal stroke is like a mass of clouds in battle formation, every hook like a bent bow of the greatest strength, every dot like a falling rock from a high peak, every turning of the stroke like a brass hook, every drawn-out line like a dry vine of great old age, and every swift and free stroke like a runner on his start.*

Innate strength of the strokes, of course, is not to be acquired by the application of brute force, nor is it to be effected by rapid motion. The strength that goes into a stroke is generated from the arm and carried through to the writing surface via the suspended elbow, the firm wrist, the rigid fingers, and eventually the upright brush. Calligraphers have been complimented for their 'strength big enough to carry a *ting*' (the weighty bronze utensil with three legs used in formal ceremony). But sheer muscular power like that of a boxer or wrestler is not what is called for. A good calligrapher should be able to impart strength into his strokes so that 'the strength penetrates through the paper'. A well executed stroke should not look like a dry leaf floating on a pool of water. It should sink through the paper on which it is written. We have in our time seen reproductions of works of art done with the most ingenious scientific methods. When the reproductions are hung side by side with the originals, the first thing that strikes us is that in the reproductions the characters seem to be floating on the surface while those in the originals appear to merge with the paper into an organic unit. The difference obviously lies in the fact that one is 'printed' and the other is 'written'. The ability to 'write', to apply the brush to the paper, comes from the most sensitive mastery of the brush. (As I am writing these lines, I notice in an American literary magazine that the word 'calligraph' is used as a verb. It is perhaps the right word to use in a book on Chinese calligraphy.)

The Chinese speak of an artist, calligrapher and painter alike, as a master of brushmanship and inkmanship, *yu pi yu mo*. By this they mean the calligrapher's ability to regulate and control the amount of ink absorbed in the brush and applied to the paper in order to achieve the desired artistic effect. We have seen that the strokes of some of the calligraphers, such as Liu Kung-ch'üan and Huang T'ing-chien, are taut and sinewy, while those of other calligraphers, such as Yen Chên-ch'ing and Su Shih, are broad and heavy-set. The *fei po* style of Ts'ai Yung, leaving white streaks in the strokes,

---

* Translation by Lin Yutang.

is done by carrying the brush rapidly over the writing surface. Tung Ch'i-ch'ang is the master of the 'thirsty brush'. Whatever the technique of ink-manship, innate strength is always found. Su Shih, in particular, is praised for his ability to 'conceal a needle in a bundle of cotton'. Although we do not actually see the needle, we somehow feel its presence in the strokes. Too much ink poorly applied results in what the lady Wei Shuo called 'ink pig'.

The concept of *yu pi yu mo* is a question of making 'the ink support the brush and the brush support the ink'. The calligrapher should strive to make both brush and ink play their respective roles properly so that they both con-tribute their share to the artistic qualities of the end result. A stroke with too much brush and not enough ink (*yu pi wu mo*) means that the role of the brush has been over-played, that the traces of the brush are excessively exposed, with the result that the stroke appears acrid and astringent, like the dead branches of an ungraceful tree. On the other hand, a stroke with too much ink and not enough brush (*yo mo wu pi*) means the subordination of the brush to the ink, resulting in a formless mass, a nondescript blot. The task of the calligrapher is to bring about the suitable supplementation of brush and ink in an effort to produce strokes that are clear and luminous, lively and well-nourished. Having said that, we must hasten to add that, while the tenets of brushmanship and inkmanship are well understood and agreed upon, individual calligraphers are completely at liberty to work out their own formulas to sustain their personal styles. There is a world of difference between a stroke by Su Shih and, to take an extreme example, one by Emperor Hui-tsung. And yet both are consistent with the basic principles of brushman-ship and inkmanship.

A Chinese character is a pattern of pure lines. It is a linear design. The calligrapher's task is to make the line intimately expressive of form, a task to be performed by the mastery of brushmanship and inkmanship. After going through the process of the intellectual analysis of the elements of the charac-ters, the calligrapher arrives at a point where a sensuous perception of totalities is in order. The beams and pillars are there for him to build the architectural monument. This is the construction of the character, what the Chinese call *chieh tzŭ*.

A character is a composition of strokes properly arranged as a framework for the revelation of a calligraphic style. In the practice of calligraphy the target is the duality—the structure of the character contrasted to its use as a vehicle with which to display the features of a style. While the calligrapher is not allowed freely to alter the basic structure of the character, he is at liberty to try out new forms and combinations—to slant a stroke slightly, to distort a square gently, to move an element somewhat out of its customary place, to substitute one type of stroke for another, to leave a space unfilled. In trying out these experiments, he is always guided by certain basic formal concepts which he can violate only at his own peril. The T'ang Emperor T'ai-tsung

[201]

commended Wang Hsi-chih's calligraphy by comparing the characters done by the Tsin master to 'clouds which appear isolated and yet linked, the soaring phoenix and curling dragon which appear reclining and yet upright', thus underlining Wang Hsi-chih's own dictum that 'geometric forms are not characters'. Emperor T'ai-tsung in this statement reveals himself to be a true connoisseur of art by lending weight to experimentation in form, to the combination of repose with the suggestion of potential movement, and to the perfection of symmetry by balance and compensation. Sir Kenneth Clark, in discussing the statues of Polyclitus, believes that one can easily reduce them to the rods and sheet-metal of modern sculpture and they would still work. The same thing may be and has been done to the Chinese character. For the Chinese character, like no other fruit of the human mind, has a life of its own, a mysterious organic quality, which may be used abstractly as an abstract painter uses paint. A character is itself a form and, consequently, a definite object. In creating the form, the calligrapher is in effect creating a being.

A Chinese character may have within itself the rhythms of movement, yet it always comes to rest at its true centre. The construction of the character, *chieh tzŭ,* is guided, according to the Chinese, by a series of opposites: 'forward and backward', 'confronting and backing away', 'rising and falling', 'light and heavy', 'condensed and dispersed', 'strong and weak', 'dry and wet', 'fast and slow', 'sparse and crowded', 'fat and lean', 'thick and thin', 'connected and disconnected', 'joined and detached'. The Ch'ing critic Chou Hsing-lien, who made up the above list of opposites, bluntly stated: 'These are the essentials of calligraphy; without them, it will be the work of the devil'. If we were to express Chou Hsing-lien's ideas in plain English, we would summarize them by the words 'balance', 'symmetry', 'tension', 'contrast', 'harmony', 'proportion', 'confrontation', and 'yielding'. In this connection, it seems worthwhile to reiterate the point that, no matter how the character is constructed, it must come to rest at its true centre. Huang T'ing-chien said:

The old masters, even Chang Hsü, always managed to make the character stand squarely on the paper. A character which is out of balance cannot be considered a character at all. An improperly placed dot is like a beautiful maiden with a blind eye. A badly done hook is like a warrior with only one arm.

A Philistine may go about saying that he likes the calligraphic style of Mi Fu and does not like that of Yen Chên-ch'ing. The judgment cannot be that simple and subjective. It involves the all-important question of taste. How taste is acquired and by what inner pattern we unfailingly recognize it are questions which no one is in a position definitively to answer. But it is something basic to the full appreciation of Chinese calligraphy and should not be dismissed lightly.

'A people of taste, or a period of taste', Sir Herbert Read said, 'is always one in which there exists a system of education or upbringing based on the acquisition of integrated physical skills.' In no other field is this truer than in that of Chinese calligraphy. The mastery of brushmanship and inkmanship is a rigorous discipline that every Chinese calligrapher must go through. It is at bottom a question of acquiring physical skills. A young man may be extraordinarily gifted; if he cannot wield the brush and apply the ink properly and competently his gifts must seek fruition outside the domain of calligraphy. All the good calligraphers are efficient technicians. There is no exception to the rule. The programme of training we described in the previous chapter is the system of education referred to by Sir Herbert Read. It is the soil on which standards of good taste are grown.

The ultimate test of good taste is in many respects empirical. The great works of the past are studied and modelled after, and from them the feeling of good taste is derived. This is what Chao Mêng-fu called 'archaic elegance'. Chinese critics are fond of using the term *ku p'u* as a mark of superior quality. *Ku* is the air of archaism hanging over and enveloping a work of art, reminding us of the old masters and indicating that the calligrapher is on intimate terms with them. *P'u* is the quality of simplicity, of the lack of conscious effort, of spontaneity, even of a measure of crudity and artlessness. The emphasis on the twin principles of *ku p'u* is in a sense an appeal for the exercise of restraint, a warning against stylistic extravagances, not to say a denunciation of the pursuit of novelty for novelty's sake. To the Chinese, a true artist always tries, consciously or unconsciously, to keep his skills under measured control, to avoid pedantry, and to guard himself against spilling over the boundaries of decency. A common way to describe bad calligraphy is to compare it with a country lass's makeup—too much and too colourful. Winckelmann told us that the highest beauty should be free from all flavour, like perfectly pure water. The connoisseurs of Chinese calligraphy can certainly subscribe to that statement without reserve.

Huang T'ing-chien once said: 'A person in this world may do anything he pleases, but he should not be vulgar (*su*); if he is vulgar, he is beyond salvation.' The concept of *ya* (in good taste) and *su* (vulgar), which runs through the entire fabric of Chinese society, is one of those things which defies accurate definition but which can always be felt, whether it is in a personality or in a work of art. Applied to the art of calligraphy, a calligraphic piece, to the Chinese, is the revelation of the personality of the artist, his individuality and integrity as a member of society. As each stroke goes into the building up of a character and each character flows on to the next, a man's inner being is revealed in the process. As the Ch'ing critic Chu Ho-kêng has said: 'Calligraphy is a craft, and its first essential is the personal integrity of the calligrapher.' To the Chinese, an artist is a noble person who conducts himself in accordance with the highest moral standards. Foremost in the Confucian

[203]

scheme of ethical values is the sense of loyalty, the enlightened devotion to the sovereign one serves and the tenacious defence of what one considers to be the best interests of the State. If such a person happens also to be an artist, such as Ch'u Shui-liang and Yen Chên-ch'ing, his work will be most highly prized for the combination of art and morality therein manifested. On the other hand, if an artist, however accomplished, is considered morally unworthy, as in the case of the Sung calligrapher Ts'ai Ching, his name will be banished from the roster of merit. Chao Mêng-fu's reputation, as we have seen, is somewhat blemished because, as a scion of the House of Sung, he chose to serve the Mongols. He did not suffer the ignominy of Ts'ai Ching only because his artistic achievements are too impressive to be ignored.

Many calligraphers were retired scholars and recluses. They professed to have no patience with the restraints of the social order and the vulgar mediocrities of bourgeois existence. They therefore took themselves out of the mundane world to lead a life of calm contemplation and abstract meditation in the midst of mountains and streams, clouds and mist. Such a man was Wang Hsi-chih who, after serving in a number of official posts, gave up his government career in disgust and devoted the rest of his life to the enjoyment of Nature as an emotional projection of his own elevated and refined sentiments. His was the choice between *ya* and *su,* between good taste and vulgarity. Having made the choice, it is inevitable that his art should be dictated by it. All this, it seems, is the Chinese way of affirming the aphorism that the style is the man himself or Ruskin's statement that 'all lovely art is rooted in virtue'.

The road to a personal style is lined with pitfalls. A style may include a great deal of inherited elements; it may even be a composite of many styles. But the artistic worth of a particular style is always determined by its purity, what Chou Hsing-lien called the 'face', which alone belongs to the calligrapher, as personal to him as the timbre of his voice or the twinkle of his eyes. However, in the calligrapher's search for his own 'face', he is always in danger of over-exerting himself, of indulging in embellishments for the sake of being different. A certain measure of mannerism and affectation in calligraphy is permissible; an overdose will become an oddity which should be avoided by all means. Some of the Ch'ing calligraphers, notably Ching Nung and Chêng Hsieh, are balancing themselves dangerously on the razor's edge because they seem to be consciously disfiguring the characters to make them different. In contrast, the styles of the Han and Wei tablets, done by nameless men who made no claim for fame, are peculiarly satisfying precisely because of the lack of conscious effort.

It should not be inferred from the above that Chinese calligraphy is invariably in good taste, not by any means. With the lone exception of the hapless Pao Shih-ch'ên, we have confined ourselves only to the calligraphers whose works we consider worthy. However, the Chinese landscape is full of calligraphic specimens that are shockingly poor and in bad taste, which may be seen in exhibitions and even in museums and galleries. Well may a connoisseur say with Macaulay: 'So great is the taste for oddity that men who have no recommendation but oddity, hold a high place in the vulgar estimation.' We call it in China 'barber shop art'.

Chapter Thirteen

Calligraphy as an Art (2)

In his admirable discussion of abstract art and abstractionism, Etienne Gilson, the distinguished philosopher and historian, discovers a tendency 'to simplify the complexity of the visual images, to reduce them to a small number of constitutive elements, and to substitute for the stylized representation of natural objects, or beings, certain structured wholes, made up of plastic equivalents, whose signification lies in themselves rather than in their relation to things'. Substantially the same tendency, it may be said, is discernible in the long evolution of the Chinese script from the primitive pictographs at the dawn of history to the sophisticated *ts'ao shu* of Yü Yu-jên in our day. In the end, the characters in the Chinese written language, in whatever script, have become what Gilson called 'structured wholes, made up of plastic equivalents', and are used by the calligraphers, as the Western artists use the nude, as ends in themselves, or, in the jargon of current art criticism, as means of creating significant form. To the calligrapher, the Chinese character is more than the departure for a work of art. It is a form of art.

What is peculiar to Chinese calligraphy is that, instead of banishing the older scripts as new ones came forth, all the scripts, ancient and modern, exist simultaneously and are included not only in the professional calligrapher's repertoire but also in the programme of calligraphic training. The Chinese believe that each major script has its own *fa* (method) which is peculiar to itself. *Fa* consists of two elements: the special technique of brushmanship required to execute characters in the particular script and the structural organization of the characters in the particular script. Our knowledge of the different scripts, from *chuan shu* to *ts'ao shu*, readily informs us that the range of *fa* between the different scripts is indeed enormous and fundamental. It is considered important and essential for a calligrapher to be thoroughly at home with the *fa* of each one of the scripts, at least the major ones, in order that he may obtain command of the basic techniques. Among the major scripts, the *chuan shu* and *li shu* have always been regarded as the foundation upon which calligraphic art is based, and all calligraphers at one time or another practise the two scripts. The Tsin, T'ang and Sung masters, unfortunately, have left us very few manuscripts done in the two scripts. But there should be no doubt that all of them had worked hard on the two scripts to train their hand. The official biography of Chao Mêng-fu in the *Yüan Shih* (History of the Yüan Dynasty) said of him that 'in *chuan shu, Chou wên, pa fên, li shu, chên shu, hsing shu* and *ts'ao shu*, he was the master of all time'. This statement may appear to be somewhat extravagant, but it was with Chao Mêng-fu that we began in earnest to have calligraphers who did manuscripts in many, if not in all the major scripts. We have seen such an example in Wên Chêng-ming's *Ch'ien Tzŭ Wên* in four scripts (Fig. 48a). We have also seen Têng Shih-ju's calligraphy in the major scripts (Fig. 52). In the Ch'ing Dynasty, when the ancient tablets were the fashion of the day, this practice became even more prevalent to the extent that no calligrapher was considered truly worthy unless he was able to do characters in at least the major scripts, sometimes in the minor ones as well. A display of parallel scrolls in different scripts is designed not only as a demonstration of the calligrapher's versatility, which is important enough, but also as a graphic affirmation of the general belief that in Chinese calligraphy no script is really dead and that each has its own peculiar contribution to make to the art of calligraphy. It serves to underscore the principle that calligraphy, like all enduring forms of art, is a continually evolving process so that each fresh departure is a development, with behind it an accumulated weight of ideas, to carry the next experiment still further.

The importance of the older scripts has been still further emphasized by the generally held concept that calligraphic excellence is defined as the calligrapher's ability to employ the *fa* of one script in doing the characters in another script. Thus Chung Yu's calligraphy has often been praised because his *chên shu* carries the flavour of *chuan shu*. Wang Hsi-chih, as we have seen, began his lessons in calligraphy with the lady Wei Shuo who was somewhat of a *li shu* expert. In his more mature years, he went still further back to model after the ancient tablets. While he lamentably did not leave us with a single specimen of his calligraphy in *chuan shu* and *li shu,* the critics are in general agreement that much of the archaic elegance of his style came from the older scripts. The prevailing fashion of the T'ang and Sung calligraphers was to go back only as far as Wang Hsi-chih and no further. But we are able to detect traces of the old scripts in their styles, most notably those of *chuan shu* in Yen Chên-ch'ing and *li shu* in Ch'u Shui-liang, to mention only the two most apparent cases. Chang Hsü and Huai-su, in doing their *ts'ao shu,* freely employed the technique of *hsiao chuan,* complete with wiry lines and rounded corners. The real high-water mark of the incorporation of *chuan shu* and *li shu* technique into the modern scripts, quite naturally and expectedly, came in the Ch'ing Dynasty when the study of the ancient tablets came into general vogue. The calligraphy of Chao Chih-ch'ien is one of the best examples of how the technique of *li shu* may be employed in *chên shu* with complete success (Fig. 53). Another example is the incorporation of *li shu* and *pa fên* technique in *chên shu* and *hsing shu* by the influential Ch'ing calligrapher Ho Shao-chi (Fig. 64).

The question may be asked: Why is it so desirable to employ the technique in doing one script to doing characters in another script? No one, it seems, has supplied a satisfactory answer to the question. Somehow the matter is taken for granted by the Chinese critics. In the voluminous literature of Chinese calligraphy, we come across over and over again the statement that so-and-so's calligraphy is good because he is able to apply the technique of one script to another, with no further explanation supplied. We have never been explicitly told why such a mixture of technique is almost automatically the ticket to fame. The answer to our question, we venture to think, may be found in the fact that, when the critics talk about mixing techniques, their primary consideration is the application of the technique of the old scripts, *chuan shu* and *li shu,* to the modern scripts, particularly *chên shu.* This kind of mixture, in the eyes of the connoisseurs, is to lend a touch of archaism to the calligrapher's style, and a touch of archaism, antiquity-minded as the Chinese are, is always something much to be desired. Speaking of Chinese painting, Chao Mêng-fu wrote in a colophon:

The most desirable quality in a painting is the air of antiquity enveloping it. If it is not there, the work is not worth much, however skilfully done it may be. . . . People now are totally oblivious of the fact that a work without an air of antiquity is full of faults and not worth looking at.

The same concept, the same veneration for the old, it appears, may be applied to calligraphy. Specifically, the air of antiquity Chao Mêng-fu spoke about can only be achieved by introducing, however subtly, the techniques of the older scripts to the modern ones. To be able to do that implies that the calligrapher is on intimate terms with the older scripts, an unmistakable indication that he has gone through the rigorous programme of training expected of a man who claims to be a calligrapher. It is for this reason that, in the talk about mixing techniques, we only hear of the application of the technique of the older scripts to the modern ones. We have never heard of a calligrapher being praised for application of *chên shu* technique to *li shu.*

A calligraphic style, even Wang Hsi-chih's, is a derivative of some older

[208]

Fig. 64   Ho Shao-chi: *Calligraphy in Hsing Shu*

styles. No calligrapher ever claims that he has developed a style entirely on his own. The calligrapher uses the characters as vehicles for the revelation of his personal style. But he will be the first to admit that he owes it to some old masters who in turn owe theirs to some even older masters. As far as *chên shu* is concerned, this tracing of origins eventually goes back to Chung Yu, although many would be perfectly happy to go back only as far as Wang Hsi-chih. If we are concerned with the older scripts, and modern calligraphers are generally so concerned, we may go way back to the dawn of history, including the inscriptions on the oracle bones. Calligraphers are proud of the ancestors of their styles, and it is up to the critics to work out the genealogy for our enlightenment. If the detective work is well done, the man is considered a competent critic and the owner of the style will be flattered. If the solution is off the mark, confusion ensues, as in the case of Tung Ch'i-ch'ang described above, where the whole business degenerates into a senseless exercise. All this may be illustrated by a story Pao Shih-ch'ên told of his encounter with Liu Yung (Liu Shih-an), a respected calligrapher of the Ch'ing Dynasty, which is included in Pao Shih-ch'ên's book *I Chou Shuang Chi,* presumably as an example of his sharp eye in detecting the sources of calligraphic styles. Pao Shih-ch'ên, according to his contemporary Ho Shao-chi, was extremely proud of his prodigious knowledge of calligraphy and was prone to be argumentative. Pao Shih-ch'ên tells that he met Liu Yung on a boat at Kiangyin and the two men had a long discussion on the merits of the works of the old masters. They were in complete agreement. At one point of the dialogue, the following exchange (which we present in abbreviated translation) developed:

LIU: What you have said about the old masters is all very judicious. Would you care to say something about my calligraphy?
PAO: Your style is derived from Tung Ch'i-ch'ang.
LIU: Why do you undervalue me like that? I pride myself in having achieved a measure of archaism in my calligraphy. I like to think of myself as a descendant of Chung Yu.
PAO: Do you claim that you have actually seen the works of Chung Yu? Specimens of Chung Yu's calligraphy extant are either copies or forgeries. You certainly would not condescend to model after those things. Your style is derived from Tung Ch'i-ch'ang. In his later years Tung Ch'i-ch'ang was approaching an archaic elegance. Your style is too clever. So you are not as good as Tung Ch'i-ch'ang.
LIU (after a long pause): My labours of many decades have been exposed and discredited by this one remark of yours.

We have quoted this exchange between Pao Shih-ch'ên and Liu Yung, not because the protagonists are of any particular importance, but because of the attitudes assumed by the two men which are illustrative of certain basic aspects of Chinese calligraphy. After going through the programme of training, which is prolonged and arduous, a calligrapher wants his public, and especially the knowledgeable critics, to think that he has drawn from the best sources, which are synonymous with the oldest sources. In the dialogue quoted above, we can almost feel Liu Yung's painful disappointment when Pao Shih-ch'ên flatly stated: 'Your style is derived from Tung Ch'i-ch'ang.' There was really nothing wrong with Tung Ch'i-ch'ang for he was easily the most outstanding and influential calligrapher in the early part of the Ch'ing Dynasty. The only trouble from Liu Yung's point of view was that Tung Ch'i-ch'ang was a late-comer while his idol, Chung Yu, lived fifteen centuries earlier and at one time influenced no less than Wang Hsi-chih himself. It was all a matter of trying to be the descendant of a long line founded by an illustrious ancestor, and Liu Yung was obviously hurt by what Pao Shih'ch'ên said. While we can understand Liu Yung's disappointment, Pao Shih-ch'ên was right in saying that Liu Yung's calligraphy is inferior to Tung Ch'i-ch'ang's. No sensible person would dispute such a statement. Pao Shih-ch'ên's critical appraisal of Liu Yung was later endorsed by K'ang Yu-wei.

A person who has gone through the period of training, including *chuan shu* and *li shu,* may be regarded as a finished craftsman, if he is at all gifted. But he is not yet a calligrapher. What constitutes greatness in the art is a question which does not lend itself to a ready answer, but the curious thing is that there seems to be a surprising degree of unanimity among the Chinese art historians and critics as to who are the truly great calligraphers, which indicates that there are generally accepted standards by which calligraphic proficiency is judged. Time, also, has not made spectacular reversals in taste and appraisal. Few, if any, writers on Chinese calligraphy will dispute the names we have included in this book, although claims may be made for a few whom we have left out. Fashion in calligraphic styles may have its ups and downs in different periods of history. Even Wang Hsi-chih was at times somewhat over-shadowed. But no one would argue that an eclipse in popular favour is necessarily a diminution in artistic worth. Like an eclipse, it is but a passing phenomenon and its full glitter will soon be restored.

'No nation,' said Mario Prodan, the Italian student of Chinese art, 'has produced more literature on art than the Chinese'. It is in this massive literature that we seek the answer to the question as to what constitutes greatness in calligraphy. Chinese art books generally fall into several broad categories, although they are not mutually exclusive. It seems profitable for us to make an overall survey of the field before we try to answer the question we have posed for ourselves. Literature on calligraphy may be divided into the following categories:

1. Manuals, books of instruction, teaching the novice how to hold the brush, where to start, how to proceed, what to emphasize, what to avoid, and so on. The manuals are full of technical terms which are quite untranslatable;

many of them are much too obscure to be of any practical use. Some of the manuals were written by the great calligraphers, including such big names as Wei Shuo, Wang Hsi-chih, Ou-yang Hsün, Yen Chên-ch'ing, Chang Hsü. Manuals published in more recent times are usually excerpts from and commentaries on the old manuals plus the author's own observations on the works of the calligraphers of more recent date. There are hundreds of such manuals, and none is regarded as standard. Some calligraphers feel that they should be ignored altogether because they are likely to restrict the learner's capabilities. There is much to be said for this point of view.

2. Catalogues of collectors and connoisseurs, often with critical appraisals by the authors. The Chinese are fond of making notations of the art treasures in their possession, giving the names of the artists, the titles of the works, the colophons and seals attached to the works, their previous owners, and in the case of the Ming collector Hsiang Yüan-pien, the prices paid and the profits made. A work of art usually passed through many hands. From the catalogues we are often enabled to trace its peregrinations, and by comparing the notations made by the various collectors, determine whether or not it is a genuine article. Entry into a catalogue of a famous collector is known in Chinese as *chu lu,* which is one of the most important clues we have in ascertaining authenticity. The collector's notations are also invaluable in helping us to form an opinion on the artists' worth. The most famous catalogue of calligraphic pieces is probably Mi Fu's *Shu Shih,* while the most comprehensive is the *Shih Ku T'ang Shu Hua Hui K'ao* compiled by the Ch'ing collector Pien Yung-yü. We owe to these assiduous compilers of catalogues our present knowledge of the works of the calligraphers, great and near-great, from ancient times to the present day. It may be mentioned in passing that the *chu lu* in the imperial collections, from Emperor Hui-tsung's *Hsüan-ho Shu P'u* to Emperor Ch'ien-lung's *Shih Ch'ü Pao Chi,* is often not as reliable as those of some of the private collectors, especially when the collectors themselves were famous artists, a situation brought about no doubt by the inevitable bureaucratic inefficiency connected with the vast collections of the royal households. On the other hand, some of the private collectors, most notably Mi Fu, were inclined to make their *chu lu* too opinionated, if not cantankerous, to be entirely trusted. The art dealers are the most avid readers of these catalogues and any work of art they offer to sell is accompanied by a table of *chu lu* like the pedigree of a thoroughbred. Where is the art lover who can resist buying a Wang Hsi-chih original once owned by Chung Shao-ching?

3. Colophons and poems in praise of artists and their works. Lovers of calligraphy are in the habit of writing colophons to the works they have seen. Sometimes the colophons are critical essays of great merit, and are mounted as appendages to the scroll. When the colophons are done by men such as Su Shih, Mi Fu, Chao Mêng-fu and Tung Ch'i-ch'ang, and transcribed in

their own hand, they are often more treasured than the works of art themselves. A great deal of critical opinion may also be gathered from literary works dealing with the art of calligraphy. The most famous essay on the subject is the *Shu P'u* by Sun Ch'ien-li. In this remarkable work, Sun Ch'ien-li described in beautiful language the finer points of the art of calligraphy, gave advice to the beginners, offered his critical opinions on calligraphers past and present, even disputed the veracity of an ugly story connected with Wang Hsi-chih. The great T'ang poets have also left us with quite a number of long poems singing the praise of calligraphers and their art. Li Po, the romantic poet, was particularly fond of Huai-su's *ts'ao shu*, rating the eccentric monk highly. Tu Fu, on his part, developed a passion for the *pa fên* script, while Han Yü was thrilled by the archaism of the stone drums. The examples set by these giants in the world of Chinese literature has been eagerly followed by the men of letters of subsequent generations, and literary works in prose and poetry praising artists and works of art have become an important department in Chinese art criticism.

4. Histories of calligraphy. In the field of painting, Hsieh Ho, a minor painter in the Southern Ch'i Dynasty, published around the year 500 a book entitled *Ku Hua P'in Lu,* which has become a classic. To most art historians, Hsieh Ho's book is important for the Six Canons (*lu fa*) of painting he laid down at the beginning of the book. A close examination of the book shows that Hsieh Ho's primary purpose was not to set up the *lu fa*, which he enumerated casually in the introduction with no explanation at all. What he really tried to do was to set up six levels (*p'in*) of artistic worth which were designated numerically. He then went about allocating the painters known to him, twenty-seven in all, to the different levels, justifying his allocation by a few general remarks. Hsieh Ho's idea of establishing an artistic hierarchy of merit somehow caught the imagination of Chinese art critics and many books along similar lines were written in the subsequent centuries, bringing Hsieh Ho up to date. The man who adapted Hsieh Ho's idea to the art of calligraphy was Chang Huai-kuan, author of a book entitled *Shu Tuan,* published in the first part of the eighth century. Chang Huai-kuan himself was a calligrapher extremely proud of his own achievements. He claimed that in *chên shu* and *hsing shu* he was the equal of Yü Shih-nan and Ch'u Shui-liang, and that in *ts'ao shu* he would dominate the field for a few hundred years. However, his claim appears to be totally unjustified. Posterity has not accorded Chang Huai-kuan even a minor place in T'ang calligraphy. But his book *Shu Tuan* has exerted quite a bit of influence on calligraphic criticism.. His innovation was to reduce Hsieh Ho's six levels to three which he called *shen* (divine), *miao* (wonderful) and *nêng* (skilful), thus setting up a hierarchy of calligraphic excellence. Following Hsieh Ho's example, Chang Huai-kuan then proceeded to allocate the calligraphers up to his time to the three levels—25 to the 'divine', 98 to the 'wonderful', 106 to the 'skilful'.

Chang Huai-kuan offered no explanation or justification of his allocation scheme, nor did he give us any precise definition of the three levels. Speaking of the various types of art critics, Thomas Bodkin, in his book *The Approach to Painting,* has this to say about a certain type:

Another type of critic conceives his function to be judicial rather than legislative, and arrogates to himself the duty, not of guiding the artist, but of pronouncing judgments of success or failure. These critics are characterized by their uselessness. They have no mandate from either the artist or his public to award reputation of success or failure.

Hsieh Ho and Chang Huai-kuan, together with their many followers, were critics of this type, and we are quite prepared to describe them in Bodkin's terms. We use their books only for the names of calligraphers they supply us, and in this sense they are sources of art history.

We have been combing this vast literature on calligraphy in search of an answer to our question: What constitutes greatness in calligraphic art? Why do certain calligraphers stand out above the others?

In going over the field, we have come across literally thousands of names of persons whom the art historians consider deserving enough to be mentioned in general surveys. We are fully convinced that each and every one of them is a highly polished technician. The English painter Constable once said: 'There has never been a boy painter, nor can there be; the art requires a long apprenticeship, being *mechanical,* as well as intellectual.' Precisely the same may be said of the art of Chinese calligraphy.

In going over the literature, we have also wrestled with the numerous abstract and abstruse terms in the vocabulary of the manual-writers and critics, as well as the endless analogies they make to natural objects and phenomena. Our search, we regret to say, has not been particularly rewarding. Chinese art writers are notoriously lax in supplying precise definitions to the terms they habitually use. They also have the tendency to use the same set of terms and employ the same analogies to calligraphic works the styles of which appear to us to be vastly different. For instance, the term *ch'iu ching,* referring to mastery of and maturity in brushmanship, has been applied to the art of practically all calligraphers and painters of note and we are at a total loss as to exactly what the term signifies. Similarly, analogies of calligraphic styles to the soaring dragon and wriggling serpent are so frequent that they really have no meaning at all. Chinese calligraphic criticism, generally speaking, has been more in the nature of critical assessment than critical argument, as evidenced by Chang Huai-kuan and his followers. Hsieh Ho allocated the Tsin painter Ku K'ai-chih to the third level, a critical appraisal which has been seriously challenged by later writers. No comparable misjudgment has been made with regard to Wang Hsi-chih's place in calligraphy, which seems to imply that, as far as calligraphy is concerned, the standards are more widely accepted than those of painting. Our only problem is to find out what the standards are.

In a colophon Su Shih casually remarked that in his opinion the T'ang painter Wu Tao-tzŭ was the greatest painter he knew of because the T'ang master was able to 'manifest new ideas within the framework of established methods'. It has occurred to us that this is the answer to our question on calligraphic standards. Su Shih's idea has been elaborated by subsequent writers on calligraphy. For instance, Sung Ts'ao, a critic in the early part of the Ch'ing Dynasty, said:

There are really no set rules in calligraphy. But we must begin by following the methods of the old masters before we can hope to develop something new out of them. If we succeed in bringing out something new, we will become old masters ourselves. We will then be in a position to legislate for others to follow.

Similarly, Fêng Pan, another Ch'ing critic, said:

If we wish to change the old methods, or to discard them, we must first know what they are; and if we do make a change, we must be sure that it is a change for the better. A calligrapher must have his personal style, but that does not mean ignoring the old masters. Those who do so are ignorant of what calligraphy is.

In our survey of the masters of Chinese calligraphy, we have seen that each and every one of them has something new, something different, something distinguished, to offer. All of them are of course thoroughly grounded in the physical skills required. They are also on the most intimate terms with tradition, the weight of which never seems to be too heavy on their shoulders. But over and above all these, and within the severe limitations under which they labour, they are able somehow to present us with an image which is not only technically proficient but also revelatory of a refreshing beauty all its own. They are the men who have taken over tradition and have enriched it—to bring forth new forms, new ideas and new truths. Their styles are indeed original, but original in the sense that they have kept within the boundaries of good taste. These are the men we have discussed in this book, from Wang Hsi-chih to Yü Yu-jên.

Chapter Fourteen

Calligraphy as an Art (3)

When we look at a calligraphic piece, our attention is naturally first drawn to the individual characters forming the piece, noting particularly the script in which it is done. But our eyes will also be cast over the whole display— the imaginary chain linking the characters into lines, the relation between one line and another, the space left uncovered, the balance and contrast of the whole piece. All these factors are of equal importance in contributing to the overall appeal of the work before us.

There are certain limitations to the calligrapher's choice of scripts. If he wishes to do a piece of *chuan shu* or *li shu,* the main body of the piece must be uniformly in that script. He is not permitted to mix the scripts, although he is free to sign and inscribe it in another script. With the three modern scripts—*chên shu, hsing shu* and *ts'ao shu*—the calligrapher may do a bit of mixing, but it should not be overdone. Fortunately, the world of Chinese characters is one of such limitless arrangements and combinations that each piece has, almost automatically, the freshness and excitement of discovery.

In stringing *chuan shu* or *li shu* characters into lines, the calligrapher, as a rule, is obliged to allocate equal space to each character. Generally speaking, *chên shu* characters should also be done in this way. Some calligraphers prefer to draw light lines on the paper forming squares or rectangles of uniform size and then to fill each square or rectangle with one character, thus maintaining the same number of characters in each line. We have seen an example of it in Ch'u Shui-liang's transcription of the *Han Ming Ch'ên Chuan Chan* (Fig. 29). A recent example is a scroll done by Wang Chuang-wei

[216]

(Fig. 65), one of the best *chên shu* calligraphers of our time. Like a string of evenly matched pearls, a line of characters done in this fashion appeals to our sense of uniformity and orderliness. There is here no problem in the management of spatial harmony and the emphasis is placed on the calligrapher's ability to make characters with many strokes appear in perfect balance with characters with only a few strokes. Formal *chên shu,* of course, may be done without drawing squares or rectangles on the paper and a certain measure of irregularity is often quite appealing. A good example is Wang Hsi-chih's *Hsiang Han T'ieh* (Fig. 66), a delightful little manuscript in which the Tsin master, after a frost, asked about his sovereign's health. Characters standing like beads of an abacus should not be regarded as good calligraphy. Some measure of irregularity is much to be desired. Wang Hsi-chih clearly was trying to achieve just that.

The trend towards asymmetry, quite naturally, is more marked in manuscripts done in *hsing shu.* The old masters have improvised a number of ways to underscore the element of variousness in their works. One of the ways is to write the same character slightly differently each time it appears in the text. For instance, the character *chih* (of) appears nineteen times in the *Lan T'ing Hsü* (Fig. 18), and Wang Hsi-chih did it in as many different ways without running into the danger of making it grotesque, a feat which has delighted the lovers of calligraphy no end, and which has been copied by many other calligraphers in subsequent centuries. Another way to introduce variousness into a calligraphic piece is to diversify what may be called the weight of the strokes forming the characters, doing some strokes heavier than others. All these devices are splendidly illustrated by Mi Fu's transcription of the *Li Sao Ching* (Fig. 67), the immortal elegy by Ch'ü Yüan. In this remarkably well preserved manuscript, which was photographically reproduced for the first time in 1958 in Taiwan, we can see that Mi Fu, in a script which is halfway between *chên shu* and *hsing shu,* has given us a most exciting demonstration of his calligraphic achievements, employing every trick in the bag to enhance the manuscript's artistic appeal, while keeping everything under tasteful control. The devices under the calligrapher's command are many and varied. Like 'method acting', their employment in a work of art is a form of contrived spontaneity which must at all times be conditioned by measured restraint.

It is in *ts'ao shu* that the calligrapher enjoys the maximum degree of freedom which appeals so much to the poets. There are practically no rules or conventions governing what he can do and cannot do. He may vary the size of the characters at will. He may link or separate the strokes in any way he pleases, even joining the characters together in a continuous swoop of the brush. He may turn squares into circles. He may indulge in violent thrusts and emphatic simplifications. As we look at the *ts'ao shu* by an accomplished master—Wang Hsi-chih, Wang Hsien-chih, Huai-su, Sun Ch'ien-li,

[217]

Huang T'ing-chien, Hsien-yü Shu, Yü Yu-jên—we feel that it would be wrong for us to call the irregular shapes before our eyes distortions or deformations. They are really reconstructions because they do not impress us as shapes and forms pulled out of proportion by whim or incapacity, but rather as distinct types, harmonious throughout, created in a new pattern and on a new scale as parts of a spiritual context in which they function to perfection.

Of paramount importance in executing a line of characters is what is known to the Chinese as *hang ch'i,* the flowing continuity of the characters as they take their places in the line. The characters forming a line should not stand there like a row of tin soldiers. They should be joined together as a coherent and articulate production. Flow of line, it has been said, is the most musical element in the visual arts. Wang Chuang-wei, the modern calligrapher whose *chên shu* we have just seen (Fig. 65), believes that, of all the arts, East and West, Chinese calligraphy is most akin to music. Indeed, in a fine calligraphic scroll, the patterns of alternating shapes and forms do have their internal rhythm which may be measured like bars of music. The whole piece is pulsating with movement that varies in tempo from second to second; one part expands, another contracts, as if it is breathing. It teases the eye unmercifully, making it jump from one character to another, from one line to another, until finally the entire composition is comprehended.

As our eyes dance over the piece, we become aware of the space that is left uncovered. It has been said that, 'of the formal elements of design this gift of spacing is China's greatest contribution to the world's art'. Laurence Binyon, the British specialist of Asian art, who made the above statement, was talking about Chinese painting. But the statement is equally applicable to Chinese calligraphy, perhaps more so because the calligrapher has much fewer formal elements to play with so that he has to exert more effort to bring about the saliences and hollows to attain the highest aesthetic appeal in his work. Spacing in Chinese art is known as *pu po,* which has been defined by a modern Chinese critic as 'the proper relationship and the organic integration between one character and another, one line and another, even one scroll and another'. When we look at the finer examples of Chinese calligraphy, even a casual piece such as Wang Hsi-chih's letter after a snowfall (Fig. 21), we become conscious of the fact that the pieces are deliberately composed, the individual characters taking their places in a pre-ordained scheme of things, flawlessly articulated, gracefully dimensioned, leaving nothing to chance. We range our eyes over the whole display and we are left with the sensation that we are looking at a finished product in which there is complete harmony between the parts of the whole, with the black strokes of the characters and the white areas left unfilled in such mysterious balance that our eyes rest in willing contentment within its bounds. A calligraphic piece, therefore, is a demonstration of style *and* composition whose successful resolution is a

[218]

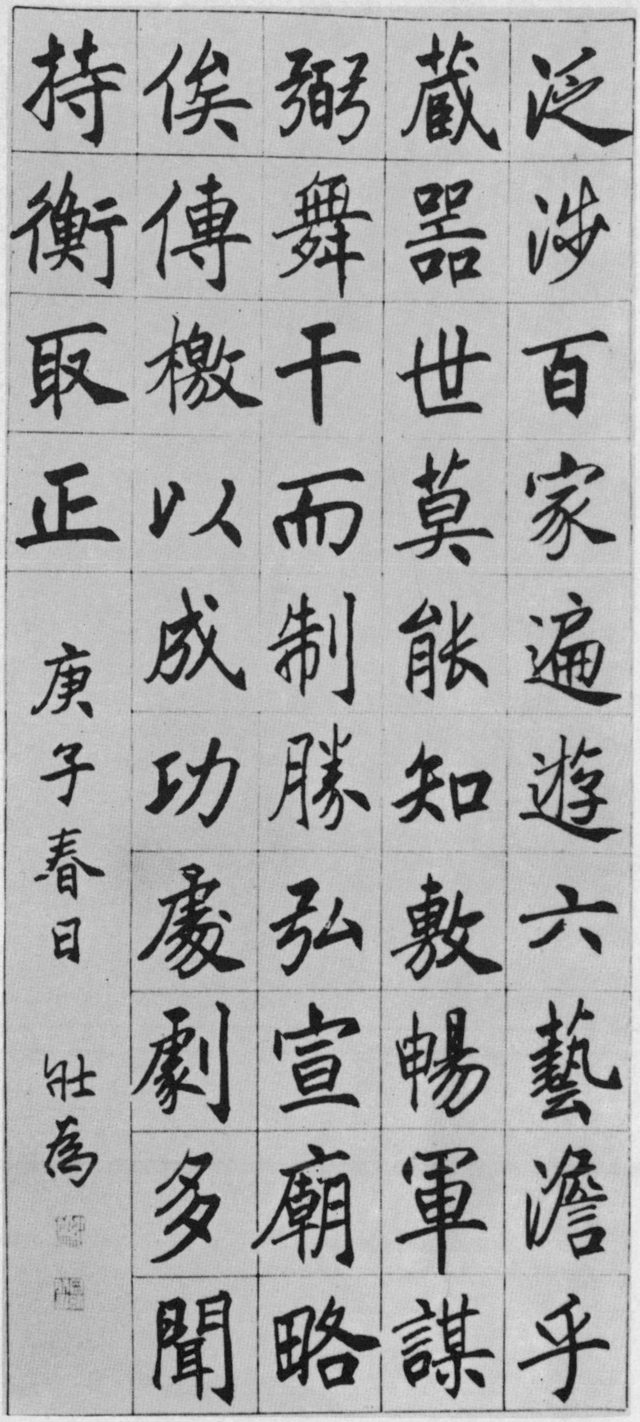

泛涉百家遍遊六藝澹乎
藏器世莫能知敷暢軍謀
�舞干而制勝弘宣廟略
俟傳檄以成功慶劇多聞
持衡取正　庚子春日　壯為

Fig. 65　Wang Chuang-wei: *Calligraphy in Chên Shu*

triumph in artistic management. These are the things we look for in the masterpieces.

As we gaze at them, we seem to sense the motion of the brush as it glides over the writing surface and the element of timing of such motion. The Chinese characters are done with a brush soaked with ink over a surface (paper or silk) that is slightly absorbent. As the brush comes into contact with the surface, the amount of ink that is imparted is dependent upon the length of time the brush remains at that particular point. If the brush is guided across the surface rapidly, the amount of ink imparted on the surface will be small. If the brush pauses, however momentarily, at a certain point, the amount of ink deposited upon and absorbed by the surface will be larger. It follows that the calligrapher must time his strokes in such a manner that the right amount of ink is deposited at the right places. This calls for expert control. A painter in oil may retouch or over-paint his canvas. A calligrapher is allowed no such liberties. When a stroke or a character is done, its defects, if any, cannot be corrected. The Western painters have told us that they often do not have the finished product in mind when they take up the brush. Picasso once said:

I don't know in advance what I am going to put on the canvas, any more than I decide in advance what colours to use. Whilst I work, I take no stock of what I am painting on the canvas. Every time I begin a picture, I feel as though I were throwing myself into the void. I never know if I shall fall on my feet again. It is only later that I begin to evaluate more exactly the result of my work.

Picasso's experience is shared by Braque, who told us:

A picture is an adventure each time. When I tackle the white canvas I never know how it will come out. This is the risk you must take. I never visualize a picture in my mind before starting to paint.

How different are these statements from what the Chinese calligraphers and painters have told us! In a previous chapter, we have cited Yü Yu-jên's advice: 'Conceive of an image of the finished character in the mind before applying the brush to the writing surface.' This principle is known in Chinese as *i tsai pi hsien,* 'concept before the brush', and is equally applicable to calligraphy and painting. Yü Yu-jên was only repeating what the old masters, beginning from Wang Hsi-chih, said over and over again. Kuo Hsi, the famous Sung landscape painter, explained the principle in these words:

It is really like an expert craftsman carving a zither out of a piece of *tung* wood. . . . Even when the piece of wood is still lying on the ground, and the

[220]

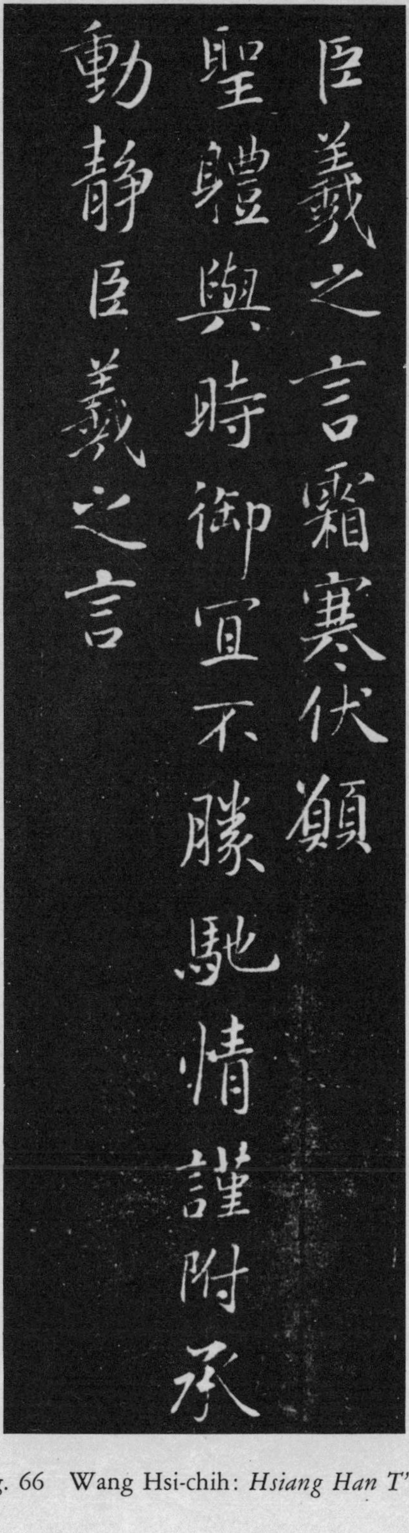

臣羲之言霜寒伏願
聖體與時御宜不勝馳情謹附承
動靜臣羲之言

Fig. 66   Wang Hsi-chih: *Hsiang Han T'ieh*

branches and leaves have yet to be cut off, the image of the completed zither is already in the mind of the maker.

Nothing, it appears, is more of an anathema to the Chinese artist than a work made up in a piecemeal fashion, even in a calligraphic piece, which is composed of characters and·nothing else. It is quite clear that the main consideration in this case is the peculiar qualities of the various mediums used by the Chinese. The calligrapher, or the painter, not only has to form a complete image of the finished product in his mind before he takes up his brush, but also to determine beforehand the speed with which each part is to be done. Once the action starts, and the brush begins to glide over the surface, he can no longer afford the luxury of the slightest hesitation or indecision. The Chinese creative process may be described by Li Po's immortal song about his friend Huai-su, presented here in prose translation as follows:

The *ts'ao shu* of the young monk Huai-su is the very best in the realm. The fishes of Peiming rise from his ink-pool; the tip of his brush kills all the Chungshan rabbits. It was cold in the eighth and ninth months of the year. The drinkers and poets were assembled in his house. There were several trunks full of paper and silk; the ink juice shone from the slabs made of Hsüanchow stone. The drunken monk leaned on a bed made of ropes, and in a few moments he had finished several thousand sheets. It was like the strong wind before a sudden storm, or the flower-petals and snowflakes blown by the gale. He rose and stood against the wall; his hand went on without any pause. Enormous characters began to form lines, and I heard the cries of the gods and spirits, as I saw the dragons and serpents running: to the left and to the right, fast like a flash of lightning, or like the battle between Ch'u and Han. How many families there are in the seven prefectures of Hunan! And each family has scrolls and screens by this man! Wang Hsi-chih and Chang Hsü are famed for this art. Chang Hsü is dead and does not count. Our master's art is not modelled after the old, and we prize the old because it is natural. There is no reason to admire the dance of Lady Kung-sun.

In our consideration of this aspect of Chinese calligraphy, the temptation is irresistible to compare it to what is known as 'action painting' in Modern Art, to regard a calligraphic piece as a record of the muscular urges of the hand that holds the brush, to see it as the outcome of the battle between the mind and the hand of the artist. The Chinese artists, calligraphers and painters alike, have often talked about *hsin shou hsiang yin,* a concept which may be interpreted as the co-ordination between the mind and the hand. It implies that the artist has a mental image of what he proposes to commit to paper. His problem is to make what he eventually commits to paper conform as much as possible with what he has in mind. In this sense, a calligraphic piece is a type of automatism, a realization of an artistic concept through the application of sophisticated brushmanship. When the calligrapher's art is mature, his work is a grand display of linear ecstasies.

[222]

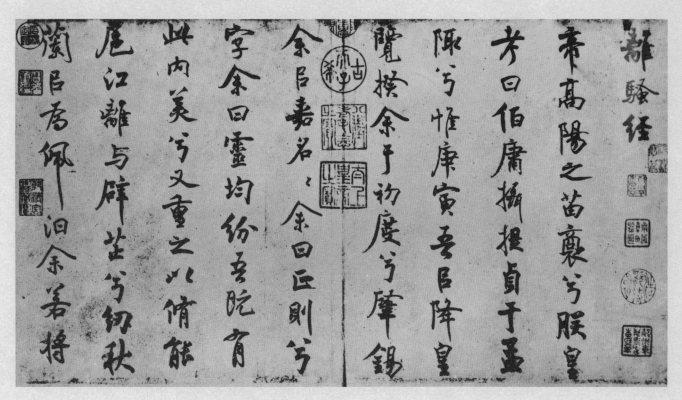

Fig. 67   Mi Fu: *Li Sao Ching* (first portion)

To the connoisseur of Chinese calligraphy, a work also has its appeal in the materials used. We have noted how fastidious the calligraphers are in the choice of their brushes. If the calligraphers are careful in their choice of brushes, they are even more so in the choice of ink. In remote antiquity writing was done with lacquer. Juice derived from ground graphite was later used. When calligraphy became an art in the Ch'in and Han period, ink came to be made with soot derived from burned tree-branches mixed with glue of animal origin. In the history books, we read of the high-quality ink produced in the Han period at a place named Yü-mi (now Ch'ienyang Hsien of Shensi Province) because the pines grown in that district were particularly suited to make ink. Soot collected from the burned branches of the *tung* tree, a favourite theme of the painters, is also used to make ink. Cheaper varieties are made of burned pig-fat. The burning of the ingredients is done in indoor furnaces and the soot is collected from the surrounding walls. The best ink is made of the soot farthest away from the furnace because it is the most refined. Terms such as *yüan yen* (far soot) and *kao yen* (high soot) have been used to describe ink of the best quality.

The soot collected is mixed with glue made out of ox-horn, deer-horn, fish-scale or donkey-skin. After the mixture of soot and glue is prepared, the next step, and the most important step, is to pound the glutinous substance into a thick, well-blended paste. Wei Tan, tutor of the great Chung Yu, besides being a famous calligrapher, was noted for his ink-making. He used to pound the mixture in an iron utensil thirty thousand times. After the pounding the paste is cut up into small pieces and placed in moulds which give them the desired shape and decorations. The ink-sticks, now in their final stage, are left to dry and solidify.

Many calligraphers and painters make their own ink. All sorts of theories and superstitions attend their task. First of all, they go about finding what they consider to be the best materials. It is the general belief that the gnarled and weather-beaten branches of the pine trees found in the famous scenic spots of the country yield the finest soot. Glue made out of horns of animals captured in their natural habitat is preferred. The element of exoticism has become a fetish. Su Shih used to make ink himself with graphite from Korea and glue from the animals of Khitan. In the process of burning wood for soot, he almost burned his house down. Besides soot and glue, precious materials are added to improve the quality and enhance the value. Wei Tan, besides pounding the mixture thoroughly, also added musk and mother-of-pearl to the mixture.

As far back as the Han Dynasty, special officials were appointed by the Emperor to take charge of the manufacture of writing materials for the royal household. In the T'ang Dynasty, ink-making became an exalted profession and good ink-makers, such as Tsu Min, were universally revered.

By far the most renowned ink-maker is Li T'ing-kuei of the Period of Five Dynasties. The man's surname was originally Hsi. The Southern T'ang ruler was so impressed by his ink-making that the surname Li, the surname of the royal household, was bestowed upon him as a special honour. According to Li T'ing-kuei's formula, to each catty (*chin,* equal to 1-1/3 lb) of pine soot he added three ounces (*liang,* one *chin* is divided into sixteen *liang*) of ground mother-of-pearl, one ounce of ground jade, one ounce of Baroos camphor, plus a quantity of raw lacquer. The glutinous paste resulting from the mixture was pounded, not thirty thousand times as Wei Tan did, but one hundred thousand times. In moments of extravagance, Li T'ing-kuei also mixed into the compound such expensive materials as rhinoceros-horn, pomegranate-peel, gamboge, croton-oil bean and cinnabar. The ink-sticks he made were said to be 'as hard as jade and stone' and 'could be immersed in water for three years without damage'. Every stick of Li T'ing-kuei ink bore his signature, sometimes his full name, sometimes only the character 'Kuei'. The dragon motif was his favourite design. The best ink-sticks he fashioned were decorated with dragons with two rows of fins. In his book *Mo Shih* (History of Ink), Ma San-hêng, the Ming patriot, listed two hundred and forty-eight ink-makers by name, among whom the best known was Li T'ing-kuei.

The test of good ink, generally speaking, is the lustre it manifests when applied to silk or paper. The Sung painter Ch'ao Yüeh-chih, in his book *Mo Ching* (Ink Classic) said:

The best ink has a purple lustre; a black lustre is second best; a white lustre is the least desired. Ink quality is determined by both the lustre and the colour. Durability (the ability to retain lustre and colour without fading) is the highest virtue. Lustre growing out of the glue is not the best quality. When struck, the ink-stick should give a clear and resonant sound. A heavy and dull tone is the mark of inferiority. A good ink-stick should be reasonably heavy. New ink-sticks are not as good as old ones. When aged for more than ten years, the ink-stick should be as hard as stone. The older it is the harder it becomes. The soot becomes blacker with age. When it is very black it gives a purple lustre. The glue becomes firmer with age. A firm glue promotes a brighter lustre. This is why new ink-sticks are not as good as old ones. Ink-sticks which have not passed three summers should not be used. Old ink-sticks are prized not only for age but also for quality. Size and shape do not matter.

Good ink-sticks are worth their weight in gold. A genuine Li T'ing-kuei, if extant, would be priceless. The fastidious calligraphers have ink-sticks made to their own specifications. The ancient ink-sticks were spherical. Cylindrical and rectangular solids are more common now. Good ink-sticks are richly decorated with border designs and inscriptions, even pictures, generally coloured in gold and blue. Following the practice of *tou ch'a* (tea competition) in the Sung Dynasty, during which various varieties of tea were tasted and compared, scholars and artists also held sessions of *tou mo* (ink competition) where writings done with different types of ink were tested and collated. Su Shih, the proud owner of a genuine Li T'ing-kuei, used to transcribe his own literary compositions with various types of ink, carefully recording the details for future examination. One of his friends tried to improve his calligraphy by drinking good ink as a beverage.

To prepare liquid ink for writing, the ink-stick is ground gently in an upright position on an ink-stone in a pool of clear water. According to the Ming painter-calligrapher T'ang Yin, the water should be at room temperature, water drawn directly from the well would be too cold for the purpose. As the grinding proceeds, a viscid, black solution is gradually formed—ink. T'ang Yin also told us that the hard tuft of the new brush should first be softened in clear water before dipping it into ink.

The ink-stone (*yen*) to the calligrapher is like 'a mirror to a beauty'. In the Han Dynasty, ink-stones were made of jade or tile. T'ang ink-stones were usually made of pottery. After much experimentation, certain types of stone were found to be the most suitable material. Good ink-stones are adorned with carvings, such as winding dragons, prunus branches or lotus leaves. Incised inscriptions are sometimes included, generally on the back. Ink-stones come in all shapes and forms. Some of them suggest the Greek lyre, the crescent moon, the peach, the fish. From the Sung Dynasty onwards, stone used to make ink-stones has come from two principal sources—Tuanchow in Kwangtung and Hsichow in Anhwei. Tuanchow stone is good because its exposure to underground water has made it porous. A good Tuanchow ink-stone is so smooth that one can hardly hear the sound of the grinding. The sensation of grinding an ink-stick on a Tuanchow ink-stone, according to one expert, should be like melting wax on a hot plate. As a rule, the Tuanchow ink-stone is purple-black, but it can also be bluish-black. A rare type is called 'banana white' after its colour. The Hsichow stone is generally bluish with clearly observable veins. The texture is not as fine and smooth as Tuanchow stone, but it possesses a remarkable quality of yielding ink more quickly. Mi Fu, who wrote a book on the subject, listed and described the better and the rare ink-stones he came across one by one, noting the shape, the carving, the colour, the maker, the owner, the veins. The antiquity-minded have ink-stones made of the bricks and tiles of old tombs and palaces. As collectors' items, ink-stones are often given descriptive names—'dragon-tail', 'ice cracks', 'fluttering silk'. If the markings are circular, like knots in wood, they are called 'eyes', which are identified either by their colouring (cinnabar point, rainbow tail) or by their odd shapes (mynah eyes, sparrow specks). There are hundreds of varieties.

The man who first did calligraphy on silk was probably Ts'ai Yung of the Han Dynasty. From that time on, silk material, known as *chüan,* has been one of the principal surfaces for writing and painting.

In the early days, the silk used was unprimed and the weave was coarse. The early T'ang painters made a number of experiments with the process of priming. One method, allegedly inaugurated by the great figure painter Wu Tao-tzŭ, was to immerse the silk in a hot glucose solution after which a sizing talc made of chalk or starch was beaten into it with a flat spatula until the surface was smooth and bright enough to reflect light. Another method, attributed to the T'ang painter Chou Fang, was to beetle the silk on polished stone until the interstices had been filled in and the silk showed a smooth continuous surface. Priming with glue mixed with alum came into general use in the Period of Five Dynasties. It was said that, when the priming was completed, the silk appeared as white as snow and as pure as stream water. In the Sung Dynasty, silk woven for the royal household was a type of dense and heavy fabric with a polished, jade-like surface. Two methods of weaving silk existed side by side. One method was to use double threads for both the warp and the weft; the other was to use a single thread for the weft and a double thread for the warp.

Hsü Shên's dictionary *Shuo Wên Chieh Tzŭ,* issued in 100 A.D., contains the character *chih,* 'paper', which bears the radical *ssŭ,* 'silk'. This bit of information has led some scholars to speculate that 'paper' in the early days was made of silk refuse. According to classical histories, Ts'ai Lun, an official of the Han court, was the 'inventor' of paper, and the date of the momentous invention was fixed at 105 A.D. The paper Ts'ai Lun made was composed of linen waste, old rags, fishing nets and tree-bark. It was probably unsized. The large-scale manufacture of paper probably exhausted the supply of the raw materials very quickly. To meet the demand, new materials were found— hemp in Szechuan, young bamboo in Fukien, husks of millet in Chekiang, corn and rice stalks in Central China, water-fungus in the coastal areas, mulberry, ramie and osier in North China. The tragic Emperor Hou-tsu of the Southern T'ang Dynasty (the great lyric poet Li Yü who was also a calligrapher and painter of impressive merit) had a specially high quality paper made for the use of the galaxy of artists assembled in his court. It was called *Ch'êng Hsin T'ang* paper after the name of the palace hall in which the Emperor and his court artists used to congregate. Paper used for writing and painting in the early days was unsized, and was therefore somewhat absorbent. The sizing process was developed in the T'ang Dynasty at about the time when silk began to be primed. It consisted of the application of an agent—usually glue but sometimes gypsum or rice-flour—which had the effect of hardening the paper and protecting it against the inroads of moisture. The *Ch'êng Hsin T'ang* paper was sized. It was slightly yellowish and very thin and smooth, 'as thin as the membrane of the egg, as strong and clean as jade'.

For display and safe-keeping, calligraphic pieces are mounted on paper or silk into scrolls or albums. Mounting works of art is a highly specialized craft and is as important a department as the framing of pictures in the West. To show respect to the works of art, some collectors, particularly the Emperors, were in the habit of using expensive materials such as brocades for the borders, ivory for the ends of the rolls, camphor for the box. The Japanese are fond of using silk or paper of various colours for the borders. The Chinese generally prefer plain white. The experts in mounting are also cleaners and restorers. Works done on silk are likely to turn brown and the threads break off. Special methods have been developed to 'wash' the works and occasionally the missing parts are filled in, a process known as 'mending'.

We have gone into this long and yet necessarily superficial description of the material aspects of Chinese calligraphy for the purpose of emphasizing what Eric Newton, the English art historian, has called 'the medium and its effect on the work of art', which he defined in his book *The Arts of Man* in these words:

The invisible, inner world of experience, the artist's secret possession, is limited only by his capacity for experience. But once the artist crosses the frontier between emotion and creation, choice is forced upon him. The main problem is no longer the end but the means. For him the 'what?' of his creative imagination is gradually invaded by the 'how?' of his creative hand. Briefly, he has to choose a medium (usually it is chosen for him by the requirements of his patron or the nature of the task imposed on him) and once he has done so the age-old struggle between opportunity and limitation begins. Out of that struggle the work of art is born. Stubbornly the medium imposes its will on the artist while he, like a skilful jujitsu wrestler, turns its stubbornness to account, making each medium work *for* him to produce effects unattainable by any other means, even while it is working *against* him by refusing to behave as his creative imagination would perhaps have liked.

In a previous chapter, we have discussed the capabilities and limitations of the Chinese brush and the preferences of various calligraphers which are more or less dictated by their own individual styles. A calligrapher has a choice of doing his work on silk or paper. As a general rule, the calligraphers prefer paper to silk while the painters prefer silk to paper. The gorgeous paintings of the T'ang and Sung periods are mostly on silk, while the calligraphic pieces of the same period are usually on paper. The most famous calligraphic work on silk is, of course, Wang Hsi-chih's *Lan T'ing Hsü*. According to historical records, the material the Tsin master used was 'paper made of silk cocoon', a type of paper manufactured out of silk refuse. Mi Fu, who preferred paper to silk for both calligraphy and painting, has left us a transcription of some poems on a piece of rare Szechuan silk. Calligraphers were frequently called upon to transcribe epitaphs for engraving on stone. In order to prevent distortion by stretching in the engraving process, paper was obviously the more suitable material. Like the artists in the West, as Eric Newton said, the medium is sometimes chosen for the calligrapher by the

[228]

requirements of his patron or the nature of the task imposed on him. In the T'ang Dynasty, both calligraphers and painters were called upon to adorn the walls of palaces, temples and shrines with their works. Wall writing, like wall painting, was very much the fashion of the day, as we have seen in the case of Huai-su as related in Li Po's song. Yang Ning-shih, we may recall, also did a great deal of wall writing. There is a picture, originally done by Li Kung-lin, showing Mi Fu making inscriptions on a slab of stone in the garden. All the wall writings, unfortunately, have been irreparably lost.

The calligrapher, like the painter, has the choice of primed or unprimed silk, sized or unsized paper. This choice is by and large determined by his calligraphic style. Primed silk and sized paper have hard and smooth surfaces. They are only very slightly absorbent, so that the ink does not blur easily on them. These qualities quite naturally appeal to the artists employing firm and fine brushstrokes. It was therefore not an accident that the T'ang figure painters Wu Tao-tzŭ and Chou Fang experimented so enthusiastically with silk priming. Nor was it an expensive habit for the Sung painter Li Kung-lin to use *Ch'êng Hsing T'ang* paper for his pictures done in 'iron wire lines'. The T'ang calligrapher Ou-yang Hsün insisted upon using 'strong, thin, white and smooth' paper for his works. Unprimed silk and unsized paper, on the other hand, are porous and highly absorbent, allowing ink to blur easily. These are the materials preferred by Su Shih and Mi Fu, who wished to achieve special aesthetic effects through modulation and controlled timing. The choices are dictated by the requirements of the artists' style in which no patron, however discriminating, should be allowed to interfere.

The use of high quality materials is a factor which contributes greatly to our full enjoyment of the works of art. We do not wish to see the artists defeated in what Eric Newton called 'the age-old struggle between opportunity and limitation'. In looking at a work of art, style and composition are, of course, the primary considerations. But at the same time, we are excited by what may be called the subordinate aspects—the jade-like smoothness of a sheet of *Ch'êng Hsin T'ang* paper, the metallic lustre of Li T'ing-kuei ink, all of which seem to dazzle our eyes across the centuries. Chang Hsü and Huai-su, when drunk, sometimes wrote with their heads or hats. Mi Fu experimented with the seed-case of the lotus as a brush. Tung Ch'i-ch'ang has left us calligraphic scrolls done on satin. One Ch'ing artist, Kao Ch'i-p'ei, fascinated us by doing calligraphy and painting with his fingers and finger-nails. K'ang Yu-wei, in doing extremely large characters, used the broom instead of the brush. All these are oddities which delight us but should not be taken seriously. Our pleasure becomes total only when we see works of art done by the masters in their prime with mediums best suited to their styles. Malraux has talked enthusiastically about the 'museum without walls' made possible by the modern methods of reproduction. Unfortunately there are certain features of Chinese calligraphy, most notably the lustre of ink, what the

Chinese call *mo kuang* or *mo ts'ai,* which no camera can capture. We have placed emphasis on this point because these features are essential to the complete appreciation of the art of Chinese calligraphy.

Chapter Fifteen

Enjoying Calligraphy

Chinese calligraphers have been extremely prolific in their output. The ravages of wars, accidents and natural disasters have of course taken their heavy toll, and some collectors have committed unpardonable crimes against the items in their possession. But what has survived still staggers our imagination. The *San Hsi T'ang Fa T'ieh,* which covers only the manuscripts (not tablets) in the period between Chung Yu of the late Han Dynasty and Tung Ch'i-ch'ang of the late Ming Dynasty, runs to thirty-two volumes. Tablet rubbings are issued in individual volumes by private publishers, and there are thousands of them.

Our interest in Chinese calligraphy urges us to explore the whole field in pursuit of a thorough understanding of the full range of the artistry of the masters, old and new. But that is an impossible task. We can concern ourselves only with a fraction of a fraction of what the calligraphers have left us. We have to make choices, and they are bound to be personal. Fortunately, we have an enormous literature of calligraphic criticism to guide us, and calligraphic excellence, though never sharply defined, is something which is readily recognized. Our experience has been that the more we study the works of the acknowledged masters, the more sensitive we become to their appeal. We may differ with some of the critical assessments here and there. A few calligraphers who enjoyed tremendous fame in their time may appear to us to be rather mediocre, even incompetent. This may be due to the fact that too few of their works have come down to us. We often find it difficult to draw the line of distinction between genius and talent. But by and large, the standards are sound and reliable, judicious and trustworthy, and if we concentrate ourselves on the truly representative works of the universally acknowledged masters, we may indeed fulfil our ambition of seeing and enjoying the very best that the past has to offer.

We propose to divide the calligraphic works we have seen and discussed into two broad categories which we shall designate as the 'major' and the 'minor' works. In the first category, we shall include works which the calligraphers have done with an eye to posterity, and in the second category works which they have done in their more relaxed moments. By studying the works in both categories, we hope to be able to comprehend the creative process in Chinese calligraphy and thereby to get an idea of what the art is all about.

MAJOR WORKS

Tablets. Beginning from the Ch'in Dynasty, calligraphers have been called upon to transcribe texts to be engraved on stone tablets in commemoration of important events or in memory of the dead. The tablet texts are formal and solemn documents done with great care either as a tribute to a friend or in response to a commission by a patron. The usual practice is for the calligrapher to transcribe the text on paper and the transcription is then pasted on the polished surface of a stone slab to be engraved. Since the engraver has to cut through the paper in the engraving process, the original transcription cannot be preserved, and what we are left with are rubbings made from the tablet with characters in white against a black background. However, to save the original transcription, a process has been developed whereby the transcription is traced by a craftsman and the traced copy is committed to the stone. The Chinese engravers are expert craftsmen who have developed their skill to near perfection, and their engraving is as faithful to the original as is humanly possible. This may be illustrated by Wang Hsi-chih's *Hsing Jang T'ieh* (Fig. 68), which we reproduce both in the manuscript and in the engraved rubbing form. A careful comparison of the two offers us a splendid example of the engraver's craftsmanship. Some students of Chinese calligraphy, including Mi Fu, are inclined to undervalue the rubbings, calling them 'second-hand calligraphy'. While it is undoubtedly true that nothing can take the place of the original, rubbings have played a most important role in the growth of Chinese calligraphic art, both in informing us about the scripts and styles and in providing easily obtainable copies to model after. In the previous chapters we have taken quite a number of tablet rubbings as illustrations, beginning with the *I Shan Pei* attributed to Li Ssǔ (Fig. 11) through some of the T'ang masters such as the *To Pao T'a* by Yen Chên-ch'ing (Fig. 30b) down to the large characters by Chao Chih-ch'ien (Fig. 53a), covering a span of about two thousand years. The tablets are mostly in the formal scripts— *chuan shu, li shu* and *chên shu*—and only rarely in *hsing shu*, almost never in *ts'ao shu.* They are all representative works of calligraphers, known and

行穰帖玉宣和時如出董思

Fig. 68a Wang Hsi-chih: *Hsing Jang T'ieh* (in manuscript form)

unknown, and calligraphic specimens of first-rate importance. In terms of influence upon Chinese calligraphic art, they are at least on the same level as the Tsin masters.

Transcriptions. The greatest treasures of Chinese calligraphy are the transcriptions of literary works composed either by the calligraphers themselves or by other men of letters. When a calligrapher feels the urge to do a major work, his first consideration is to find a text to transcribe. If he happens to be also a man of letters, as so many calligraphers are, he is tempted to transcribe a literary composition of his own. There is something terribly exciting about a literary composition transcribed by its author who is also a calligrapher— two works of art combined in one. It is like a composer playing his own composition, a playwright starring in his own play. The greatest work of this kind is, of course, Wang Hsi-chih's transcription of his own essay *Lan T'ing Hsü,* copies of which we have seen (Fig. 18). Others are Chung Yu's *Chien Chi Chih Piao* (Fig. 16), Huai-su's *Tzü Hsü T'ieh* (Fig. 33a), Sun Ch'ien-li's *Shu P'u* (Fig. 35), Su Shih's *Ch'ih Pi Fu* (Fig. 39), Huang T'ing-chien's *Sung Fêng Ko Shih* (Fig. 41), to mention only the most outstanding. If the calligrapher does not happen to be a literary man, or if he does not wish to transcribe his own literary compositions, he may choose any text at hand. We are familiar with the many transcriptions of the *Ch'ien Tzǔ Wên* from Chih-yung to Yü Yu-jên. Among the other texts are Wang Hsi-chih's transcription of the *Yüeh I Lun* and *Huang T'ing Ching* (Fig. 17), Chung Shao-ching's transcription of the *Ling Fei Ching* (Fig. 36), Mi Fu's transcription of the *Li Sao Ching* (Fig. 67), again mentioning only the most prominent.

It is indeed most regrettable that in our 'museum without walls', we are only able to produce small portions of these extraordinary works, some of which are very long. The excitement of reading the texts of classical literary works (most Chinese have learned them by heart) transcribed by great calligraphers in their exquisite hand is lost to us. Many calligraphers have advised us that, in doing transcriptions of this nature, the mind must first be cleared of all mundane thoughts and the task should be approached with solemnity and seriousness, 'as in the presence of a superior man'. Although such advice may not be followed by a calligrapher like Huai-su, the fact remains that all these are the artists' major works and may be enjoyed in full measure only when the whole text is before us, as in the case of Wên Chêng-ming's transcription of Ou-yang Siu's essay *Tsui Wêng T'ing Chi* (Fig. 48b). Those who love Chinese literature and Chinese calligraphy would be well advised to consult such collections as the *San Hsi T'ang Fa T'ieh,* so that they can read and see the masterpieces at the same time.

MINOR WORKS

Colophons. Colophons done by the calligraphers on works of other calligraphers are source materials for art criticism. They are also works of art in

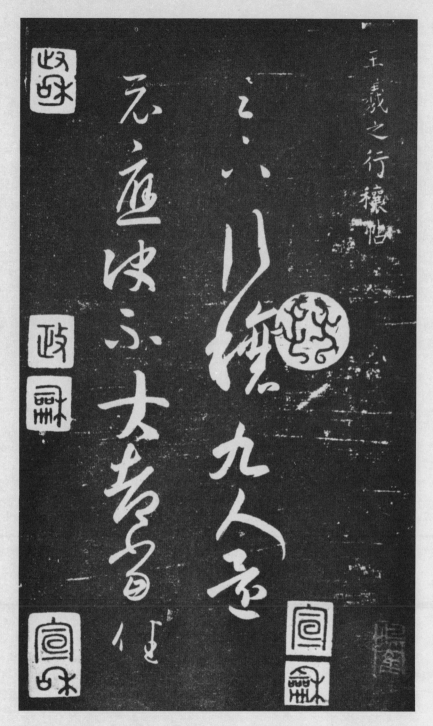

Fig. 68b   Wang Hsi-chih: *Hsing Jang T'ieh* (in engraved rubbing form)

themselves. The calligraphers are inspired by a sense of awe when they write colophons to the masterpieces of the past, and it is human nature for them to try to do their very best. Among the numerous colophons we have, three have been chosen as illustrations: Mi Fu's colophon to Ch'u Shui-liang's copy of *Lan T'ing Hsü* (Fig. 69); Chao Mêng-fu's colophon to Wang Hsi-chih's letter after a snowfall (Fig. 70); and Tung Ch'i-ch'ang's colophon to the *Shêng Chiao Hsü* (Fig. 71). We have chosen these three examples because the juxtaposition of the great calligraphers of the Sung, Yüan and Ming periods with the Tsin master Wang Hsi-chih has a peculiar appeal to the lovers of Chinese calligraphy, what Keats has called 'the entanglements and enrichments' of art. It goes without saying that all three colophons were done with the loving care to which the works they were commenting upon were entitled.

Letters. By far the bulk of the manuscripts extant are letters which, we may presume, have been preserved by their recipients because of the artistic eminence of the writers. The Ch'ing Emperor Ch'ien-lung formed the San Hsi T'ang, 'Hall of Three Rarities', in 1746 as the repository of the calligraphic works in his collection, and all three of the rarities are letters by Tsin calligraphers—Wang Hsi-chih's letter after a snowfall, Wang Hsien-chih's *Chung Ch'iu T'ieh,* and a letter by a less known Tsin calligrapher Wang Hsün (Fig. 21, Fig. 24, and Fig. 72). The letters, done casually and without any conscious effort, are splendid examples of the calligraphers' art in their more relaxed moments, and may be studied jointly with the more serious works. In addition to the three letters of the Tsin masters, we have seen some others by Ts'ai Hsiang (Fig. 38), Mi Fu (Fig. 43b), Chao Mêng-fu (Fig. 46c), and Chao Chih-ch'ien (Fig. 53b).

Drafts. Just as we treasure the drawings of the great artists of the West, we look upon the drafts the Chinese calligraphers have left us as yet another aspect of their art which is revelatory of their styles. Unfortunately the number of drafts we have is rather limited. In a sense, Wang Hsi-chih's *Lan T'ing Hsü* is a draft which has been copied by the T'ang calligraphers including its several corrections. Many critics hold the view that Yen Chên-ch'ing's draft of his obituary of his nephew (Fig. 31) is his best work, although the piece is littered with corrections.

Copies. In the previous chapters we have referred often to the Chinese calligraphers' habit of copying the works of others. When done by an accomplished calligrapher, the Chinese are inclined to regard the copies as originals of the copier. The most copied work undoubtedly is the *Lan T'ing Hsü,* and since the original had gone into Emperor T'ai-tsung's tomb, the later copies are really copies of copies. And yet Chinese collectors and connoisseurs have always treasured the copies by the famous calligraphers. We may now buy anthologies of the various copies of the *Lan T'ing Hsü,* and if we compare them carefully we will find that the copies have taken quite a bit of liberty

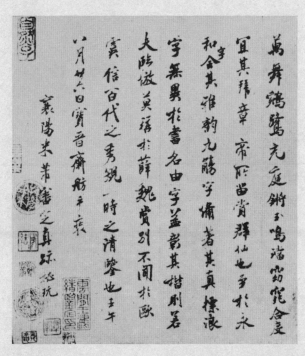

Fig. 69   Mi Fu: *Colophon to Ch'u Shui-liang's Copy of Lan T'ing Hsü*, dated 1102

with the copies originally done by Ch'u Shui-liang and Ou-yang Hsün, even to the extent of altering the arrangement of the text.

Miscellaneous items. Under this heading we include calligraphic works which do not properly belong to the above categories—such as couplets (*tui tzŭ*), parallel scrolls in sets of four, six or eight (*p'ing*), album leaves (*ts'ê yeh*), round or folding fans (*shan mien*), and other pieces which the calligraphers have done to give to their friends or for their own amusement.

These, then, are the calligraphic treasures of China, one of the richest heritages of mankind, for us to see and enjoy. They are mostly found in collections, royal, private or museum. All of them have gone through the test of authentication by armies of experts, who may or may not be artists in their own right. The authentication of works of art, in China as elsewhere, is a special branch of knowledge, a science in itself. Some of the great artists, notably Mi Fu, Li Kung-lin, Tung Ch'i-ch'ang, among others, have been highly regarded for their prodigious knowledge and sharp eye. On the other hand, some of the most famous collectors—Hsiang Yüan-pien, Wang K'o-yü, Liang Ch'ing-piao, Pien Yung-yü, An Ch'i—were either artists of indifferent achievements or no artists at all. In our days, the experts are the museum directors whose business it is to take charge of the collection and make purchases. It may be said that, generally speaking, art dealers play a much smaller role in China than in the Western countries. Many dealers catering to buyers from the West are really handlers of antiques rather than of works of art, and since few Western lovers of Chinese art are interested in calligraphy at all, these dealers are a blank as far as calligraphy is concerned.

It is quite impossible in a book like this to go into the many and intricate problems involved in the question of authentication. What we can do is to give a general view of the overall situation and to indicate in a most summary way the facets of the question and the pitfalls that may be expected. The Chinese use the term *chien shang chia* to describe the experts on works of art. The term *chien shang* is a composite of the term *chien pieh* (to discriminate) and the term *hsin shang* (to enjoy). We may say that our present concern is more on *hsin shang* than *chien pieh*.

Too much attention, it seems, has been directed to the physical form a Chinese work of art assumes. To a considerable extent, the Japanese art dealers may be held responsible for this situation. All Chinese, Japanese and Korean works of art are mounted for display and preservation. A work of art may be mounted and remounted many times. The Japanese terms *kakemono*, meaning an upright scroll, and *e-makimono*, meaning a horizontal scroll, have come into general use, and have sometimes been wrongly taken as terms denoting two different forms of art. In Chinese, they are called *li chou* and *shou chüen* respectively. They denote merely the way a work of art is mounted, and in re-mounting it may turn into something different. For instance, a tablet is an upright slab of stone, so the rubbing of the inscription is an upright

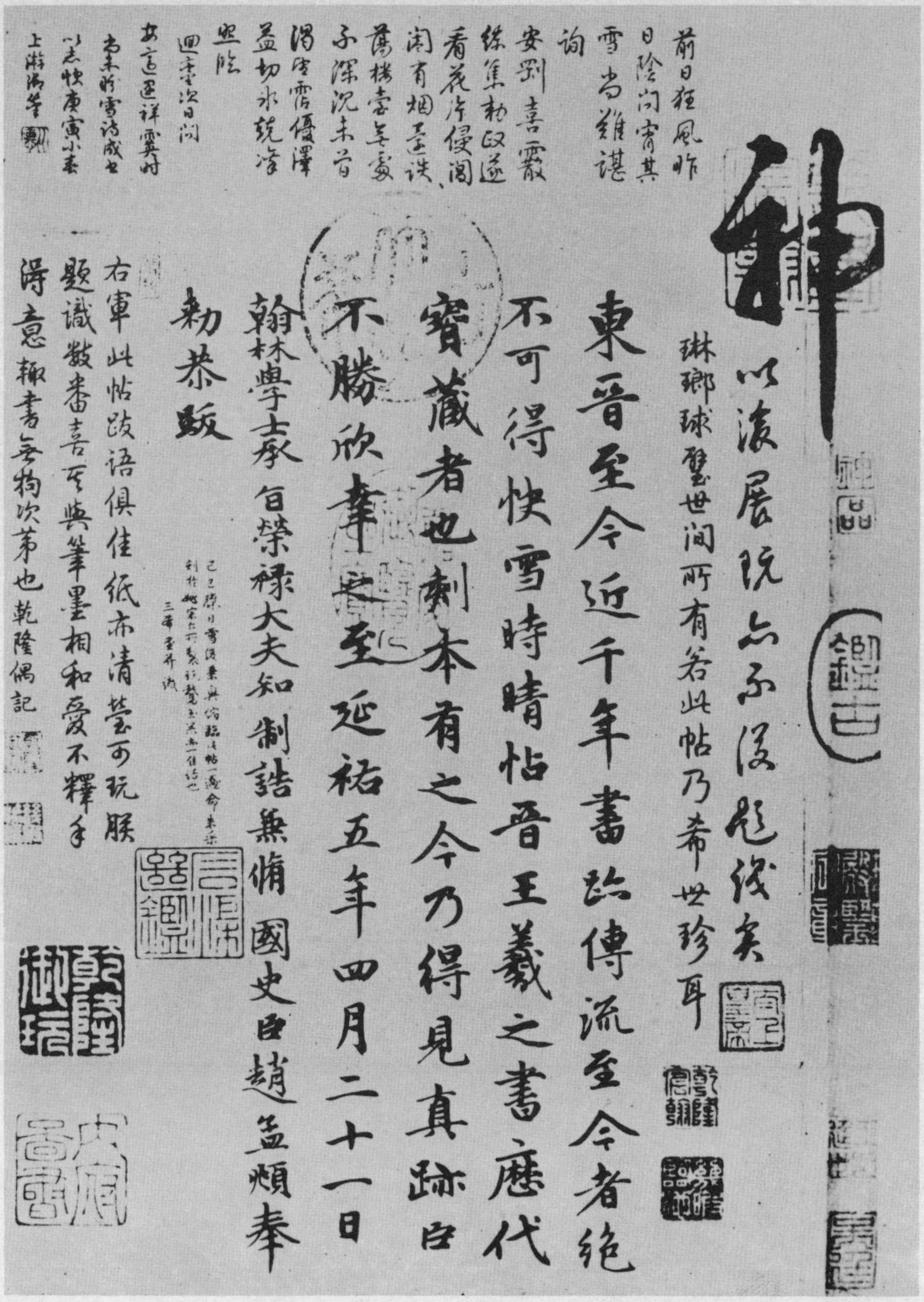

神

Fig. 70 Chao Mêng-fu: *Colophon to Wang Hsi-chih's K'uai Hsüeh Shih Ch'ing T'ieh,* dated 1318

scroll—*kakemono*. But for the sake of convenience, the rubbing is often cut up and mounted in the form of a horizontal scroll—*e-makimono*. The Sung Emperor Hui-tsung, a most ardent collector, inaugurated the practice of mounting small items such as letters and fans into albums (*ts'ê yeh*), while other collectors may have these items joined into scrolls, either upright or horizontal. A most outrageous practice on the part of some collectors is to cut a large work of art into sections. The most notorious case is a long horizontal scroll (*shou chüen, e-makimono*), a figurative painting called 'Springtime in the T'ang Palace', which has been attributed to no less than Chou Wen-chü of the Period of Five Dynasties, although it is most probably a Sung copy. One of the owners of the scroll decided to cut the scroll into five sections and, mysteriously enough, at least four of the sections found their way outside China. At the present time, the four sections are in four different places— the Florence Museum in Italy, the Fogg Museum in Harvard University, the University Museum in Philadelphia, and the private collection of the British student of Chinese art, Sir Percival David. The location of the fifth section is unknown. Sir Percival believes that the scroll once belonged to a man with five sons. Upon the man's death, the scroll was cut into five sections, bequeathing one section to each son. R. H. van Gulick, the Dutch expert on Chinese art, in his book *Chinese Pictorial Art as Viewed by the Connoisseur,* has given us examples of how even an upright scroll (*li chou, kakemono*) can be successfully dissected. Admittedly, it is a little more difficult to dissect a calligraphic piece, what with the text, the signature, and so forth. But if a scroll is a transcription of a number of poems, dissection is not entirely beyond the realm of possibility. As Etienne Gilson said, 'the owners of paintings sometimes do curious things to them to improve their quality', or perhaps to heighten their monetary value.

Chinese experts generally believe that it is easier to fake a painting than a calligraphic piece. They think a faked calligraphic piece can be readily detected. Their confidence is based on a number of factors.

To begin with, a calligraphic piece usually bears the artist's signature, whereas painters began to sign their works, and only in very obscure corners, as late as the Sung Dynasty. It is true that the Han and Wei scribes who did the splendid tablets did not see fit to reveal their identity to us. But beginning with Chung Yu of the late Han Dynasty, all the calligraphic pieces, including the tablets, bore the calligraphers' names. A most interesting case is the long scroll *Nü Shih Chên T'u* (Admonitions of the Palace Instructress) now in the British Museum (Fig. 73). The painting in the form of *shou chüen* consists of a series of illustrations of the essay *Nü Shih Chên* composed by a prominent literary man Chang Hua. At the beginning of each section of the scroll, the text of the illustrated portion of the essay was transcribed. As it now stands, the scroll ends with the signature of the great Tsin painter Ku K'ai-chih. The experts are in general agreement that the signature is a

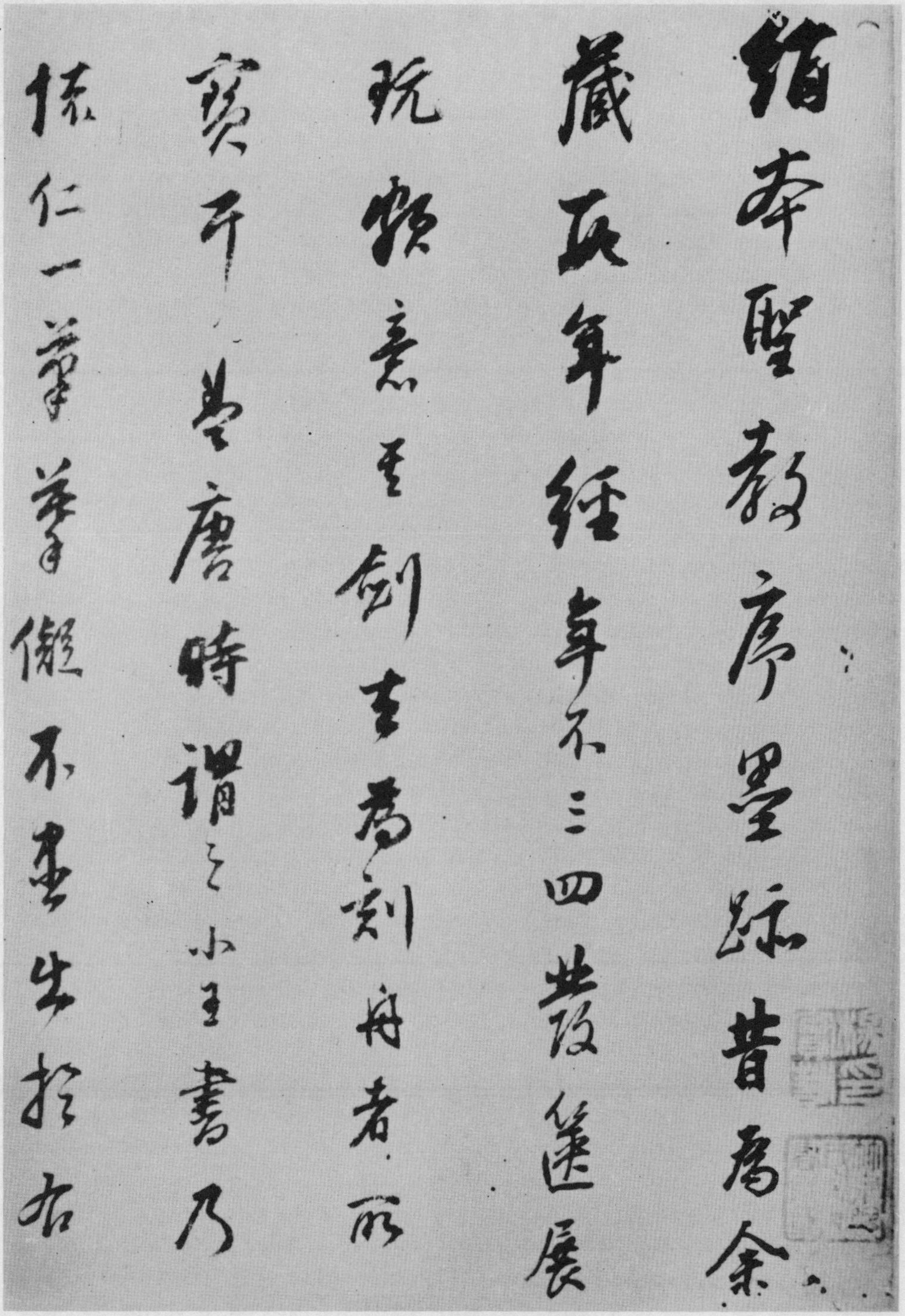

循本聖教序墨跡昔為余

藏戊辰年經手不三四歲篋展

玩頓意主刻去為別舟者所

竇于學唐時謂之小王書乃

悵仁一筆筆懈不畫生於右

Fig. 71　Tung Ch'i-ch'ang: *Colophon to Shêng Chiao Hsü*, dated 1634 (first portion)

forgery. The scroll itself, however, could have been painted by Ku K'ai-chih. What intrigues the student of Chinese calligraphy is that the transcription of Chang Hua's essay on the scroll is in small *chên shu.* The question is: Who did the calligraphy? One theory maintains that the transcription as well as the illustration were both done by Ku K'ai-chih. Another theory is that the transcription was done by no less than Wang Hsien-chih, who was Ku K'ai-chih's contemporary. Although we have no way of solving the riddle, the fact that big names like those of Ku K'ai-chih and Wang Hsien-chih have been involved in the speculation is something worthy of note in itself.

Mi Fu, who ought to know, has categorically asserted that it is possible to trace (*mo*) a painting but impossible to trace a calligraphic piece. Ku K'ai-chih has left us with a set of detailed instructions on how to trace a painting. According to the art historian Chang Yen-yüan, during the reign of Empress Wu Tsê-t'ien, all the paintings in the royal collection were traced and mounted in exactly the same way as the originals. Mi Fu's contention notwithstanding, calligraphic manuscripts have often been traced either with the purpose of having extra copies available (several versions of the *Lan T'ing Hsü* and a number of Wang Hsi-chih letters are admittedly traced copies), or for the sake of saving the original manuscripts from destruction in the process of stone engraving. For instance, all the manuscripts reproduced in the anthologies published before the invention of photography, from the *Shun Hua Ko T'ieh* to the *San Hsi T'ang Fa T'ieh,* were traced for the purpose of engraving. It is indeed remarkable what a wonderful job the craftsmen did, and their expertise raises a question for the connoisseur: How to tell the difference between a traced copy and an original?

The connoisseur, faced with such a perplexing question, is driven to find his answer in other aspects of the work of art under scrutiny. One of the first things he examines is the qualities of the materials used. He is of course fully familiar with the types and qualities of the silk and paper used in different periods and preferred by different calligraphers. Fortified by such technical knowledge, he proceeds to challenge the faker. Is it likely that such-and-such a calligrapher, doing his work in such-and-such a period, used paper of such-and-such a quality? He has no problem with the honest tracer and copier for they would not have taken the trouble to duplicate the materials used. The deliberate faker, however, is an animal of a different colour. The Ch'ing Emperor Ch'ien-lung once did a colophon on a long horizontal scroll attributed to Mi Fu, which bore many seals of the collector Hsiang Yüan-pien. In a note to the scroll the Emperor said: 'As I inscribe the poem on the scroll I become aware that the paper is not of Sung quality, so the scroll is a fake and Hsiang Yüan-pien is wrong in his attribution'. Emperor Ch'ien-lung may be a bit over-confident, but this is the sort of problem that the connoisseur is always tackling. Over a period of many hundreds of years, the techniques of silk-weaving and paper-making did undergo important

[242]

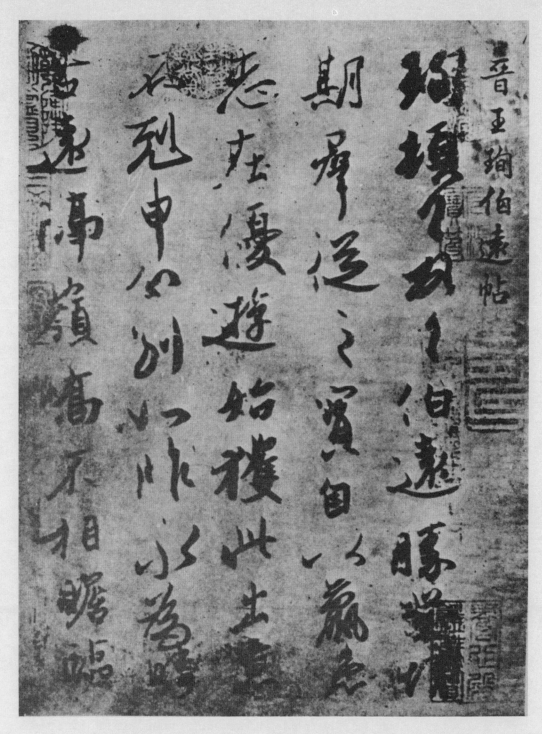

Fig. 72   Wang Hsün: *Po Yüan T'ieh*. Wang Hsün (349-400) was a well-known political and literary figure of the Tsin Dynasty

changes and there is always the matter of aging which is very difficult to duplicate artificially. It is for the connoisseur to know such things, to see the differences, and to come to his own conclusion on the authenticity of a work of art. It may be said that the Chinese have as yet made little use of the modern scientific methods in the field of calligraphy and painting, although they have been using them quite extensively in other fields, such as in the study of the ancient bronzes. This is probably due to the confidence on the part of the connoisseur that, in calligraphy at least, he is quite able to hold his own against the faker.

In his eternal battle with the faker, the connoisseur's arsenal contains many other potent armaments. From the references (*chu lu*) in art histories and collectors' catalogues, the connoisseur is able most of the time to follow the travels of a work of art from hand to hand, from period to period. The references are detailed descriptions of the works of art. All that the connoisseur has to do is to check the work of art under scrutiny against the references. A faker, however clever and careful, is bound to make a slip here and there, and the connoisseur will catch him. The painstaking labours of the art historians and collectors have helped much in defeating the faker's game.

It used to be an established custom in China to avoid using characters forming the names of the reigning monarchs or of one's ancestors. The custom is known as *pi hui*. If such characters must be used in a text, the usual practice was to write them slightly differently, such as omitting a key stroke. This is one of the places where the faker may be exposed. Let us suppose that a calligraphic piece allegedly done in the reign of the Ch'ing Emperor K'ang-hsi is under scrutiny. If the connoisseur finds in the piece the common word *hsüan* written without abbreviation, he can be very sure that the work is a fake because the character *hsüan* is part of Emperor K'ang-hsi's personal name. Tung Ch'i-ch'ang's courtesy name also has the character *hsüan* in it—Tung Hsüan-tsai. For this reason, Tung Ch'i-ch'ang's works signed in his courtesy name had to be excluded from Emperor K'ang-hsi's collection, even though the Emperor was a great admirer of Tung Ch'i-ch'ang's calligraphy. The same principle applies to the characters in the names of one's immediate ancestors. In examining a work of art, the wise connoisseur would take careful note of the name of the Emperor in whose reign the work was supposed to have been done. He would also check the names of the artist's ancestors up to and including his great grandfather. If he finds the characters which should be avoided or abbreviated in the work under scrutiny, he is in a position to proclaim it a fake, for no calligrapher is so careless as to commit such an offence which is punishable and in poor taste. The famous scroll 'Ten Views of the Thatched Hut' attributed to the T'ang scholar-painter Lu Hung has been declared a copy because the inscriptions on the painting contain characters which should be avoided or abbreviated. There is no appeal against such a conviction.

故曰翼翼矜矜福所以興靜恭自思榮顯所期

歡不可以瀆寵不可以專生愛則極遷致盈必損理有固然美者自美翩以取尤冶容求好君子所仇結恩而絶寔此之由

Fig. 73 Ku K'ai-chih: *Nü Shih Chên T'u*

The great T'ang poets Tu Fu and Chang Chiu-ling, according to art histories, were in the habit of inscribing their poems on works of art. The practice, however, did not gain general currency until the Sung Dynasty when Su Shih and Mi Fu did calligraphic inscriptions on their own paintings. This should occasion no surprise since the two men were highly accomplished in both painting and calligraphy. The juxtaposition of the two arts on the same work heightens its artistic value, a sort of mutual accentuation, which also has the effect of making the job of the faker doubly difficult. Inscriptions on calligraphic pieces either by the artist himself or by others, however, are less common than on paintings for understandable reasons. Colophons to calligraphic pieces are often done in the postface or in the vast space which the mounter has left for this purpose. Since it has been the habit of Chinese collectors and connoisseurs to write colophons, a masterwork, especially one in the form of a horizontal scroll, may be followed by yards and yards of colophons by all sorts of people in different periods. The contents of a colophon may be anything—a poem in praise of the work's artistry, a record of its peregrinations, a research essay on the artist, even a picture illustrating its text. If a work appears to a connoisseur to be questionable, he has no hesitation in saying so in his colophon, carefully giving the reasons for his belief. The colophons are the nightmare of the faker. He cannot submit his fake to the public without also faking the colophons. An old work by an acknowledged master without colophons simply cannot be believed. If he includes colophons in his fake, he will have to fake the calligraphy of many famous artists, which is an impossible task. Imagine the man faking a scroll by Su Shih and having also to fake colophons by Chao Mêng-fu and Tung Ch'i-ch'ang! No faker can be that resourceful. A knowledgeable connoisseur invariably examines the colophons first. This is where the faker is most likely to reveal his failings.

Another aspect of art peculiar to the Chinese is the seal. In ancient times, seals were used for the purpose of identification and certification. The Chinese today still stamp their seals on letters and even cheques in lieu of signatures. The stamping of seals on works of art began in the Tsin Dynasty, but it did not become a standard practice until the Sung Dynasty. Many works of Ts'ai Hsiang, Huang T'ing-chien, Su Shih and the Emperor Hui-tsung were stamped with their personal seals. Mi Fu was in the habit of stamping many seals on his works, seals he carved himself. It was Mi Fu who said that 'no fake is possible with a seal, the faker can always be detected'. Seals carved in the Sung Dynasty were usually made of rock crystals and jade. It was Chao Mêng-fu who started the practice of carving seals made of ivory or stone. He also established the *hsiao chuan* as the script for seal-carving. In the Ming and Ch'ing period, seal-carving became one of the favourite hobbies of the calligraphers and painters. It was a time also when Chinese artists were fond of giving themselves all sorts of appellations. There was virtually no limits to what might be carved on seals: the various names by which the artist was known, the names of his residences and halls, names of localities in which he resided, even sayings and proverbs. Some of the Ch'ing calligraphers—Chin Nung, Têng Shih-ju, Chao Chih-ch'ien, Wu Chün-ch'ing—were as famed for their seals as for their calligraphy. A calligraphic piece or a painting in monochrome is a composition in black and white. A few seals here and there in bright red offer a pleasing contrast and, in the eyes of the Chinese, add much to the work's appeal. And if the work is also accompanied by inscriptions and colophons by famous calligraphers, its value will further be enhanced (Fig. 74a and Fig. 74b).

The practice of Emperors stamping their seals on works of art in their collections began with no less a figure than the T'ang Emperor T'ai-tsung, whose seal bore the characters *Chêng-kuan*, the appellation of his reign. The Sung Emperor Hui-tsung quite expectedly followed the practice with a seal bearing the characters *Hsüan-ho*. It remained for the Ch'ing Emperor Ch'ien-lung really to make a nuisance of his seals. The Emperor, second to none in his love of art, not only formed the habit of stamping all six of his seals on practically every work of art that came to his attention, but insisted that at least one of the seals must be stamped in the most prominent place, right at the top centre, as a mark of his august stature, while the other seals were scattered all over the place, often on the elements of the work of art themselves. Besides stamping his seals indiscriminately, Emperor Ch'ien-lung was also fond of writing colophons (most of them in indifferent poetry) on the work of art itself, in a calligraphic style allegedly modelled after that of Tung Ch'i-ch'ang but singularly undistinguished. The Ch'ing Emperor was really the greatest despoiler of China's art treasures. Even the last Manchu Emperor Hsüan-t'ung (Henry Pu I), who was only a few years old when he ascended the throne, felt compelled to put a stamp or two on the works of art in the Palace Collection, works he could not possibly have seen or understood.

The practice of stamping collector's seals on works of art was followed by some of the collectors and connoisseurs, among whom the Ming collector Hsiang Yüan-pien was the most notorious. According to a modern Chinese student of art, Na Chih-liang, Hsiang Yüan-pien had at least ninety-three seals which he stamped more or less indiscriminately on the contents of his vast collection. He was the proud owner of three Wang Hsi-chih manuscripts. There were some fifty seals on them. Hsiang Yüan-pien also stamped some seventy seals on Huai-su's *Tzǔ Hsü T'ieh*, and some forty on Huang T'ing-chien's *Sung Fêng Ko Shih,* both of which were once in his collection. Fortunately, the mounters had provided enough blank space so that the great works were not greatly defaced. The seals are found mostly at the beginning and at the end of the scroll. They are also to be found at the point when two sheets of paper were mounted consecutively, as a measure to certify the continuity of the scroll (see Fig. 33a). The practice of stamping seals has been followed by most modern collectors such as Liang Ch'ing-piao, Pien Yung-yü, An Ch'i, and lesser figures down to the present day.

Since we have it on the authority of Mi Fu that a faked seal will always be detected, the seals belonging either to the artists or the collectors are invaluable checking points in the determination of the authenticity of the works of art. No matter how much we resent the ubiquitous seals, we must admit that a genuine seal stamped on a work of art, be it one that belonged to Su Shih or Mi Fu or Emperor Hui-tsung, does bolster tremendously our confidence in the authenticity of the work.

The art world of China, as that of any other country, is full of scoundrels who try to get the better of us. In spite of the many tools we have to defeat him, the faker keeps on flooding the market with his wares. One Ming faker, Chang T'ai-chieh by name, besides faking works by the great artists of China, even composed a catalogue of his collection to mislead the connoisseur—a sort of spurious *chu lu*—which fortunately was also quickly exposed. Nevertheless, the art market is still extremely active in the transaction of fakes, and entire collections have been assembled with them. It is not within the scope of this book to go into the techniques of faking, but some general remarks may be made concerning the subject. Some of the artists, among them Wên Chêng-ming and Tung Ch'i-ch'ang, were notorious for their tolerance of the imitators and fakers. They were often willing to sign their names and stamp their seals, even to make inscriptions, on works imitating their styles. To them, such a practice was a form of charity and was openly justified, as in the case of the Ming painter-calligrapher Shen Chou, on the ground that 'the fakers have the right to make a living too'. Some other calligraphers, besieged by requests for their works, saw nothing wrong in asking their friends and disciples to produce works on their behalf, a practice known as *tai pi*, 'vicarious brush'. Modern artists, generally speaking, are inclined to shun such practices. When Yü Yu-jen died in November, 1964, it was pointed out in the eulogies that never in his long life did he ever resort to the practice of the vicarious brush to meet the torrential demands for his calligraphy. However, there are many fakes of Yü Yu-jen's calligraphy, even shop-signs in the city of Taipei where he resided. When he spotted one of them, his admirers told us, all that he did was to do a shop-sign himself and have it sent to the shop-owner with no thought of prosecution or recrimination. Such a spirit of tolerance is traditionally regarded as a virtue of the true artist and, under the circumstances, we have only ourselves to blame if we are not knowledgeable enough to tell the difference between good and bad calligraphy.

The faker's bag of tricks is wellnigh inexhaustible. He can buy up the seals of the artists and the collectors and stamp them on his fakes. He can of course fake the seals. It has been reported that there are now six sets of Emperor Ch'ien-lung's seals in Hongkong and all of them are fakes. The faker, with

Fig. 74a   Seals Carved by Famous Calligraphers. The three seals in the column on the
right are by the Ch'ing calligrapher Têng Shih-ju; the four in the next
column are by the Ch'ing calligrapher Chao Chih-ch'ien; the topmost seal in
the column on the left is by the Ch'ing calligrapher-painter Wu Chün-ch'ing
(Wu Ch'ang-shih); the last three seals in the same column are by the contemporary painter Ch'i Huang (Ch'i Pai-shih)

the connivance of the mounter, may remove genuine colophons and attach them to fakes. He may distribute genuine colophons attached to one scroll to a number of fakes. All these tricks, and we have mentioned only the most obvious, apply to both paintings and calligraphic pieces. Fortunately, because it is easier to fake a painting than a calligraphic piece, the scourge of faking is much more serious in painting than in calligraphy. A Ch'ing Dynasty collector and connoisseur, Chang Ying-wên, told us:

When we examine old calligraphic pieces, we must first clear our minds of all extraneous matters. We must not approach the task absent-mindedly and in haste.

We first examine the brushmanship, the character-construction, the spirit animating the piece, the inter-relationship between its component parts.

We then study the artificial and the natural aspects of the piece, to find out which aspects are derived from the true revelation of the artist's genius and which aspects are the result of the artist's deliberate efforts directed to enhancing the work's artistic appeal.

After going through these tests, we should be sixty to seventy per cent sure whether the work is genuine or not.

The next step is to examine the colophons, old and new, to find out how the work has been handed down from person to person, from period to period.

The last step is to scrutinize the collectors' seals and the quality of the paper or silk.

After these tests, we can draw our conclusion regarding the work's authenticity.

If the characters in a work are well constructed but the traces of the brush are defective, we know it is a traced copy.

If the traces of the brush are there but the composition is defective, we know it is a copy.

If the characters do not flow one into another, if they stand on the paper like beads of an abacus, we know it is made up of assembled characters.

If a reproduction is made by first outlining the characters of the original (*shuang kou*), there is a chance that the traces of the outline may still be seen. If the whole piece lacks spirit, it too can be felt. All these are not difficult to detect.

Furthermore, the old masters, in their application of ink, whether wet or dry, heavy or light, always managed to make the ink penetrate through the paper or silk. If the ink appears to float on the surface, the piece must be a fake.

Some writers on Chinese art have chosen to draw a parallel between calligraphy and graphology. A strong protest seems to be in order. We confess that we do not know very much about graphological techniques, but we do know that calligraphy is an art, as much an art as painting, and cannot be taken as something from which the artist's personal traits and fortunes can be read. 'A graphologist,' Sir Herbert Read said, 'will find a person's hand-

Fig. 74b Chao Mêng-fu: *A Goat and a Sheep*. This small painting, now in the Freer Gallery of Art, Washington, D.C., depicts the two animals without background. However, the painter, Chao Mêng-fu, included in it an inscription to the left in his exquisite calligraphy which complements the picture admirably. Emperor Ch'ien-lung, besides spattering the painting with his many seals, also added a colophon to it at the upper right-hand corner. The Ming collector Hsiang Yüan-pien also stamped a number of seals on the painting

writing significant, and will generally prefer to look at it upside down in order not to be distracted from a contemplation of its form as distinct from its literal meaning.' All that we have to say is: Whoever has thought of looking at a calligraphic piece upside down!

A proposition has also been advanced to the effect that when we look at a calligraphic piece, we should pay little if any attention to the text and concentrate our attention on the artistry with which the characters are executed and the piece composed. It is certainly true that the texts of the inscriptions on many ancient works of art, such as those on the bronze vessels and stone drums, are quite difficult to understand. Quite a number of the ancient artifacts are in such an advanced state of decay that many characters are missing from their inscriptions. It is also true that the texts of the tablets, including those composed by prominent men of letters such as Ts'ai Yung and Han Yü, are singularly lacking in literary merits largely because they were paid for by their patrons as unqualified eulogies of the dead. The Ming scholar Ku Yen-wu was certainly right when he said: 'To compose flattering epitaphs for the rich and the powerful was how men of letters made their living.' The *Chi Chiu Chang* and *Ch'ien Tzŭ Wên,* which the calligraphers were so fond of transcribing, have no literary value to speak of. They were composed as chants for school children to recite as vocabulary exercises. However, we cannot deny that we do derive a great deal of pleasure seeing and at the same time reading a transcription of a literary masterpiece by a great calligrapher, such as Wang Hsi-chih's *Lan T'ing Hsü*, Su Shih's *Ch'ih Pi Fu,* Mi Fu's *Li Sao Ching,* or Wên Chêng-ming's *Tsui Wêng T'ing Chi.* In these cases, the texts have a part to play in arousing our emotions towards the work of art, a state of aesthetic pleasure to which some modern Chinese critics have applied the psychological theory of empathy quite convincingly.

The problems of the connoisseur with which we have so far concerned ourselves—signatures, materials, references, colophons, seals—important as they undoubtedly are, are the technicalities involved in ascertaining the authenticity of the works of art, and have nothing to do with the central problem before us: the aesthetic value of the works of art themselves. The art experts, preoccupied as they ought to be with the exacting tasks of identification and authentication, have often lost sight of this central problem. They are prone to go by what Constable called 'the rule of name'. They seem to imply that, if a piece has been proved to have been done by some old master, then it should be good. They are inclined to forget that even Wang Hsi-chih's art did not come into full flowering until after he had reached middle age. If we were writing Wang Hsi-chih's biography, or an account of the development of his art, we would of course be paying equal attention to all the specimens of his calligraphy, even his practice sheets when he was a child if we could get them. But this is not our present purpose. We are interested more in

Wang Hsi-chih's art because we want to enjoy it than in his life or in the tortuous path by which he reached the pinnacle of perfection. Most Chinese calligraphers are surrounded with legends, and the subject of each vignette has become a part of the pageant of history. Many of the calligraphers were eccentrics (Chang Hsü, Huai-su, Yang Ning-shih, Mi Fu); others were towering political figures (Yü Shih-nan, Ch'u Shui-liang, Yen Chên-ch'ing, Yü Yu-jên); still others were retired scholars (Wên Chêng-ming, Tung Ch'i-ch'ang, Têng Shih-ju, Chao Chih-ch'ien). The Chinese art historians simply cannot resist reminding us of the official positions their heroes occupied, and official titles have frequently been used to identify them, as in the case of Wang Hsi-chih (Wang Yu-chün) and Chao Mêng-fu (Chao Wei-kung). Do these titles matter? We have been told over and over again that Yen Chên-ch'ing's calligraphic style is solemn and austere because of the high position he occupied in the T'ang court. But Mi Yu-jên (Mi Fu's son) was also a very high official, and his calligraphic style, like his father's, is anything but solemn and austere. Both Wang Hsi-chih and Tung Ch'i-ch'ang were not successful in politics. Are we then to assume that there must be some affinity between their calligraphic styles? Art historians have been reading too much biography into calligraphic styles. Fortunately we have not yet been infected by the maudlin romanticism of the psycho-analytic biographers. No one has so far advanced the proposition that Chao Mêng-fu's style differs from Tung Ch'i-ch'ang's because the former was a devoted husband while the latter had many concubines.

The preoccupation with technicalities has sometimes resulted in a disregard for aesthetic values. A case in point is Mi Fu's transcription of the *Li Sao Ching* (Fig. 67). The work bears no signature or seal, which is rather unusual with Mi Fu. For a long time, it remained unnoticed in the royal collection. The Ch'ing Emperor Ch'ien-lung, in a colophon dated 1744, after taking due notice of the absence of signature, said of the work: 'The artistic merit (of the work) should be obvious to all; what difference does it make if it is unsigned?' In a further colophon done in 1778, the Emperor opined: 'Since I have ascertained the authenticity of Mi Fu's *Li Sao Ching,* I have come to the conclusion that it is the best sample of Mi Fu's calligraphy in my collection, the *Shih Ch'ü Pao Chi.*' Emperor Ch'ien-lung showed good sense in rating the work so highly. But Mi Fu's *Li Sao Ching* was still excluded from the *San Hsi T'ang Fa T'ieh.*

'Art is not a lollipop, or even a glass of kümmel,' said Sir Kenneth Clark. 'Knowing what one likes,' he argued, 'would not get one very far. Looking at pictures,' he continued, 'requires active participation, and, in the early stages, a certain amount of discipline.' The ideas of Sir Kenneth have certainly received abundant support from the Chinese art critics and historians. The Yüan writer, T'ang Hou, said:

[253]

People nowadays (the Chinese always deprecate the present in favour of the past to make a point), in looking at paintings, do not seek instruction from a teacher and do not consult the records. If they like a painting, they say it is good; if they don't like a painting, they say it is bad. But if one asks them the reason for their reasons, they cannot offer an answer.

What is true with painting is equally true with calligraphy, perhaps more so. There are, of course, many ways of looking at and enjoying calligraphy, and a work of art exists on many levels. To the true connoisseur, each work makes its own impact on its own terms. For instance, the three works—*Huang T'ing Ching, Lan T'ing Hsü* and *K'uai Hsüeh Shih Ch'ing T'ieh*—are all by Wang Hsi-chih, but each has its own individuality and it is to be appreciated on that count. They arouse totally different emotional responses from us because we have been educated to the context in which they were done. Fortified by such background information, we are led ineluctably from the initial impact to closer scrutiny, and as we know something about Wang Hsi-chih's life and temperament, his progenitors and training, his time and its outlook, his monumental influence upon posterity, our perceptions become further sharpened until in the end we have established an identity with the works themselves, or as a Chinese painter of grasshoppers said, 'I don't know whether I am a grasshopper or the grasshopper is I.' The joy then is complete.

In a thing like this, there are of course no set rules to guide us. But we should first of all rid ourselves of all prejudiced preferences. The Han imperial consort, Chao Fei-yen, was a beauty with a light, slender body. The T'ang Emperor Hsüan-tsung's consort, Yang Yü-huan (Yang Kuei-fei), was somewhat corpulent. Comparing the two female beauties to calligraphic and painting styles, the Ming calligrapher-painter Hsü Wei said: 'If their masters had changed places, the ladies would not have pleased them. But an outsider would find them both lovely. That is the way the true connoisseur judges calligraphy and painting.' Su Shih and Huang T'ing-chien were contemporaries, but their calligraphic styles are totally different. What Hsü Wei asks us to do is to like them both, and all others, and forget our own petty likes and dislikes. Whether we agree with him or not, this is the way the Chinese have been enjoying the art since time immemorial. The Chinese art world has not seen nearly as many changes in taste as in the West.

The enjoyment of calligraphy, to the Chinese, is an art in itself. With the exception of panels on walls and screens, Chinese calligraphic pieces are generally mounted in scrolls and albums which are stored away on shelves and in trunks. As far back as the Tsin Dynasty, the enjoyment of works of art on special occasions became a pastime of the scholars and connoisseurs. Huan Hsüan, a powerful politico-military figure of the Tsin Dynasty, used to show his art collection to his guests at banquets. On one occasion, one

梅花道人
畫巨軸絕
少此幅氣
韻生動布
置古雅大
類巨然非
王蒙所能
夢見也
其昌題于
鑑堂

Fig. 74c   Tung Ch'i-ch'ang: *Colophon to Landscape by Wu Chên.* Wu Chên (1280-1354) was a great landscape painter of the Yüan Dynasty. In writing the colophon to this enormous scroll, Tung Ch'i-ch'ang carefully avoided writing on the painting itself

of the guests, while munching a pretzel, soiled the work of art he was examining. Huan Hsüan thereupon laid down the rule: 'No pretzels served at banquets, and guests are requested to wash their hands first.' Throughout the centuries, the Chinese have held art enjoyment sessions. On a bright, sunny day, a group of art-lovers would gather at the house of the collector. A prized scroll would be unrolled (Fig. 75). Attentive eyes would be focused on the work, admiring the artistry and at the same time scrutinizing meticulously the brushmanship and inkmanship. This would be followed by the examination of the quality of the materials used, the colophons, the seals, the mounting. A lively discussion would ensue as to the work's artistic worth. Art histories would be consulted for references to the work; the seals would be checked against accurate facsimiles of the originals. After many hours of collation, the poets in the gathering would compose verses describing the work while the experts would draft commentaries pointing out its finer qualities. The proud owner would be preparing the ink and the brushes. At an appropriate moment, the guests would be invited one by one to inscribe their poems and commentaries on the mounting of the work. Anticipating what would happen, most of the guests would have brought along their personal seals, which would be stamped one by one. In a session like this, which could last a whole day, only a few works would come under scrutiny. The examination would be thorough and no critical opinion lightly advanced. One can well imagine how horrified these men would be if they were taken on a tour of a modern museum or exhibition. The Ch'ing painter-calligrapher Wang Chien sternly admonished: 'Do not show works of art to those who do not understand them!' Chang Ying-wên, the connoisseur, was even more fastidious. He told us that it was his practice not to show items in his collection (1) in artificial light, (2) on a rainy day, (3) after drinking, (4) to vulgar people, and (5) to women.

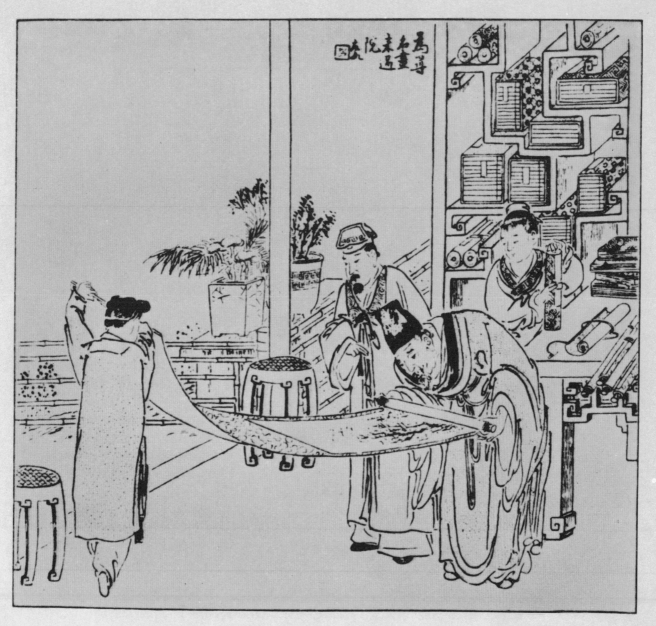

Fig. 75 *Enjoying Works of Art*. This woodcut shows two venerable gentlemen examining a scroll. Notice the old gentleman's close attention to the details of the painting. The shelves in the background are loaded with scrolls and books. There are also other scrolls and albums on the table. The page near the table is seen tying up a scroll

Chapter Sixteen

Calligraphy and Painting

Tung Ch'i-ch'ang once said: 'Those who are good in calligraphy are also good in painting, and those who are good in painting are also good in calligraphy, because the two arts are really one and the same thing.' This statement did not originate with Tung Ch'i-ch'ang. The T'ang art historian Chang Yen-yüan was probably the first person to say it categorically in connection with his account of the painter Wu Tao-tzŭ. It is a statement that has been unquestionably subscribed to by practically all art historians and critics. However, its exact meaning invites close scrutiny.

We begin with the question of origins. As we have said, Chinese legend has it that Ts'ang Chieh was the father of the written language and Shih Huang was the father of painting. Both figures were officials of the legendary Huang Ti, and were therefore contemporaries, implying that calligraphy (at least writing) and painting got their start at the same time. One commentator of the Eastern Han Dynasty, Kao Yu, without any supporting evidence, flatly stated: 'Shih Huang was Ts'ang Chieh.' Mario Prodan has pointed out that it is a 'Chinese idiosyncrasy never to inquire too deeply into a historical fact'. On the legends concerning Ts'ang Chieh and Shih Huang the proposition that calligraphy and painting shared the same origins (*shu hua t'ung yüan*) has been accepted since the T'ang Dynasty.

We are on safer ground when we explore the remote beginnings of the Chinese written language. In all probability, the first characters the Chinese devised were pictorial representations of the objects or phenomena denoted. The *P'ei Wên Tsai Shu Hua P'u*, the monumental encyclopaedia on calligraphy and painting compiled by order of the Ch'ing Emperor K'ang-hsi, asserted: 'Although painting began in the Ch'in and Han period and reached maturity in the Period of the South and North Dynasties, its real beginning may be traced to the primitive pictographs of remote antiquity.' Since a pictograph is by definition a picture and a character at the same time, the theory that calligraphy and painting shared the same origins begins to make sense.

One of the basic arguments advanced in support of the theory is that, in both calligraphy and painting, brush and ink are the principal instruments and mediums of the artists. The calligrapher talks about brushmanship and inkmanship. So does the painter. Both the calligrapher and the painter are linear artists. The line is their major means of expression. But there is danger in pushing this argument too far. Although many Chinese paintings are black-and-white monochromes, Chinese painters do use colours in their works, and colours are not the concern of the calligraphers, except the lustre of their black ink. Hsieh Ho's fourth canon of painting, 'apply the right colours to the right objects' (*sui lei fu ts'ai*), does not apply to the art of calligraphy at all.

The good calligraphers, as we have seen, pride themselves on being able to use the *chung fêng* (holding the brush in an upright position throughout) to do the characters. The painters, on the other hand, are allowed to slant the brush in many ways. The modelling technique known as *ts'un*, so basic to landscape painting, is often done with a slanted brush, sometimes at a sharp angle to the painting surface. Holding the brush in such a fashion is unthinkable in calligraphy. The figure painters, especially those specializing in 'iron wire lines', are prone to stick to the *chung fêng* in doing the human contours and flowing draperies. The landscape painters, however, cannot afford to confine themselves to this one technique. The brushmanship of the painter is, therefore, more varied than the calligrapher. Whether this makes painting a higher form of art is a moot question in the same category as the argument between Da Vinci and Michelangelo about sculpture. In his art history, Chang Yen-yüan told us that Wu Tao-tzŭ had learned the technique of *ts'ao shu* brushmanship from Chang Hsü and that Wu Tao-tzŭ gave up calligraphy in favour of painting. Chang Yen-yüan himself also dabbled in both calligraphy and painting and he wrote extensively on both subjects. He candidly admitted to us:

In calligraphy I have not been able to get the secrets of brushmanship and my character-structure (*chieh tzŭ*) is poor. I have thus brought shame to my family, something for which I am remorseful all through my life. My painting also does not bring out what I have in mind. I do some painting only to amuse myself.

In Chang Yen-yüan's mind, there seems to be no question as to which is the more exacting art. But after telling the story about Wu Tao-tzŭ learning

[259]

brushmanship from Chang Hsü, Chang Yen-yüan drew the conclusion: 'We now know the brushmanship is the same for calligraphy and painting.' He did not explain why and how.

A theme peculiar to Chinese art is that it is considered an unusual accomplishment if an artist succeeds in employing the technique of one branch while working on another branch. We have encountered this theme in full measure in our discussion of the mixture of the techniques of the various scripts, such as the introduction of *chuan shu* and *li shu* techniques to *chên shu*. The same theme has been applied in respect of the interchangeability of calligraphic and painting techniques, particularly brushmanship. The critics seem to take it for granted that if an artist is able to use calligraphic techniques in painting, or painting techniques in calligraphy, he has accomplished something very worthwhile and commendable. Chao Mêng-fu once asked the painter Ch'ien Hsüan: 'How do you describe scholar's painting?' Ch'ien Hsüan answered: 'The style of *li shu*.' Why is it so good to paint pictures with the brushmanship of *li shu*? What does it entail? How does one do it? These and similar questions Chao Mêng-fu and Ch'ien Hsüan have left unanswered.

Is it historically true that great calligraphers have been great painters, and great painters great calligraphers?

Wang Hsi-chih and Wang Hsien-chih, we have been told, were both painters. They were said to be particularly good in painting animals. Wang Hsi-chih also painted his self-portrait. He liked to adorn his fans with small scenes, presumably landscapes. All this we read in art histories. Not a single painting by members of the Wang family has come down to us. More interestingly, Wang Hsien-chih's style in *ts'ao shu* was said to have exerted a great deal of influence on the painter Lu T'an-wei, rated by Hsieh Ho as the most outstanding painter of the time. The T'ang art historian Chang Huai-kuan reported that Lu T'an-wei once did the sleeve of a Buddhist figure the folds of which were executed in one continuous stroke of the brush with six or seven turns. This, according to Chang Huai-kuan, was Wang Hsien-chih's *ts'ao shu* technique. Here we have an early example of the application of calligraphic technique to painting. The sixth century painter Chang Sêng-yu reportedly wielded his brush like a weapon of war, making jabs and thrusts with great power, suggesting that he had taken his cue from the calligraphic manual written by Wang Hsi-chih's tutor, the lady Wei Shuo. The paintings of Lu T'an-wei and Chang Sêng-yu, alas, have all perished. The important thing about them is not that they were calligraphers but that they used calligraphic brushmanship in their paintings.

Except for the story about Wu Tao-tzŭ learning calligraphic brushmanship from Chang Hsü, T'ang calligraphers and painters were two different breeds. The T'ang calligraphers we have named—Yü Shih-nan, Ou-yang Hsün, Yen Chên-ch'ing, Ch'u Shui-liang, Chang Hsü, Huai-su, Liu Kung-ch'üan,

Li Yung, Hsü Hao, Sun Ch'ien-li, Chung Shao-ching, Li Yang-ping—were not known to have done any painting worthy of note, while the celebrated T'ang painters, Yen Li-pên, Han Kan, Wang Wei, Li Ssŭ-hsün, Li Chao-tao, Chang Hsüan, Chou Fang—had no calligraphic achievements to speak of. The same applies to the calligraphers (Yang Ning-shih) and painters (Ching Hao, Kuan T'ung, Huang Ch'üan, Hsü Hsi) of the Period of Five Dynasties. The only exception was the Emperor Hou-tsu of the Southern T'ang Dynasty (Li Yü). According to art histories, the Emperor was able to mix the technique of painting bamboos with the techniques of calligraphy. Oddly enough, he claimed that 'only Liu Kung-ch'üan has that kind of brushmanship', while Liu Kung-ch'üan was never known as a painter of bamboos or of any other subject.

The Sung Dynasty was the Golden Age of Landscapes. Among the outstanding landscape painters of the period, Li Ch'êng, Tung Yüan, Chü-jan, Fan K'uan, Hsü Tao-ning, Li T'ang, Liu Sung-nien, Ma Yüan and Hsia Kuei were not known to be calligraphers. Among the Sung landscapists, Kuo Chung-shu was an epigrapher and was good in the old scripts (*chuan shu* and *pa fên*), while Kuo Hsi was said to have employed *ts'ao shu* technique in doing the trees in his landscapes. Among the painters of other subjects in this period, Li Kung-lin, a specialist in human figures and horses, and the Emperor Hui-tsung, a specialist in flowers and birds, were both credited with introducing the technique of painting into their calligraphy. Li Kung-lin's works, featuring the 'iron wire lines', were essentially a demonstration of the *chung fêng* technique in calligraphy. His insistence upon painting only on the highly sized *Ch'êng Hsin T'ang* paper of jade-like smoothness was an indication of his style of fine lines with extraordinary innate strength. Emperor Hui-tsung, on his part, chose to use brushes of long tufts to do his meticulously detailed studies of flowers and birds, brushes he also used to execute characters in his own 'slender gold script'. Two of the outstanding calligraphers of the Sung period, Ts'ai Hsiang and Huang T'ing-chien, were not painters.

Mi Fu was the first man in Chinese art history to have achieved great and equal distinction in calligraphy and painting. We have dealt at some length with his most impressive contribution to the art of calligraphy. In the field of painting, his stature is no less imposing. In many ways, the dreamy landscapes he created anticipated by almost two hundred years the so-called *wên jên hua* (scholar's painting) which reached the acme of inventiveness, individuality and refinement in the Yüan Dynasty represented by such painters as Huang Kung-wang and Ni Tsan, a school of painting which has become indelibly identified with the Chinese but which has exerted a tremendous influence upon China's neighbours, particularly the Japanese. Because Mi Fu was a calligrapher and a painter at the same time, it was almost inevitable that there should be an interchange of techniques. One of his trademarks in painting was the piling up of ink and pigment washes and stains of varying sizes and

[261]

shapes to create through profuse accumulation masses of different tonal values which were to be taken as hills and trees shrouded in mist and haze, creating a mood and an atmosphere pregnant with tantalizing mystery and bucolic sentiments, a world undisturbed by the grime and toil of man. His style of painting is considered almost impossible to emulate (it has been emulated with a measure of success only by his son Mi Yu-jên and the Yüan painter Kao K'ê-kung) because it is the product of an indistinguishable fusion of calligraphic and painting techniques, a breathtaking manifestation of pure genius. To the Chinese addicted to the doctrine of interchangeability of techniques, Mi Fu's achievement is of the highest order. He has demonstrated to the satisfaction of all parties concerned the close affinity between calligraphy and painting, an affinity which most Chinese art historians and critics, from Chang Yen-yüan down, have assumed to exist and to be a mark of unmitigated excellence. Mi Fu has proved that they have been right.

The appearance of Mi Fu was indeed a moment of triumph, an hour of fulfilment, in the history of Chinese art. He heralded the beginning of an era, which has lasted down to the present day, in which what might be called the twin arts of the brush have become inseparably joined. A tradition has been established for calligraphers to dabble in painting and for painters to dabble in calligraphy. However, few men have been able to achieve distinction in both. Among the many calligraphers we have mentioned, only three men after Mi Fu may be regarded as legitimate inhabitants of the house he built —Chao Mêng-fu, Wên Chêng-ming, and Tung Ch'i-ch'ang. The landscape is strewn with minor figures: some calligraphers whose painting is worthy of attention, some painters whose calligraphy deserves a passing consideration. The title of 'three superlatives' (*san chüeh*)—good in poetry, painting and calligraphy—has been bestowed upon a number of men from time to time, such as the Ch'ing flowers and birds painter Yün Shou-p'ing and the Ch'ing landscape painter Wang Yüan-ch'i. But the peak of success was scaled only by Chao Mêng-fu, Wên Chêng-ming and Tung Ch'i-ch'ang. The latter's statement that 'those who are good in calligraphy are also good in painting, and those who are good in painting are also good in calligraphy', however stimulating and gratifying, is clearly a gross exaggeration born of his own massive achievements. Most artists would be quite happy if they succeeded in getting somewhere with one of the arts.

The most fertile field for the interchange of calligraphic and painting techniques is that of ink bamboo painting, which is a separate category by itself. If a story in the history books is to be believed, the T'ang Emperor Hsüan-tsung, a calligrapher of no mean stature (Fig. 34), once painted a bamboo branch in ink by tracing its shadow on the paper screen window. The same idea, we have been told, occurred to a lady named Li (Li Fu-jên) of the Period of Five Dynasties, whose calligraphic attainment, if any, is unknown to us. It is generally agreed among art historians that Wên

T'ung of the Sung Dynasty, Su Shih's good friend, was chiefly responsible for elevating the painting of ink bamboo into an art form and for turning it into a major pastime of calligraphers and men of letters. Emperor Hui-tsung's catalogue of painting, *Hsüan-ho Hua P'u*, which classified the painting of ink bamboo as a separate category, said: 'Ink bamboo painting is not done by the professional painters but by poets and calligraphers.' Wên T'ung, an outstanding scholar of his time, devoted ten years of his life to the practice of calligraphy, trying his hand at all major scripts. His application of calligraphic brushmanship to ink bamboo painting brought him instantaneous fame.

Su Shih's admiration for Wên T'ung's artistry was complete and unqualified. He, too, made use of his calligraphic brushmanship in ink bamboo painting. It is very easy for us to see the similarity between Su Shih's bamboo painting (Fig. 76) and his calligraphic style. There could be no mistake about it. The leaves are arranged as if they were strokes of a character; bunches of leaves are inter-related as if they were characters in a calligraphic piece. The maximum emphasis is placed upon composition, leaving a great deal of space uncovered—a manifestation of the principle of *pu po* in calligraphy. On the art of ink bamboo painting, Su Shih wrote:

When painting the bamboo, it is best to have the whole thing in mind. Withhold the brush first and contemplate the plant carefully. When you see something that you wish to commit to paper, follow the impulse instantly. Allow your brush to pursue the image relentlessly as the buzzard swoops down when the hare emerges from its hole. A slight hesitation and the image will be gone forever. Wên T'ung taught me to do ink bamboo painting in this way.

Here Su Shih was reiterating the principle of *i tsai pi hsien*, 'concept before the brush', so fundamental to calligraphy. Wên T'ung was trying to tell him to apply the principle to ink bamboo painting. The phrase *ch'êng chu tsai hsiung*, 'the finished bamboo in the mind', has become an idiom in the Chinese language, meaning 'preconceived ideas or foregone conclusions'.

Ink bamboo painters in the subsequent centuries are too numerous to enumerate. One of the best known is expectedly Chao Mêng-fu who laid down the principle: 'Mastery of the art of bamboo painting demands mastery of the art of calligraphy.' He went on to explain: 'In ink bamboo painting, the stalks should be done in the manner of *chuan shu*, the branches in *ts'ao shu*, the leaves in *chên shu* and the joints in *li shu*.' In another connection he added: 'Rocks should be painted in the manner of *fei po*, and tree trunks in *Chou wên (ta chuan)*.' Chao Mêng-fu was a major painter—landscapes, figures, horses—and he occasionally also did a few branches of ink bamboo. His wife, *née* Kuan Tao-shêng, was fond of painting the young and tender bamboo in spring, sometimes shaded partly by a floating haze. Instead of painting only a branch or two, she preferred to depict the plant in groves stretching across the length of a long scroll.

[263]

Chinese ink bamboo painting has lately fascinated the art world of the West, and a great deal of its strange appeal has been attributed to its affinity with calligraphy. Eric Newton said:

There is nothing in European art to match those Chinese renderings of bamboo leaves in which the brush, loaded with Chinese ink, trails off at the end of a stroke as it arises from the paper, leaving behind a record of its passage like a gradual decrescendo in music.

Newton went on to credit such effect to 'the oriental veneration for brush-work as such, so that calligraphy itself becomes an art'. At the same time, Paul J. Sachs, after examining an ink bamboo painting by the Yüan artist Wu Chên, felt that it 'should serve as a reminder that in certain fields we of the West have everything to learn from the East'.

The Ming painter-critic Li Jih-hua said: 'I have often reflected on the principles of painting and I have come to the conclusion that one must be skilful in calligraphy before one knows how to wield the brush.' The Ming calligrapher-painter T'ang Yin said: 'Most of those who are skilful in calligraphy are also skilful in painting because calligraphy has taught them how to manoeuvre the wrist and to wield the brush without hindrance.' These statements, and many others, are meant to lay particular emphasis on brushmanship in calligraphy and painting. It is generally assumed that since calligraphy involves the several scripts, each of which is to be executed with its own type of brushmanship, the skill demanded of the calligrapher is to that extent more exacting than of the painter. The modern painter Huang Chün-pi once told his pupils: 'Since all of you know how to do characters with the brush, you should also be able to paint.' A good calligrapher, as we have seen, is supposed to employ the different types of brushmanship to do characters in the different scripts. It is therefore not much of a jump for him to employ his skill in brushmanship to painting pictures. The ultimate goal, of course, is to be in the company of Mi Fu, Chao Mêng-fu, Wên Chêng-ming and Tung Ch'i-ch'ang.

The introduction of calligraphic technique into painting is particularly desired. The Chinese are inclined to think that the four men we have just listed were great calligraphers first before they were great painters, or that they were great painters because they were great calligraphers. Following Chang Yen-yüan's concept, there seems to be no doubt in the minds of most knowledgeable Chinese that, between calligraphy and painting, calligraphy is the more exacting discipline. In the nature of things, there are some calligraphers who do not care to paint, including such prominent men as Hsien yü Shu, Chu Yün-ming, Têng Shih-ju and Yü Yu-jên, to name only those who came after Mi Fu. There are other calligraphers who only dabble in painting without pursuing it seriously, such as Su Shih and Chao Chih-ch'ien. But among those who take both calligraphy and painting seriously,

Fig. 76   Su Shih: *Ink Bamboo*. The painting is dated fifteenth day of the eighth month
(Autumn Festival when the moon is brightest), 1075, with the notation:
'Painted under moonlight for amusement'

the prevailing idea seems to be to introduce calligraphic brushmanship into painting instead of the other way round. The reason for this may be found in what Chao Mêng-fu called archaic elegance. The ancient scripts—*chuan shu, li shu* and *chang ts'ao*—are tastefully archaic in Chinese eyes. The peculiar brushmanship required to do these scripts, when introduced into painting, adds an archaic flavour to the painting and thereby enhances its aesthetic appeal. Tung Ch'i-ch'ang told us that 'the scholars have often brought archaic characters in *li shu* and *chang ts'ao* into their paintings'. The Ch'ing calligrapher-painter Wu Chün-ch'ing has gone even farther back and has endowed his studies of flowers and birds, trees and rocks, with the forms of the stone drum script. All these efforts have but one purpose: to promote an air of archaism into painting. If one happens to agree with Chao Mêng-fu that archaic elegance is *the* goal to pursue in art, then one is bound to accept his prescription of introducing calligraphic brushmanship into painting, especially the type of brushmanship used in doing the old scripts. If the *fei po* and the *Chou wen* scripts are archaically elegant, why not employ them in doing rocks and tree trunks? If the *chuan shu* and *li shu* carry an antique flavour, why not adapt them to the stalks and joints of the bamboo? Why not, indeed?

In our discussion of the interchange of techniques, we have mentioned only two persons who have introduced their painting technique into calligraphy —Li Kung-lin and Emperor Hui-tsung. Regrettably we do not now have any specimen of Li Kung-lin's calligraphy, so we are not in a position to pass judgment on the artistic worth of his calligraphy. Emperor Hui-tsung's calligraphy, though refreshingly original, is too mannerist and effeminate to rank with the truly great. Generally speaking, while critics such as Chou Hsing-lien talk excitedly about the interchange of technique, 'calligraphy in painting and painting in calligraphy', the emphasis leans heavily on the introduction of calligraphic brushmanship into painting, the examples of Li Kung-lin and Emperor Hui-tsung notwithstanding.

When people such as Mi Fu, Chao Mêng-fu and Tung Ch'i-ch'ang talk about Chinese painting, they are referring particularly to *wên jên hua* in which category all three of them are highly distinguished. *Wên jên hua,* it may be said, is a form of Chinese Impressionism, what the Chinese call *hsieh i* (literally 'writing down the idea') indulged in by men of letters as a pastime and strictly for their own amusement. In typical Chinese fashion, these painters do not claim to have founded a new school of painting. Instead, they protest loudly that they are the true followers of the great masters of landscape painting of the past, Wang Wei of the T'ang Dynasty, Tung Yüan of the Northern Sung Dynasty. Tung Ch'i-ch'ang is a key figure of this school; he is also its most persistent and vociferous propagandist. At the same time, he is an ardent advocate of the interchangeability of calligraphic and painting techniques.

The question naturally arises: Is the interchange of techniques applicable to all schools of painting? On this question opinion differs. Tung Ch'i-ch'ang has brought considerable controversy into the art world of China by proposing to divide Chinese landscape painting into the Southern School and the Northern School, and he has made it very clear that his sympathies are entirely with the Southern School headed by Wang Wei and Tung Yüan. Because he denounces the Northern School in no uncertain terms, we can well understand why he does not care to go into the question as to whether or not calligraphic techniques may be introduced into that school of painting. What irks us is that he has also failed to touch on the question in respect to the Southern School. With the exception of Kuo Hsi and Kuo Chung-shu, no one has told us that the Southern School owes its enormous reputation to the admixture of calligraphic and painting techniques. As a matter of fact, up to Mi Fu, none of the Southern School painters had been known to be a calligrapher. Tung Ch'i-ch'ang's more or less arbitrary division of the landscape painters into the two schools and his intense dislike of the painters of the Northern School (including such illustrious names as Li Ssŭ-hsün, Li Chao-tao, Chao Po-chü, Chao Ling-jang, Li T'ang, Liu Sung-nien, Ma Yüan and Hsia Kuei) have been heatedly challenged by art historians and critics. The point that concerns us in this connection is that, in drawing a line of distinction between the two schools of landscape painting, Tung Ch'i-ch'ang has neglected to relate it to the other theory he advances, namely, the interchange of calligraphic and painting techniques. And we know as fact that, up to Mi Fu, the outstanding painters of both the Southern and the Northern School of landscape painting were not in any way distinguished in calligraphy. We are, therefore, compelled to come to the conclusion that the question of the interchange of techniques boils down ultimately to that of the overriding importance of brushmanship in both calligraphy and painting. Calligraphy and painting are indeed the twin arts of the brush.

The calligraphers and painters of China come from all stations of life— Emperors, Ministers of State, Viceroys of Provinces, scholars, hermits, recluses, Buddhist monks, Taoist priests, ladies of leisure. But, to the Chinese, they have one thing in common: they are all persons of lofty character and metaphysical insight. We have quoted Liu Kung-ch'üan's saying: 'When the heart is upright, the hand will be upright.' All Chinese are in agreement that 'a person of low character cannot wield the brush properly'. Tung Ch'i-ch'ang has told us that a true artist must have 'read ten thousand books and travelled ten thousand *li*'. He is a man who 'holds the universe in his hand', whose works 'carry the smell of books'. Whether he is a calligrapher or painter or both, his *ching chieh* ('conceptual vista', a term which the Chinese have applied to all sorts of things) is on a higher plane than that of the ordinary person, because it is only from that height that he can engage in creative activities of genuine and enduring qualities. The earliest calligrapher Li Ssŭ told us: 'The *tao* of calligraphy is communion with Nature.' The T'ang calligraphers Huai-su and Yen Chêng-ch'ing, in comparing calligraphic strokes to water leaking through the ceiling and cracks on the wall, were laying emphasis upon the element of naturalness or the lack of artificiality in calligraphy. The ideal of the artist is to become identified with the organic processes of Nature and to create his work in the same spirit. In going about his artistic pursuit, his aim is to cultivate an affinity between the dignity of the human person and the amplitude of Nature. Tung Ch'i-ch'ang even went so far as to assert that a true artist is bound to live a long life. Calligraphy and painting, in the Chinese conception, spring from the same set of artistic impulses. A work of art, whether a massive landscape of Tung Yüan or a casual note of Mi Fu, is the embodiment of the 'conceptual vista' of the man who has through it revealed to us the totality of his personality. As a Chinese poet said:

> Set forth your heart, without reserve,
>   As your brush will be inspired.
> Calligraphy and painting serve a single aim,
>   The revelation of inner goodness.
> Here are two companions,
>   An old tree and tall bamboo,
> Metamorphosed by his unreined hand,
>   Finished in an instant.
> The embodiment of a single moment
>   Is the treasure of a hundred ages,
> And one feels unrolling it a fondness,
>   As if seeing the man himself.

Chapter Seventeen

Modern Trends

A Chinese Catholic priest recently found in the library of the Vatican a slip of paper bearing thirteen Chinese characters written by the Ch'ing Emperor K'ang-hsi. The characters form a sentence saying: 'The people of the West are most honest; this is because they are well grounded in knowledge.' Notations of the Vatican librarian indicate that Emperor K'ang-hsi wrote the simple sentence in 1690 and the missionary Antonius Thomas, S.J., who was in the service of the Manchu court, sent the slip to Rome, and it arrived at the Vatican in 1699.

The remarkable thing about this relic is that the characters were written with 'a Western pen', most probably quill and ink—the earliest instance we have of Chinese characters written with Western writing instruments. The characters are in small *chên shu* and are quite pleasing. That Emperor K'ang-hsi should have made such a flattering statement about the people of the West is not particularly surprising to those who know the history of the early contacts between Europe and China. Emperor K'ang-hsi had an open mind towards the men and the importations from the West. When the Italian Catholic missionary Matteo Ricci (known in China as Li Ma-tou) brought to China pictures of Christ and the Virgin Mary at the beginning of the seventeenth century, a minor storm broke out in the art circles of China. The Chinese had never seen anything that was so starkly and startlingly realistic. They were amazed by the chiaroscuro and the chromatic pattern of the pictures. Regrettably we have no record of the identity of the pictures. They could have been copies of the religious paintings of the Renaissance. Addicted to the *wên jên hua* of the Yüan and Ming period, the Chinese artists expressed doubt whether such accurate and lifelike representations could be properly called art. They were inclined to regard them as works of artisans whose training in brushmanship was deficient. But the Emperor K'ang-hsi, himself a calligrapher and painter of some merit, liked the European pictures very much. He even compared them to the works of Ku K'ai-chih! And his curiosity in things of the West also drove him to try out the quill and ink.

The Chinese writing instruments—the brush, the ink-stick and the ink-stone—cannot be easily carried around. A poet once complained in verse that he could not tell his family that he was well while travelling because he could not write on horseback. The introduction of the fountain-pen into China wrought a fundamental change in Chinese writing habits. Students are still required to practise calligraphy with the brush in the traditional way. Lessons on calligraphy are telecast on the Taipei TV station regularly. But when the students are taking notes in classes and answering questions in examinations, they prefer the fountain-pen. The Chinese are now manufacturing fountain-pens on a mass-production scale. No matter how much the eclipse of the traditional brush is lamented, no sensible person will contend that the fountain-pen should be outlawed. The recent perfection and popularization of the ball-pen is another step in the same direction. The poet can now drop a post-card to his family while flying in a jet-liner. The latest news is that the Hu K'ai-wên Company, the most famous brush- and ink-maker of China, has just gone bankrupt.

In the old days, calligraphic training was basic to the large army of men employed as copyists in public institutions and publishing houses. The monumental book compilations of the Ming and Ch'ing Dynasties were all copied by hand. The Ming compilation, *Yung-lo Ta Tien*, started in 1403, consisted of 11,995 volumes. The Ch'ing compilation, *Ssŭ K'u Ch'üan Shu*, started in 1772, consisted of 36,275 volumes. These compilations, together with their duplicates, were all transcribed by hand! So were all the documents, public and private. In the early days of the Republic, the Chinese typewriter was invented. Because of the nature of the Chinese language, it is a rather clumsy machine and no portables are possible. In recent years, all sorts of experiments have been carried out to improve the Chinese typewriter, from the IBM of the United States to the private endeavour of the author Lin Yutang. As it now stands, the Chinese typewriter is good enough to be used by all government agencies and the larger commercial establishments. Most Chinese documents and letters are now typed, not written by hand. A teletype machine is well on its way to general use. All this mechanization tends to depreciate the necessity of calligraphic training and practice, and calligraphic standards have understandably fallen disastrously low.

Meanwhile, ours is an age of mass education and illiteracy eradication. In the days of the great calligraphic masters, only a fraction of the people could

Fig. 77 *Mei Shu Tzŭ* ('Art Characters'). The characters read: 'Seeing the World Through Cartoons'

read and write. Literacy was the monopoly of the privileged few. The master-pieces of calligraphy were locked up in royal and private collections with no means of reproduction except through stone engraving and woodcut. Now, ninety-six per cent of the children are attending school, and illiteracy is rapidly becoming a thing of the past. The calligraphic masterpieces are on public display in museums and reproductions of near perfect fidelity can be had at very reasonable cost. And yet the Chinese people today are writing with fountain-pens and ball-pens and typewriters, which rule out the refinements of brushmanship and inkmanship altogether. Many modern scholars regard calligraphic exercises in the old way a sheer waste of time and energy and training to execute characters stops as soon as the pupil has acquired a work-ing vocabulary. The famous calligraphers of the past are now known to the students as historical figures, not as models from which to learn calligraphy.

In has occurred to a most versatile young man in Hongkong, Wang Chih-p'o, a calligrapher of talent and promise and, of all things, a motion picture pro-ducer and actor, to advance the proposition that, although we no longer use the traditional brush, there is no reason why we should also abandon all standards of good calligraphy when we write with fountain-pens and ball-pens. Of course, the tenets of brushmanship and inkmanship as they were understood in the old days can no longer be maintained. For instance, there is no way to grip the fountain-pen in an upright position, although we can do it to some extent with a ball-pen. There is also no way to regulate the volume of ink on the nib. We cannot apply a fountain-pen to the absorbent surface of a sheet of Hsüan-ch'êng paper without producing a messy blur. But Wang Chih-p'o maintains quite correctly that writing with a modern instru-ment does not mean that we have to give up some other aspects of good calligraphy, most notably stroke arrangements and character structures. With a fountain-pen and ball-pen, it is quite possible for us to compose characters and calligraphic pieces suggestive of the styles of the old masters, if we are familiar with their formal aspects. Wang Chih-p'o has published a calligraphic manual teaching people how to execute Chinese characters correctly and artistically with the fountain-pen. He advocates the choice of a soft nib in order better to simulate the modulatory strokes produced by the pliable brush. It is truly amazing that, of the eight rules of good calligraphy laid down by Yü Yu-jên, seven of them may just as well be applied to writing with modern instruments, the only exception being that concerning *chung fêng*. It may be argued that calligraphy minus brushmanship and inkmanship is no longer an art. In the traditional sense, such an argument is irrefutable. But a reasonable amount of training, consisting mainly in placing emphasis upon the formal structure of the characters, does help to produce characters which are in conformity with the traditional norms of good taste. At the least, if and when such training gains currency, we can be spared the painful experience of reading

[272]

Fig. 78 *Abstract Calligraphy*. Taken from a Christmas card printed in Hongkong in 1963, done by an artist named Ch'iu Chien-chang. The two highly stylised characters are *kung hsi*, roughly 'congratulations'

letters and manuscripts written in characters which are not only atrociously ugly but frequently illegible.

At the turn of the century, some Chinese began learning Western painting in Japan. Later, some found their way to the cafés of Montmartre and Montparnasse. Besides introducing Western art into China, a few of these men undertook to turn Chinese characters into decorative patterns, known as *mei shu tzŭ* (art characters) which are widely used for commercial purposes (Fig. 77). The characters are usually drawn, not written, with the aid of geometrical instruments and parts of the characters are deliberately distorted for alleged artistic effects. Lately, some people have been experimenting with what is called 'Abstract Calligraphy' (Fig. 78), supposedly inspired by Surrealism and Constructionism in Modern Art. Meanwhile, designs purporting to be Chinese characters appeared in Western paintings, the best known being those in Van Gogh's 'Plum Trees in Blossom' and 'The Bridge After Hiroshige'. Many similar characters have appeared in paintings depicting scenes of the East (Fig. 79) and on backdrops of plays such as 'The World of Suzie Wong'. These characters are almost always wrongly constructed and the strokes are done in complete ignorance of calligraphic principles. The overwhelming majority of them are illegible to the Chinese or the Japanese. Even as pure designs they are quite irritating to the eye.

All these things, quite understandably, infuriate the traditionalist who persists in believing that calligraphy must continue to be China's basic aesthetics with all its standards and refinements kept intact. If the art of calligraphy has been responsible for the prevailing good taste that has permeated Chinese society for so long, its decline, it follows, will inevitably usher in an era of ugliness and vulgarity, and this is something which must be avoided at all costs. He very naturally takes a measure of satisfaction in the knowledge that some artists in the West are beginning to take interest in Chinese calligraphy. Although he cannot say exactly how the Western painters are influenced by Chinese calligraphy (works under the label of Calligraphic Expressionism are still quite foreign to him), he is nevertheless prepared to stress the point that, at this critical juncture, the cultivation of the art in China herself should be pursued as assiduously as before.

The scene, however, is not nearly as black as the traditionalist pictures it to be. It has, in fact, many bright spots. In the old days, an aspiring calligrapher would be considered very fortunate if he were able to see and model after a few originals by the great masters at first hand. Now, he can examine them all in the museums and galleries. With the aid of photography, the masterpieces are reproduced with amazing fidelity on mass production basis. The novice no longer has to rely on stone engravings and woodcuts. Thus, the best that the past has to offer is available to the multitude, a situation which contributes powerfully to the propagation of good taste among the populace. If calligraphy in the traditional sense is no longer practised as extensively as before, there is always a group of men who are prepared to spend a lifetime on it, not as a means for personal advancement but for its own sake. Few in our society have chosen to be poets or painters or musicians and yet these few have written the history of their arts. It is quite safe to assume that ultimately the same standard will stay with regard to calligraphy too, in Chinese and Japanese societies.

Fig. 79 *Chinese Characters on Western Painting*. A painting, of a street scene in Macao by an American artist, James Thomas. Most of the characters are wrongly constructed

extensively as before, there is always a group of men who are prepared to spend a lifetime on it, not as a means for personal advancement, but for its own sake. Few in our society have chosen to be poets or painters or musicians, and yet these few have written the history of their arts. It is quite safe to assume that substantially the same situation obtains with regard to calligraphy. There are in China and Japan associations dedicated to the art. Even in Korea and Vietnam, where the adoption of an alphabet has dealt a fatal blow to calligraphy as such, there are still a number of people who continue to practise it. These are the men who love calligraphy and are in love with it. Like the poets and painters and musicians, they will be providing us with great works in the days to come. Calligraphy is not a lost art, not by any means.

Index

Chinese words (except those which, like Nanking, Kiangsu, are written in English without syllabic division) are indexed according to their first element, without reference to the aspirate, if any exists.